Margins of Insecurity

Minorities and International Security

Margins of Insecurity

Minorities and
International Security

edited by
Sam C. Nolutshungu

University of Rochester Press

First published 1996

University of Rochester Press
34-36 Administration Building, University of Rochester
Rochester, New York, 14627, USA
and at P.O. Box 9, Woodbridge, Suffolk IP12 3DF, UK

ISBN 1-878822-63-2 (Hardback)
ISBN 1-878822-75-6 (Paperback)

Library of Congress Cataloging-in-Publication Data

Margins of Insecurity : minorities and international security /
edited by Sam C. Nolutshungu.

p.   cm.
Includes bibliographical reference and index.
ISBN 1-878822-63-2 (alk. paper) — ISBN 1-878822-75-6 (paperback)
1. Marginality, social. 2. Minorities. 3. Security, International.
I. Nolutshungu, Sam C.
HM136.m267 1996
305.8—dc20
95-51461

British Library Cataloguing-in-Publication Data
A catalogue record for this book
is available from the British Library

This publication is printed on acid-free paper
Printed in the United States of America

TABLE OF CONTENTS

PREFACE

A number of crises since the end of the Cold War have demonstrated in very dramatic ways the catastrophic insecurity of ordinary people in circumstances where states—and the international system of states—are either unable to provide protection or are themselves the principal sources of violence. Ethnic cleansing in former Yugoslavia, genocide in Rwanda, and a whole range of outrages against civilians on all sides in the wars of Somalia, Liberia and Chechnya—these are not the kinds of situation that have traditionally been central to conceptions of "international security" used by leaders of major powers and academic specialists. Yet, whenever such crises erupt and make the headlines, both leaders and public opinion recognize in them a problem of "international security" on which they feel motivated to act in some way or other. There are at least two reasons why this is so. One is simple compassion: the feeling that the plight of some embattled group of ordinary people is very much the business of other people the world over, or that it ought to be. The second, is a belief, not always clearly defined or argued for, that such situations must, sooner or later, impact upon the security of the system as a whole, and, therefore, on states and peoples who may, at first, not appear to be involved. This one-world sentiment is, of course, fundamental to virtually any concept of a *system* of international relations and to many of the moral claims that states make on individuals and that people make upon each other and upon their own and other states in international relations, in war and peace. Yet, despite the conventional appeals to human rights that emanate from virtually every corner of the globe, it is exceedingly rare for such intuitions to be translated into effective security policies and arrangements that even begin to treat the situation of real persons, rather than abstract "nations" coterminous with states, as a decisive criterion of international action.

During the Cold War, ideology, on both sides, fudged the issue of the distinction between state and popular interests or the uneven representation of different categories of people within the security projects of states. Internal conflicts could, more or less plausibly, be linked to the security policies and interests of great powers which always seemed both well-defined and comprehensive enough to exclude nothing that mattered. No similar framework of viii interpretation (or misconstruction) is available any longer. What emerges, in each case, as insecure is not a well-defined system of international relationships, or even a power balance between states, but categories of people within states, or straddling state boundaries, who have limited or no access to the protection of their state and of the international community. Such people, whom we characterize as "marginal", are many and diverse and the factors that make them vulnerable are also numerous and varied.

The essays which follow emerged out of a series of workshops on the International Security of Marginal Populations sponsored by the Committee on International Peace and Security of the Social Science Research Council, through a grant from the John D. and Catherine T. MacArthur Foundation which were intended to contribute alongside other initiatives of the Committee to an approach to international security that goes beyond the traditional emphasis on the interests and relations of states, and gives due weight to the security of people.

The attempt to broaden reflection on international security unearthed a multiplicity of ways in which different categories of people are marginal to the states in which they live and the various forms of insecurity confronting them. The concern with redefining the agenda of international security is the starting point of this multi-disciplinary, multifaceted, inquiry.

The focus on marginal populations connects the issue of international security to a wide range contemporary concerns in various disciplines and fields of study—with minorities, but not just demographic minorities; some of the marginal people are in the majority in their countries or regions; with ethnicities, even though ethnicity, however defined, is not always the decisive criterion of exclusion; with identities, though these, too, are not always focal to the preoccupations of those who are marginalized or who marginalize; and with class which is embedded in other distinctions with which it also competes as a criterion both of exclusion and of mobilization against marginality. Some marginal groups are dispersed among several states, like the Kurds, some live astride international frontiers or at the borders of their countries; some are indigenous people at the periphery of developed states as in the circumpolar North, or in the developing countries of central America where their struggles have acquired prominence even if state policies continue to seek to keep them at the margins; others, like homeless African-American men are the victims of the interplay of racism and economic change, others still, like North African immigrants in Europe are affected by industrial change in their host countries and the responses of host populations to such change in the context of the continual incitement of global "civilizational" antagonisms. Racism with its various appeals to blood and culture—and civilization—is seldom absent from such crises as much when the specific needs and aspirations of marginal people are denied as when their essential otherness and incompatibility are proclaimed.[1] Some groups are rendered more insecure because they resist marginalization others because they embrace distinctness. Many are caught in the problems of failed or unfinished nation-state building projects.

The complexity of response of marginal groups both in terms of identity formation and of what Loic Wacquant has called the silent riots of everyday life (*les émeutes silencieuses de la vie de tous les jours*)" is a common theme of all the papers.[2] So is the presence of violence—the most dramatic form of insecurity—implicit or explicit, actual or potential in both the projects of integration and exclusion as pursued by both states and dominant populations on one hand and by different elements of marginal populations. Complexity of identity and of response implies an equally complicated pattern of sites and occasions of insecurity both in the larger context and within the marginal populations themselves. For that reason, neither the insecurities nor the marginalities that are of interest are restricted to those of the big stage only: of the clash of cultures and civilizations, ethnicities and classes. We share with Bourdieu his concern for small scale wretchedness as well as cataclysms of mass privation.[3]

The introduction explores in some detail the central issues and identifies some of the conceptual problems of a state-centered notion of international security which is bound to overlook the interests and needs of large categories of people, particularly, those already marginal in other ways within states or the system of states. The situation of marginal people dramatically illustrates the reality of a problem of vulnerability that is often generated by the very efforts to gain security for states and the system of states. While state-centric notions presume a certain community, if not identity, of interests in international security between state and people, the identification of marginal populations who are rendered insecure largely by, or through, the states under which they live, provides an effective entry point into a critical reorientation of international security concerns, in favor of a more realistic balance between the interests of states and those of persons.

"Marginal people" may be more or less conscious of themselves as having a collective identity but that need not always be so, or the identity relevant to any particular form of marginality may be non-evident or indeterminate, or may be one of less general salience than other identities that may be attributable to them. The fact of their exclusion and special treatment, more than any essential objective characteristic which they may or may not have in common, or any shared subjectivity, is the decisive issue. Marginality in its disadvantageous forms—as distinct from mere identity or difference—is an imposed condition, the result of the practices of others, or of the action of state and society upon those who become marginal. Ultimately, individuals identify themselves or are identified—according to variable, not to say arbitrary, criteria and conventions—with collectivities which, for their part, often have shifting boundaries and changeable real or imputed characteristics. The imposition, assumption and rejection of identifications are central to the politics of marginality and assimilation.

In the opening chapter, David Laitin advances a formal model of marginality and security, focussed on the costs and benefits of assimilation—with its varied and complex meanings—as they might appear to individuals in potentially or actually marginal groups. This enables him to identify a number of relationships between such groups and dominant populations and, particularly between dominant elites and the leaders of the dominated whom they recognize as well as the coercion which may be involved. The dependence and collaboration of marginal elites are generalizable features which are also invoked by other contributors to the book.

The two chapters which follow, by Rémy Leveau on Moslems in France and Zoltan Barany on the East European Roma deal with cases of marginality in Europe which are deeply rooted in the past but which also highlight some of the most challenging issues of citizenship and human rights in the two Europes of East and West, undergoing different but related processes of profound social and political change. The problem of assimilation and integration looms large but so also does the conditioning effect of the larger regional and international context with its new opportunities as well as dangers for people at the margin of the emergent political constructions.

Nowhere are margins more troublesome than in the Near and Middle East. Hamit Bozarslan examines the situation of the Kurds who straddle several international boundaries and fall foul of various nation state building projects in their region. Having been once closer to the center in the Ottoman Empire they are now distinctly marginal and insecure amid national and international violence. Jonathan Boyarin's chapter on Jews and Palestinians highlights the danger of creating new centers and margins through the very solutions that each side favors for escaping its own marginality, and, warns of the marginalizing effects of the conceptualization of the world in terms of centers and margins. Like Bozarslan, he illustrates the inadequacy of nation-state building projects as responses to marginality, casting doubt on the conventional recourse to the principle of national self-determination in such situations.

By contrast, Charles Hale and Alfred Darnell, in their chapters, deal with contexts where national claims to autonomy and self-determination have acquired a new and arresting importance—in the contestation of indigenous peoples seeking to escape marginality. Darnell concentrates on state practice

in dealing with indigenous people, manipulating ethnic boundaries and cate-
gories and deciding the material claims and claimants that can be entertained. Hale sees claims to autonomy as dominating a particular phase of struggle in which the language of the state is turned against it while indigenous responses to domination and their relation to Left movements in Latin America are re-examined and reconfigured.

Kim Hopper's chapter brings the focus back to the throbbing center of the global economy, namely the United States of America and examines a form of marginality that has grown dramatically in the US and is on the increase world-wide: homelessness. He analyzes the particular situation of African American men marked out for marginality and insecurity by poverty and race.

The international system depends on territorial boundaries which, even when they are not contested, are often privileged sites of insecurity. The margin has an altogether more palpable significance for people who find themselves at the border between states, and with the creation of states and of new political and economic unions the issue has a growing and urgent importance. Anthony Asiwaju examines the difficulties faced by people at the borders of states, marginal whether or not they straddle those borders, victims of their geographic situation. On the basis of his comparative review of initiatives in Europe, America and Africa, Asiwaju concludes that "multilateralism matters" and sees a positive role for states in reducing marginality through a policy of international cooperation which actively involves the borderlands people.[4]

The contributors to this study are drawn from different disciplines and fields of study. They bring to the subject of this book distinctly different perspectives, methodological preferences and empirical observations. The aspects of marginality discussed range widely and so do the areas of the world that are involved. And yet, we cover a limited range of issues in a large subject area—we believe, a crucial one—in a way that makes it possible for us to communicate with each other despite the intended pluralism of the study with respect to methodology, disciplines, and areas of reference.[5] The book does not pretend to provide a comprehensive catalogue of griefs of all the endangered peoples of the planet—few, indeed, are those who are not in any danger at all—and their many contexts of marginality, but by illustrating the dynamics of marginality and insecurity in a few cases it offers insights that can be applied to many other as well.

The dominant theme that emerges from all the contributions is that of the need to treat the state-people relationship as profoundly problematical in the area of international security—now, perhaps, more than ever—and start- ing from there to search for new, more appropriate forms of political associa-

xii tion that can improve upon the nation-state as we have known it so far and the system of states based on its paradigm. In being critical of states and state-centric approaches to security all the authors, nevertheless, share the recognition that states cannot simply be ignored as a matter of methodological taste or preference, bypassed or abstracted away in a serious account of the security of persons. States are central to both the security and the insecurity of peoples. The state remains critical: when it intervenes in social conflict, at home or abroad, to create security or insecurity for some and not for others; when it refuses, in obedience to ideology or the needs of domination, to offer economic protection to those who are vulnerable, or to contribute to economic amelioration nationally and internationally; when it loses the capacity to act as in those cases where the state itself has become marginal.

This study is the result of the research planning activities of the Social Science Research Council's Committee on International Peace and Security. Without the encouragement and assistance of the Council and the Committee this project would not have been realized. The staff of the Social Science Research Council, particularly, Paul Erickson and Arhun Elhance, have been a major help in coordinating various aspects of the work of the Marginal Populations Group. At an earlier stage, Cary Fraser, then on the staff of the Council, played a decisive role in coordinating the group and was a valued participant in its deliberations. Lori Gronich who joined the Council at a later date was also both an effective organizer and an insightful participant in our deliberations. We are also indebted to Aristide Zolberg who was a very active participant in the early stages of the project but who was later forced to withdraw by the pressure of other commitments.

Notes

1. The counterpart of this situation in law as it affects indigenous people is illustrated by Patrick Macklem, "Ethnonationalism, Aboriginal Identities, and the Law" in Michael D. Levin ed., *Ethnicity and Aboriginality: Case Studies in Ethnonationalism*, Toronto, 1993, 9-28
2. Loic J. D. Wacquant, "De l'Amérique comme utopie à l'envers" in Pierre Bourdieu, ed., *La Misère du monde*, Paris, Editions du Seuil, 1993
3. Pierre Bourdieu, ed., *La Misère du Monde*, Paris, Editions du Seuil, 1993, p. 11
4. The phrase is taken from John G. Ruggie, ed., *Multilateralism Matters: The theory and praxis of an institutional form*, New York, Columbia University Press, 1993.
5. Interest in the problems of oppressed minorities and indigenous peoples is growing and many valuable studies have emerged in recent years. Examples include: Ted Robert Gurr, *Minorities at Risk: A Global View of Ethnopolitical Conflicts*, Washington DC, United States Institute of Peace Press, 1993; *Cultural*

Survival, State of the Peoples, Boston, Mass., Beacon Press, 1993; Elizabeth Kempf ed., *The Law of the Mother: Protecting Indigenous Peoples in Protected Areas*, San Francisco, Sierra Club, 1993, Michael D. Levin, *Ethnicity and Aboriginality*, already cited.

Introduction

INTERNATIONAL SECURITY AND MARGINALITY

Sam C. Nolutshungu

This collection of essays is a response to the increasingly widely recognized need to broaden the study and understanding of security beyond a narrow emphasis on the security of states or interstate systems, to take fuller account of the fate of individuals and human collectivities under the national, regional or international security arrangements of states. Above all, the project of this study arose out of a recognition that there exist many marginal populations who, either because of their own characteristics and circumstances, or by the nature of states and international relations, suffer particular problems of insecurity which are not disposed of when those of the states to which they belong are resolved.

States are often identified with distinct peoples so strongly that the possibility of a major divergence of the interests of the two, particularly, in their relation with other states and other peoples, is largely obscured. More-over, the state is identified with a single "people" or "nation" regardless of the diversity of the population living under it or the conditions of its "unity" under the state which may include domination and repression. The tradition goes back to the very beginnings of states and, in modern international relations it is implicit in the characterizations of the law of nations such as may be found in Victoria's idea of international society as being made up of a community of communities", the "complete" communities being those en-joying sovereignty or independent statehood, and in the Grotian conception of international relations which continues to have considerable currency.[1] The strongest identification of states with distinctive communities is linked with nationalism, but, it is also evident in democratic notions of popular sover-eignty where "the people" are conceived in unitary terms.

States And People

It is often implied that there is (or should be) an organic unity between the people and their state, or, at least one of representation in a strong sense— where the state generally (some exceptional cases notwithstanding) represents at the international level, either the views or the interests of its population, or both. One variant of this position asserts that if people constitute a distinct political community they are entitled to independent statehood if they desire it as an expression of their autonomy which Walzer, for example, urges as a supreme international principle in his influential study, *Just and Unjust Wars*.[2]

Indeed, and this is, of course, not Walzer's view, a strong association of a state with its people (which could be called the "democratic fallacy") is an indispensable condition of the justification of war insofar as its destruction and violence are visited not only on the agents of states—even within the most conscientious application of Just War principles of discrimination—but on populations and their vital assets as well. One does not go to war against Saddam Hussein, as in a medieval duel or tournament, but against Iraq. Without some unspoken belief in their complicity or duty to remove their offending leader (whatever role others—foreign leaders and states—may have had in sustaining him in power), how else could one justify the bombardment of Baghdad and the economic privations imposed on Iraqis before and after the Gulf War (even with all the "humanitarian" constraints in their targeting and scope)?[3] In 1939, the Allied Powers fought not against Hitler and his henchmen, but "the Germans", not Hirohito and his generals but "the Japanese", and so on. To be sure, those who give battle and those who are embattled, do, for the most part, share the conflation of state and people, leaders and led, and so give apparent plausibility to the claim that the fate of the state is also properly their own.

If the convention of fudging the distinction between "people" and "state" is imposed by the need for ease of communication and action (e.g., in ordinary American English usage "country", and "state", and "nation" are virtually interchangeable), it is, nonetheless, often misleading. States, presiding over diverse and unequal societies, simply are not always representative of, or responsive to, all sections of their populations; nor are state interests always coterminous or congruent with popular interests.

The point has been made many times. In Marxist theory the state, born of class conflict, while pretending to raise itself above society and its conflicts remains partisan in the class struggle, even when it asserts its autonomy as in the paradigm case of Bonapartism. From a quite different perspective, the notion of raison d'Etat as a major thread in modern history was emphasized in the seminal study by Friedrich Meineicke.[4] Even within the contemporary literature of international security the specificity of state interest has been underlined in various contexts.[5]

Once mentioned, such objections are all readily acknowledged as commonplaces. What is less easily accepted, however, is that they have radical implications for the idea of international security and that they call into question the conventional assumptions not only as they apply to some,

Sam C. Nolutshungu

perhaps, undemocratic, or miscreant states and their peoples, or the "Third
World" as a special political universe, but, in principle, all states and all
international orders of security based on states.

To be sure, the disarticulation of the various security interests of persons,
groups of people, regimes and states is most evident in those instances where
states are being formed, transformed or destroyed: or where they seem permanently suspended between these conditions. Here, not only are the basic terms
of political association yet to be established, but even the territorial extent of
the state and whom it encompasses are also contested, often violently. We see
it clearly, too, in openly divided societies where political power is competed
for among leaders of rival antagonistic ethnic, confessional or racial coalitions,
or where class relations are so polarized that the security of rulers and ruled
hardly defines a common interest (as between peasants and landed classes in
revolutionary China in the face of Japanese expansionism).

Yet, even in established, democratic states, there are significant categories
of people whose interests are, at various times, badly served by the states in
which they live or who consider themselves to be marginal. This is the case of
Arabs in Israel, ethnic Koreans in Japan. In addition, even in the most
democratic polities, consensus about security policy often amounts to no
more than submission to decisions taken under conditions which preclude
informed consent. Security debates are opaque and lend themselves to distorted communication perhaps more than any others in a democracy. Typically, discussion is constrained by intimidatory appeals to loyalty that limit
questioning and silence certain forms of opposition. "National security"
dictates a hush-hush discourse in which knowledge is mystified in a cult of
technical expertise, and public information characterized by selective disclo-
sure and, often, misleading suggestion. Trust rather than agreement or understanding is demanded. But trust can be misplaced or deceived so that the form
of government alone cannot suffice to establish the convergence of the interests and wishes of citizens with those of their rulers. Besides, it is a fact of
democracy that governments are chosen by majorities against the wishes of
minorities that are often substantial, and quite what the majorities can be said
to have voted for among the security policies that follow the election of their
leaders is, for the most part, pretty obscure. "Consensus", then, as generally
understood, can barely carry the full moral weight of specific consent to
policies, nor less provide evidence of the unity of the interests of regimes or
states with those of people.

In all cases, situations can be envisaged in which the security of the state
imposes particularly severe burdens on some groups of people. The means
which the state employs to secure itself may involve repression of a part of its
population (as with the internment of "aliens' in war time, or large-scale

population removals). Stockpiles of war materials, or development and testing of weapons may expose populations to hazards no less severe than those that would arise from any probable external attack—a constant concern in the period of nuclear competition between the US and the USSR, but by no means a negligible matter even after the Cold War with the danger of the proliferation of nuclear, chemical and biological weapons still existing. In some cases of conventional conflict, the closure of international borders in response to security considerations may inhibit vital economic mobility for certain sections of the population or impose repressive regimentation of borderlands people.

If state security policies do not serve or represent all their citizens equally or well, the costs of such policies, even when they are not inherently biased against minorities, fall unequally and disproportionately on communities within states. Although difficult to assess, in each case, the uneven distribution of the economic and social burden of state security across populations and regions, and, indeed, classes, is relevant to all states. The former Soviet Union is not the only state whose economic development was distorted by the arms race and finally undermined by costly regional wars. In the United States, too, the burden falls unevenly and the effects of fiscal deficits, external indebtedness, monetary instability and the curtailment of socially necessary expenditures bear particularly heavily on social categories already rendered vulnerable by structural changes in the economy, like the "homeless people" who are the focus of Kim Hopper's chapter.

The very assertion of territorial sovereignty with the enforcement of interterritorial boundaries has proved subversive of the economic well being and the life-styles of nomadic peoples, as in the case of the Tuaregs in the Sahel who have in recent decades found themselves at odds with the several states (Mali, Niger, Burkina Faso and Algeria) to which they were assigned at the end of European colonial rule.[6] The creation of would-be national states with firm boundaries, not only produced the conflictful modification of relations of dominance between them and the sedentary populations from whom the leaders of these new states were drawn, but also provoked a crisis in the order of class domination within the Tuareg population itself which exacerbated their sense of insecurity and reinforced their attitude of suspicion and resistance towards the emergent states. To be sure, such transformations could not all be avoided unless Sahelian populations were to be preserved in aspic; but, they do illustrate a way in which the creation of states engenders both marginality and insecurity.

Although their circumstances and histories differ radically from each other, all "transnational peoples" are adversely affected by rigid territoriality. The Roma, in Eastern Europe, though never a dominant force in any state yet a large presence in several, suffer not only division among various states, but in a tradition well established in Central and Western Europe and the United States as well, they face hostility within states for their itinerancy.[7] Here, too, the re-structuring of European states, with the attempted creation of new democracies, following the collapse of the Soviet Union and the post World War II security order it guaranteed, has markedly increased the anxieties for this population which shared the fate of the Jews under the Nazis.

In Africa, militarization and the proliferation of personal arms have contributed to the rapid conversion of social conflicts into armed confrontations, and add to popular insecurity and to the creation of refugee populations, marginal by any definition. The effects of global economic development, in the shadow of forty years of arms races, regional conflicts and low intensity wars through which the post World War II international security order was maintained, remain to be assessed. At the very least, some of the marginalizing effects of development in the world economy might have been ameliorated if more resources had been available for productive investment in less developed countries and the growth of international trade not constrained by ideological and strategic considerations. If the Cold War may, indeed, be considered a "security order", then, its global economic costs and their impact on the evolution of societies may well have laid the foundation for the insecurity—economic and military—so acutely felt on the threshold of the "new world order."[8]

The chapters which follow develop this line of inquiry in various ways by identifying categories of people in the present international system who, for various reasons, are not integral to their states, are in various senses, which we define, marginal, and who suffer particular insecurity on that account, and whose situation, therefore, dramatically illustrates the need to distinguish the interests and conditions of security for persons and states. The overwhelming conclusion that can be drawn from all the contributions is that, in any account of security, "unity" and "representativity" between state and people is not given but has in each case to be established, in some cases, over and over again, and that methodologically, to assume them is to preempt and occlude the question of who benefits and who loses from any security policy, regime, or order. The eventual integration of marginal groups is by no means assured, nor is the harmonization of interests in security guaranteed, and, certainly, not without violence and insecurity as part of the process.

Despite the considerable attention that has been paid in recent years to the role of non-state actors and transnational movements in international relations, it is rare to find the security interests of states separated, even conceptually from those of the people under them, less still, the international security of persons and groups of people rather than states made the focus of attention. Some authors, like Barry Buzan, have, indeed, urged a view of national security that encompasses a wide range of human concerns.[9] Others have insisted on the importance of domestic politics and transnational movements bearing on security, over and above the interstate phenomena that have dominated the study of international security. Such interventions qualify the preeminence of the role of the state and the methodological primacy of the interstate level of analysis. Many of the contributors to this study point to unresolved theoretical problems implicit in the view of state-and-people that persists even when these insights have been added as qualificants or elaborations.

In the first instance, a focus on the security of groups of people, or of marginal populations, specifically, challenges the idea that the problems of security linked to conflict between states are, inherently, of greater consequence than those that are encountered within states. The fate of Jews, Gypsies and Slavs in Nazi Germany would still have been an unparalleled catastrophe even had there been no involvement of other states and no international war.

Secondly, the state as the provider of security for those enclosed within its borders is questioned rather than presumed. The notion that there is no security for people outside the protection that their state can provide or obtain for them in the international system is viewed with a measure of skepticism. Indeed, an observation made, almost in passing, by Kolodziej in a critique of some approaches to security, namely, that the state itself may be a source of insecurity is amply illustrated for the marginal populations under review.[10] What can be said of individual states can also be said about interstate arrangements, regimes or systems insofar as they privilege certain states and forms of statehood.

When the idealization of the state-people relationship is subjected to critical scrutiny in these ways, important questions are raised about political association, about particular state forms, like the modern nation-state, and, above all, about their connection to the problem of security at the most fundamental level. The transformation of imperial state systems, ever prone to insecurity at their margins, and the emergence out of their turbulent peripheries of new would-be nation-states, as well as the attempted redesigning of the imperial political centers as nation-states in their own turn, have been at the heart of the problem of security.

Three times in this century major redesign of imperial systems has been attempted along these lines. After the First World War, with the collapse of the Hapsburg, Romanov and Ottoman Empires, old sources of aggression and instability were removed in favor of new states which did not take long to testify to their own capacity for instability and to become variously targets of aggression and new aggressors. The international system came to be defined as

Sam C. Nolutshungu

a system of nation-states, with only such states assured legitimacy within it. The anticipated and desired order was expressed in doctrinal terms in the idea of national self-determination. No sooner had this Wilsonian order begun to emerge than it was thrown into confusion in the events that led to the Second World War. In the crisis ridden order sustained by the balance of Soviet and American power which ensued, the same principles of state legitimacy prevailed. If the mechanisms through which the balance of power was maintained (e.g., foreign penetration and armed interventions and the satellitization of states), belied doctrine, the model was, nevertheless, applied with undiminished fervor to an ever-widening circle of territories and peoples—now, with the encouragement of the United Nations.[11] Self-determination was granted to, or asserted by, the colonies of the former European empires, in a process which, from Indochina to Angola, was marked by a series of regional wars—producing states that were prone to further internal and external instability. At the end of the Cold War, the former possessions of the Austro-Hungarians, Turks and Russians, have once more become prominent as areas of insecurity in all senses, internal and external.

What is at issue is not whether imperial systems were more secure, or security-giving, or more stable than nation states, which, quite evidently, they were not: but, two quite different considerations. The first is that the process of transformation through which new states are consolidated, responding to new doctrines of legitimacy and security, is, like the reordering of power relations to which it responds, turbulent and protracted with no guarantee of a happy issue. The second is that in the light of its failure in so many cases to deliver security we have to question whether the nation-state, specifically, is, in a general sense, any more satisfactory as a basis of world order than what preceded it. In the very effort to conform with the prevalent model of statehood, the builders of states have, in many cases, created marginality and insecurity as the necessary consequence of their efforts and, a *fortiori,* their failure, a point made very forcefully by Hamit Bozarslan with regard to the situation of the Kurds. We are bound to wonder, moreover, at the paralysis of political thought which seems to leave us with no alternatives to consider.

The forty years of Cold War now ended, which, for the most part, were dominated by the possibility of nuclear war, highlighted the ultimacy, if not the primacy of the problem of war, even as measures to stabilize power balances under the Cold War produced regional crises, exacerbating the internal conflicts of states, leading to the militarization of the planet and the proliferation of the means of destruction. Festering strife, in the Balkans, in an ever widening area of the African continent, in various of parts of the former Soviet Union, in South and South East Asia and Central America, drives home a similar lesson. If the danger of "major war" has, indeed, receded, the prevalence of violence in politics, national and international has in no way declined.[12]

The conflict over the remains of what was once Yugoslavia highlights the plight of populations without protection from any state, some prey to the remnants of the very state that was once supposed to be their protector. The disintegration of the state in Somalia has demonstrated in the most dramatic way, the exposure of vast numbers of people not only to the dangers of violence from contending bands of warriors and bandits in a manner reminiscent of medieval Europe, but to hunger and disease on a cataclysmic scale. In the process of the disintegration and reordering of states, groups of people suffer both the lack of protection from any state and extreme vulnerability to the abuses of competing political and military formations with or without any real capacity to build states.

Both Yugoslavia and Somalia draw attention not only to the absence of protection for some populations by any state, but to the possibility of states that, in their present condition, can barely provide an acceptable degree of security in any sense to anyone; states that are marginal.

It is of considerable interest that the history of both states is dominated by the security maneuvers of great powers. Yugoslavia's very federal structure was an admission that the principle of self-determination through the nation state could not be applied consistently to all peoples without detriment to the security order favored by the victors of the 1914-18 War.[13] After the Second World War the security interests of the victors once again favored its continued existence despite a bloody civil war, and in the Cold War its defiance of Stalin won it Western support against external coercion and spared it from Western anticommunist pressures that might have exacerbated its divisions. With the end of the Cold War, Western tolerance for the communist hegemony of Serbia disappeared leading to the precipitate recognition of new claims for self-determination which contributed to the subsequent tragedy.

The "national question' in Somalia was imposed by the machinations of colonialism and by territorial concessions made by great powers to its more important neighbors. But it was the Cold War which, at first, restrained Somalia's ambitions, and then, later, made possible Siad Barre's irredentist adventure to regain the Ogaden, and, when that failed, sustained him in power. The proliferation of liberation movements as well as the militarization of this very poor desert state, led directly to the catastrophe which followed the fall of Barre, no longer capable of attracting external support on Cold War grounds.

Yet, even amid all these reminders of the ever present danger of war, domestic and international, most of the time, most states, are not directly at war, either at home or abroad, and the insecurities that confront their peoples and, indeed, the states, themselves, are of different kinds and are experienced as important not only because they might under certain conditions result in war. As the Horn of Africa, particularly, demonstrates, the dangers include both natural and manmade catastrophes, economic and ecological. In non-military domains, too, the state can by its complicities as well as its omissions visit insecurity on some of its population—in the disposal of toxic wastes as threatens to happen in several African countries, in both the toleration and the maladroit control of the narcotics industry as has been the case in places as diverse as Burma, Thailand and Colombia and the United States.

So far as the economic disasters are concerned, they have to be seen against the background of a large and diverse body of scholarship which has emphasized the force of global processes which outweigh the capacities of national economies and states to influence their own development (as in dependency theory and the world system school), or the increasingly transnational character of decisive economic agents and influences (as in the literature of interdependence).[14] The simultaneous incorporation and marginalization of national and local economic systems in the world economy is mirrored in the contradictory incorporation and marginalization of people within national economies. The special attention devoted to "indigenous peoples" by the UN and the ILO, and latterly by various nongovernmental organizations, recognizes the particular hardships endured by such populations historically as colonialism and the penetration of capitalist relations of property and exchange destroyed or reduced to a vestigial existence what were once distinct economic systems.[15] Deforestation today threatens not only Indians in the Amazon but also the much diminished populations of "Pygmies" in central Africa, ever the objects of studies in *physical* anthropology, but almost totally ignored in recent years by social science.[16]

Global economic processes, state-building and state securing initiatives combine to produce alienation not only when they threaten cultures but also when elements of an established or remembered way of living become the means of survival, resistance or rebellion as with various movements of religious fundamentalism. But, such responses can also occur at minutely local levels and yet have potentially far reaching consequences for international security.[17]

In a different way, in the polarized development of North and South (and to some extent, the formerly communist East and the West, as well), states also function to police the boundaries between places of economic progress and well being and their hinterlands of stagnation and poverty. Conditions in the poorer countries generate pressures favoring emigration while insecure strata in the prosperous countries resort to racism not only against new and prospective entrants, but also against those long settled in the host country.

International Security and Marginality

The changes in Eastern Europe and the Soviet Union which have produced new waves of migration to the West have provided further occasion for manifestations of militant racism in Europe which add to the climate of insecurity affecting all distinct minorities. Discriminatory curbs on immigration, including deals between prospective host countries and the governments of the countries of origin, may reinforce rather than reduce prejudice. It is very much open to question who benefits, in terms of enhanced security, from the fulfillment of this function in each case. But the flow of illegal immigrants into the advanced countries many of whom venture into the high seas in the most perilous conditions are one measure of the insecurity which ensues.

States, indissociable from the system of states of which they are a part, so very far from being dependable providers of security to their peoples, are, themselves, often the sources of insecurity and the conduits of international and transnational violence (whether in the form of the proliferation of arms or of armed criminality), and that is so in the attempts made to maintain or refashion them, in the formation of states that does not always succeed and in their involution.[18]

Can we, then, cast aside a well established preference for placing the state at the center of the maintenance of order and security? The state remains, by its own action, and by its place in the system of states, the privileged *subject* of security. It places its own, as it were, at the core of any political (as distinct from economic, ecological, etc.), conception of security. That is assured by the system of war in which the states system is embedded. By the "system of war" we denote the relations among agents that make war and the means of war (e.g., military formations and security systems and military-industrial complexes at one end, and transnational as well as national armed movements, private armies whether of warlords or of international criminals at the other). For, despite the multiplicity of the forms and agencies of war, states continue to command an unrivalled capacity to wage war.

In his review of strategic studies in the United States, Stephen Walt, probably, expressing the dominant view, defined the object of his field of study as the "threat, use, and control of military force. . . the conditions that make the use of force more likely, the ways that force affects individuals, states, and societies, and the specific policies that states adopt in order to prepare for, prevent, or engage in war".[19] In this way he reaffirmed at once the state as the privileged subject of security and the centrality of the problem of war.

It is, indeed, the importance of war (in the various ways in which it is conceived) and the unique place that states occupy in it—that accounts for the state-centric view of security. The philosophical tradition that associates the emergence of states with the "descent of order upon disorder" is a long

and influential one, extending from St Augustine to Thomas Hobbes and
beyond. The central function, and the justification of state authority is the suppression of violence and disorder among individuals, which is, essentially, little different from war among states (hence the judicial analogy in Augustine's just war—the just war enforces the law; and the comparison of the state of nature and international anarchy in Hobbes).[20] Nudging the two together, one might say that via the legal analogy, external war is reconciled with the principles of order within the state, and through the idea of war, the domestic authority of the state is justified.

An extended idea of war—i.e. of its nature, prevalence, decisiveness across various other forms of social relation—favors a corresponding role and significance for the state. Yet, the association remains vulnerable to the double objection that war does not begin and end with the state and that states are not the only war makers, a point persuasively made by Alain Joxe.[21] According to Joxe, states, do indeed, come into existence to respond to necessity, i.e., the threat of death, but it is hunger as well as war that poses the threat. The state encloses a collection of people, let us say a "community", according to a set of "criteria" which are, ipso facto, exclusionary: religious, economic, political and military, so that necessity (and, therefore, insecurity) and the response to it is never merely military, nor the states' military role either ultimate, or, indeed, assured.[22] Nevertheless, the assertion of continuity between internal and external war has the merit of challenging the arbitrary methodological (and ideological?) distinction between internal and international domains of security. It *is* continuity, almost, identity—more than *analogy*—that is suggested by both Augustine and Hobbes, and, indeed in every view that associates internal and external sovereignty via a link between the monopoly of the legitimate use of force at home and the legal or moral capacity to make war abroad. The "criteria" of Joxe's argument are the sources of both internal and external conflict as they are, incidentally, also the poles of inclusion and exclusion which define and generate marginality.

If the state is privileged in security matters by its role in the coordination of collective effort for production (economy) as well as destruction (war) the continuity between the external and the internal domain nevertheless involves a contradiction that cannot be resolved even at the level of theory and which suggests that the order created within entails (indeed, presupposes) the disorder without. For, if the state emerges to control and subdue violence in or for a community (apart from keeping hunger at bay), it does so by monopolizing the means of violence (or by attempting to do so), which is to say that it becomes the supreme arbiter of force within society. But, then, it confronts other states with equal claims and none able decisively and for long to achieve a similar monopoly of the use of force among states. The potential for (private) violence and anarchy supposedly conquered within the community of the state, is simply recreated among states while, within their boundaries, people remain subject to each state's own potential for violent and anarchic conduct in the familiar forms of tyranny and misrule.

Force is critical to the existence and functioning of the state internally and in the international domain, but it is never decisive in creating order and security, or, to put the same matter somewhat differently, its order and security pass through insecurity and disorder. The problem of security is not solved. The spheres of insecurity and security are re-ordered within and among states, contingently, through balances of power, to be sure, but also through the cooperative accommodations which are also imposed by necessity. It is not the privileged control of force alone, but also the role of coordinating collective effort at home and accommodation abroad which assures the state a pre-eminent role in security whether narrowly defined in relation to military threats or, more broadly, in terms of whatever imperils vital human interests.

Cooperation and Security

"International security", in this light, evokes a problem rather more complex than the dilemma of the egoist state of the realist imagination. In practical politics, the notion applies to both the security of a state or group of states and the security of the states system as a whole. Indeed, the concept echoes, at times, not too distantly, ideas of *collective security* which even more boldly assert a shared or shareable interest

Even as an ideal, collective security is never universal. States may have a common interest in a system that discourages or punishes "aggression." If this were sufficient to define "international security" there would be no conceptual problem in viewing it as a collective good (provided, always, that there could be agreement on the definition and identification of "aggression"). However, insecurity derives not only from the fact of aggression, nor even from actual aggressive intentions, but also from capacities: the capacity of a state to defect from cooperation at some future date, in the situation where no one can be completely assured of the motivations of others, is a source of insecurity that to a greater or lesser extent provokes rivalry: not only the competition of arms races but rival conceptions of how the common international security is to be organized and managed; of the levels and forms of autonomous national security within the overall order; of the implementation of the principles of international security. The potential for independent action whether in the form of defection or of "oversubscription" or "undersubscription" to common efforts to discourage "aggression" is, in itself, a source of insecurity for others.

To the extent that every international security order depends on a status quo, indeed, on conventions of state legitimacy, such arrangements are inherently biased against those who in each region or country would be better served by alternative political arrangements. Both in the Middle East and in the Balkans, several of the states accepted as essential to the post World War II order were imposed on divided populations and could only be sustained and consolidated at the expense of marginalized minorities. For such minorities the international security order could hardly be considered a good—especially, in the light of the measures deemed necessary to maintain it within states (of political and cultural repression), and by the rival great powers (militarization, armed intervention, support for repressive regimes, and so much more).

In no historical system of international security are the gains of membership distributed equally or proportionately by any criterion. Some states are more exposed to insecurity either because of their geostrategic situation, or because their own security contributes relatively little to the overall order, or because their own insecurity reduces their capacity to bargain for a greater level of collective protection. "Collective security" was never a public good.

It is true that, in spite of rivalries and inequalities of advantage, there may yet be conceivable an enveloping order in which most states would be secure from external attack and within which conflicts would be contained and managed, just as, in the bilateral case, it has been argued that means can be found of reducing the "security dilemma".[23] At a practical level, the Cold War reflected these unreconciled aspects of security as both a single country quest in competition with others and a common good, alternately in the series of crises in the Superpower relation and in the attempts at accommodation, ultimately, even in the desperate bargain of "mutual assured destruction" as a basis for shared security. That was accompanied by conflicting expectations that accommodation among the Superpowers would enhance security even for, and among lesser powers, and, alternatively, that regional conflicts, including those in which the Superpowers were directly involved, could be dealt with separately. Détente came to grief because of such conflicting aspirations.[24] Needless to say, whichever way they are interpreted, in the strictest bilateral sense or more broadly, such arrangements do not solve the problem of insecurity, durably or comprehensively. They are vulnerable to changing perceptions of the bargaining power of each side, and they may increase the insecurity of states that are not parties to the bargain.

The security bargain is, therefore, not stable, nor does it assure international security in a general sense—either as a collective condition of states or of people within individual states. Whether or not accommodations create security within the bilateral relationship is often a matter of opinion that can be decided only after the passage of time, when, perhaps, it no longer matters.

Not only is there no self evident point of congruence of the security needs of all states in a system, between states and their populations there is, equally, no reason to suppose that the conditions of the external security of the state are consistent with those of the safety of all or most of its people. Internal security beyond the protection of persons and their goods as e.g., under common law, is, notoriously, an area of profound disagreement in many states.

Security, international or national, is, therefore best thought of not as a stable general condition that can ever be achieved once and for all, or a good that can ever be shared to the satisfaction of all but those of ill will. Rather, where it exists, it is a matter of contingent accommodations always subject to renegotiation or repudiation, and always vulnerable to changing objective conditions affecting aspirations and capacities of states and persons.

Applied to people rather than to states, the conditions of international security become even more indeterminate, quite as much as the threats against which people might wish to be secured are, in principle, illimitable. The threat of destruction is assuredly a compelling point of departure, but it would be arbitrary to restrict "destruction" to its most material senses only: of death from hunger or physical violence. Throughout history, people have sometimes preferred both to other insults and privations as in the classic resistance of Melos to Athens.

One could limit the range by referring only to threats to values generally agreed to be ultimate within a state or a system of states, but such consent is likely to be hypothetical even for democracies; or one could consider only "core values" but then one would have to specify the "core" without mere stipulation or excessive reliance on an ideological preference. We would be nearer to some objectivity if we defined as "core values" those conditions that are generally necessary for the pursuit of most values (of whomever it was whose security were being considered, leaving it as contingent how far these applied to other persons, and as a matter of opinion whether such values were more or less worthy of defence than those of others, or than other values of the same people). Security would, then mean, for each person or collectivity, assurance against threats to such core values. However, even threats are seldom unambiguous or objective.

This would seem to imply that at the heart of our inquiry there is no object: we are in the domain of perceptions and of preferences and uncertain judgements about the conditions of their satisfaction. But, that would be going too far: some perceptions are well-founded, some preferences reasonable in the light of those perceptions, and some judgements wise. The chal-

Sam C. Nolutshungu

lenge is to determine which ones and to distinguish when "security" is a political concept worth arguing about and when it is merely a weasel word.

Statesmen brought the concept of "international security" into currency a long time ago and nowhere more resonantly than at the founding of the United Nations. In the Charter, the idea appears in the phrase "international peace and security". The separation of "peace" from "security" only appears to occur when the threat of aggression is encountered, when security measures are to be taken to restore peace. International peace and security are associated with many other desirable things, such as economic and social development and the advancement of human rights, but in the institution of the Security Council, and in the discourse of Chapter 7, security assumes a distinctive profile.

It is in this domain that the right of states to act in their own defence—the ultimate expression of state egoism—is affirmed, the inequality of states recognized and underlined, as in the voting powers in the Security Council, and the manichean opposition between security and aggression enshrined. Proof, if any were still needed, that international security was not imagined to be a universal good. We know, of course, that the overriding concern of the founders of the UN was with the potential resurgence of the defeated powers. It was the failure of the old aggressors to rise again and revert to type that made the UN so largely incongruous in the subsequent epoch where "international peace and security" rapidly acquired a unilateral and more explicitly sectarian meaning between Superpowers and their rival alliance systems, universalism remaining merely as propaganda or bombast.

The phrase in which "peace" and "security" seem welded together may have been meant to warn against the separation of the one from the other, or the mistake of supposing that the one could stand for the other: almost a coded recognition that things to be done to obtain security might be incompatible with peace; or that the pursuit of peace alone might fall short of providing security. Yet in this double negation ambiguity is assured, even if the use of the two in apposition produces a cliché that discourages further, critical, exploration of intentions.

It is doubtful whether in its most common usage, including that implicit in the naming of a Committee of the Social Science Research Council, the phrase has since departed much from its at once felicific and ominous, declaratory and obfuscatory, meanings. Could it, in toto, or in two separate parts of peace and security, ever be a scientific concept, or is it, ultimately, an historic phrase fit only for interpretation by the elaboration of the contexts of its use, its shifting, contradictory, and often, hidden meanings?

Where, however, the Charter restricted itself almost exclusively—with the cautious but extensive exception of Article 51—to a collective notion of

International Security and Marginality

international security, the narrower idea has since attracted as much if not more attention. No doubt, in the minds of many people, international and national security are complementary (if not additive) notions: the more national security there is, the more international security there will be also. Yet, if narrower, and whether or not burdened with a universalism quite alien to its spirit, the concept of national security has been no more precise than the grander international idea. Nor has its association with peace and all the other proclaimed international values been any less elusive.

In the work recorded in this book there is no assumption that the problem of international or national security is ever definitively solved; or that the conflicts of interest that produce it can ever be laid to rest. Different manifestations and contexts of insecurity demand critical appraisal and, in some cases, suggest if not their remedies, then clearly, the conditions that make them worse. While avoiding, in this way, an objectivist or empiricist reification of "international security" the different contributions approach the problem from what we hope is an unusual perspective which distinguishes itself mainly in two ways. The *subject* of insecurity is neither the international system, nor the state, nor, even, society, but human groups within societies. What is at issue is not only the inadequacy of *national* security arrangements, but forces that transcend state boundaries.

The international character of this insecurity owes to the fact that its sources are not unique to individual states but are attributable to system wide influences at the international level and to the very division of people into political communities that is constitutive of the international system. The relationship between the international system and the entities that compose it is not a passive one, rather, in various ways the international system favors and promotes, both in doctrine and practice, certain forms of internal political organization.

In some cases, like those of displaced people, the effects of past arms races, continuing trends in the world economy, and the consequences of the present remodelling of states are crucial to the generation of insecurity. Some of the marginal populations are, in many cases, astride conflicted international borders or divided among several mutually hostile or suspicious states. At the same time, their very insecurity leads to the conscription or enticement of members of these populations into international conflicts that become more intractable by that very fact and which do little to improve the security of such groups. The situation of the Kurds both in the war between Iran and Iraq and in the 1991 Gulf War is a poignant illustration.

The struggles of some of the populations under study have acquired a transnational aspect of growing importance notably for those who despair of finding relief within the existing framework of nation states. At the same time,

Sam C. Nolutshungu

intergovernmental organizations and transnational interest groups, whether under the banner of human rights or out of a concern for the environment, have featured prominently in some of the campaigns of indigenous peoples especially in Latin America. There, as Charles Hale's analysis shows, where identity politics is part of an historic political *reclassement* in which traditional popular political blocs are challenged and reconfigured under the dual impact of the eclipse of Marxism and the new hegemony of economic liberalism, the transnational may provide more efficacious options of struggle for indigenes than traditional national movements of resistance.

The shape of the international system, the balances of power among great states, the rules of the game of politics, and the distribution among peoples and classes of wealth and misery are unlikely to be determined by the fate and struggles of what are, after all, minorities or conquered peoples. Yet, with the end of the Cold War and its representations of politics in the world, its forms of opposition and solidarity, and of violence, the politics of marginal populations and their struggles within the boundaries of states or in transnational movements or as complicating factors in international conflicts, cannot fail to influence the options of state behavior in the realm of security and the dynamics of their popular legitimation. *A fortiori,* the remaking of states and the states system that is now afoot will continue to raise, in many dramatic, and sometimes, catastrophic ways, the problem of security as it affects human groups in all their diverse cultural and material circumstances.

Once we abandon the idea of the state as a unitary subject and approach security from the perspective of the situation of people we are confronted with a welter of problems of identification and attribution of entities and their interests which convention, if not common sense, disposes of quite summarily in the case of states as subjects. Beyond the solitary individual, every candidate is questionable not only as an object of study but also as an entity with sufficient coherence and distinctness as a subject of security: "nations", "ethnic groups", "classes", "races", or the "marginal populations" of our study. The problem is not unique to the domain of security however but applies to all social inquiry. The indeterminacy that it highlights with respect to who or what is secured is itself an inherent problem of social or collective life. In a state-centric view all this is, as we have suggested, understated or merely ignored.

Who is Marginal?

Marginal populations are distinguishable minorities within states whose integration to the society and state is markedly incomplete so that their participation in either is partial, intermittent, or subject to special qualifications and restrictions. Marginal populations are "minorities" in a political sense, but they need not always be so numerically. To cite just one example, the Bahutu make up 82 per cent of the population of Burundi but have, until very recently, been extremely marginal politically.[25] They may, by some definition or other, be ethnic groups but "ethnicity" is not always a criterion: caste, class, religion, geography, and ecology may have a more specific salience even though all these attributes generally correlate highly with the rather catch-all category of "ethnicity". Ethnogenesis or the definition of groups by themselves or by others in ethnic terms is sometimes the result rather than a precondition of their distinctive relation to the larger community.[26] Although marginality implies discrimination, the problem cannot be reduced to one of ethnic or racial discrimination alone.

Marginality has a double aspect. In one respect, marginal groups are distinguishable from the larger population by their shared characteristics (e.g., culture, language, religion), or their situation (social, economic, geographic, and so on). Otherwise, there would barely be any point in singling them out for study. However, such characteristics are not unequivocal, nor are they entirely objective. Moreover, whether such attributes are or should be signifi-cant—to what extent, and in what ways—are, very often, highly disputed issues. The boundaries of group belonging are often blurred and shifting, and, only too often, imposed on individuals to whom they may be neither self-evi-dent nor desirable. Similarly, the forms and options of association within the group and with members of other groups in the larger society are varied and ambiguous. Indeed, the unicity of the marginal population is usually an ideological and political construction. Likewise, neither belonging to a group nor marginality of a group are original conditions, and they may change over time. While the postulate of objectivity is clearly necessary from a methodo-logical point of view, it carries a danger of reification of which all the contributors are explicitly aware.

More important than its own characteristics, what distinguishes a group is its relationship to the state and to other groups in the society of which it is a part (as "other", "different", "distant", "alien", "recalcitrant", etc.). Its objectivity in this respect lies not in the fact that it is empirically observable in an immediate way but in that it is discoverable by inquiry into the ways people understand and express their social existence. It is hidden or revealed in the ways that people think of society and their part in it, of the state and its articulations to people under their various identifications of class and culture, and even mere physical location and appearance. Marginality describes a relationship which is ultimately not reducible to empirical phenomena. There are no unique characteristics which determine marginality. Indeed, the differ-entiating features around which people are marginalized in one society may

Sam C. Nolutshungu

not have the same significance in another. Gender and sexual orientation may be examples. Nor would it serve much purpose to regard all those who are distinct or who suffer any disadvantage in a society as "marginal". While that would perhaps serve to underline the very important point that few people are ever completely integrated into their society or state, our intention is to distinguish groups whose relationship to the state and society is significantly different from that of other groups. We also wish to distinguish marginality from a temporary alienation or weakness of a group, or the temporary or contingent weakness of state performance, or the incompleteness of an otherwise ongoing process of integration, and to focus on enduring relationships. We have a particular interest in those categories of people for whom being marginal in their own societies makes integration into the *system of states* fundamentally problematic.

Marginal populations are usually disadvantaged or oppressed, but in some cases, their oppression may be no greater than that of most other groups, or it may be counter-balanced by material advantages which derive from the situation of marginality itself. These may include mutual support within the group, or, in the case of transnational populations, access to support from kindred populations in other countries, or articulation to transnational financial and commercial networks, and, in the case of caste systems in some countries, monopoly access to skills and occupations prohibited to the fully integrated or dominant population. Although, it does appear that in most cases, marginality is associated with hardship, the situation is sufficiently complex to discourage us from defining it simply as one of oppression.

This reserve is justified by three additional considerations. First, marginality is not total or general. A group may be marginal in some respects, but not in others: e.g., politically but not economically. If Sikhs are considered by their nationalists to be marginal in India in political terms, it can hardly be said that the same applies to their economic situation or their role in the military. Likewise, a group may suffer cultural repression without specific political and economic disabilities being imposed on it.

Second, marginality is not always unilaterally imposed on a group that otherwise wishes to be fully integrated. Populations may wish to maintain aspects of distinctive ways of life for various reasons; or, else, marginality may be enforced by strata of the marginal population with a vested interest in their own roles that can exist only under conditions of marginality. This is central to the problematic of assimilation which is the focus of David Laitin's contribution and which, in various ways, is addressed in other chapters as well. It bears some relation to the phenomenon of collaboration under foreign occupation or colonization. When collusion between internal dominant elements and an external ruling class is very extensive (or, when there is convergence between the group's own efforts to sustain or assert its identity and those of others to exclude it), a one-dimensional view of marginality in terms of domination and subordination becomes unsatisfactory.

Finally, marginality may define a relationship with other people in a general way, as well as a specific relation to the state. In the former case, it is, often, quite implausible to consider the whole of the non-marginal population as dominators when most of them may be victims of some form of oppression in their own right. In such cases the oppressor needs to be identified rather more precisely: it may be an elite or class, a coalition of internal and foreign elements, an alliance of marginal and non-marginal elites, or a regime or system which defies identification in representational terms (i.e. as belonging to or serving a particular population—except in the most relative terms as e.g., to mean that it serves (or pleases) such people rather more than it does the marginal ones). Yet, the forces that construct and accentuate distinctness and boundaries may not originate from the structures that dominate or oppress, or, in current social science parlance, not in the state but in "civil society". The same is true of conflict and violence among groups: although it implicates the state in important ways, it may neither be initiated by the state nor helpful to its own specific needs.

Zoltan Barany, in his chapter on the East European Roma (Gypsies), lays particular emphasis on societal attitudes in his account of centuries long marginalization of the Roma which has persisted despite major social and economic transformations and radical changes of regime. Even where post-communist regimes have favored liberal policies towards the Roma, as in the Czech Republic, hate crimes against the Roma have increased alongside a resurgence of anti-semitism.[27]

In short, domination and oppression point to a specific complex of relationships that may be a part of marginality and marginalization but they do not define the situation of marginality, while the existence of marginal groups and their treatment may be little more than incidental to the sets of power relations that constitute dominance and the forms of oppression in a political order or society.[28]

Indeed, the notion of marginal populations is difficult to apply to states where virtually no part of the population can be said to participate in any meaningful way either because the state is an alien imposition (e.g., an externally supported dictatorship or autocracy), or is dominated by a narrow stratum relying on force and a favorable web of external relationships (as in Zaire), or where the state has all but disappeared as in Liberia and Somalia today, or is overwhelmed by brigands and armed bands as in Mozambique in the middle and late 1980s and Chad in the early 1980s; or, more typically, in many parts of the Third World, where the level of development of the

Sam C. Nolutshungu

economy and of the state itself is such that the contact between the state and most of the people is superficial and episodic, the state being for the most part, a superfluous encumbrance. In these cases, it would seem, it is the state that is marginal.

Some states are marginal in international relations. They are, through their internal conflicts, or by self-closure, or by the action of other states, or by their general weakness, unable to participate gainfully in international relations. The *populations* doomed to live under them are then marginal in the measure of their exclusion from world society. While world society is a rather loosely integrated, somewhat ethereal thing in which participation is tenuous for most and manifestly unequal, it does, nevertheless, represent a point of reference over and above "national" societies. Indeed, given the integration of the world economy, transnational political and ideological movements, and the proliferation of international regimes and institutions, marginality within the state can be ameliorated or aggravated by the society or the marginal group's articulation to transnational and international webs of affiliation both governmental and non-governmental. Even though the contributors to the present work mostly focus on marginal populations within states, they invoke the larger regional and international contexts, being aware that a view of marginal populations as subjects of international security (which opposes itself to the more familiar state-centric approaches), requires that neither the national state nor the society it encloses be considered the ultimate points of reference for the definition of marginality.

It may give some concreteness to the preceding analysis to enumerate, rather summarily, some of the categories of people we envisaged when the project began and to take in review some of main lines of argument which emerge from the chapters which follow.

1. A marginal group may consist of a distinct population regionally concentrated within one country. "National minorities" claiming a right to self-determination are usually of this type. Many groups, however, have neither a project for independent statehood nor the practical possibility of realizing one.

2. Members of a group may not occupy a distinct region but may be scattered throughout the territory of the state while being, nevertheless, distinct and subject to marginality. Jews in pre-war Europe and the Roma (Gypsies) fall into this category.

3. Some diasporas are associated with marginality: where the population concerned is regarded or regards itself as belonging elsewhere; or where a population marginal in the state of origin regards itself as coextensive with such a diaspora, with the interests of the two not being integrated to those of

either the state of origin or the diaspora states. Palestinians are one contemporary example.

4. Indigenous peoples as conventionally understood by both the UN and the ILO are marginal in most places where they may be found. The identification of such people as "indigenous" implies the existence of a significant section of the population in each case which lives an "indigenous" way of life. "Indigenous" came into circulation to replace "primitive", partly as a euphemism and partly to reflect a more respectful regard for such ways of life but the nomenclature remains unstable, reflecting shifting political perceptions and claims.[29] Though often characterized in terms of their cultures and their relations with the environments which they inhabit, "indigenous peoples" are invariably populations that came under foreign conquest and dispossession and were either poorly integrated into the would-be modern, capitalist political economy, or integrated in a special way that suppressed individuation and valorized their collective identity whether in property relations and the organization of labor or as part of their exclusion from citizenship and the system of rights pertaining to the conqueror population. Historically, they were, literally, at the frontier, i.e., the margin of the expansion and diffusion of modernity. Quite often, however, the character of "indigenous" is applied to persons as an inherited attribute without much regard to the actual degree of their social or economic integration, or to the extent to which their own way of life persists. Some indigenous groups, whether among Indians of the Americas or Pygmies and hunter gatherers of other continents, are, clearly, more "indigenous" than others.

5. Multistate populations who straddle international boundaries so that they either consider no single state as their homeland, or are not considered by any single state as fully integral to its people, are often marginal in, at least, one of the states. Among the best known cases are the Kurds who are the focus of Hamit Bozarslan's chapter, but Baluchis and, Sri Lankan Tamils are also in this situation. "Transnational" peoples who may not occupy contiguous territories across international borders but who, while having a distinct identity as a people, are dispersed in several states, provide another example. The borderlands people whose situation is explored by Anthony Asiwaju are another category of people who are made anomalous by the territoriality of states.

7. Communities of displaced persons can acquire something of a permanent character without ever being assimilated to the host state or community. Some are recognized officially by states and international organizations as being entitled to protection under international law, but the definitions are technical and exclude internal refugees and what are increasingly referred to as "economic refugees". The assumption that refuge is temporary, accompanied

Sam C. Nolutshungu

by the expectation that the persons affected will eventually be reinserted in their countries of origin may encourage a reluctance on the part of host states to facilitate integration even where the prospects of reinsertion under humane conditions are remote.

8. Labor migrants, whether legal or illegal, may be subject to laws in the host countries which, even when their sojourn has been prolonged, place obstacles to their integration and the acquisition of rights of citizenship. The supposed temporariness of their presence may encourage periodic agitation by sections of the host population and by political leaders and demagogues against immigrants while the toleration of their presence continues to be treat- ed as a matter of unilateral discretion by the host society. This is a problem that confronts many advanced industrial countries, but is of particular importance in the contemporary European context with which Rémy Leveau's chapter is concerned.

9. Underclasses in industrial and industrializing societies face marginality. Many of these fall into the category of homeless people, old and young, investigated by Kim Hopper. Among them is the burgeoning population of "street children," lacking state protection and support, often the victims, in every country, of unspeakable misuse.

The list could, no doubt, be lengthened and the examples multiplied. But the present study is not concerned to produce a survey of marginal popula- tions or marginalizing situations. It seeks to identify some central problems and to develop lines of thinking that may be of general application.

Approaches to Marginality and Security

What marginality is, or does, cannot entirely be settled by definition. We gain a fuller idea of its meanings by exploring its various aspects in the different contexts of its occurrence. In this spirit, the authors do not merely apply a list of questions, mechanically, to different marginal populations and countries in order to compare and contrast findings across a set of case studies. Rather, they tackle different aspects and situations of marginality and their implications for security. Within its own remit each paper is comparative but across papers comparative argument is indirect and implicit, rather than schematic or mechanical. There are no shared methodological presuppositions except for the requirement of conceptual and analytical rigor in whatever approach is used. Yet, the chapters communicate closely with each other for all their diversity of subject and method.

David Laitin deals with the problematic of assimilation.[30] Rejecting a view of identity as primordial and preferring one that sees it as capable of being assumed (chosen)by individuals, acting rationally in their own interests, among a plurality of available alternatives, he approaches assimilation in terms of its costs and benefits for each individual who decides to assimilate. Using a modified version of Schelling's tipping model, he postulates that these change as the number of assimilated individuals increases in such a way that when a certain point is reached defections from the marginal group should increase substantially as the costs fall relative to the expected benefits for each individual. Elaborating on the "costs" and "benefits" involved, he advances a series of hypotheses which he then proceeds to evaluate in the light of historical situations involving Gypsies and Jews in Europe and Russia, Untouchables in India, and Gastarbeiters in West Germany before the fall of the Berlin Wall.

The procedure enables Laitin to highlight a number of important analytical points. For individuals as well as for groups there are varying degrees of assimilation while the content of assimilation (i.e. what counts as assimilation) is complex and variable. Both the dominant population and the marginal minority are internally differentiated in such a way that various elites and strata in each group may have conflicting interests in removing barriers to assimilation or maintaining boundaries, for reasons linked not only to beliefs and values but to the economic consequences of change.

A great part of the insecurity of marginal populations arises from the violence provoked by assimilation as it threatens diverse vested interests. Violence may be directed against the would be assimilators, or the non-assimilated, or both; but it can also arise within the marginal population out of the efforts of certain elements to preserve marginality.

The focus on costs and benefits for a diversity of actors provides a *grille de lecture* that can be applied to situations of marginality which are not restricted only to the confines of single states but may encompass regions in different continents, in different historical epochs. Many of the ideas developed here to analyze the complex interaction of marginal and dominant populations are developed and illustrated in other contributions, notably those of Bozarslan and Leveau.

Bozarslan's analysis of the Kurdish situation shows assimilation in a sharply contrasted light. Despite some softening of state policies in recent years, the Kurds in the states issued out of the Ottoman Empire, have not characteristically been given a choice to assimilate but compelled to do so. Assimilation is not variegated but categoric. It relates not nearly so much to culture as to politics. It is little more than the renunciation of the option to organize around a distinct political identity. This denial is linked to the exploitation and underdevelopment of Kurdish territories which is motivated by both economic and political considerations.

The problem of assimilation-marginality presents itself, however, as pre-eminently political, arising out of the failed attempts of these relatively new

Sam C. Nolutshungu

states to consolidate their unity as nation-states. That produces, on the one hand, the nationalism of the states—all the more truculent for having failed to institutionalize nations or to develop complementary mechanisms of legitimation—and, on the other, the reactive nationalism of the Kurdish minorities.

Being "transnational," Kurds nevertheless have to organize their nationalism within the framework of nation states, their leaders entangled in clientelistic accommodations with individual states, and when they operate regionally, they do so under the manipulation of leaders of states with regional ambitions. Such ambitions, themselves, undermine efforts to consolidate national sovereignty for each state as the subversion entailed in the manipulation of sub-national marginal groups like the Kurds not only contributes to interstate violence but on the rebound, practiced reciprocally, challenges the sovereignty of each state.

Zoltan Barany sees the problems of the Roma aggravated by the devastating interruptions of state creation and economic development in Eastern Europe in modern times. Latterly, the economic difficulties faced by these states in their transitions to capitalism have at once revived traditional xenophobia and provoked migration of Roma across international boundaries, notably, to Germany, where it excites hostility to the Roma. While Barany sees steady progress with succeeding system-types so far as the political rights of the Roma are concerned, the persistence of traditions of hatred and exclusion raises questions as to the conditions in which those rights can ever be fully exercised or the security of their bearers assured.

The politics of identity revolve around the politics of mobilization at two levels: within states in the contestation of alienated urban strata whom the Kurdish movements were able to organize ideologically and politically, and to arm; and regionally and internationally, in the continuing attempts to define and redefine interstate capacities and relations. Because of their insertion into this international arena, transnational marginal groups acquire a particular interest in a time of global reordering of international relations not only for states but for non-governmental organizations and transnational interest groups, which have also become important, as Charles Hale points out, in the politics of identity of indigenous peoples in the New World.[31]

Where the teleology of state formation and a continuing purchase of marxist radicalism characterize the situation in the region of the Kurds, in Latin America the ideas of struggle are being debated and redefined in the context of a changed global and regional context.

Jonathan Boyarin demonstrates the power of a critical analysis of conventional political conceptions and their uses. He analyzes the discourse of marginality, particularly the binary opposition between margin and center which he takes to be implicit in it, and illustrates not only that "margin" and "center" change with time, but that, at one and the same time, they may refer to different aspects and sets of relationships so that people and places that are part of the center in some ways may be at the margin in others, at local, national and global levels, while their position can change radically in time. Israeli (and other) Jews and Palestinians are both, in their different ways, marginal peoples. Since the creation of the Jewish state, Israelis have felt, and continue to feel, insecure in various ways. Ethnocentric state creation fails to solve the problem of insecurity and marginality but, instead, reproduces, somewhat absurdly, the very system of binary oppositions between margins and centers that generates insecurity, and which it is supposed to remedy.

If the formation of the Jewish state is an attempt to overcome Jewish marginality, in its turn, it constitutes the Palestinians as a marginal population. Yet, within itself, Israel has produced several marginal situations: of certain categories of Jews like Orientals and Russian immigrants; of Arab Israelis, marginal to both the Jewish state and the Palestinian diaspora (yet capable of placing themselves at the "center" of struggle as through the Intifada); and, territorially, Arabs and to a different degree, Jewish settlers as frontiersmen, in the occupied territories. On the other hand, Palestinian aspirations to statehood, though imposed as a necessity by the facts of international political life and the prevalence of nationalism and the nation state in the world (and, for that reason, deserving of support), bid fair to produce a state that generates margins of its own as it contrives to create a Palestinian center. Boyarin implies that the ways in which margins and centers tend to be conceived embody extensive claims concerning the conditions of security and well being of people which are, quite often, simply false in a way that discredits the discourse of "national self-determination", to the extent, at any rate, that it depends critically on such expectations.

People have multiple identities, or, rather, compound and subtle ones for it is not a matter of distinct self-definitions donned for different situations and occasions. It is rather that self-awareness always contains all the facets of being and belonging which the dichotomy of marginal and non-marginal as well as ethnocentric notions in state building (in Bozarslan's terminology, *les doctrines fondatrices* i.e., "foundational doctrines") seeks to separate out and polarize.

Against the background of rising hostility to non-European immigrants in Western Europe, Rémy Leveau examines the situation of North African immigrants in France, taking their responses to internal and international crises affecting Arabs and Islam, as revealed in opinion surveys, as an indication of their disposition to the host community and states. There is overwhelming political identification with France, yet, the climate of hostility towards immigrants provokes a kind of "ethnogenesis" in which some of the

Sam C. Nolutshungu

immigrants defiantly and defensively assert their own distinctness. Their integration has been complicated by regional and global developments: the deteriorating North-South relation, the collapse of communism and the influx of immigrants from Eastern Europe to the West, the changing labor needs of European capitalism, and, in an earlier age, the demands of the colonial empire, which, at one point, encouraged immigrant labor, and the decline of working class politics and proletarian solidarity (as in the example of the city of Marseilles). In the united Europe that might emerge, integration of these populations in one country will not necessarily spare them marginalization and discrimination in another, o at the regional, European, level. Once again, the foundational doctrines which may be adopted for a European political system will help or hinder not only in terms of the internal criteria of acceptance applied to immigrants already in Europe but also in the orientation of the New Europe they may dictate towards the countries and cultures of origin from which these populations may not wish to dissociate themselves completely.

The problems of state-building have been the major sources of displacement, particularly in Africa, in the wake of the dissolution of empires, and, as in the Middle East and Eastern Europe where there is a strong association between state-building initiatives and the creation of new, or the reactivation of old marginalities and insecurities. In the third world, generally, revolutionary pressures, always international as well as national in their causes and their consequences, continue to be felt, expressing themselves in a variety of idioms and modes of mobilization: sometimes expressed in familiar nationalist terms, at other times embedded in religious fundamentalist movements, and, as in Mexico, in the coalescence of identity and class politics in a dramatic invocation of memories of peasant rebellion.

The theme of global change is taken up in the study of homeless people by Kim Hopper. The new homeless in the United States are produced, in large part, by secular changes in world capitalism notably by the disappearance of certain categories of work in late capitalism and with them the redundance of certain productive human capacities. Embedded in the "durable realities" of racism and poverty, homelessness among African-Americans on the present scale is a relatively recent form of marginality.

Finally, administrative preoccupations, over and above the interplay of political consciousness, demands and action, define a terrain of marginalization and resistance. Two papers, by Alfred Darnell and Tony Asiwaju, in quite different contexts and with different foci, draw our attention to the imperatives of administration and its biases. Indigenous peoples in the circumpolar North, discussed by Darnell, like borderlands peoples around the world—the subject of Asiwaju's chapter—confront the state pre-eminently as an administrative anomaly. In the case of the indigenous people, their identity and demographic size tend to be determined by administrative procedure with a bias towards minimizing the numbers and so bounding the obligations of the state. With many of them astride the distinction between indigenous and non-indigenous, an ambivalent situation bound to be reproduced through the generations, the preference of states is to make a dichotomous determination and one that effectively limits the size of the anomalous population and the financial obligations of the state towards it. The intrusion of capitalist relations of property facilitated by state policy further structures their choices from without while creating scope for deals with coalitions of indigenous elites and external capitalists which may disadvantage future generations.

Borders, for many countries, are remote from the centers of bureaucratic control, while the people at or astride the frontier complicate the policing and control of the international movement of goods and persons. Administrative suspicion towards borderlands people and heavy surveillance of their homelands by "a multiplicity of state security agencies" are accompanied by a lack of responsiveness towards them on the part of political authorities at the center. But borderlands differ in type and are subject to different regimes. Their problems can be alleviated by transborder cooperation regimes of which an outstanding example is Western European integration as it has developed since World War II—in short, a certain modification of the national state and a softening of the territorial boundaries so essential a part of the Westphalian system.

Asiwaju's solution draws attention back, however, to new borders that may be created and jealously guarded—between regions—as Leveau suggests may be the case between Europe and its South, a view supported by the expectation that as global processes dispose many in the poorer regions of the world to migrate to the centers of production and exchange of an integrated world economy, admission policies there will become more restrictive. In the end, the source and the theater of marginality, is the international system itself.[32]

A New Politics?

Taken together, the contributions to this work indicate ways of thinking about international security which are not merely additional to the most prevalent approaches but which invite a radical reconsideration of the relationship between states and people in relation to security appropriate to our times which are characterized by dramatic state failures and by development of a world system that is profoundly subversive of some of the basic ideological claims of

Sam C. Nolutshungu

states regarding people. We may now indicate the outlines of an emerging argument that still awaits theoretical elaboration.

Shifting the focus from states as subjects of security, and from insecurity as represented by the threats they pose to each other, implies more than a simple substitution of "the people" contained in the state for the state itself. It raises a problem of definition of people or categories of people other than those which are derived either from the fact of the existence of the state or from state-building aspirations. Although individuals are assuredly valid foci of attention, our concern requires the identification of meaningful collectivities (groups, communities, etc.), as well. Such an undertaking is closely related to the identifications that people make of themselves and are, therefore, never innocent of the "identity politics" which, too, is necessarily an object of study. The question of "whose security" asserts itself as central to the study of international relations demanding detailed consideration? We have chosen to look at only one category which is, nevertheless, inclusive of a wide range of types of identity.

The contexts of security and insecurity change of necessity once the subject is changed. The distinction between "national" and "international", meaning inside the state and outside it, then becomes question-begging and inadequate. Indeed, the insecurities that some categories of people suffer acutely all the time, sometimes, comparable in all respects to the vicissitudes of war, are discovered to be within states, or, while being within states, to implicate the international system in important ways. The state may be a context of insecurity, but sometimes it is a region—the Middle East, the Horn of Africa, or Southern Africa, or what have you, that, by its very configuration, creates the conditions of insecurity for certain categories of people. Sometimes, it is the great globe itself in the way it is divided and administered, and ideologically constructed. International security, then, ceases to belong to a distinct domain of "international relations" even if this is broadened to include the influence of non-state actors and nonpolitical affairs.

Likewise, the sources of insecurity are less determinate. Threats issue not only from states but from other people acting, sometimes, with the complicity of the state, at other times, in defiance of it (as in the attacks on refugees and immigrants in Europe).

Some of the severest forms of hardship result not from politics (except in so far as it fails to intervene helpfully), but from the impersonal operation of the world economy and its impact on the material conditions of survival and well-being, and on the possible forms of association and solidarity among people (and peoples). The questions that are relevant to the security of marginal populations cover, potentially, all the issues of uneven development within countries and among them. With respect to indigenous peoples and what used to be called "traditional societies", they involve the penetration of world capitalism and property rights and patterns of resource use. But they also bear on the manner in which claims to collective goods (e.g., the environment, resources of the seabed, etc.), are formulated and recognized. Faced with such issues, some states, like the marginal ones to which we have adverted, are helpless, their very existence perpetuating the manner in which the effects of world development are distributed.

The private trade in arms, narcotics and restricted animal products as well as the smuggling of immigrants represent economic processes that are growing and whose effects in terms of violence, destitution and degradation for communities across the world are significant, and by all indications, growing. The various ways of unloading toxic waste on ill-governed countries—and the pollution problem, generally—are yet another aspect of world economic development with potentially far reaching effects for marginality and insecurity. To some extent, the state, indeed, several states are often implicated in these transfers through neglect or collusion.

The insecurity of marginal people is, in most cases, a problem of oppression and exploitation: but marginal people are not all oppressed or all of the oppressed. Marginality is primarily about participation (or relative exclusion from participation) in gainful cooperation with others which includes institutional representation, fair inclusion in the schemes of social protection and support and in the system of rights applicable to each context. The problematic of marginality and insecurity, therefore, invokes the politics of belonging where this entails rights of participation. This brings it close to the problematic of citizenship except that in contemporary use this notion always presupposes the very system of nation-states that is under suspicion in this work.[33] It invokes the "politics of identity" that several of the contributors refer to, except that the assumption, denial or manipulation of identities always presupposes a real, material world, in which identities make a difference but which is not comprehended in the "identities" themselves. One cannot dispense with "structures" in understanding identities any more than one can understand choices without the stable constraints the previous choices of oneself and other agents impose.

The discourse of identity, belonging, and citizenship, gains in meaning and poignancy when it is related to the real world—and it is the world, in the literal sense, which is at issue. It then ceases to be the mere contemplation of the subjective doomed, in its own turn, to be forever subjective. Global change has, as we have noted, been described in various ways by international relations theorists of various kinds both in terms of the inadequacy of traditional ideas of sovereignty and the nation-state and with respect to the integration and subordination of "national" economies in a world system now free from the challenge of even an ideological alternative. If the emphasis on questions of identity and marginality has anything specific to contribute, it is awareness of the definition of subjects and reference contexts as absolutely central not only to the description and analysis of marginality and security but to meaningful action regarding them. Whether one (i.e., an individual or group) refers oneself to the locality, the state, the region or the world cannot be settled by conventional notions of state, people and international relations but is in each case a political action (a *prise de position*) by the self or others, but so also is the definition of the collective self.

More, we are challenged to be particularly sensitive to the marginalizing processes of the contemporary world with its multivalent internal frontiers: collapsing in the face of some forces and closing securely against others—whether these be boundaries of citizenship, of economic exchange, of employment and survival. Cutting across the relations of oppression and exploitation which have dominated the relationships between human groups in the creation of the modern world, and which mainstream international relations and security studies barely recognize and have yet to integrate fully into their concerns, a new contrast has clearly emerged. It is the opposition between those who have a large share of the fruits of the collective work of societies and international society and those who barely participate; and, even more fundamentally, between those who have a role at all in the human effort that is necessary and those who have become superfluous. If warfare was always based upon some portion of the population being under certain conditions, expendable, those who made up that part were, nonetheless, essential to the system of war for that very reason. Increasingly, now, many young male persons from disadvantaged classes, especially, are merely superfluous contributing no more to purposeful destruction than to economic production. A large part of national and international violence, in which they are expended, whether in the form of the breakdown of civil order or organized crime, does little to enhance their salience in society while it makes no economy of lives.

All countries have now adjusted to significant proportions of their populations living outside the margins of whatever collective effort still sustains the idea of society. There is no better indication of this than the fact that the ethical commitment to full employment, once an unquestioned ideal, has weakened to an unprecedented degree in this century while notions of citizenship premised on solidarity and participation in a common patrimony have fallen victim to economic (rather, economistic) ideologies that render it merely procedural and formal. In a sense, that underlines a decline of the ideal of integration, also. Yet, being integral pays: and for that reason, it matters greatly where one belongs—not only in the subjective sense of self-identification but also in the mastery of the contexts to which it is gainful to belong. It

International Security and Marginality

is, surely, no surprise that, under these conditions, we witness a recrudescence of forms of intolerance and violence from which progress had been thought to have delivered us: xenophobia and racism, religious intolerance, and the wholesale murder of superfluous children (the so-called "street children") or their exposure through organized crime or by mere neglect to hunger and deadly disease—also a variant of "identity politics".[34]

The papers in this book raise grave doubts as to the adequacy of the state as a provider of security. For marginal populations, but, perhaps, for others, too, it may be necessary to look elsewhere: "elsewhere", within national societies, and "elsewhere", beyond them, to new possibilities of association and solidarity that recognize, in creative ways, the possibilities of the contradictory integration of the world which, at once, incorporates and marginalizes. That points to a new politics of groups and collectivities manipulating different contexts of belonging and security and their articulations: a *world politics* rather than merely international relationships. It is not that the state has become irrelevant to security and can be ignored. It is, rather, that, in the various ways indicated in the chapters that follow, it is inadequate, and sometimes, harmful. It is in the recognition of its limitations and attempts to qualify and establish counterweights to the role of states and the system of states that progress in international security, seen, primarily, as the security of persons, may lie.

Notes

1. Ernest Nys ed., *Francisci de Victoria De Indis et De ivre belli relectiones,* (tr John P Bates) Washington, The Carnegie Institution of Washington, 1917. Hedley Bull, "Grotian Conception of International Society" in Herbert Butterfield and Martin Wight, *Diplomatic Investigations,* London, Allen and Unwin, 1966

2. M. Walzer, *Just and Unjust Wars: a moral argument with historical illustration,* New York: Basic Books, c 1977

3. For some discussion of the ethical issues confronting America at the time, see Robert W Tucker and David C. Hendrickson, *The Imperial Temptation: The New World Order and America's Purpose,* New York, Council for Foreign Relations Press, 1992

4. *L'Idée de la raison d'Etat dans l'histoire des temps modernes,* Genève, Droz, 1973

5. Robin Luckham, "Security and Disarmament in Africa" Alternatives 9 Fall 1983; Carlos Egan, National Security and Human Rights Abuse: Argentina's Dirty Wars in Edward E Azar and Chung-in Moon, *National Security in the Third World: The management of internal and external threats,* Aldershot, Edward Elgar,1988; Brian L. Job, "The Insecurity Dilemma: National, Regime, and State Securities in the Third World" in Brian L Job ed., *The Insecurity Dilemma: national security in the Third World,* Boulder: Lynne Rienner, 1992, and Edward

Sam C. Nolutshungu

A. Koldziej, "Renaissance in Security Studies? Caveat Lector!", ACDIS *Occasional Paper*, September 1991, University of Illinois at Urbana-Champagne. **33**

6. Cf Mano Dayak (avec la collaboration de Michael Stuhrenberg et de Jérôme Strazzula), *Touareg, la tragédie,* Paris: Jean-Claude Lattès, 1992, a partisan account and the review of it by Adamou Idé, "Lettre à un prophète annoncé" in *Africa International* No 251, July 1992; see, also, "Touaregs, les Kurdes de l'Afrique" in *Le Nouvel Afrique-Asie,.* No 26 November 1991

7. Cf. Nicolae Gheorghe, "L'Ethnicité des Tsiganes Roma et le processus de transition en Europe de l'Est" in *Etudes Tsiganes* No 2/91; See also, P. Williams, ed., *Tsiganes: Identité, Evolution,* Paris? Syros, 1989

8. Of related interest, Björn Hettne, "Security and Peace in Post-Cold War Europe" *Journal of Peace Research,* vol 28, no 3, 1991, pp 279-294

9. Barry Buzan, *People, States, and Fear: The National Security Problem in International Relations,* Chapel Hill, University of North Carolina Press, 1983

10. Kolodziej, op cit

11. Alfred Cobban,National Self-determination London: Oxford University Press, 1945 and *The Nation State and National Self-determination* (revised edition) New York, Crowell, 1970. In a vast literature, see, also Eisuke Suzuki, "Self -Determination and World Public Order: Community Response to Territorial Separation", *Virginia Journal of International Law,* 16:4 Summer 1976, pp 779-862; Patrick Thornberry, "Self-determination, minorities, human rights: a review of international instruments" *International and Comparative Law Quarterly,* 38: October 1989, pp 867-889; Edward Morgan, "The Imagery and Meaning of Self-Determination" *New York University Journal of International Law and Politics,* 20: 2 Winter 1988 pp 355-403; Dov Ronen, *The Quest for Self-Determination,* New Haven: Yale University Press 1979; and Charles Beitz, *Political Theory and International Relations,* Princeton: Princeton University Press, 1979, pp 92-105 for persuasive criticism of the "principle". See also, Daniel P Moynihan, *Pandaemonium:Ethnicity in International Politics,.* New York, Oxford University Press, 1993, and Gidon Gottlieb, *Nation Against State: A New Approach to Ethnic Conflicts and the Decline of Sovereignty,* New York, Council on Foreign Relations Press, 1993

12. John Mueller, *The Retreat from Doomsday: The Obsolescence of Major War,* New York: Basic Books, 1989; also, "Changing Attitudes Towards War: The Impact of the First World War," *British Journal of Political Science,* 21: January 1991

13. M.S. Anderson, *The Eastern Question,* London, Macmillan, 1966, pp 287 et seq; Walker Connor, *The National Question in Marxist-Leninist Theory and Strategy,* Princeton NJ, Princeton University Press, 1984

14. I. Wallerstein, *The Politics of the World-Economy: The States, The Movements and The Civilizations,* Cambridge, Cambridge University Press, 1983; Robert O. Keohane and Joseph Nye, *Power and Interdependence: World politics in Transition,* Boston: Little, Brown, 1977

15. Cf Lee Sweepston, "The Indian in Latin America: Approaches to Administration, Integration, and Protection" *Buffalo Law Review,* 1978: 27: 4 pp 715-755

16. Cf Robert Bailey, "Development in the Ituri Forest of Zaire" Cultural Survival, Spring, 1982; Colin Turnbull, *The Mbuti Pygmies: change and adaptation* New York: Holt, Rinehart, and Winston 1983; Lucien Demesse, *Techniques et économie des Pygmées Babinga,* Paris: Institut d'ethnologie, Musée de l'Homme, 1980. The non-technical literature about these people has become very scanty. Cf Luigi Luca Cavalli-Sforza, *African Pygmies,* New York, Academic Press,1986

17. Of related interest, Michel Seurat, "Le quartier de Bâb Tebbâne à Tripoli (Liban): étude d'une 'asabiyya urbaine" . . . unpublished

18. Cf R.Cohen, "Warfare and State Formation: Wars make States and States make War" in R.B.Ferguson (ed), *Warfare, Culture and Environment,* New York, Academic Press, 1984

19. "The Renaissance of Security Studies" *International Studies Quarterly,* 35:1991, pp 211-239

20. Marcus Dods: The Works of Aurelius Augustine: Vol II: *The City of God, Book XVII,* Edinburgh, T&T Clark, 1871; Michael Oakeshott ed: *Thomas Hobbes, Leviathan, Book I* (London: Collier Macmillan, 1974)

21. Alain Joxe, Voyage aux sources de la guerre, Paris: Presses Universitaires de France, 1991, esp p52

22. Op. cit.

23. Robert Jervis, "Cooperation under the Security Dilemma" *World Politics,* 30:2 January, 1978

24. Adam Bromke, *Détente or Cold War II: East-West relations after Afghanistan,* Toronto, Canadian Institute of International Affairs, 1980.

25. On the construction of the groups, see Jean Pierre Chrétien, "Hutu et Tutsi au Rwanda et au Burundi" in Jean-Loup Amselle et Elikia M'Bokolo, *Au Cœur de l'ethnie,* Paris, Editions La Découverte, 1985

26. Cf the situations described by Nicolae Gheorge for the Roma, op cit and by Chrétien, *op cit,* for Burundi.

27. Cf. Reuters, RTw 02/08 2123 "Right-Wing Groups on the Rise in the Czech Republic"

28. The phrase "the marginal situation" is not intended to invoke the quite different problematic in the sociology of race reflected in, e.g., H.F.Dickie-Clark, *The Marginal Situation: a sociological study of a Coloured Group,.* London: Routledge and Kegan Paul, 1966

29. To "native", "aboriginal", "indigenous", Canadians have added the terminology of "First Nations". See Michael D. Levin, ed., *Ethnicity and Aboriginality: Case Studies in Ethnonationalism,* Toronto, University of Toronto Press, 1993

30. See also his related paper, prepared for this project, published as "Marginality: A Microperspective" *Rationality and Society,* 7,1, 1995 31-57

31. See also his earlier paper for this group, published as Charles R. Hale, "Between Che Guevara and the Pachamama: Mestizos, Indians and identity politics in the anti-quincentenary campaign", *Critique of Anthropology* 14:1 1994, 9-39

32. These themes are taken up and developed in the concluding chapter.

33. See Thomas H. Marshall, *Citizenship and social class, and other essays,* Cambridge: Cambridge University Press, 1950. G.Andrews (ed), *Citizenship,* Lon-

don, Lawrence and Wishart, 1991; B.Turner, "Outline of a theory of citizen-ship" *Sociology,* 24: 2 There is a somewhat different emphasis in the anti-discrimination discourse in continental Europe as an antithesis to belonging by blood which is heavily focussed on rights of domicile, movement within states and the European Union, and employment, but egalitarian notions of social solidarity are generally shared. "Citizen rights" have been understood and applied according to prevailing patterns of dominance in society, a point made from a feminist point of view by Ann S. Orloff, "Gender and the Social Rights of Citizenship: The Comparative Analysis of State Policies and Gender Relations" in *American Sociological Review* 58:3, June, 1993

34.   See, among many, Yves Marguerat and Danièle Poitou (eds) *A l'écoute des enfants de la rue en Afrique noire,* Marjuvia (Marginalisation des jeunes dans les villes africaines), Paris, Editions Fayard,1994; see also Michel Galy, "Violence, Drogue, Menidicité: En Afrique, le naufrage des enfants des rues" in *Le Monde Diplomatique,* August, 1995

Chapter 1

A FORMAL MODEL OF
MARGINALITY AND SECURITY

David D Laitin

The end of the cold war, the demise of Soviet hegemony in the Russian periphery, and ultimately the collapse of the Soviet Union, have brought to the fore nationalist movements and have as well induced large scale migrations of peoples across international boundaries. Both of these outcomes have produced "new" minority populations. In western Europe, they come as economic and political refugees. In the former Union Republics of the Soviet Union, all of which are now independent states, established minority populations find themselves having to negotiate their legal status anew. What will be the life chances for these new minorities? What can we expect in terms of assimilation, social mobility, and basic physical security? Will they join the majority, become part of a vibrant minority, or will they lapse into marginality? Is there a way that we can address these questions analytically, yet remain cognizant of historical realities?

These questions are among the most important ones to ask for anyone interested in the dynamics of the new world order, so often spoken about in optimistic terms. Optimists equate the new nationalisms with liberal anti-totalitarian ideologies; they see modern capitalism (the "market") as basically benign in the way it attracts foreign workers to join the industrial working class; they believe that human rights of minority populations can be protected internationally, through extensions of the Helsinki accords. Yet these new minorities may be in for a far more difficult time than optimists believe; they may be, given the particular mechanisms under which they are becoming incorporated into their new states, becoming the new marginals.

Through the examination of the microdynamics of assimilation and marginality, this paper develops a perspective for analyzing the new minority populations, with a focus on their security. In an earlier paper (Laitin, 1995), I presented a formal model of marginality, with an emphasis on economic ghettoization, and applied this to three well-researched cases of marginal populations: Untouchables in India; Gypsies in Europe; and Jews in Western Europe and the Pale of Settlement. In this paper, I shall first draw on the earlier paper for its formal definition of marginality. In the second section, I shall summarize the principal findings of my earlier paper, suggest a few related hypotheses linking marginality to issues of security, and provide some material from the three cases of marginality analyzed in the previous paper, to lend substance to the new hypotheses. The final section will apply the theory to a discussion of the Turkish workers in Berlin before the collapse of the wall. It will show the formal similarities and differences between the classic cases of marginality with those which exist in contemporary democratic states. To be sure, we live in a world with a variety of international treaties and non-governmental institutions that track human rights violations. But Bosnia in the 1990s—a near holocaust despite international monitoring—adds credence to this paper's contention that the future for the new ethnic minorities in Europe is not secure.

The Game Theory of Marginality[1]

Formal theory in the social sciences, basing itself on a rigid framework of methodological individualism, has given us a new perspective on ethnicity and identity change. Individuals who are born as "Navajos", "Untouchables", "Midgaans", "Igbos", "Jews", or "Shi'ites" are not stuck with their "primordial" identities. Rather, they can explore the available marketplace for ones that will provide them with better chances in life. Formal analyses, while leaving their own trail of anomalies, help to explain how purposeful action on the individual level—such as behavior to overcome ascribed status as an "Untouchable" through "sanscritization"—can have a collective outcome that undermines the reproduction of primordial groups.

From this perspective, I would like to pose a question about "marginal populations" that would have seemed impossibly naive a generation ago, because it was not a "problem" in primordial approaches. But for methodological individualists, the question addresses an anomaly. If marginality is so thoroughly demeaning, for economic well-being, for human dignity, as well as for physical security, how do marginal populations sustain themselves, and why don't they disappear through the strategic assimilation of individuals?[2]

The widely-held view on the matter of group identity, and consistent with the primordialist paradigm, is that marginal groups do not want to assimilate; rather, they wish their ethnic group to have special privileges. Consequently, marginal groups wish to secure group rights (as "Harijans", "Jews" or "Gypsies") rather than individual rights as undifferentiated Indians, Russians or Spaniards (San Román 1984:10). Even Simon Kuznets (1975:57), a card-carrying economist, explains Jewish nonassimilation in the Pale, at least in part, by "the strong desire to retain religious identity."[3]

David D. Laitin

My perspective here diverges from this widely held view about group rights. Suppose wealth and dignity are denied an individual due to that person's ascribed status. Suppose further that the costs of individual assimilation were lower than the costs of participating in a movement seeking to gain rights for the entire ethnic group, with the concomitant costs of overcoming collective action problems. Should we not then expect "defectors" from any project to enhance group rights? These defectors would seek individual exits from low status positions in the social hierarchy. The cumulative impact of individual decisions to defect would be large scale assimilation despite the preference of all defectors for the maintenance of their cultural groups. (After high levels of successful assimilation, assimilated individuals or their descendants can repackage their ethnic roots in a way that is not threatening to dominant society; but effective assimilation would have already taken place). The strategy of assimilation need not be chosen because it is collectively optimal; the strategy of assimilation should be chosen, from a methodological individualist framework, because it yields economic and status returns *to an individual* at lower cost than the route of collective action with the goal of enhancing group opportunities.

The mirror image of the widely held view claiming that marginal groups do not want to assimilate is the view, consistent with the primordialist viewpoint, that marginals can always be identified by members of the dominant society, and will face irrevocable discrimination. Cultural identities, this view suggests, are not like onions, where you strip off layers until there is nothing; rather they are like artichokes: you can strip off layers, but there remains a heart. If groups have immutable hearts, then individual actions to strip off layers of previous identities will have only limited impact as dominant society will have little trouble in identifying and discriminating against defectors.

Rational choice approaches to identity challenge the primordialists on this very image. While the onion view is oftentimes inadequate to explain aspects of identity politics (Laitin 1986), it is worthwhile to accept the assumptions of the instrumentalists if only to explain why assimilation in some contexts occurs quickly, while in others, the barriers seem insurmountable. It would be tautological to argue, as a primordialist perspective often implies, that cultural identities are artichokes where assimilation fails but are onions when assimilation succeeds.

What is Assimilation?

For someone to have assimilated, it does not necessarily require becoming indistinguishable from the dominant population in language, religion, appearance, dress, customs, and taste. Rather it means that someone has made sufficient changes in one's public appearance (on these dimensions) such that people from the dominant society, under normal conditions, consider that person as a member of their society, and as a credible claimant, *ceteris paribus*, in the marriage and labor markets. The "choice" to assimilate, then, is really a plethora of choices, that may carry over generations, to publicly portray oneself and one's family as part of the community of the dominant cultural group in society.

However, this process cannot be seen as mere adoption of the cultural practices of dominant society by members of the nonassimilated communities. After all, dominant society often appropriates cultural forms of its own marginals. For example, it is considered an essential aspect of Gypsy culture to carry on the *flamenco* tradition in Spain and the medieval folkloric melodies of Russia (McLane 1987; Lemon, 1990:3). Yet in the 1980s in booming Madrid, young professional Castilian women would drag their husbands to flamenco dance classes in order to partake in "Spanish" culture. For Gypsies, then, it is ambiguous as to what cultural practices need to be changed in order to become Spaniards.

The ambiguities in the process of assimilation are most apparent in the bait-and-switch games that are so common in social life among heterogeneous populations. Assimilators in the marginal population are often made to feel like Alice on the Queen's chessboard: the faster they move, the more the nonmarginal society changes so that the social gap between them and the majority population grows. The common story of such practices is one that points to the strategic behavior of members of dominant society changing their cultural practices to confuse potential assimilators with a moving target. But strategic behavior by members of dominant society is not even necessary for bait-and-switch, as the following two examples demonstrate.[4]

Consider's first Cohn's description (1955:67) of the outcaste Camars, where exogenously induced cultural change within dominant society acts as a barrier to assimilation: "The small changes in family structure that can be noted among the Camars, especially among Camars who have attained some education, are not changes in the direction of a Western-influenced family but changes in the direction of a more orthodox 'Hindu' family. Camars are trying to tighten the authority of the father and place restrictions on the wife. While the Thakur (patron caste) wife is coming out of seclusion, the Camar wife is being put into seclusion." Cohn also observes (p. 74) that Camars are sanscritizing their diets, while upper castes are relaxing their rules. So adopting the cultural practices of dominant society leads not to assimilation but rather to continued isolation.

David D. Laitin

after emancipation where the very process of assimilation creates new barriers between the dominant society and assimilating Jews:

> The Jews who took the Enlightenment on its word and identified emancipation with refinement of manners and, more generally, with self-cultivation, had become cultural fanatics. In every Western nation they were the ones who treated national cultural heritage most seriously . . . Trying to excel in the complex and often elusive task ahead, they sung the praises of national monuments and masterpieces of national art and literature, only to find that the audience comprised mostly people similar to themselves. They read avidly and voraciously, only to find they could discuss what they read only with other *aspiring* Germans or Frenchmen like themselves. Far from bringing them closer to assimilation, conspicuous cultural enthusiasm and obsessive display of cultural nobility set them aside from the native middle class and, if anything, supplied further evidence of their ineradicable *foreignness* . . . The self-destructive tendency of assimilation also affected occupations[;] legal or medical careers . . . offered particular attractions to assimilating Jews . . . The unplanned outcome . . . was . . . an overrepresentation of Jews in the professions, and a new set of arguments to prove the Jews' permanent distinctiveness. The abandoning of traditional Jewish occupations, which from the assimilants' viewpoint meant *Entjudung* (de-judaization of 'men as such') appeared to the baffled native public more like the process of *Verjudung* (judaization of heretofore gentile areas)." [This was a] 'Catch 22' plight [for which] there was no guaranteed escape.

Such dynamics make a simple definition of assimilation as adopting nonmarginal cultural practice quite problematic.

In light of these phenomena, perhaps the best way to think about assimilation, here relying on Barth (1969), is to consider the cultural *content* that differentiates groups as always changing. These changes can be explained as interested behavior by members of dominant groups to establish and maintain *boundaries* between themselves and members of subordinate groups. My approach to assimilation is not inconsistent with a focus on boundary maintenance. If the content of culture is contingent and fluid, as Barth maintains, assimilation can best be defined as the process of adoption of the ever-changing cultural practices of dominant society with the goal of crossing a fluid cultural boundary separating marginal groups from dominant society.

The "Tipping Game"

We can now return to our core question: under what conditions do ethnic, caste, social, and religious groups that are denied rights available to the rest of the population disappear as a result of the cumulative "exit" from those groups by strategic individuals who redefine themselves as members of one of the more favored groups? The mirror question is: under what conditions do the costs of individual exit become so prohibitive that these culturally-defined yet subordinate groups reproduce themselves? The key test of any model that provides answers to these questions is if it can simultaneously account for heavy constraints against assimilation along with the continued success of some groups in assimilating.

An adaptation of Schelling's (1978:chap. 7) "tipping game" provides a partial but compelling set of answers to these questions by highlighting individual payoffs for assimilating that are a function of the percentage of former members of their community who have already assimilated. Consider Figure 1, which represents a situation of a cultural minority within a society with a dominant majority. The game involves binary choices for minority individuals (here, to assimilate or not) who have an incentive to coordinate with each other (as the average payoff for coordinating with members of their cultural group is higher than defecting from it). There are two stable equilibria (in which no one assimilates and in which all do) along with a tipping point, signified by "k". At "k" any small movement in one direction should induce a cascade in that direction towards a 0% or 100% equilibrium.

This model portrays the logic of assimilation in a stunning way, for a number of reasons. First, it captures the "sliding slope" phenomenon of assimilation. Initially, it seems that an immigrant community or an otherwise separate group will remain distinct forever. Then, after a generation or so of contact, suddenly it seems that there are no constraints at all holding back assimilation. Frisians became British; Picards French; Germans American; Sicilians Italian; Ugongs Thais; and Egyptian Nubians Egyptians.[5] Nativists in the majority group cease fearing that a "foreign" group will overrun them; those people holding on to the "old" culture wistfully mourn the extinction of their language and their distinctive way of life.

Second, the tipping game captures the complex coordination problem in making identity choices. At either equilibrium, many individuals might reckon the other equilibrium to have higher individual or collective payoffs, but it would be irrational for someone to switch unless one was convinced that others would switch as well.

Third—and crucial for this chapter—the model allows for an analytic comparison between assimilation patterns in "minority" as opposed to "marginal" populations. It is assumed here that all cultural minorities will face barriers to assimilation, such as discrimination in the job and marriage markets. However, a special subset of minorities (i.e. marginals) face additional burdens that lock them into a permanent situation of political, social

David D. Laitin

and economic degradation. By developing this distinction, I hope to uncover the reason why for some groups assimilation occurs rapidly; whereas for others, it never gets going at all.[6]

Figure 1.1, as was suggested, is a representation of the minority dynamic. Suppose this model represents the choice situation of 17th century Catalans (a minority nationality in northeastern Spain, but clearly not a marginal one) of whether to become "Spaniards". The Catalans had always been part of an economically vibrant region of Spain, and although they were politically dominated by Madrid, they had considerable rights and impressive material resources. The choice for them was whether to educate their children as Spanish-dominant Spanish-Catalan bilinguals or whether to educate them primarily in Catalan. At the early points in the game, where only a few Catalans had switched to Spanish as their principal language, it was irrational for any Catalan to switch to Spanish-dominant bilingualism. But past some tipping point, arbitrarily set here at 50% who made Castilian the principal language in their repertoire, it then becomes irrational *not* to do so. In this tipping game, the value of the equilibrium of nonassimilation at 0% is not much lower than the value of the alternate equilibrium of assimilation at 100%. Assimilation into Spanish culture was indeed a collective action problem; but it did not entail the perception of insurmountable barriers.

Now consider the marginal situation portrayed in Figure 1.2. The characteristics of this game are different, in at least two regards. First, even though the payoffs for individuals at non-assimilation at 0% are far lower than that of assimilation at 100%, the gap in payoffs between assimilation and the status

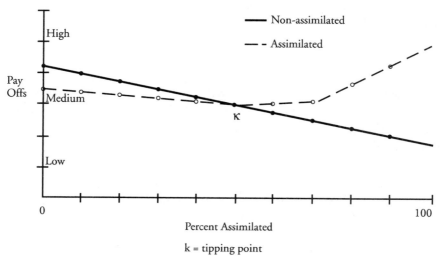

Figure1.1. Tipping game for minorities.

k = tipping point

A Formal Model of Marginality and Security

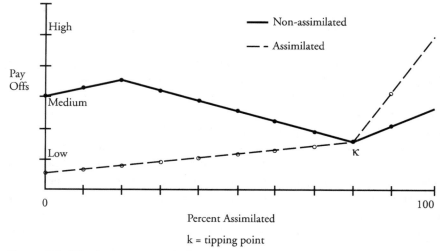

Figure 1.2. Tipping game marginals.

quo is much greater for the marginal than for the minority. Second, the tipping point comes much later, meaning that it will take movement by far more people to the assimilation column before it will be rational for the average member of the nonassimilated community to assimilate. This means that even the expectation that there will be some others assimilating at the same time will not be sufficient for a member of a marginal community to risk assimilation.

We must now ask, what makes for the special configuration of Figure 1.2? We shall do this in the following section, in the course of deriving hypotheses from the model.

Hypotheses on Marginality

To answer this question about the particular shape of a payoff function for marginal populations, it is necessary to analyze how that function is derived. Petersen (1989), in examining the choice of ethnic minorities to join the armed forces of the country in which they live, conceives the payoff function to be an aggregation of three variables: the economic benefits of an army job; the social stigma that the minority group places upon its own members for having joined the armed forces of the dominant society; and the probability of greater social acceptance in the dominant society of the minority if its members prove their loyalty through enlistment.

In my first paper on marginality (Laitin, 1995), I relied on these three variables to generate hypotheses differentiating "minority" and "marginal" populations. In regard to economic benefits, a principal finding of that paper was that marginal groups are often "consigned" to a low status role that has higher economic returns than an entry level job would provide in the higher status economy. While the average economic returns to marginals, I argued, would be far less than for nonmarginals, the individual payoff for a marginal worker in a consigned economic role will be higher than what would be received in a job on the bottom of the occupational ladder of dominant society.

In regard to social stigma—that is the social cost imposed on potential assimilators by fellow members of the disadvantaged group—I suggested that internal monitoring (i.e., performed by members of the marginal population) of potential assimilators slows down the assimilation process. Monitoring, the tipping model suggests, is weak when elites of unassimilated communities can get positions in the dominant society that are equal in status to their former positions in the dominated society. Relying on my earlier research on 19th century Russia and the Soviet Union in regard to assimilation by non-Russians into the Russian nationality, I referred to those elites who could get high status positions in the dominant society "most favored lords", and demonstrated why they had little incentive to monitor assimilation among lower status members of their own nationality group (Laitin, 1991).

The third variable, social acceptance by dominant society, refers to the degree of acceptance in dominant society received by those who avidly seek assimilation. One obvious hypothesis in this domain is that racial or other physically apparent distinguishing characteristics of the non-dominant population permit members of the dominant society more easily to police entry, and to raise its costs.

The Question of Security

The hypotheses summarized in the previous section, and a set of related hypotheses, all derived from a consideration of the formal attributes of the "tipping game", received mixed levels of support based on the examination of the experiences of Gypsies, Jews, and Untouchables. Indeed, many of the hypotheses required extensive reformulation to make sense of the data. Here, rather than developing those hypotheses any further, I shall seek to draw out implications of the model for questions concerning the security of populations who are not of the dominant cultural or nationality group.

The basic insight derived from the model focuses on the rising average benefits for the nonassimilators as the first 10-15% of the marginal population attempts to assimilate. This occurs because at early stages of assimilation, members of the marginal group see their community identity at risk, and give high social status to those who have the opportunity to switch, but do not take it. Meanwhile, the payoffs to those who assimilate remain low, as low paying jobs in the high-status economy yield less than normal jobs in the "polluted" job sectors. Also, early assimilators will lose status among their own, and will face barriers to social acceptance in dominant society. With these incentives, assimilation will be slow, and only those with expected payoffs far greater than the average will attempt to make the switch.

But after a while the gap begins to close, and members of both dominant and marginal society begin to see the implications of an approaching tipping point. As the tipping point approaches, a variety of groups will feel threatened. Elites within marginal society will see their own constituencies beginning to disappear, and they will fear that their representational role before state authorities will no longer be needed. Less well-to-do members of the marginal population will begin to see basic social norms breaking down, and will want to set sanctions against assimilationist probes (Akerlof 1984, 35-36). Also, members of dominant society who are economically at the bottom of the employment ladder (the "red-necks" in American parlance, vis-à-vis African Americans) will feel threatened by marginal assimilation for two reasons. First, their status was predicated on the belief that although they were poor, they were not social scum, as were the marginals. Second, as marginals enter the dominant society's job market, there will be a downward pressure on wages, thereby economically threatening the red-necks.

The implications for security of marginality, based on the formalized tipping model, are as follows:

Hypothesis 1: The physical security of marginal peoples will be lower than for the population at large because elements in both the dominant and marginal communities are threatened by assimilationist success. Those threatened by assimilationist success—whether from the dominant or dominated groups— have an interest in monitoring all attempts by marginals to pass as members of the culturally dominant society. Heavy monitoring tends to take the form of vigilante protection groups, whose members harass potential assimilators. Harassment can easily spiral into "tarring and feathering", lynchings, and other forms of violence. In sum, high incentives to police assimilation among people in both the marginal and dominant population heighten the security risk faced by marginals.

Hypothesis 2: Early assimilators will face security threats most strongly from two specific groups: the elites among the marginal population (who do not want to lose their constituencies, and bargaining power as mediators between the marginal populations and political authorities); and also the lower strata among the majority population (who, like the American rednecks in regard to African Americans, will be threatened if marginals enter the job ladder of dominant society).

Hypothesis 3: A few successful and wealthy assimilators among the marginal population can, if visible to all, induce pogroms aimed against the non-assimilated, as they are easier targets in that they can't afford protection.

Hypothesis 4: A threshold of assimilations (say 10%) may activate the threatened lower strata among the majority population to punish the first nine percent who assimilated, and had previously been quietly accepted (but not forgotten, at least by some).

Hypothesis 5: The actual threat of insecurity plays itself back into the tipping game in raising the expected disutility of assimilation, at least in comparison to the expected payoffs for the protection of remaining a member of the marginal community.

Unfortunately, data on the security of marginal populations, differentiating them based on levels of assimilation, and comparing their security with members of the dominant society, are unavailable. A data gathering project with these variables in mind would be valuable; if such data were collected, we could assess for marginal populations their levels of physical, economic and social security under conditions of assimilation and nonassimilation as compared to the population at large. A world-wide monitoring of the life chances of marginal populations would allow us to identify security threats in a relatively objective manner—that is to say, without prejudice as to whether members of the group wish to assimilate or whether the culprits for the erosion of security come from the majority or marginal population. The knowledge which would come from such an effort could only help to address the problem of the insecurity of marginal populations in the world today. In the context of this chapter, I cannot fulfill such a broad agenda; but in the following section, I shall begin to illustrate and elaborate on some of the principles from this theoretical discussion with historical material on three marginal populations. No attempt here is made to justify these examples as typical, or as representative. Rather, I have taken three well-known cases of marginality in order to probe whether the approach taken herein provides a compelling, or at least a plausible, perspective.

Security and Marginality

In regard to security, little need be said in regard to hypothesis 1: the livelihood of marginal populations is egregiously insecure. Jews and Gypsies have faced expulsion, pogroms and mass murder for centuries in Europe. For Jews, even the relatively peaceful migration to the United States in the late 19th century had a pattern, involving very low male-female ratios, that was more typical of "refugee or relief" migration than the standard form of international labor migration (Kuznets, 1975:94). The Gypsies were so marginalized that unlike the Jews, they got no compensation from Germany after the holocaust (Puxon, 1973:5). Untouchables have been the victims of communal violence as a regular part of their lives, especially if they attempt to attend (after it became their legal right) a Hindu temple or other place that was open only to the pure (Chandrasekhar in Mahar, 1972:xi-xii).

The evidence in the sources that were consulted for this paper were not specific enough to assess the validity of hypotheses 2, 3 and 4. Indeed, in support of 3, Borrow quoted a Spanish Gypsy saying that "those who are rich keep aloof from the rest, will not speak in Calo, and will have no dealing but with the Busné [non-Gypsies]." This, Borrow reckons (1893:134) puts the poorest Gypsies in greater peril at the whims of the economy and the police. For Jews in Europe, the Peace of Utrecht in 1713 undermined their crucial role as war financiers. Bankruptcies abounded; Jewish poverty resulted, as well as greater numbers of conversions. But as Jews began to compete in the regular labor market, Israel (1985:chap. 10) reports, the threatened nonmarginal workers put pressure on their states to expel all Jews. Israel isn't clear whether the non-assimilators were as vulnerable as the assimilators, but hypothesis 3 would expect that to occur. My guess is that closer scrutiny of the historical record from primary source material will show triggering mechanisms aimed at the marginal community based on the number of marginals who have assimilated, but such data are not available.

The historical record confirms the intuition about the threat faced by marginals coming from a variety of social actors, oftentimes in strange coalitions, making protection extremely difficult. What is interesting about these coalitions is that they are extremely unstable, and cannot lead to concerted action. In fact, it could be suggested that the difficulty of stabilizing such coalitions is an important source of wildcat acts of harassment heaped on marginals by unsatisfied members of these coalitions, who seek to make marginal people pay a cost for their assimilationist probes.[7]

None the less, these strange alliances are often in the making. A number of accounts suggest the complicity across the marginal/nonmarginal divide, in what might be called a pact of cultural reification. Various social alliances, with different implications, have been attempted to further this project. The first is the alliance of majority aristocrats with elite marginals against the interests of the state. High caste Konds, Bailey reports (1960:128ff, case 35), ally with the elite of the outcaste Pans in order to keep nonelite Pans with legal rights granted to them by the state from asserting themselves against the caste ordering. A similar alliance in 16th century Spain bonded the aristocratic *hidalgos* and elite Gypsies, the latter providing illegal goods and prostitutes for the wealthy and newly-landed aristocrats. This alliance tended to subvert the policy of the Habsburg kings to assimilate Gypsies into the sedentary population.

For the Jews in 19th century eastern Europe, the pact of cultural reification was the product of a second type of social alliance, that between state authority and elite Jews. In this alliance the state protects the non-elite Jews against the aristocrats, many of whom wanted to purify their countries by eliminating the Jewish population. Jews were then ruled indirectly through a Jewish-run organization known as the Kahal, and through a salaried "crown rabbi". Kahal leaders got exclusive rights to decide local court cases and otherwise extort from the local population in return for keeping their own communities quiet. They secured these rights by providing central government officials with gifts, sometimes amounting to 85% of the Kahal's budget. By restricting local Jews from appealing to state courts, Kahal leaders in coalition with state authorities equated assimilationist strategies with criminal activity (Lederhendler 1989:33; Levitas 1981:chap. 6).

Both of these coalitions, between aristocracy/elite marginal or between state officials/elite marginal, only involve part of the marginal elite and a segment of the nonelite apparatus. In England, for example, the government was internally divided on the question of Gypsy education for thirty-eight years. From 1870, a variety of Cabinets sought to pass a compulsory education act for children of travellers; but local Members of Parliament resisted, fearing voter wrath if those children actually went to the schools in their district. It was not until 1908 that the legislation was finally enacted.

There is as well the possibility of an anti-assimilationist pact between blue-bloods and red-necks. This social alliance exists independently of elite marginals. While my case studies show that such alliances have been unimpressive in holding back assimilationist tendencies among the nonelite marginals, they have revealed the frustration of a variety of actors who are threatened by the possibility of marginal assimilation. In India, for example, the Untouchables, through collective action, won many government concessions for protected jobs and social programs; as a result, many low caste Hindus, instead of allying with Brahmins to limit those state offerings, began to clamor for their own classification as backward. Appalled by this, Prime Minister Indira Gandhi pleaded in 1981, that "we should be against making backwardness a vested interest. We thought the word 'backwardness' would gradually go out of our vocabulary but we find more and more people seeking to get listed as backward" (Chandrasekhar, in Mahar 1972:xxxviii). Nearly two decades later a backlash developed against the scheduled castes, in what

A Formal Model of Marginality and Security

might well have been a Brahmin/low (but not out-)caste alliance. While this alliance has been neither stable nor powerful, the anger which it reveals can only work to bring fear into the hearts of Untouchable communities.

In regard to gypsies in England, a "blue-blood"/"red neck" alliance did not form. Poor anglo-saxons have nothing but antipathy for the Gypsies, and have sought to keep the "travelers" and "troublesome van dwellers" socially isolated. Gypsies have as a consequence of this political action been prohibited from local pubs in many areas. Meanwhile the blue-bloods don't face many Gypsies in their taverns, and they have a romantic attachment to the "true Gypsies", the real travelers. They are far more unhappy with Gypsies who are partially assimilated, whom aristocrats call "mongrels". Disagreement between high and low status Englishmen over what is objectionable about Gypsies has prevented any sort of concerted anti-assimilationist alliance. The physical security of Gypsies, under these conditions, is less threatened.

As for the Jews in the pale, for two centuries, the Russian nobility successfully protected the Jews against the wrath of the Russian nobility. None the less, an alliance between the local notables and peasantry ultimately did emerge, and it was the source of the pogroms that helped to induce over a million Jews to emigrate to the United States. The lesson here is ominous for marginal populations: your grandchildren may pay a heavy cost for assimilationist activities that you take today.

Marginal populations face threats from within and from without; early assimilators never reach full security; and nonassimilators may face pogroms due to the assimilationist attempts of others. These multiple threats faced by members (and former members) of marginal population explain a pattern which most clearly differentiates them from mere cultural minorities: marginal populations, both assimilated and nonassimilated, face randomized threats to their security. These apparently random acts of violence work to bond marginal communities together in self-protection rings. The unpredictability of violence aimed at them, even if they successfully "make it" in dominant society, lowers the expected payoff of investments in social mobility within dominant society. Random and apparently unpredictable violence against marginals becomes a dominant concern for all people with traceable roots to marginal groups, and this in turn holds marginals together as tightly knit communities.

The apparent randomization of threat is well-documented in the literature on marginals. In a review of legislation aimed a Gypsies from 1530 to 1908 (Mayall, 1988: Appendix i), we see periods of toleration in a cycle with harsh laws aimed directly against Gypsy practices. A decree by Edward VI in 1551-2 forbade traveling salespeople from their work without a license; under George III, that decree and similar ones were repealed. But George IV in 1822

David D. Laitin

in his Turnpike Roads Act, enjoined Gypsies from encamping on the side of the road. Two years later a Vagrancy Act defined palmistry as a form of vagrancy. In periods when Gypsy livelihood (economic security) was threatened, a climate could be felt, in which lower strata members of the majority society could harass violently, and with impunity, members of the identified minority.

In Russia, Lemon (1990:23) argues, part of what makes Gypsies marginal is that they live at the whim of state definition. In the 1920s, she notes, the state fostered a Romani renaissance, but when *korenizatsiia* (local rooting) gave way to *zblizhenie* (merging of peoples) and later to the ideology of *sliianie* (the fusion of all peoples into a nation), suddenly nothing could be published in Romani, and the language schools were closed. In the liberal period of the 1950s, a state order forbade wandering completely, and it has been suggested that this was the only crime in the Soviet state that was based upon nationality. In the late 1980s, under *glasnost'* (openness), Romani schools began to reopen. Perhaps it would be difficult to show that the Romani suffered worse than other groups under Soviet rule; but the pattern of cyclical changes in their status is common to all marginal populations.

The history of Jews in Europe is one of long periods of successful incorporation into society, with moderate levels of assimilation, and then sudden reversals, with mass expulsion or mass murder following. In 1096, Jews were massacred by the Crusaders in the Rhineland and Bohemia. They were expelled from England and France in 1290 and 1394 and were accused of causing the Black Death in 1348-9 Germany. They faced massive pogroms in Spain in 1391, and were expelled a century later, many going to other west and central European countries. The exodus to eastern Europe began in the 16th century, due to mass expulsions in France, Germany and Italy. This thorough-going rejection of Jews coincided with the liberal renaissance era, and not the middle ages. As for the Reformation, Luther first thought his challenge to church authority would win over the Jews to conversion. But he became increasingly frustrated with Jewish obduracy, and by 1537 he was in favor of expelling Jews form Saxony. Erasmus was even more anti-semitic than Luther, showing that humanism and modernism correlated with anti-semitism. If the reformation turned on the Jews, so did the Pope amidst the counter reformation, despite pre-Reformation accommodation of Jews by the Vatican (Israel, 1985:5-17).

Jews in the Pale faced similar arbitrary acts against them. Under Nicholas I, Jews were forcibly conscripted into the Russian army at rates higher than Russians, after a long period in which they had been exempted from service. Alexander II remedied these inequalities, but late in his reign, new laws aimed directly at the Jews were passed. The crown rabbis were forced to come up with conscripts, and fearing community reprisals, they often kidnapped Jews

A Formal Model of Marginality and Security

from other towns to meet their quotas, and this turned Jew against Jew (Levitas, 1981:chap. 4). From 1825-1855 in the Pale, Howe reports (1976:6-7), more than 600 anti-Jewish decrees were enacted, expelling them from villages, censoring their books, meddling in their schools, conscripting them in the army, and prohibiting them from certain occupations. While other aliens could acquire Russian citizenship after five years of residence, Jews required as well the "Tsar's grace" (Levitas, 1981:chap. 2).

Long periods of economic prosperity and physical security for marginal populations have not reduced their security situation within any country. Assimilation does not purchase protection from arbitrary laws and officially accepted pogroms. Marginal individuals need to make private arrangements to protect themselves against harmful legislation and popular action. This potential ordeal draws marginals inward toward each other, and lowers the probability that any individual would make a clean cultural break from his or her marginal roots. The question of security, for marginals and their assimilated descendants, never recedes far from their consciousness.

Applications of Theory For The Post Cold War World

The flood of immigrants into western Europe from Poland, the former German Democratic Republic, Czechoslovakia, the former Yugoslavia, Romania, and Russia, into countries that don't consider themselves lands of immigration, is causing some consternation among observers who foresee these migrants as facing generations of marginality. Are these fears justified? What are the implications of marginality in liberal democracies of western Europe? To answer these questions, it is useful to examine the past generation's migrants, such as the Turks in the Federal Republic of Germany (FRG), Sicilians in Switzerland, or the Algerians in France. Based on a single dissertation (Mandel, 1988), the following discussion will address the issue of the Turks in Germany in terms of the assimilationist model of marginals presented in this paper.

Of four million "guest workers" then in the FRG, two million are Turks. They entered the job market legally, based on an interstate treaty, which specified how recruitment was to be accomplished, and which foresaw full repatriation to Turkey after the work period. Despite the fact that German authorities tried to disperse the Turkish workers so that there would not be large foreign enclaves, in Berlin a "little Istanbul" became a geographical fact in the neighborhood of Kreuzberg. The Turks, Mandel's data show, work in the low-skilled sector of the working class, and have a small but vibrant petit bourgeoisie that sells Turkish items to Turks and to cosmopolitan Germans. Life in Germany has many rewards, including full access to the extensive social welfare programs. Most of the Turks return to Turkey to marry, and then bring their whole family to Germany, and raise their children for eleven months a year in Germany, taking a long summer holiday in Turkey. The children go to German schools, though rarely in the elite stream, and by treaty they get lessons in Turkish history funded by Turkey. Many send their children to religious schools as well, and these had been funded by Saudi Arabia, allocated to the Ankara government, and then forwarded to Germany.

Reminiscent of the Indian issue of the naming of "Untouchables" (discussed in Laitin, 1995), the discourse around "guestworker" has become ideologically loaded. Turks use the term in an ironic way, to emphasize that they don't get any of the perquisites that they would provide for *their* "guests". After 1973, when the immigration treaty expired, government officials began to question the assignation of the Turks, now rather permanently settled, as guests; officials began using the term "Mitburger" or "co-citizen", but this was not taken seriously. Other terms were used, but the ironic use of "guest-worker" remains standard.

Assimilation is extremely low, and Mandel outlines the reasons for this. First, because of the terms of their migration, the German government has not promoted citizenship, though most Germans have come to recognize that many of the Turks are *de facto* permanent residents. The laws for naturalization are quite restrictive, and there are no automatic conditions to acquire citizenship. In 1974, only 374 Turks were naturalized; in 1980, the figure was 387. Without a promise of citizenship, the utility of assimilation goes way down. Second, the high birthrate among Turks compared to the Germans has created a large popular interest in restricting Turks from personal fulfillment in Germany. Despite government attempts to soften the blow of discrimination, it persists. The appearance of vigilante anti-immigrant patrols known as "skinheads" in 1991 suggests that there is strong popular pressure against foreigners being accepted as citizens.

A third factor slowing assimilation concerns state police action. The *Ausländerpolizei* (Foreigners Police) play an intimidating role in marginalizing Turks. They can arbitrarily deny work permits to children of guestworkers, or refuse to renew the permits of Turks who have lived for years in Germany. Fourth, communications technology has enabled the Turks to live vicariously as ethnic Turks. The VCR industry in Turkey produces movies about Turks in Germany, and exports them directly. Few Turks in Germany watch state-run television, and most prefer the gerry-rigged VCR equipment that allows them to watch Turkish fare whenever they want. Finally, the Turks who do assimilate and reach professional and artistic success find themselves referred to as "Turkish artists" or "Turkish intellectuals". Mandel notes (p. 312) that "a further paradox is the fact that while the *Gastarbeiter* find it demeaning to be

A Formal Model of Marginality and Security

labeled and assigned an identity solely on the basis of their labor, the elites strive for this yet are denied it." In light of these factors, the Turkish identity will long remain "marked" and separate from German identity, assimilation will remain costly, and therefore Turks in Germany will share many attributes of a marginal group.

A significant difference between the Turkish population in Berlin and the cases of marginality reviewed in this paper is that of intergenerational tensions among the Turks. Mandel reports that the children of migrants are unwilling to "return" to Turkey, and fear that their parents might accept a buy-out of their rights to live in Germany. Despite hearing the Turkish language in "Little Istanbul", the children are barely able to speak it without significant code-mixing with German. In annual visits to Turkey, the children find Turkish morés to be far more rigid in Turkey. They consequently feel foreign in their supposed homeland; they are called "Almancilar" (German-like) by their Turkish peers. Their parents try to preempt this sense of alienation by sending their children to Saudi-sponsored Qur'anic schools in Berlin, even though most of the parents were completely secular when they initially migrated. It is hard to believe that these schools will have a great cultural influence; already they have been beset with scandal, such as evidence that Turkish officials accepted Saudi bribes to set these schools up. Careful examination of the life-chances of this generation is essential before we can come to any conclusion about the reproduction of marginality.

Even more important from the perspective of the model, Turkish workers have not moved into lucrative sectors of the German economy that give them greater expected utility than entry level jobs in the standard economy. There is no suggestion in Mandel's work that the petit bourgeoisie engaged in selling Turkish products and movies work in a prosperous subeconomy, providing an insular mobility ladder for Turks like banking had for medieval Jews, or sweeping has for contemporary urban Indian Untouchables. The incentives for the next generation of German-born Turkish workers will be to compete with Poles, east Germans, and Russians for unionized employment in the former West Germany. This analysis strongly suggests that the sources of marginalization will not be internal to the immigrant community, but most strongly from the pact of cultural reification, made up mostly of members of the dominant "German" society, but also including Turkish state and Saudi religious authorities.

Even if the pact of cultural reification were to succeed, however, the existence of the European Commission of Human Rights and other international bodies will make it virtually impossible for marginal groups in the next generation to face the horrors that Jews and Gypsies faced a half century ago. Democracy in Germany is more fully institutionalized today than it was in

David D. Laitin

the 1930s, seriously diminishing the possibility of state-induced terror against its own workers. Turks won't be the victims of a new holocaust in Germany. In western Europe, the security of marginal populations is less perilous today than it was in the 1930s.

But the lessons of marginality in regard to security are such that we should not expect regular and systematic threats to the security of marginal groups, but rather irregular, sporadic and often vicious attacks coming at unpredictable moments. The geographical isolation, combined with the low status and continued cultural practice, make the Turks easy targets for xenophobic movements among the majority population. The pact of cultural reification includes the far right wing which sees the Turks as a threat to German cultural purity, elements in the left who want to promote Turkish culture as a liberating force, and the Turkish government (aided by the Saudi religious elites) that has taken an interest in keeping this population "Turkish". The policing of this pact is carried out by "skinheads", by *Ausländerpolizei*, and by first generation immigrants who cling to the myth of return. Through this project, Turks in Germany remain "marked". This does not suggest unencumbered assimilation; nor does it speak well for their future security.

Conclusion

Marginality, the analysis in this paper suggests, has different dynamics from mere minority status, and the situation of marginality enhances levels of security threats faced by peoples living in lands whose dominant culture is different from theirs. In the post Soviet world of high ethnic tensions, we should expect greater levels of population movements, often involving large conglomerations of marginalized groups, especially into the more settled states of western Europe and north America. The post Soviet world, then, might well be a world of lower nuclear threats to states and to the urban populations of the superpowers, but it will likely be a world of greater security threats to populations that find themselves facing high barriers to assimilation into the national cultures of the states in which they reside. Indeed, in the period between the initial drafting of this paper (November, 1991) and its preparation for publication in this volume (March, 1995), the terrible consequences of marginality in so-called civil societies of the west have been grotesquely revealed. These issues demand continued attention by students of international security.

Acknowledgments

The author benefitted from comments on earlier drafts by Sam Nolutshungu, Charles Hale, Jonathan Boyarin, and Roger Petersen.

A Formal Model of Marginality and Security

Notes

1. This part is drawn directly, without further reference or inverted commas, from Laitin (1995).

2. Bauman (1988:66) disputes the logic holding that because identities are socially and politically constructed, they are "any more contingent, flexible, or manipulable by individual efforts. If anything," he argues, "the opposite is true." My point here is simply that this issue would not get seriously raised from a primordial framework.

3. Kymlicka (1976:176), too, a sophisticated analytic philosopher, uncritically highlights a natural human resistance to assimilation that is not subject to calculation.

4. Bourdieu (1984) analyzes with great subtlety the degree to which adoption of new cultural norms by dominant classes in their attempts to maintain class boundaries is a self-conscious activity. See, e.g. pp. 246-56.

5. Many of these cases are documented in papers in Dorian, 1989.

6. The implications of the tipping game developed in this paper represent only the tip of the iceberg. A whole variety of phenomena can be interpreted through its lens. For example, the model can neatly represent a role for a tiny percentage of the original minority population to hold on to the old ways, or the old language even when mass assimilation is under way. They are the "lonely philologists and half-forgotten poets" (Laitin 1988) who keep the old culture alive, in a rather archaeological way, and pass the traditions on intergenerationally to receptive individuals. These people have skills or interests that give them much higher than average returns for non-assimilating. Their pay-off at 99% assimilated could be higher by choosing not to assimilate than by choosing the reverse. If assimilation is nearly complete, these hold-outs begin to be considered socially irrelevant, even by people with roots in the once-marginal culture; but if a national revival occurs, these poets have kept alive the seeds of a counter-hegemony, and can form a useful alliance with new dynamic sectors that have an economic interest in separation. This and other implications of the tipping model cannot be raised here. I have discussed other aspects of the tipping model in (Laitin 1994).

7. In Laitin (1995), I emphasized only the instability of the coalitions that I shall be describing, and suggested that the instability weakened my theory, as the pressures against assimilation of marginals were concomitantly weak. Here I am using the data on that very instability to give a reason for why frustrated members of these coalitions might take violence into their own hands, thereby adding to the insecurity of marginal populations, and raising the costs of assimilation. The data that disconfirmed the theory in the previous paper is being used to give it strength here. Further work in specifying the model is clearly required.

References

Akerlof, George (1984) "The economics of caste and the rat race and other woeful tales" in Akerlof, *An Economic Theorist's Book of Tales* (Cambridge: Cambridge University Press)

David D. Laitin

Bailey, F.G. (1960) *Tribe, Caste and Nation* (Manchester: Manchester University Press)

Bauman, Zygmunt (1988) "Entry tickets and exit visas: Paradoxes of Jewish identity" *Telos* 77:45-77

Barth, Frederick (1969) *Ethnic Groups and Boundaries* (Bergen: Universitets Forlaget)

Borrow, George (1893) *The Zincali: An Account of the Gypsies of Spain* (London: John Murray)

Bourdieu, Pierre (1984) *Distinction* (Cambridge, MA: Harvard University Press)

Cohn, Bernard S. (1955) "The Changing Status of a Depressed Caste" in McKim Marriott *Village India* (Chicago: University of Chicago Press):53-77

Dorian, Nancy ed. (1989) *Investigating Obsolescence: Studies in Language Contraction and Death* (Cambridge: Cambridge University Press)

Howe, Irving (1976) *World of our Fathers* (New York: Simon and Schuster)

Israel, Jonathan I. (1985[1989]) *European Jewry in the Age of Mercantilism: 1550-1750* (Oxford: Oxford University Press)

Kuznets, Simon (1975) "Immigration of Russian Jews to the United States: Background and Structure" *Perspectives in American History*, IX:35-124.

Kymlicka, W. (1989) *Liberalism, Community and Culture* (Oxford: Clarendon)

Laitin, David (1986) *Hegemony and Culture* (Chicago: University of Chicago Press)

Laitin, David (1988) "Language Game" *Comparative Politics* 20:289-302

Laitin, David (1991) "The National Uprisings in the Soviet Union" *World Politics* 44:139-77.

Laitin, David (1994) "The Tower of Babel as a Coordination Game: Political Linguistics in Ghana" *American Political Science Review* 88:622-34

Laitin, David (1995) "Marginality: A Microperspective" *Rationality and Society* 7, 1 (January): 31-57.

Lederhendler, Eli (1989) *The Road to Modern Jewish Politics: Political Tradition and Political Reconstruction in the Jewish Community of Tsarist Russia* (New York: Oxford University Press, 1989).

Lemon, Alaina (1990) "Performance, History and Becoming Civilized: Roma (Gypsies) in the USSR and the Moscow *Teatr 'Romen'* Dissertation Prospectus, University of Chicago.

Levitas, Isaac (1981) *The Jewish Community in Russia, 1844-1917* (Jerusalem: Posner and Sons)

Mahar, J. Michael, ed. (1972) *The Untouchables in Contemporary India* (Tucson: University of Arizona Press)

Mandel, Ruth Ellen (1988) " 'We Called for Manpower, But People Came Instead': The foreigner Problem and Turkish Guestworkers in West Germany" Ph.D. Thesis, University of Chicago, Department of Anthropology.

Mayall, David (1988) *Gypsy-travellers in nineteenth-century society* (Cambridge: Cambridge University Press)

McLane, Merrill F. (1987) *Proud Outcasts: The Gypsies of Spain* (Cabin John, Maryland: Carderock Press)

Petersen, Roger (1989) "Rationality, Ethnicity, and Military Enlistment" *Social Science Information* 3:564-98

A Formal Model of Marginality and Security

58 Puxon, Grattan (1973) *Rom: Europe's Gypsies* (London: Minority Rights Group)

San Román, Teresa (1984) *Gitanos de Madrid y Barcelona: Ensayos sobre acultaración y etnicidad* (Bellaterra: Universidad Autótoma de Barcelona)

Schelling, Thomas (1978) *Micromotives and Macrobehavior* (New York: Norton)

David D. Laitin

Chapter 2

A MOSLEM POPULATION IN FRANCE

Rémy Leveau

During the 1980s various well-known figures began to speak openly of rejecting the Moslem populations living in Europe. In France, Jean-Marie Le Pen, the leader of the National Front made the most of this theme to change his small group into a political party which obtained 11 percent of the vote in different elections since 1983, up to 15 percent in the first round of voting in the 1995 presidential election, and could still do better judging by the negative reaction to Islam and immigration reported in surveys. Even the former president, Valéry Giscard d'Estaing, who began his term of office in 1971 by inviting Malian street cleaners to the Elysée, came to see an invasion and the need for a reform of the nationality code based on the jus sanguinis principle.

In November 1989, the president of the "Generlitat" of Catalonia, Jordi Pujol, speaking of the Islamic veil affair which was rocking France, declared during a conference on migration in the Western Mediterranean are that it was very difficult to integrate the Moslem population of Europe. In May 1991, during a visit to Notre Dame of Fatima, Pope John Paul II declared that the culture of Europe should be Christian.

Faced with the growing demands for permanent settlement made by the descendants of migrants from North Africa, Turkey, the Indian sub-continent (and very soon, Egypt) who are appearing in Berlin and Barcelona, Milan, Marseilles and Manchester, the nation-states of the European Community adopt contradictory policies which combine a grudging acceptance with restrictive conditions and even a disguised rejection. For their part, these groups have, since the early seventies, expressed their wish to remain, negotiating the process of their integration while developing minority behaviors that are generally badly received by the native population. The loss of their original cultures is, in many ways, already far advanced due to a long and compulsory schooling, a life-style in which consumerism and the media have more influence on youth behavior than the traditional culture handed down by their parents. But, if the loss of identity is deep and rapid among young people, the acquisition of a new identity is much slower and more chaotic.[1]

The colonial heritage which applies to North Africans in France, and especially Algerians, or Indians and Pakistanis in Britain plays a particular part. It makes the acquisition of a common language and shared values easier, but it carries the memory of violent conflicts in the struggle for independence. It should also be remembered that traditionally it contributed to integration through the diffusion of French culture and through the experience of fighting together in the two World Wars—and even in colonial wars (the French conquered Morocco with predominantly Algerian troops). But the colonial system was broadly characterized by an unwillingness to allow local elites to accede to positions of responsibility contrary to its assimilationist discourse.

The situation in the France of today is certainly not comparable but the recollection of a difficult past affects the memory of the groups. Identification with a particular city or neighborhood is much stronger than attachment to a state. To take up French nationality still partly implies a betrayal of one's father or a conversion. In colonial Algeria in the 1930s the ulemas forbade it and few dared to disobey. Today, all that is needed is to ensure that in becoming French one does not break with family traditions. Employing religion to signal an identity appears, in this light, to be a minimal strategy, widely used but not to the exclusion of others. The individuals or groups who resort to it are those who lack access to the standard and quicker ways of upward social mobility through education and economic achievement.In general, the predominant preference is for integration but it is difficult to analyze since it contains within it an element of provocation with regard to the value systems of French society, in apparent contrast with an overall attitude of loyalty that dominates even in times of crisis. Two surveys of Moslem opinion in France, one conducted in November 1989 during the affaire of the Islamic veil, and the other in January-February 1991 in the midst of the Gulf War, support these claims.[2]

The first case related to an internal crisis concerning the wearing of the veil in the class room which the French educational authorities considered an act of proselytism forbidden by law in public schools. The second was a conflict with an Arab and Moslem state in which France though not the main adversary was militarily engaged at the initiative of its head of state.

During the crisis of the veil, 66 percent of the sample of the Moslem population was against any special status being given to Moslems as far as marriage, divorce, or custody of children was concerned. In the same way, 93 percent of this sample thought that one could be perfectly integrated into French society and practice Islam privately. Furthermore, 72 percent declared that if someone close to them abandoned the Moslem religion they would continue to see him leaving him free to make his own choices. A similar percentage would accept intermarriage with a non-Moslem. Beyond that, some 25 to 30 percent of the sample, depending on the questions asked,

adopted decidedly secular views. 45 percent even went so far as to oppose the
wearying of the veil in school and 49 percent opposed the public call to
prayer.

The majority mainly favored integration with a concern for collective
visibility an attitude that corresponds to the strategy of the intermediary elites
who emerged out of the associational movement. In this way, 95 percent
claimed ties to Islam, 70 percent by faith and 20 percent through memory. 90
percent were in favor of giving their children Moslem names and 72 percent
desired some form of representation for French Moslems. A slightly larger
number said they were in favor of the building of mosques and the wearing of
the veil in the street.

One may then infer a desire for visibility within a respect for the rules of
French society which the French, however, interpret, with many misgivings,
as community spirit seeking to assert itself in the public, i.e., common, space.
Therefore, the observance of food taboos, celebration of the feast of
Ramadan, and the call for identifiable places of worship appear to some as
private conduct and to others as a series of communitarian signals. In a
process of collective acceptance of the rules of the host society the use of
religion as a beacon by a group which has no other legal means of getting
recognition might appear as a way of rejecting the host society when, in fact,
it represents more of a conditional acceptance of that society. This approach
entails going through the public school system, identification with local
institutions and an attitude of reverence towards the president of the Republic, symbol of protection against the hostile forces of parties, bureaucracy and
society.

This approach to belonging would be confirmed in a situation of an
external crisis and war which put to the test their confidence in the person of
François Mitterrand.In these exceptional circumstances, he was viewed favorably by 67 percent of French moslems doing better than any leader, Arab,
moslem or foreign (Saddam Hussein obtained only 26 percent). Even more
respondents recognized that the President had tried to avoid war. They were
sensitive to the fact that "he did not agree with the Americans" whom they
considered mainly responsible for the conflict. But, if 71 percent thought that
Saddam Hussein should have accepted French peace proposals, only 21
percent supported the despatch of french troops to Iraq.Of those (26 percent)
who declared their support for Iraq, only 20 percent said they would be
willing to help that country actively. In that last group, 62 percent would limit
their support to the signing of petitions, 58 percent would participate in
demonstrations, and only 2 percent would actually be ready to use violence.
A certain radicalism might appear where Israel, Americans, or moderate Arabs
are concerned, alleging a Zionist plot. Their analysis and categories come

largely from Western tiers-mondisme (or a Western pro-Third World radicalism). They adopt a prudent, wait-and-see attitude when their relationship with France is at stake, and, in general, have no illusions concerning Saddam Hussein's personality and disposition.

What, then, might be the significance of this external solidarity which also functions as a marker for a sub-group whose essential problems lie in their relationship with French society? The majority of the sample consisted of pacifists who would have preferred a simple condemnation of Iraq without military action. The crisis evinced a strong sense of solidarity with external forces, undoubtedly an important element of group identity; but it was managed with a concern for realism and caution and did not challenge the legitimacy of the decisions of the head of state on which their integration depended. In such times of crisis the elites, including those with a secular background, tend to stress identity and community all the more effectively to present themselves as intermediaries in relation both to the state and to other groups. Their discourse reflected a pessimistic expectation that their followers would reject compromise, an expectation encouraged by the fact that it was such an attitude of rejection that was voiced most provocatively at football matches with the cry, "Long live Saddam Hussein," in suburban confrontations with police, and in graffiti on the subway. By contrast, the families that preached prudence and who kept their youngsters at home during tense moments did so discreetly.

During these periods of tension, the public authorities seek out intermediaries from the group who can play the role of volunteer firemen ready to put out the expected fires. Drawn largely from the members of voluntary associations, these intermediaries then emerge as the self-styled guardians of an imaginary contract of mutual respect and good neighborliness between communities. They volunteer to defend a social peace the maintenance of which they closely link to the stability of their own role as intermediaries. There is a great risk that when the crisis passes, these same firemen may themselves fan some flames in order to preserve their role. The perverse mechanisms which characterize the relationship between the state and the intermediaries it has itself created as the spokesmen of the marginalized social groups are reproduced in order to maintain contact and to ensure tranquility in different ways. In this way, after the Gulf crisis, the President and the Prime Minister would receive the representatives of the "Comité de Réflexion sur l'Islam en France" and of the Jewish Community to thank them for having worked for calm and social peace. Their appeals to calm over the Gulf war were considered to have made some contribution to peace in the urban neighborhoods also. Subsequent flare-ups were seen as confirming this line of reasoning.

Rémy Leveau

Taking the long view and based on the analysis of further surveys one is led to believe that the intermediaries were not needed at all. If crises adduce strong affirmations of loyalty on the part of minorities (who are required at such times to show their support of the system more than other people), they also reveal the suspicion in which the group is held by the majority, its vulnerability and its marginality.

During the controversy over the veil the same questions had been put a sample of the general French population as those put to a sample of Moslems whose responses we earlier analyzed. The median position revealed by this poll could be summarized as follows: the presence of Moslems in France is acceptable on condition that it is discreet or, better still, a good Moslem for the French is an invisible person who does not stand out from the rest. The same could apply to a Catholic, a Protestant, or a Jew. Thus, 82 percent thought that the Moslem religion ought to remain a private matter and should in no way be granted a special status. A majority of people believed that the more one was integrated into French society the less Moslem one would be, and they would not allow Moslem chaplains to be appointed in the school system or food taboos to be respected in public institutions (e.g., schools, the army, and prisons). The wearing of the veil was rejected by 75 percent and the call to prayer by 86 percent. In short, almost three-quarters of the sample would accept the integration of Moslems only on condition that they converted to a secular outlook and adopted without argument the established values of French society. About half of the sample considered such a development unlikely while one third of the population, including people who said they supported left-wing and extreme left parties, were fundamentally hostile to any idea of integration, adopting positions quite close to the principles of the National Front.[3]

There is, then, a strong opposition to those affirmations of identity which, as we have seen, a part of the Moslems movement toward integration. So far as French society at large was concerned, at the end of the 1980s, the recognition that immigrants with a Moslem culture had come to stay in France permanently led to renewed support for a centralized state and secular values. Yet, the renunciation of specificity need not lead to unquestioning acceptance of French society in its present state. After all, Moslems, unlike the Jews and protestants, did not participate in the republican political compromise which laid down the principles of French society at the end of the last century. However, things are not heading toward a confrontation since both the immigrants and the host population affirm through their more representative elites a desire to transcend the conflicts inherited from colonialism or imported from outside.

A Moslem Population in France

At the same time there is among the Moslem elites increasing talk of a "plot" which applies to both the internal conflicts in which they are involved and the external ones which affect them. Whether part of a logic of subordination or the language of those who are excluded, more apt to endure events than to act on their own account, this discourse may also reflect various economic, political and social tensions. But it already appears in many respects to be the explanation of those who are dominated and marginalized within the system. Consideration of one local situation, that of Marseilles, which shows the dysfunctions of the French system, may provide some clues.[4]

That city comes nearest, in the French social and political context, to an American ethnic model. It was settled in the 19th century by successive layers of immigrants from the Mediterranean basin who kept for quite a long time the collective memories of their origins. Today the city is home to nearly one million people, 100,000 to 110,000 of whom are Moslems—twice the national average. They are concentrated in the northern parts of the city where their living conditions are worse than those of the French lower classes. 58 percent of the North African youth under 24 years of age have no jobs. Poorly integrated into the world of labor, the North African population is further marginalized by its residential location. They cannot be said to live in ghetto, however, since no ethnic group predominates in any given locality and none has the majority of its members in any one place. Neither do they command any shared amenities. Nevertheless they are to be found in areas which have been abandoned by the middle class and where the sense of identity and working class pride which characterized Marseilles in the 1950s is disintegrating. A cleavage between natives of the city and immigrants replaces the former divisions of social class, a fact that is manifest in the steady rise of the National Front at the expense of the traditional parties, feeding on the fears of an electorate that associates immigration with insecurity. It is in such a context that the assertion of Islam along communitarian lines may also be the reflex response of fear of a group defending itself and seeking to regain the dignity which work is no longer sufficient to provide.

The mosque becomes a kind of community center, the hub of networks of solidarity, sometimes managing relations with local institutions through cultural and religious associations. It performs an educational function with young people, assures contact with the authorities and progressively pushes aside the pressures on immigrants from their countries of origin while still making use of the transnational networks at its disposal. Local rivalries between communities may also relate to economic interests linked to religion. The question of "hallal" meat is a major religious and financial issue in Marseilles which provokes attempts by different intermediaries to gain control of its supply with state assistance and to excommunicate rival. Legitimacy

Rémy Leveau

is gained by consummate skill in manipulating religious symbolism, relying
on the outside world but taking care not to alarm the political authorities.

During the municipal elections of 1989 an independent socialist, R Vigouroux won by calling for recognition of the ethnic and religious diversity of the population and by giving to some little known Moslems a political recognition which he denied to leaders of more important associations. He even went so far as to commit himself to the partial satisfaction of some local religious demands but without risking the displeasure of important sections of his constituency, like Jews and Armenians, the community-minded elements among whom could enter into serious conflict with the Moslems. The mayor of Marseilles did not do more than recognize Moslems that he, himself, had raised to prominence conceding as little real power to them as possible. The way immigration had become politicized to the benefit of the National Front made it impossible for him to go much farther than symbolic recognition. But, equally, he could do no less.

If marginalization in Marseilles owes to the economic situation it may also be the result of a social and political construction that exhibits the "perverse effects" of the French model of integration. The case of the "harkis"—Moslem former soldiers or auxiliaries of the French army brought back after the Algerian war in order to shield them from the revenge of the National Liberation Front (known by its French initials, FLN) is exemplary in many respects. Together with their families they numbered 100,000 in 1962-63 and now they make up a group of about 500,000 people. Having chosen the French side during the war, they remained French citizens after 1962. But they did not choose to come to France and the French authorities accepted them reluctantly, placing them in lumbering camps in the south of France where some of them still live with their families. To be sure, many of these French Moslems have managed to escape from that system of isolation, control and assistance, and have worked and succeeded outside. Some very successful examples can be found especially among the second generation. But these often choose to distance themselves from their original group and often disown it. Many of the children of the harkis can be found in such strongly integrationist associations as France-Plus. Those who have remained in the camps are subjected to strongly clientelistic politics and their forms of political participation are very similar to what existed in colonial Algeria. On the basis of the service they rendered and being fully French they demand special jobs, quotas and help for their children up to the third generation and beyond.

Courted at election time, they have the feeling of being left to themselves afterwards and they blame the government for doing too much for immigrants—along similar lines as Jean-Marie Le Pen. Economically and socially marginalized, in debt, seeing some of their children succumb to drugs and

A Moslem Population in France

delinquency, they are attracted by violent symbolic action that draws attention to themselves in order to obtain grants and subsidies which, however, will never satisfy their expectations or compensate them for the adverse conditions of integration, psychological and material, they suffered initially.[5]

While some sons of harkis fought as professional soldiers in the Daguet Division during the Gulf War, others spoke favorably of Saddam Hussein. In order to pay their "father's debt" some young people go to Algeria to do their military service under the terms of the 1983 Franco-Algerian Agreement which allows migrants' children to choose one or the other country without losing their nationality. From time to time revolts break out in the camps: administrative commissions are appointed to recommend definitive solutions to the problem of the integration of the harkis. We may wonder whether the model of perverse relations with French society that has developed over the years will extend to other North African groups who have become French citizens but who are marginalized with their economic and social hopes frustrated.

Internal and external crises, while they provide an opportunity for testing the loyalty of these groups, can also increase their marginality. They create an unequivocally negative image in French society which represents Islam as an intolerant, hostile religion. This stigma attaches, without distinction, to every person and group of Moslem culture and accentuates their fears and their anti-integration reflexes. External crisis also creates anxiety and affects the Moslems' outlook on their future. In a survey of February 1991, 55 percent of the Moslems were anxious about their future in France while 70 to 80 percent declared that France was the country in which they wished to live. Five percent said they wanted to live in another European country and only 10 to 20 percent wished to live in their family's country of origin. But more than 80 percent thought that the Gulf War would mean more controls and more racism, more difficulty in getting jobs, and would add to the daily complications of life. More than 60 percent still feared an increase in expulsions. Paradoxically, this percentage was higher among Moslems with French citizenship which indicates the importance of perceptions that may be irrational from a juridical point of view but which correspond to a sense of rejection that goes back to the notion of a plot and to the stigmatization of a group which will fall back on external ties of solidarity.

As they become aware of the permanence of immigrants of Moslem culture some groups within the majority population see themselves as a threatened minority and behave accordingly. That identity response is most evident among social categories that feel economically insecure who tend to blame the immigrants for it. The part of the working class suffering unemployment will tend to consider the latest arrivals as unacceptable because of cultural differences. Neither the fact that many of the followers of the National Front formerly supported the Communist Party nor the fact that many of their ancestors arrived in France as immigrants spares the Moslem immigrants from the racism of the National Front. A similar discourse is sometimes prevalent among peasants who are going through hard times even though for the most part they have very little contact with immigrants. These attitudes feed on rumors about the role of immigrants in the underground economy, drug trafficking and urban violence. The language of rejection presents itself as refusal of an integration that amounts to the assertion of a right to share.

It is precisely when the immigrant adopts the compulsory code of conduct (i.e., seeks to assimilate) that he or she provokes the strongest racist response on the part of the majority groups who consider themselves a threatened minority on account of the immigrant's very presence.[6] This will not prevent some of the immigrants from succeeding in leaving their group by achieving individual preeminence in various ways, or to make their way unnoticed as part of the urban crowd. Intermediaries who partly play the collective game of identity preserve for themselves individual ways of escape from marginality in spite of racism. On the other hand, those with few individual or collective opportunities are steered towards the very forms of communal withdrawal condemned by the French system's integrating ideology.

If, indeed, all the factors analyzed indicate a major tendency towards integration in the political culture of the new generation, there are, nevertheless, some ambiguities which merit specific attention pointing to both individualistic behavior that seeks to escape the logic of exclusion and to collective response of a neo-communitarian kind.

"Beurs"—as the young second generation North Africans are familiarly known—have a political culture that cannot be seized as an undifferentiated whole, but it is possible to identify some key features on the basis of qualitative studies and opinion polls. Local attachments in the modes of address and accent and identifying with a particular sports team or club are forms of integration, sometimes in conflict with each other, but which would merit further study. Along with the President of the Republic, the mayor is, no doubt, the figure of authority most present in their political imagination, often to complain to about policies applied to themselves which they consider hostile or inadequate. In most cases it is such policies, or their failure, as they relate to housing and employment, which are responsible for creating the conditions of exclusion and for provoking collective neo-communitarian answers.[7]

Gender relations may provide deeper insights into this approach by focusing it on the family.[8] Traditionally, studies of the political culture of young Moslems or their strategies have focused on boys because they are the most visible actors. Girls have tended to be ignored after mention of some commonplaces: they are more capable of benefitting from the school system, are less exposed to the drug problem and delinquency, and have less family conflicts regarding their personal freedom. They are better represented in opinion polls which indicate that they are rather in conformity with the ways of the larger society, especially with the behavior of girls of their age from the popular classes. A study done in Dreux indicated that girls were less resentful towards society and more open to political participation.[9] Their attitudes toward family values, procreation, and sexual partner showed profound changes compared to the traditional values brought by their parents from the Maghreb and applied even more strictly for having been transplanted.

In a context of exclusion in which girls manage to get out of some its problems better than boys, the latter will tend to use the traditional model in order to ensure stricter control of their sisters. Their own austerity may be interpreted as a reaction towards French society which rejects them as well as towards those within their group of origin who succeed in avoiding exclusion and marginalization. By reimposing constraints in the name of tradition they substitute themselves for their parents who have failed or may even, in some cases, appear as accomplices to their daughters. To compel recognition by all they base their claim to authority of the Shari'a.

A bloc emerges of some 15 to 30 percent of the samples which, according to the type of questions asked, gives neo-communitarian responses. In 1991, 15 percent favored a conflict in the Gulf which would turn into a war between Israel and Arab countries.[10] A similar number (14 percent) said in 1993 that they associated with or approved of Moslem extremists. One could not, however, infer from that a structured process of identification with the Algerian Islamic Salvation Front (French initials, FIS), however, because the image of that country is so poor among migrants. The language of provocation relates and is addressed to France and still corresponds to a claim for integration. Neo-communitarianism emerges in this context also to the extent that there is an investment in the neighborhood as the only valid point of reference for young males unable to escape exclusion. Having assumed that position they cleverly invest it with meaning by relating it to religion, all the more so when they realize its power to scare society and attract its attention.

In September 1994, at the beginning of the school term, tensions surfaced again over the issue of the veil as in November 1989. This time the authorities feared that the situation would be exploited by associations under the influence of the Algerian Islamic Salvation Front (the FIS) among the immigrants in France, with the concern, once again, that the minorities might be used to relay violence from outside. However, to the surprise of many observers, a new poll indicated that those favoring integration had increased

Rémy Leveau

since 1989 among both the French natives and the immigrants. The two groups got along better on one side by reducing the external signs of particularism and, on the other, by being more tolerant. More people in both groups accepted mixed marriages. The FIS was largely viewed as negative (60 percent) and only 9 percent wished it would come to power in Algeria compared to 68 percent who were against it. Support for an opening to Algerian refugees fleeing the civil war was moderate (31 percent) and most migrants would be in favor of maintaining the present procedures or, at most, allowing in those with family members already living in France. Allegiance to the head of state was very high (86 percent), as at the time of the Gulf War.

Closer study suggests a more varied reality overall, however, and among groups of young people between the ages of 16 and 24 behavior that was more strongly communitarian as the EHESS studies showed.

Finally among Moslem immigrants those from the Maghreb stand in some contrast to their counterparts from other parts of the world, e.g., Turkey who tend to be more markedly communitarian. The existence of a common cultural space with the French, in the country of origin as well as n France, may explain why North Africans integrate more easily than the Turks who keep to themselves.

Unlike North Africans, Turkish immigrants lack a common language and clear points of shared historical experience with French people. We found, when studying Turkish migrants in 1992, that they tended to behave in a very pragmatic way towards their surroundings. The Turkish migrant knows what is useful to him, such as the hospital, the bank, city housing. But he ignores everything which has an abstract character such as newspapers, the political class, the city hall, and even the school.[11]

That community is subject to strong internal control. The size of the population 201,000 according to official statistics, probably between 250,000 and 275,000 if one adds those who have acquired French nationality and those who do not have any legal papers, and its very high concentration is a specific area both facilitate the establishment of control and mechanisms for imposing sanctions. The large number of women who say that they have been forced to wear the veil testifies to the effectiveness of those sanctions.

Social control may also go along with the predominance of a political organization. Dreux would seem to provide a perfect example of that situation. The PKK has controlled the Kurdish community there for years. In other (rather isolated and sporadic) cases Islamist groups have succeeded in exercising both social control and a political monopoly. In such cases, however, the organizations become intermediaries between the community and French society. In other respects, though omnipresent, those Islamist organizations do not , for the time being, display any hostility towards France which is still considered as giving more religious freedom than Turkey.

The political life of Turkish immigrants in Europe is in the hands of "federations" at the European level which implies that the community's fate is dependent on decisions coming from elsewhere. Whether a migrant lives in Sweden or France, he or she is politically dependent on Germany. This is particularly true of the PKK, the Islamists (Kaplanci and Milli Görüs) as well as the Turkish extreme right.

So far inter-communal clashes such as those seen in Germany have not occurred. The size of the community does not allow for a repetition of the German experience. But there is evident a clear polarization of the community around the crucial problems relating to the state of origin and Turks and Kurds are led more and more towards a transplantation of ethnic conflicts into Europe rather than integration.

Finally, this community has developed a strategy for marriages which is largely contrary to the integration process as far as the second generation is concerned. Everything indicates that there is a determination to bring in new blood rather than allow integration to proceed. The model of the matriarchal family is imposing itself strongly among Turkish migrants in France, especially in the provinces. This is in part aimed at re-establishing bonds of authority badly shaken by the fact that boys go to school and are, more and more, compelled to marry early.

The evolution of the European situation—the reunification of Germany, the opening to the East, and the ratification of the Schengen Agreements of 1991—transformed the field of migration.[12] On the one hand, European states became more determined to control the movement of people and tended to create more mechanism to do so. On the other, there was the greater freedom of social actors which largely favored migration from Eastern Europe.

The Schengen and Maastricht Agreements create a new European political space within which nationals of countries that are not members of the European Union will, in theory, be confined to their country of residence within the EU. There are signs of a very deep sense of frustration among North African elites who feel marginalized when they have to obtain a visa to go to Germany or England unless they adopt French nationality. In time, the evolution toward common policies regarding refugees and toward the harmonization of immigration procedures and visa requirements should, logically, provoke a Europe-wide debate on the question of immigration.

There is a likelihood of ethno-cultural refugees seeking admission into the European Union in the years to come if the troubles in Yugoslavia and tension among minorities in Eastern Europe increase. If the elites leave these

Rémy Leveau

countries because of these problems or to flee from bad living conditions, then, together with refugees fleeing in search of freedom there could be a pool of migrants numbering several million people. In European countries, public opinion is likely to consider requests to immigrate made by secular Moslems threatened by Islamist movements (or by refugees from conflicts for which Europeans bear a heavy responsibility) as new blows to their collective identity.

Faced with these changes, states seek to toughen their control by applying their visa policies more stringently to the countries of the South than to those of the East. Reuniting families, mixed marriages, and ordinary travel will all become problematic as soon as people from Moslem countries are involved. A model of migration along American lines with the creation, in the long run, of a federal department of immigration, may emerge at the European level, calling into question the various national models of integration but without openly developing into a clearly defined system of quotas.

These developments may, so far as the elites are concerned, provide a kind of transnational social mobility but they may, equally, create new exclusions internally -for the old minorities already settled—and externally—for the states from which the new waves of migrants come.Given that immigration, at present, takes the form of a double insertion, in the language of the surveys, "here and over there," i.e., immigrants maintain an active association with their countries of origin, these policies of cutting off and withdrawal are baneful and may produce a double radicalization of the countries of origin and of immigrant groups. The stigma that falls on the whole minority when operations of control and repression are undertaken against Islamist groups in France is likely to provoke a radicalization of the whole group and may touch off reflex responses of solidarity.

It might have been thought that there would be greater scope for the recognition of their identity as a group within the wider Europe. For some there is some hope, but Europe appears for many of them as a constraint and a new humiliation, especially because of the Maastricht Agreements, but also because of the restrictive practices towards foreigners that all European governments develop in times of crisis.

If they do not choose to adopt the nationality of one of the Community's member countries, the immigrants from Moslem countries will, therefore, be excluded from the new political and economic space of Europe. Because they live in Europe, they share in the dream of a common enterprise but they will be confined, by way of a visa system much stricter than in the past, within the borders of the state within which they live, while people from other Community countries will have the right to settle and vote in France, being treated on the same footing as nationals. The advantages gained by Spanish and Portuguese people will make the North Africans and Turks feel even more marginalized. The situation leads them to break rules that they consider to be unfair and discriminatory. This weighs all the more heavily on the elites and established civic (associatifs) intermediaries, whether secular or religious, who would like to stay without having to face the problem of changing nationality.

At the popular level, changes in visa and control procedure may affect relationships with the countries of origin. For young people in North Africa it will be much more difficult to dream of leaving their country as the controls are applied more stringently everywhere including Southern Europe. Perceptions of envy and hostility increase but it will never be possible to cut off further immigration altogether. More than one million people every year transit through Spain during the summer without taking into account other means of entry by air or by sea.

Family arrangements which gave former immigrants the possibility to be at one time in France and at another in North Africa will be more difficult and the rigidity of procedures will increase hostility on both sides, at least, as long as it appears as a measure imposed by Europe unilaterally without negotiation with the countries of origin. For young people, Europe is part of their hope for change and for overcoming the constraints of nation-states. It could provoke more fears if the construction of the new Europe now under way involved for North African immigrants 'entry conditions that they felt to be discriminatory compared to actual or imagined treatment of Eastern countries even as Europe is perceived to be party to the injustice meted out to Bosnia's Moslems.

If fears and violence lead immigrants from Moslem countries to withdraw into their own group, if they do not find in Europe the space for pluralism and tolerance they expect, they will be deprived in the present without no hope that the future will be any better. They will then be twice as marginalized and frustrated.

Notes

1. Didier Lapeyronnie, L'individu et les minorités - la France et la Grande Bretagne face à leurs immigrés Paris, Presses Universitaires de France, 1993; Olivier Lecour-Grandmaison and Catherine Withol de Wenden, Les étrangers dans la cité - Expériences européennes ,Paris, La Découverte, 1993;Catherine Neveu, Communauté, nationalité, citoyenneté: De l'autre côté du miroir:les Bengladeshis de Londres, Paris, Karthala,1993; Rémy Leveau, Le sabre et le turban: l'avenir du Maghreb,Paris,François Bourin,1993
2. Sondage IFOP "L'Islam en France" November 20, 1989; Sondage IFOP "Les musulmans et la guerre du Golfe" February 4, 1991

Rémy Leveau

3. Rémy Leveau, "Musulmans en France: les enjeux", *Etudes*, March 1991, pp. 323-332

4. Jocelyne Cesari, "L'Islam et le politique en France: l'exemple de la population immigrée à Marseilles," Thèse Aix-Marseilles III,1991

5. *Rapport au Premier ministre de la Mission de réflexion sur la communauté rapatriée d'origine nord-africaine Paris*, May 1991, p. 42

6. Pascal Perrineau, "Le Front National, la force solitaire" in Phillippe Habert, Pascal Perrineau and Colette Yamal (eds), *Le vote sanction*, Paris, Presses de la Fondation National des Sciences Politiques, 1993, pp. 137-160

7. For discussion of this concept see Gilles Kepel, Des mouvements islamistes au néo-communautarisme, Mémoire d'habilitation -IEP, Paris, 1993

8. Report of the Study Group "Acteurs, exclus et politiques de la ville" under the direction of F Gaspard, F Khosrow-Khavar and M Wieviorka, EHESS, 1993

9. ibid

10. IFOP, 1989 and 1991

11. I am indebted for many of the observations which follow to exchanges with Hamit Bozarslan.

12. Henri Prevot, "Schengen", Commentaire, no 64, Winter 1993-94, pp. 765-770

Chapter 3

PROTRACTED MARGINALITY:
THE EAST EUROPEAN ROMA

Zoltan Barany

"We are hated from the heart, not the head."[1]

Introduction

Since their appearance in the Balkans in the 13th century the Roma (Gypsies) have constituted the most consistently marginalized ethnic group in Eastern Europe. They satisfy the principal conditions of marginality: they do not form an integral part of the societies in which they live, suffer from particular and systematic disqualifications from representation and participation in state affairs, their ethnic identity is either unrecognized or threatened, and the state has been less responsive to their needs and desires than to those of other groups. Their integration to the societies of Eastern Europe has been hindered by the uniqueness of their history, traditions, culture, language, and appearance as well as the reluctance of many Roma to adapt to changing socio-economic and political circumstances. The Roma constitute a transnational ethnic minority and not a diaspora for they do not regard themselves as belonging elsewhere (as diasporas, by definition, do).[2]

The essential argument of this chapter is that the Roma's marginal status in Eastern Europe has reproduced itself under different political system-types as well as under disparate levels of societal and economic development. Historically, the states and societies of Eastern Europe have failed to formulate realistic approaches to national integration. This problem has been aggravated by the deficiencies of state creation and economic development subject as they have been to devastating interruptions and changes in modern times.

More specifically, I argue that a) the marginal condition of the Roma has gone through significant changes and that b) this condition is the result of exclusionary dynamics in three different dimensions: political, economic, and social. Marginality is not a static condition. It has taken dissimilar forms in different historical periods and in various states: at one time the Roma may have been excluded in politics but not in the economic sphere, at another they were marginalized in the economic but not in the political sense. One relatively constant factor in their marginalization has been their social exclusion, the fact that through time and across boundaries they have been ostracized by the populations surrounding them.

Following a longitudinal overview of Romani marginality, Part II will examine state policies and popular attitudes toward and the socio-economic conditions of the Roma and will place their plight in an international perspective. In Part III the focus shifts to the states' assimilation attempts and Romani politics and the final section places the Roma's plight in an international perspective.

A Legacy of Exclusion: The Roma in Historical Perspective

Throughout the centuries the East European Roma have coexisted with a large variety of political regimes which have treated them in different ways ranging from repression to coercive integration. Yet at the end of the twentieth century they remain the most distinctive and least popular minority of the region. In a sense, appreciating Romani history is to raise the question whether they truly represent an anathema to the modern state.

The Roma arrived to the Balkans around the thirteenth and fourteenth centuries and to the British Isles in the fifteenth century following a journey that originated in northwest India approximately in 1000 AD. Throughout the migration some Romani groups halted and settled while others moved on. Today there are Roma in nearly every part of Europe as well as in Asia, the Americas, and Oceania. The Roma are neither ethnologically nor socio-culturally or linguistically homogeneous. They comprise many diverse tribes and groups based on occupational, linguistic, religious, and geographical distinctions. Although their vast majority have been sedentary for generations some have maintained an itinerant lifestyle. It is important to realize that members of the various Romani subgroups often identify themselves first with the subgroup and only second as Roma. Although there can be significant differences between Romani groups they all share their ethnic, linguistic, and cultural origins and the experience of surviving in an overwhelmingly hostile environment. For the sake of brevity I shall use the term "Roma" in this more general sense in the balance of this chapter.

In many ways the Roma have been the victims of their circumstances. Their wandering lifestyle—compelled by centuries of persecution and the fact that they were not allowed to own land—prohibited sustained agricultural activity, which was, until recent generations, the dominant economic endeavor. Thus they had developed skills in "mobile" occupations such as tin-smithing, horse breeding, and various commercial activities. Although for

a host of cultural reasons many resisted integration they generally adopted the
religion of their environment thereby creating tremendous religious diversity
of the world's Romani population.

Initially, the Roma could adapt to the medieval societies and backward
(by West European standards) economies of Eastern Europe relatively successfully primarily owing to the demand for their skills. In the areas ruled by the
Ottoman Empire they fared especially well while they were enslaved (either
working in households or on the fields) in the principalities of Wallachia and
Moldavia and were liberated only in 1864.[3] Under Maria Theresa and her
son, Joseph II, two "enlightened" eighteenth century Habsburg emperors, the
Roma received the state's attention for the first time in the form of coercive
reforms and settlement policies. By the mid- to late-nineteenth century
Romani itinerance had become an anachronism on account of accelerating
economic development and urbanization in the Habsburg Empire. Moreover,
the lifestyle of the semi-nomadic Roma had posed further challenges to the
increasingly institutionalized and strengthening state's power to control its
subjects and, especially, to collect taxes.

Meantime, in the region's underdeveloped village-centered socioeconomic systems the Roma still had an important economic role to play before
the onset of World War II. The failure of the eighteenth century monarchs at
the Roma's social integration cautioned extensive efforts of state interference
into their affairs until the early twentieth century. During the era of European
fascism integration efforts gave way to unprecedented persecution resulting in
the extermination of between 500,000 and 750,000 Roma in labor and
concentration camps.[4] For decades after the war the persecution of Roma was
essentially forgotten by all but a few.

The East European communist regimes attempted to end the social and
economic exclusion of the Roma. To be sure, they were to have no genuine
political rights but neither were members of other nationalities. The communists did not realize, however, that the Roma might not appreciate the
"privileges" about to be forced on them, such as the 48-hour work-week and
mass housing. Initially, the Roma were obviously pleased about the communists' ascension to political power with their promises of political, economic,
and social fairness and, especially, full equality for all nationalities and ethnic
groups. It soon became obvious, however, that the policies of these states,
while often well intentioned, did not endear them to the Roma. Although in
several countries of the region, including Bulgaria, Czechoslovakia, Hungary,
and Romania, the Roma numbered in the hundreds of thousands, they did
not receive the official recognition accorded to other nationalities. In fact, the
Roma were considered either as an ambiguously defined "ethnic group," or as

Protracted Marginality: The East European Roma

a social group characterized by unfathomable customs, anti-social behavior, and vagrancy.[5]

Most East European Roma welcomed the revolutions that brought about communism's collapse only to realize that the subsequent political and socio-economic changes brought mixed blessings to them.[6] They have suffered more from the resurgent nationalism and the economic difficulties accompanying the postcommunist transition process than most other ethnic groups. Generally, they are despised and discriminated against by the traditionally anti-Roma social environment and neglected or used as scapegoats by the new regimes.

The actual size of Eastern Europe's Romani population is disputed.[7] Romani activists tend to inflate their numbers while authorities are inclined to do the opposite. According to an independent source, the Romani population of East European states is as follows: Albania 62,000; Bulgaria 800,000; former Czechoslovakia 800,000; Hungary 600,000; Poland 50,000; Romania 2 million; and former Yugoslavia 800,000.[8] Owing to the high birthrate of the Roma (a result of reluctance to use contraception and the allure of state-provided per-child subsidies, in many cases the only source of regular income to Romani families), their communities have been growing more rapidly than those of other nationalities. In contrast with the stereotype of the "wandering Gypsy" most Roma have actually been settled for one or two generations.[9] The majority of the Roma are city dwellers although two or three decades ago most still lived in rural areas.[10] Since geographical isolation is a factor of the marginal condition the recent trend toward urbanization has changed the marginal character of the Roma in East Central Europe. The urban Roma are physically proximate to political and economic centers, to large numbers of fellow Roma, as well as to the intelligentsia, the only social stratum from which they can expect sympathy.

Socio-economic Conditions, Popular Attitudes, and State Policies

Although political systems have changed and so have their policies throughout the centuries, system-, regime-, and policy-variations have made little apparent difference in the Roma's circumstances. The most important reasons for the protracted marginalization of the Roma seem to be the constancy of negative popular attitudes toward them and the Roma's own reluctance to conform to social expectations let alone assimilate. Whether state policies reinforced popular prejudices toward the Roma (as they did in the imperial age, the interwar period, and during World War II) or discouraged them (as they did

The Roma's Socio-Economic Conditions

Until the belated dawn of the modern age in Eastern Europe, the Roma's traditional skills were in demand and, by and large, they were tolerated by the majority population as long as they did not try to overstep social boundaries.[11] Most Roma abided by social conventions (e.g., they addressed non-Roma [*gadje*] in the formal manner although they were spoken to in the familiar), they hardly ever rebelled against discrimination, and generally tried to make the best of their situation. Basic aspects of Romani life—such as family and personal relations with other Roma, food preparation, customs governing holidays, etc.—have remained very similar for most Roma, although the vast majority have become sedentary across the region.

One of the roots of the Romani predicament is the persistence of their remarkably low educational level which, in turn, creates other profound social problems. Until the communist period the Roma's education was neglected by the state. The communist regimes introduced the eight-year mandatory and free schooling which improved Romani education. Still, the Roma remained by far the least educated ethnic group in every East European society for reasons generally overlooked. Many Romani children could not study in their native tongue and thus were at an obvious disadvantage sharpened by often prejudiced teachers. Due to widespread discrimination by peers and teachers alike, many Romani kids left school early, especially since their parents rarely insisted that they stay.[12] Consequently, most Roma could find work only as unskilled laborers. Not surprisingly, the Roma's profound educational problems have not been solved since 1989.[13] In Romania, where the situation appears to be the worst, a large-scale study examining the Roma's conditions recently found that only 51.3 percent of the Romani children attended school regularly, 79.4 percent of the adults had no professional training, only 16.5 percent had modern professions, and the overwhelming majority lived in "incredible" poverty.[14]

The most important result of the Roma's educational exclusion is their marginal status in the economic sphere. Economic modernization had gradually rendered the Roma's traditional skills irrelevant. During the communist period, when everyone was not only guaranteed a job but by law had to hold one, most Roma became unskilled factory workers. The transition to market-oriented economies, however, has signalled a drastic decline in the Roma's economic status for one of its main features is the trimming of the labor force. Unskilled laborers are the most expendable and since 70-80 percent of the

Roma have worked in this capacity and owing to the deep-rooted prejudices in personnel departments, the Roma are the first to be dismissed. Consequently, Romani unemployment has skyrocketed and averages 60-70 percent across the region albeit in some areas it approaches 100 percent.[15]

The circle is rounded out by crime and other social ills. Since the 1989 revolutions crime rates have risen precipitously in the region, and to a large extent this has been blamed on the Roma. Criminal statistics are often unreliable, however, since they reflect arrests rather than convictions. Besides, there is no reason to believe that the Roma commit more crimes than other ethnic groups of similar socio-economic conditions. Most of their transgressions are economic in nature such as pickpocketing, purse-snatching, and burglary.[16] The Romani predicament, then, starts with inadequate education, continues with inferior work opportunities, and ends in crime and many other social problems. The result is that the East European Roma present "the typical symptoms of an underdeveloped people living within countries of (at least) a medium level of development."[17]

Popular Attitudes Toward The Roma

Clearly, the Roma have been the least popular ethnic group in Eastern Europe. Until the mid- to late-nineteenth century social interaction between the dominant group and the Roma could be controlled and was very limited. Few Roma children attended school and when they did they were ordinarily separated from their non-Roma (*gadje*) peers. Ordinarily contacts between Romani and *gadje* adults were restricted to business transactions. In sum, while the Roma were marginalized and systematically discriminated against as a matter of course, the bourgeoisie, artisans, and intellectuals—particularly as Gypsy music had acquired growing popularity—viewed them with condescending amusement.[18]

These attitudes have survived with few changes in Eastern Europe although historically a negative correlation is observable between economic conditions on the one hand and ethnic discrimination and violence on the other. Although nationalist and racist attitudes certainly did not disappear from the region under communism, their exhibition was officially prohibited and at times punished. The fall of the communist regimes, however, opened the door to increasingly unrestrained nationalist behavior which were reinforced by a number of adverse socio-economic phenomena accompanying the postcommunist transition process.[19]

Recent opinion polls have confirmed that social attitudes toward the Roma are increasingly negative. In fact, a number of surveys concluded that the Roma are by far the most disliked ethnic minority in Eastern and Central

Europe.[20] For example, a 1991 study comparing racial attitudes in the three East Central European states revealed that 78 percent of the people surveyed viewed the Roma negatively.[21] A Romanian poll indicated that 41 percent of the respondents thought that Roma should be harshly treated while one survey in Czechoslovakia disclosed that 87 percent considered the Roma's behavior provocative.[22] It appears that one of the few remaining similarities in these increasingly dissimilar societies is contempt toward the Roma.

Under communism, the state-run media in the region offered comprehensive coverage of the Roma's criminal behavior—amounting to thinly veiled ethnic criticism. Although in some postcommunist states (Hungary, Macedonia) reports concerning the Roma have improved in form and content, much remains to be done. Consistently negative media coverage aggravates social tensions and contributes to social marginalization. In Romania, for instance, the press frequently display anti-Romani prejudice and occasionally explicitly incite hatred.[23] A report presented to the April 1993 session of the Conference on Security and Cooperation in Europe (CSCE) found that even in the Czech Republic, arguably the most developed state in the region, the media presented a very malicious picture of the Roma. In most East European states Romani suspects are always identified as such in media reports covering criminal cases while the ethnic origins of their non-Romani counterparts are omitted.[24]

Many East Europeans blame the Roma for a growing number of social and economic problems. What many do not see, however, is that social problems like crime are to a large degree the results of a number of interrelated socioeconomic phenomena. Anti-Romani discrimination is so unabashed in some areas of the Czech Republic, for instance, that "No Gypsies Allowed" signs have become commonplace in bars and restaurants. Although illegal under the Czech Constitution, the local authorities simply turn a blind eye to the signs.[25] In Slovakia local decrees have been passed that sanction official discrimination against the Roma. Some Slovak villages, for instance, imposed a curfew on the Roma "and other suspicious persons."[26]

Postcommunist Regime Change, Nationalism, and State Policy

The postcommunist developments concerning the Roma confirm the dynamic nature of marginality for in this era their social and economic exclusion has increased but they have become less marginalized in the political and cultural arenas. While the negative public image and discrimination against the Roma have been challenged by at least some postcommunist polities (Czech Republic, Hungary, Poland), they have been reinforced by the emergent social problems and their economic situation has clearly deteriorated.

Protracted Marginality: The East European Roma

Perhaps the most troubling postcommunist phenomenon from the Roma's standpoint is the revival of violent nationalism. The relative lenience of the postcommunist regimes with respect to the expression of nationalist views has been interpreted by some groups as permission to display openly racist sentiments. The state cannot control these extremist groups given the lack of resources. Many have targeted their frustration at the Roma.

Physical attacks on the Roma have occurred repeatedly in virtually every country of the region. Romani dwellings have been burned down, Romani men killed, women raped.[27] As a general rule, the police are reluctant to interfere and provide insufficient protection. The governments have either neglected these problems, as in Albania or Bulgaria; or the Roma have been singled out by the regime as scapegoats and even urged to move on as in Romania.[28] Elsewhere, in Hungary and the former Czechoslovakia, politicians have not taken strong enough measures to halt the attacks perpetrated against the Roma by extreme nationalist elements.

The disintegration of the region's two federal states, Yugoslavia and Czechoslovakia, has had a particularly damaging effect on their Romani communities. The destiny of Yugoslav Roma is especially difficult to track owing to their forced participation in the war, their mass migration, and to the general turmoil in these societies.[29] Armed organizations in Serbia and Croatia have attempted to force the Roma into the war. Many have responded by abandoning their homes and migrating to more peaceful areas.[30] In the former Czechoslovakia most Roma hold Slovak citizenship but many have lived and worked for years in the territory of the Czech Republic. After the partition of the country thousands of Roma from Slovakia travelled to the Czech lands aiming to stay there owing to the latter country's better chances for economic prosperity. The Roma are also hurt by the new Czech citizenship and naturalization regulations which require at least two years of continual permanent residence and a clean police record for the previous five years. Romani leaders have demanded the alteration of these provisions given the natural mobility and disadvantaged position of their people. The Czech government has demonstrated no intention either to modify the law or to implement it differently in regard to the Roma.[31] One of the most important changes that has taken place in state policy toward the Roma in Eastern Europe is that in several countries now they are recognized as a distinct ethnic group or national minority (the Roma prefer the latter). This long overdue step was taken in Bosnia-Herzegovina, the Czech Republic, Hungary, Macedonia, and Slovakia. The Romanian government recognized the Roma as a "transnational non-territorial minority," and the new (1991) constitution gave them the right to preserve and develop their ethnic, cultural, and religious identity.[32]

Zoltan Barany

Although the institutional political marginalization of ethnic minorities has stopped everywhere except in Bulgaria, there are differences between the minority policies of East European states which are reflected in their treatment of the Roma.[33] In the highest political offices there appears to be goodwill toward the Roma. Arpad Goncz of Hungary, Vaclav Havel of the Czech Republic, and Zhelyu Zhelev of Bulgaria have met Romani leaders on several occasions, attended Romani festivals and conferences, and spoken out on behalf of the Romani people repeatedly. All have condemned discrimination against and attacks on the Roma and have criticized their governments for not doing more to protect them. These heads of state occupy largely ceremonial positions, however, and can do little more than offer symbolic support.

In general, high ranking government officials have also displayed sympathetic attitudes toward the Roma and voiced intentions to improve their conditions. Aside from some notable exceptions—e.g., the Slovak government's rejection of the Roma's demands for cultural and social development—the problems appear to be not at the policy-making level (i.e. the Minister of Interior) but at the policy implementation level (i.e. the policeman). Views concerning the Roma appear to have changed little at the latter. Thus, despite good intentions on the top, for many Roma the embodiment of state authority are the policemen, tax collectors, staffs of the local administrations, the majority of whom tend to be prejudiced.

In virtually every country of the region the central government established agencies to deal with minority affairs. Characterized by lofty ideals and intentions but limited resources and opportunities, these bodies do not enjoy much institutional prestige or political authority. Generally they are not charged with representing the interests of minorities, but to coordinate the implementation of the government's minority programs and the relevant tasks of the various government bodies.[34]

Macedonia, a newly independent republic of the former Yugoslavia where the Roma make up 3-4 percent of the population, has been the most successful East European state in shaping its relationship with the Roma.[35] President Kiro Gligorov and his governments have not only repeatedly and explicitly recognized the Roma as full and equal citizens, but have made real progress on concrete issues. Since education has been pegged as the priority, substantive issues are regularly discussed between the Ministry of Education and Romani leaders. A Romani primer has been approved, a 40,000-word Macedonian-Romani dictionary is under preparation, and a comprehensive educational program which includes two hours of Romani instruction per week will be introduced in grades one through eight. Skopje University's Department of Romani Studies is to be inaugurated in September 1995 to train teachers,

Protracted Marginality: The East European Roma

researchers, and activists. The Macedonian Television and Radio provide thirty minutes and two-and-a-half hours of programming per week, respectively, in the Romani language, which is soon to be increased. Some of these achievements came as the result of campaigning by a relatively well-organized Romani party. Although the Macedonian Roma have also suffered from the socioeconomic problems accompanying the transitions, a political leadership that is willing to take concrete steps and the general absence of overtly racist attitudes—owing to a relatively long-standing social acceptance of the Roma—have made a positive difference in their situation.

The Politics of Integration

First, it might be useful to call attention to the often blurred distinction between assimilation which denotes the outright absorption of a marginal group by a dominant group and integration which signifies the process leading to peaceful cohabitation and the retention of ethnic characteristics by the marginal population.[36] There are major differences between the "Gypsy policies" of the early years of communist and postcommunist rule in Eastern Europe. The communists initially seemed to have believed that the Roma needed the state to show them the direction leading to full-scale assimilation. Once they realized that this assumption was erroneous, they resorted to a variety of coercive measures—from the burning of Romani colonies to the sterilization of Romani women—to achieve Romani integration.

The postcommunist regimes appear to be more realistic about the situation and somewhat more knowledgeable of and sympathetic toward the Roma. Furthermore, they have faced grave economic troubles and a plethora of political and social problems, consequently, the Roma have not figured high on their lists of priorities. Although the Roma's economic conditions and social status have suffered in the transition period, it is important to note that in the issue areas under the new regimes' control the situation of the Roma have actually improved.

Assimilation Policies and Regime Change

In late-eighteenth century Eastern Europe, Maria Theresa and Joseph II introduced the first of many unsuccessful programs aiming to stop the Roma's social marginalization. They intended to "civilize" and "domesticate" the Roma by forcible settlement; by prohibiting the usage of Romani language, traditional clothing, and horse ownership; and by prescribing state education of Romani children taken away from their parents.[37] The Roma enjoyed no rights and existed on the edge of these late-feudal societies, their social and

Zoltan Barany

on the Habsburg throne were either totally oblivious to the Roma or made note of the unsuccessful yet costly "tame-the-Barbarians" campaigns of the past. In the Balkans, Romani slaves were liberated, although their social and economic conditions had scarcely improved, and many had left the region. To a large degree, a *laissez faire* stance characterized the late imperial and the interwar policies. As long as they remained inconspicuous, the Roma were left alone to fend for themselves.

Of all the system-types, Romani assimilation was an important goal only for the communists. By their very nature and in stark contrast with democracies, totalitarian regimes abhor social diversity and strive to control people. For the communist states the Romani minorities represented a seemingly unresolvable dilemma that thwarted their construction of a new society. In a plethora of publications the Roma's conditions were painstakingly described and decried, but the reasons for and the causes of their circumstances were hardly ever investigated.[38] Although there were significant variations in the East European communist states' approaches to the Roma, the goal was everywhere to settle them and to transform them into "socially useful" members of the new societies. The means to achieve this goal were carelessly chosen and implemented and often resulted in further exclusion. The communist regimes ignored the ways in which their assimilation and later integration policies could have respected the Roma's traditions. They were convinced that the Roma's integration was a prerequisite of a homogeneous society and by decreasing or reversing their socioeconomic marginalization the regimes thought to offer the Roma a great service.

Even when assimilation policies met with increasing obstacles, open discrimination against the Roma was seldom sanctioned by central authorities although the occurrence of institutionalized persecution—always for the sake of the "larger goal"—was not unknown. Local authorities, pressed by the need to produce "results" whatever the costs, exercised less prudence. In Poland the Roma's itinerance was officially curtailed, in Czechoslovakia the government pressured thousands of Romani women to allow themselves to be sterilized in return for material incentives, and Hungarian and Romanian law punished "social parasitism" and deviance from the norms of the "socialist way of life" with jail sentences or forced labor.[39] During much of Nicolae Ceausescu's quarter-century rule in Romania the Roma were simply ignored in accord with the government's declaration that the country's ethnic problems were "solved."[40] Bulgaria's policy was also forcible resettlement moving the Roma to some of the country's worst public housing projects. In the early 1980s the Roma, similarly to the ethnic Turks, were pressured to Bulgarianize their names and to abandon their customs. Yugoslav Roma fared relatively well under Tito's rule as they were recognized in the constitution as a distinctive nationality.[41]

The integration policies of the East European regimes did bear some fruit by decreasing the economic and social exclusion of the Roma. The governments and the dominant populations naturally considered these results as benefits for the Roma gained at the expense of their own sacrifice. After all, their educational and literacy levels increased substantially, they received free medical care, subsidized housing, and their living standards (by objective measures) undoubtedly improved. Nevertheless, from the Romani perspective the benefits were of often nebulous value when they were in conflict with their traditional lifestyle and values.

The postcommunist regimes do not aspire to assimilate the Roma for a number of reasons. Most of the region's governments appear to realize that such goal would be quite elusive and meet with the opposition not only of the Roma but also of the general population. Although official recognition and the granting of various opportunities for political participation have signified a reversal of the long-standing political exclusion of the Roma, in the last four years no East European party (Romani or otherwise) has offered either theoretical or practical solutions to their problems. The capacity of the postcommunist states to resolve the problems of marginality appears to be questionable.

The Roma's Reaction to Assimilation

Most Roma have resisted the various regimes' efforts to assimilate them. The reasons for this reaction may be found in the basic features of Romani culture (antagonistic attitudes toward non-Roma, close ties within the Romani community, adherence to traditions, values, customs, etc.), the centuries-long experience of discrimination and contempt from the *gadje*, and the heavy-handed assimilation and integration attempts of the past. From the Roma's point of view, assimilation signified rather bleak prospects. The state demanded that they assimilate, to lose their language and religion, and/or to integrate and drastically alter their lifestyle. The cost of integration was extremely high (such as the probable loss of traditions, culture, and language[42]) and the benefits were of disputable value. Similarly, as a result of forced (re-)settlement policies their objective housing standards may have improved but their traditional communities were often broken up in the process. Not all Roma resisted integration efforts and those who did not were often ostracized by their own people as well as the dominant population.

As a result of a limited policy of positive discrimination in the communist period the nuclei of Romani intelligentsia had developed which also signified a mixed blessing to the Romani population. A few "promising" Romani youths were selected for advanced education supported by various state programs. The result was that the state could parade these individuals as examples for the community to emulate. The Romani identity of many new Roma intellectuals vanished in the process, however, and they became increasingly reluctant to identify with and support their people. There are other signs of increasing social stratification among the Roma. Although the proportion of "middle class" Roma is still relatively small it has been slowly growing. An important distinction can be made between those who choose to retain their ethnic identity maintaining contacts with other Roma and those who try to "become white" in their manners and attitudes.

At the same time the Roma's cultural marginalization has been on the decrease. The resurgence of nationalism signalled the kindling of Romani nationalism as well. They are now free to openly voice their concerns and nurture their cultural traditions. Several large-scale museum exhibitions and ethnic festivals have been organized to familiarize the general population with Romani traditions, music, and culture.[43] With the liberalization of press and association laws, hundreds of Romani newspapers, clubs, and cultural organizations have been established across the region. In some countries, for instance in Hungary, these enjoy financial support from the government and from various domestic and foreign foundations. Elsewhere, in Slovakia, for instance, they are barely tolerated by the authorities but everywhere they exist legally. These non-political organizations play a major role in maintaining Roma's ethnic identity by keeping alive and spreading their culture, language, and traditions.[44]

The postcommunist regimes seem to have given up on their predecessors' attempts to assimilate the Roma. The more progressive East European governments believe that various social and educational programs hold the promise of improving the lot of the Roma and toward the alleviation of tensions between Roma and *gadje*. Most of these cost a great deal of money, however, and no East European state has much. In contrast with some other marginal populations, such as the Canadian Inuit, most Roma suffer only the cost of their marginal status but accrue no advantages such as positive discrimination in hiring, state-supported housing programs, etc. Perhaps the most propitious recent development is that, as a result of political liberalization, Romani communities across the region have become more active not only in the sociocultural sphere, but politically as well.

Romani Politics

In order to mollify the handful of Romani activists and to remain in a position of full control over their endeavors, some communist polities supported the creation of Romani organizations. The task of these bodies was to shape Romani cultural and social activities into a manageable and controllable institutional form. Usually they were subordinated to the "popular fronts," non-party communist umbrella organizations, and were unceremoniously abolished when they became inconvenient to the state.

The fall of communism generally ended the political marginalization of the Roma. Following the revolutions of 1989, the region's marginal populations received the opportunity to actively participate in politics. The Roma formed political organizations everywhere with the exception of Bulgaria where the new (1991) constitution did not permit the organization of political parties based on ethnicity.[45] The new Romani associations and parties have been plagued by many problems, however, most of them similar throughout the region. Like other East Europeans, the vast majority of the Roma have been politically passive not believing in their power to influence political outcomes. Internal dissension within Romani parties—a characteristic of non-Roma parties as well—has been by far the most damaging to the articulation of their interests.

Many Romani parties have been created amidst great fanfare only to fade into oblivion in a short time. Consequently, tracking them is very difficult. In some countries, such as Hungary and Macedonia, the organizations of marginal populations receive modest financial support from the state. Today there are dozens of competing Romani parties in most East European states frittering away the Romani vote at election time. Thus, despite the end to their political exclusion, Romani interests are not represented in proportion to their numbers and there are only a handful of Roma in the East European legislatures.[46] By their sheer numbers the Roma should be the strongest minority group in Hungary, the Czech Republic, and arguably in Romania and Slovakia as well; in fact, they remain politically ineffective.

Romani groups are often quite antagonistic toward each other and expecting a single Romani party (especially in countries with large and diverse Romani populations) would be unreasonable. In order to reduce the fragmentation of Romani parties, umbrella organizations have been set up in several countries to embrace not only independent political parties but also cultural and economic associations. These umbrella organizations—such as the Democratic Union of Gypsies in Romania, the Romani Democratic Congress in the Czech Republic or the Roma Parliament in Hungary—attempt to coordinate the policies of their member groups in areas of mutual concern.[47] Although they have been more effective in calling attention to Romani concerns than unaffiliated groups, they do not represent all Romani groups and there are often disagreements among the ones that they do.

Zoltan Barany

The programs of Romani parties are often determined by the aspirations of individuals; thus, there is rarely any cohesion at the political level and it is unclear who represents whom. Still, the aims of these organizations are quite similar across the region and very much like those of other minorities. They include full recognition and nationality rights, civil rights enforced by effective legal instruments, schools with Romani as the second language of instruction, affirmative action in public offices (such as local administrations and the police force), broadcast time in the state-owned media proportionate to the size of the Romani population and its fair portrayal therein, and state-supported social and economic programs to alleviate their disadvantaged position.

Thus far the Roma have clearly proved themselves unable to capitalize on their political opportunities. At the same time, mistakes in the initial period of political participation were not unexpected and growing experience should result in better organizations and more institutional cohesion. Moreover, some of the problems of Romani parties (internal dissension, lack of party discipline, etc.) are characteristic also of the parties of the *gadje* who also lack experience in political organization. Undoubtedly, there are ways to reverse the political weakness of the Romani people. For instance, there is a substantial pool of politically apathetic Roma who could be encouraged to participate in politics. There is also a number of Romani intellectuals who have either turned their backs on their ethnic heritage or have become frustrated after having seen the self-destructive machinations of rival Romani parties. There might be ways to enroll or re-enroll them as active supporters. Another chance might be to obtain the assistance of domestic or international organizations to support the education and coaching of Romani politicians.

One possible avenue toward the resolution of these problems might be to actively involve traditional Romani leaders (*bare, phure, voivode*) in the political process. In most areas they are respected by and can exert a great deal of influence on their people. Such traditional leaders have been reluctant to interact with *gadje* politicians primarily for cultural reasons. They prefer to communicate with the *gadje* through intermediaries, educated Roma—such as the sociologist Nicolae Gheorghe in Romania, the writer Menyhert Lakatos in Hungary, or the teacher-politician Lada Body in the Czech Republic—who have proved themselves successful in both cultures. Perhaps the best known Roma leaders, however, are the self-proclaimed "Emperor" (Iulian Radulescu) and the "King" (Ion Cioaba) of the Roma in Romania.[48] Their authority is restricted to the city of Sibiu and its vicinity, however, and although they have declared their intent to protect all Roma they may have done more damage than good to the Romani cause. Their ostentatious lifestyle and outlandish

Protracted Marginality: The East European Roma

statements have served to perpetuate the deluding romantic image of the Roma and to trivialize their pressing problems in critical times.

The International Context

The international facets of the Roma's plight have received growing attention in recent years. The collapse of communism opened the borders allowing the Roma to seek settling outside the region. The arrival of a large number of Romani and other immigrants, however, has forced West European states to address the problem. At the same time, a number of Romani and independent international organizations have tried to speak up for Romani interests in national and international forums.

Romani Migration and Its Effects on Marginalization

With the opening of international borders in the wake of communism the westward migration of traditionally mobile Roma was quite predictable. Arguably, many Roma have long wanted to leave but they have been prevented from doing so by the travel restrictions imposed by the communist regimes. The "new migration" of the Roma makes their plight a European problem for their destination is usually Western Europe, particularly Germany. This migration wave has resulted in the creation and re-creation of marginal populations, reinforced prejudices, and drastic increases in attacks on migrants in the countries to and through which the Roma have travelled on their journey. Their position as Romani refugees (absent of a concrete legal status) puts them into an extremely vulnerable position which has been frequently exploited. One of the major hurdles is that while citizens of the European Union can freely move within the EU, there is no consensus between member states regarding the free movement of third country nationals. This problem has been exacerbated with the great number of refugees arriving from post-communist Eastern Europe and the former Soviet Union.[49]

Tens of thousands of East European Roma, mostly Bulgarian, Romanian, and Yugoslav, have made their way to or toward Germany, chosen as a destination because of its high living standards and until recently liberal immigration policy.[50] In 1992 alone some 130,000 Romanian and Bulgarian citizens sought asylum in Germany, most of them Roma.[51] Initially, the German authorities sent many Roma who sought to enter Germany illegally across the border back to Poland where they set up camps in the border regions waiting to attempt crossing the frontier again. In May 1993 Warsaw and Bonn signed a treaty which includes $76 million in German aid to

Poland to care for refugees, improve border security, and process asylum applications.[52]

The situation of the Roma in Germany is hardly better than in Eastern Europe. Neofascist and skinhead attacks directed against them and other refugees have increased precipitously; in the first six months of 1993 German authorities reported 1,008 such attacks resulting in eight deaths, 30 percent more than in the same period a year before.[53] In 1993, the increasing number of refugees and the mounting public protest wave prompted the adoption of a new refugee policy and asylum law as well as changes to the Constitution.[54] Although many human rights groups have criticized Bonn's action, Germany itself has been in the midst of an economic recession and has faced abundant sociopolitical problems as a result of the 1990 reunification. In the meantime, the number of refugees has grown swiftly from barely 100,000 in 1988 to approximately 440,000 in 1992.[55]

In September 1992 the German Interior Ministry reached an agreement with the Romanian government arranging the deportation of Roma back to Romania that elicited widespread criticism from the international Romani and human rights communities.[56] Bonn offered $20 million to reintegrate the deported Romanian citizens but Roma did not believe that the money would be used to alleviate their problems. Deportees were escorted by members of the infamous Romanian security forces, a bitter irony that was not lost on the Roma.[57] The mass deportation of the Roma has sharpened racial tensions in Romania, where people have expressed displeasure over the Roma's return.[58] A German Foreign Ministry official claimed that the deportation policy "in no way" was aimed at any single ethnic group but against "citizens of one country who reside illegally in another."[59] Skepticism about Bonn's attitude toward the Roma was fostered by the fact that Germany was the only state refusing to sign a Council of Europe resolution urging improvement in the Roma's situation. Germany is not the only country that has deported Roma but because of its large refugee population it has received the most criticism.[60]

Migration is also a problem within East European states. Thousands of Roma have sought to settle in the more prosperous regions within the countries they reside in. As mentioned above, this problem effects the former Czechoslovakia most seriously as many Roma have moved from economically depressed Slovakia to the wealthier Czech lands.[61] Romani migration has caused tensions between Prague and Bratislava as both governments would like to shift the Roma to the other's territory.[62]

The usual route of Romanian and Bulgarian Roma toward Germany goes through Hungary, Slovakia, the Czech Republic, and Poland, where their appearance has been met by helpless government officials and enraged citizens. Another important consequence of the Romani migration is that it divides the Roma themselves. For instance, Poland's established middle-class Roma may sympathize with the refugees' plight but consider them an obstacle toward their own social integration. A Polish Romani leader said that "when the Romanian Gypsies came to Poland, I even considered going on TV and saying that they are not part of us. They dirty Polish territory."[63]

International Organizations and The Roma

In the absence of strong and effective national organizations several international organizations—some of them created by the Roma—have become increasingly active in representing Romani interests world-wide. These organizations essentially act as pressure groups and provide an indispensable service by publicizing the Roma's situation and thereby trying to improve their international security. Still, few of them have offered any specific solutions to the Roma's problems other than suggesting ways of protecting their human rights. Given the fact that their powers are very limited it is up to the given government or state authority to act upon, reject, or ignore their recommendations.

The most significant Romani supranational organization is the International Romani Union. Although this body adopted the IRU name only in 1978, IRU is a successor of the International Gypsy Committee that was established in 1965. Over 70 Romani organizations in some 28 countries are members of IRU. World Romani congresses have been held since 1971, the fourth in April 1990 at Serock, near Warsaw, Poland.[64] The IRU has not been immune to the problems—infighting, personal rivalries, etc.—plaguing national Romani organizations.

In 1979 the Roma were given observer status in the United Nations Council for Social and Economic Questions. The IRU is represented in the Council of Europe, in several other organizations of the United Nations (e.g., UNICEF, UNESCO) and has also sent a permanent representative to the CSCE meetings dealing with minorities and the Geneva Conference on Minorities.[65] A number of resolutions have been passed by various UN commissions, such as the UN Sub-Commission on the Prevention of Discrimination and Protection of Minorities, recognizing the vulnerability of Romani communities and recommending measures to guarantee their security.[66]

In August 1992, Romani leaders from twenty-two Romani organizations from ten countries established the European Roma Parliament (EUROM) in Budapest to fight discrimination and promote the culture of the European Roma.[67] The increasingly active Romani international movement has been quite successful in publicizing the Roma's situation in Eastern Europe and other regions. Considering that less than two decades ago the world's approximately 10 million Roma enjoyed neither worldwide attention nor representation, the accomplishments of Romani and other activists are considerable. Non-governmental organizations in the west such as Human Rights Watch and Amnesty International have also made serious efforts to publicize discrimination against the Roma.[68] Their endeavors have included the study of legal standards for non-discrimination, analyses and publication of specific problems, and providing political support for their resolution. These and other international organizations have managed to reduce the marginalization of the Roma in the global political arena by their attempts to organize them and by calling attention to their plight. Furthermore, they have increased the international security of the Romani people.

Conclusion

The marginal condition of the Roma has been the result of exclusionary dynamics in three separate dimensions: political, social, and economic. It is important to reiterate that the exclusion of minorities has taken a number of frequently quite dissimilar forms in various historical eras, under different sorts of political regimes, and in different states.

To some extent the Roma have been marginalized because the designs for the elimination of their marginal status were synonymous with the eradication of their ethnic identity. This disparity between goals and results indicates that the East European polities, whether dynastic, communist, or postcommunist, have not been capable of resolving the Roma's marginalization. The societal marginalization of the Roma—due to its seemingly permanent nature and often violent manifestations—has been a far more determinant and enduring factor in their exclusion than state policies.

While the state's intentions concerning the Roma have changed over time, societal attitudes toward them have remained relatively constant. The political superstructure has been unable to penetrate and transform the underlying substructure of anti-Roma prejudice. The belated arrival to or even absence from Eastern Europe of such sociopolitical movements and socioeconomic developments as the Enlightenment, Reformation, urbanization, industrialization, let alone political liberalism reinforced the conservative nature of these societies. Nationalism in the region has historically been as much directed against other nations and minorities as it was supposed to fuel the fires of their own ascension. Clearly, social tolerance has not been a traditional virtue in East European societies. In contemporary Eastern Europe, as a result of the resurgence of often violent nationalism and the persisting economic problems of the transition period most Roma's objective conditions have deteriorated.

An important factor in the Roma's marginalization is that when the choice comes down to marginal situation or assimilation they may well choose the former in order to preserve their identity. Consequently, they have remained one of the most visible minorities in Europe. The distinctive Romani language, culture, traditions, appearance, etc. and many Roma's staunch resistance to assimilation are the curse and salvation of this people. On the one hand, these qualities have rendered them readily identifiable and have conserved their marginality. On the other hand, due to many Roma's resistance to integration let alone assimilation, they have managed to maintain their distinctive ethnic identity in spite of (and, likely, due to) amazing obstacles.

Although the Roma have been part of East European societies for centuries there is still widespread ignorance about them. The enduring socioeconomic problems surrounding the postcommunist transitions, the rapid growth of the Romani population, and the political awakening of the Roma are only three of the numerous factors that might point to increasing tension between them and the dominant populations around them. Learning more about the Roma might be a first step toward alleviating that tension.

Notes

For insights, comments, and criticisms I am indebted to Gary P. Freeman, Sam C. Nolutshungu, and colleagues in the SSRC Working Group. This chapter partially draws on research published in the author's "Living on the Edge: The East European Roma in Postcommunist Politics and Societies," *Slavic Review*, Vol. 53, No. 2 (Summer 1994), pp. 321-344.

1. Romanian Gypsy activist Iulian Lepadatu quoted in *The Miami Herald*, May 4, 1993.

2. See John A. Armstrong, "Mobilized and Proletarian Diasporas," *American Political Science Review*, Vol. 70, No. 2 (June 1976), pp. 393-408.

3. On the history of Gypsy slavery, see Sam Beck, "The Origins of Gypsy Slavery in Romania," *Dialectal Anthropology*, Vol. 14 (1989), pp. 53-61; Nicolae Gheorghe, "Origins of Roma's Slavery in the Rumanian Principalities," *Roma*, No. 1 (1983), pp. 12-27.

4. For accounts of the Gypsy Holocaust or *Porajamos* see, for instance, Christian Bernadec, *L'holocaust oublie: le massacre des Tsiganes* (Paris: Editions France-Empire, 1979); Benno Mueller-Hill, *Murderous Science: Elimination by Scientific Selection of Jews, Gypsies, and Others: Germany 1933-1945* (Oxford: Oxford University Press, 1988).

Zoltan Barany

5. See Zoltan Barany, "Hungary's Gypsies," *Report on Eastern Europe*, July 20,
   1990, p. 27.
6. For a brief treatment along these lines, see Zoltan Barany, "Democratic Changes Bring Mixed Blessing for Gypsies," *RFE/RL Research Report*, Vol. 1, No. 20 (May 15, 1992), pp. 40-48.
7. See, Andre Liebich, "Minorities in Eastern Europe: Obstacles to Reliable Count," *RFE/RL Research Report*, Vol. 1, No. 20 (May 15, 1992), pp. 32-39.
8. *Der Spiegel*, September 3, 1990.
9. In Romania, for instance, the percentage of truly nomadic Gypsies is between 3-10 percent. Dan Ionescu, "The Gypsies Organize," *Report on Eastern Europe*, Vol. 1, No. 26 (June 29, 1990), p. 41.
10. See, for instance, Otto Ulc, "Integration of the Gypsies in Czechoslovakia," *Ethnic Groups*, Vol. 9, No. 2 (1991), p. 111.
11. For an examination of the ancient Romani trade skills, see Gyorgy Rostas-Farkas and Ervin Karsai, *Osi cigany mestersegek es foglalkozasok* (Budapest: OMIKK, 1991).
12. On this issue, see for instance, Josefat Zywert, Problemy mlodziezy cyganskiej w szkole podstawowej," *Kwartalnik Pedagogiczny*, No. 1 (1968), pp. 103-109; Aladar Salata, "Deti ciganskych spoluobcanov," *Ceskoslovenska pediatrie*, Vol 13, No. 3 (1976), pp. 267-271; Istvan Kotnyek, "A leghatranyosabb helyzetben," *Tarsadalmi Szemle*, No. 11 (1972), pp. 69-74.
13. See, Marta Gyenei, "A Letminimum alatt—jajhalom (I)," *Statisztikai Szemle*, Vol. 71, No. 1 (January 1993), pp. 16-32.
14. The study, "The Population of the Roma: Social and Economic Situation and Coordinates for Support Programs," was excerpted in several publications. See *Heti Vilaggazdasag*, January 2, 1993; Rompres (Bucharest), April 7, 1993; *Azi*, April 10, 1993; and *Romania Libera*, May 4, 1993.
15. See, for instance, *The European*, March 26-April 1, 1992; *Die Presse*, November 16, 1992; *Magyar Hirlap*, June 14, 1993.
16. In the Czech Republic, for instance, provincial authorities have claimed that as much as 90 percent of the crime in their municipalities is committed by Roma. See CTK, January 10, 1993.
17. Nicolae Gheorghe, "Roma-Gypsy Ethnicity in Eastern Europe," *Social Research*, Vol. 58, No. 4 (Winter 1991), p. 837.
18. This patronizing mentality can be discerned from the works of several contemporary writers and in collections of popular stories featuring the cunning Gypsy outwitting the stingy landowner. See, for instance, *Cziganyadomak* (Budapest: Jo Konyvek, 1898); and Emil Kolozsvari Grandpierre, *Elmes mulatsagok* (Budapest: Magveto, 1969).
19. On these developments, see Zoltan Barany, "Mass-Elite Relations and the Resurgence of Nationalism in Eastern Europe," *European Security*, Vol. 3, No. 2 (March 1994), pp. 162-181.
20. See, for instance, *The European*, 27-30 September 1991.
21. See "Democracy, Economic Reform, and Western Assistance in Czechoslovakia, Hungary, and Poland: A Comparative Public Opinion Survey," by Penn and

Schoen Associates, Inc., Washington, D.C., April 1991; and *The Washington Post*, May 19, 1991.

22. See the report "Prospects for the Roma in a New Europe" of the Helsinki Committee of the International Romani Union at the Conference for Security and Cooperation in Europe: The Human Dimension, Moscow, September 1991.

23. See Dan Ionescu, "Violence Against Gypsies Escalates," *Report on Eastern Europe*, June 21, 1991, p. 26. See also *Der Spiegel*, September 7, 1992; *The Los Angeles Times*, October 12, 1992.

24. See NCA (Prague), April 27, 1993; and *Le Monde*, September 4, 1992.

25. *The Independent*, January 13, 1993.

26. *Suddeutsche Zeitung*, July 12, 1993. For a more extensive report on the Slovak Roma, see Sharon Fisher, "Romanies in Slovakia," *RFE/RL Research Report*, Vol. 2, No. 42, October 22, 1993, pp. 54-59.

27. There is plenty of solid evidence, see for instance, *The Sunday Times*, April 12, 1990; *Reform* September 14, 1990; *The Daily Telegraph*, October 26, 1990; Ionescu, "Violence against Gypsies Escalates," pp. 23-26; Enache, "Die Minderheit der Roma," pp. 21-22; *The New York Times*, June 12, 1992.

28. *Los Angeles Times*, December 20, 1991.

29. See "Stop Persecution of Gypsies!" (unsigned) *Women and Revolution*, No. 38 (Winter 1990-1991), p. 3.

30. *The Globe and Mail* (Toronto), August 21, 1992.

31. NCA (Prague), April 27, 1993. See also, *The Economist*, July 31, 1993.

32. Rompres (Bucharest), April 29, 1993; and *The Economist*, May 15-21, 1993.

33. For a more detailed exposition of this point, see Zoltan Barany, "Grim Realities in Eastern Europe," *Transition*, Vol. 1, No. 4 (March 1995), pp. 3-8.

34. For articles examining the Hungarian example, the National and Ethnic Minority Office, see Alfred A. Reisch, "First Law on Minorities Drafted," *Report on Eastern Europe*, Vol. 2, No. 50 (December 13, 1991), p. 16; and the interview with Janos Wolfart in *Amaro Drom*, August 1992, pp. 5-7; and September 1992, pp. 4-5.

35. See Zoltan Barany, "The Roma in Macedonia: Ethnic Politics and the Marginal Condition in a Balkan State," *Ethnic and Racial Studies*, Vol. 18, No. 3 (July 1995), pp. 515-531.

36. I am grateful for this point to Alfred Darnell.

37. See Archduke Joseph with Henrik Wislocki, *A ciganyokrol* (Budapest: Pallas, 1894); and Willy Guy, "Ways of Looking at Roms: The Case of Czechoslovakia," in Farnham Rehfisch, *Gypsies, Tinkerers*, pp. 208-210.

38. See, for instance, Tadeusz Bartosz, "Gdzie jestes Cyganie? Cyganie w woj. kielckim," *Tygodnik Kulturalny*, No. 25 (1966), p. 7; Andrzej Mirga, "Me som Rom, tumen sam gadze," *Etnografia Polska*, Vol. 22, No 2 (1978); Jiri Bartak, "Vice svetla do 'cikanske otazky,'" *Rude Pravo*, November 1, 1968; Tomas Holomek, "Problematika Cikanu ve svetle zakone upravy," *Demografie*, Vol. 9, No. 3 (1969), pp. 210-213; Imre Sajo, "A ciganyok," *Elet es Tudomany* No. 15 (1960), pp. 471-474.

39. Kostelancik, "The Gypsies of Czechoslovakia," p. 312; Ruben Pellar, " 'Ster- **97** ilisierung von Roma-Frauen in der CSSR," *Pogrom*, 159 (May-June 1991), p. 49; and Gheorghe, "Roma-Gypsy Ethnicity," p. 835.

40. See, for instance, Trond Gilberg, "Ethnic Minorities in Romania Under Socialism," *East European Quarterly*, Winter 1974, pp. 442-443.

41. See Hugh Poulton, *The Balkans: Minorities and States in Conflict* (London: Minority Rights Publications, 1993).

42. In Romania, an estimated 60 percent of the Gypsies speak Romani in the family but most also speak Romanian or Hungarian depending on their geographical location. See *Destroying Ethnic Identity: The Persecution of the Gypsies in Romania* (New York: Helsinki Watch Report, September 1991), p. 7. In Hungary, however, 80 percent of the Roma understand no dialect of the Gypsy language. See *Beszelo*, August 10, 1991, p. 18.

43. See, for instance, *The New York Times*, October 3, 1993.

44. For an excellent general treatment of this issue, see Ian Hancock, "Gypsies: The Forming of Identities and Official Responses," *Immigrants and Minorities*, Vol. 2, No. 1 (March 1992), pp. 3-20.

45. See Luan Troxel, "The Bulgarian Gypsies: Numerically Strong, Politically Weak," *RFE/RL Research Report*, Vol. 1, No. 10 (March 6, 1992), pp. 58-61.

46. See, *The New York Times*, October 18, 1992.

47. *Koztarsasag*, July 3, 1992; *Der Standard*, August 12, 1992.

48. See *The Times*, September 2, 1992; *The Guardian*, February 22, 1993; and *The Economist*, May 15-21, 1993..

49. See F. W. Carter, R. A. French, and J. Salt, "International Migration between East and West Europe," *Ethnic and Racial Studies*, Vol. 16, No. 3 (July 1993), especially pp. 469-470.

50. Hartmut Esser and Hermann Korte, "Federal Republic of Germany," in Tomas Hammar, ed., *European Immigration Policy: A Comparative Study* (Cambridge: Cambridge University Press, 1985), pp. 165-206.

51. *The New York Times*, February 7, 1993.

52. *Suddeutsche Zeitung*, May 9, 1993.

53. *The New York Times*, August 8, 1993. For an analysis of the situation of Gypsies in (West Germany), see Luise Rinser, *Wer wirft den Stein: Zigeuner sein in Deutschland* (Stuttgart: Weitbrecht, 1985).

54. *The New York Times*, August 8, 1993.

55. *The Wall Street Journal*, February 25, 1993.

56. *The Washington Post*, September 18, 1992.

57. *Die Tageszeitung*, March 13, 1993.

58. *The New York Times*, September 26, 1992; and *The Los Angeles Times*, October 12, 1992.

59. See the *Detroit News*, November 12, 1993 cited in *Buhazi: Newsletter of the International Romani Union*, Winter 1992, p. 6.

60. See *Gazeta Wyborcza*, June 28, 1991; and *Zycie Warszawy*, August 2, 1991 about the deportation of Polish Roma by Swedish authorities.

61. *The New York Times*, November 27, 1991.

62. See *Die Presse*, January 11, 1993; *Neue Zuercher Zeitung*, January 16, 1993; *Le Monde*, January 22, 1993; and *Suddeutsche Zeitung*, February 5, 1993.

63. Quoted in *The Chicago Tribune*, February 13, 1993.

64. For a brief history of Romani international organizations, see Ian Hancock, "The East European Roots of Romani Nationalism," *Nationality Papers*, Vol. 19, No. 3 (Fall 1991), pp. 261-265. For reports on the Fourth World Romany Congress, see *The Chicago Tribune*, April 13, 1990; and *The Economist*, April 21, 1990.

65. *The Times* (London), July 11, 1991.

66. *The Romani-Jewish Alliance Newsletter*, April 1992, p. 3.

67. *The Independent* (London), August 29, 1992.

68. For a brief assessment of these efforts, see Konrad J. Huber, "The Roma: Group Identity, Political Activism, and Policy Response in Post-1989 Europe," *Helsinki Monitor*, Vol. 4, No. 3 (1993), pp. 44-51.

Chapter 4

KURDS:
STATES, MARGINALITY AND SECURITY

Hamit Bozarslan

Since the partitioning of the Middle East following World War I, the Kurdish problem has never ceased being an obstacle to the construction of states. It has been at the root of numerous revolts from the 1920s to the present,[1] and has on more than one occasion served as a touchstone of the region's instability. Although it had been steadily getting worse ever since the new state entities in the Middle East were established, the problem gained extravagant media attention in the aftermath of the Gulf War, with the exodus of more than two million Kurds from Iraq towards Turkey and Iran. The intensification of the armed struggle and Turkey's return to repression, the effective separation of Iraqi Kurdistan from the center, as well as Ankara and Teheran's military interventions in this same region, keep this among the most burning issues in the Middle East.

Let us begin with a few facts: the number of Kurds is generally estimated at 25 million.[2] The majority of this population speaks Kurmandji, while a portion in Iran and Iraq speaks Sorani. A segment of Kurds in Turkey, probably more than 1 million, speak Zazaî (also known as Dimilî), while still others, in both Iran and Iraq, speak other distinct languages or dialects. In the religious domain, we observe a division as well: if the Sunnis (of the Shafiite rite) form the majority, there are also Shiites (the Faîli Kurds in Iraq and more than a fourth of the Iranian Kurds), an important Alevi minority (in Turkey)[3] as well as Yezidi communities (in Turkey, Iraq, Syria, and the former USSR). As a general rule, these linguistic or denominational communities, which we can define as "ethnic," follow specific modes of action and relationships with the center.

The trajectory of Kurdish history in every one of the countries is inseparable from that of the states.[4] In Turkey, during the War for Independence (1919-1922), Mustafa Kemal (Atatürk, 1881-1938) increased the calls for fraternity between Kurds and Turks and for the creation of an Islamic state. Nevertheless, after the proclamation of the Republic in 1923, the Kemalist regime opted for both a vigorous Westernization policy and a rigid nationalism, leading to the banning of Kurdish tribal and cultural institutions and brotherhoods. After the wave of revolts from 1925 to 1938, a certain openness became apparent beginning in the '60s, but that came up against direct and indirect interventions by the army and the Kemalist establishment. The army takeovers in 1960, 1971, and 1980 provoked an explosive situation which, in its turn, gave rise to the Marxist guerrilla campaigns of the PKK (Workers Party of Kurdistan) beginning in 1984.[5] In 1991, the civil authorities admitted the "Kurdish reality" and tried to integrate the radical Kurdish opposition into the political system by authorizing that its candidates be inscribed in the electoral lists of the SHP.[6] But this overture was blocked on the one hand by the opposition of the army and the Counter-Guerrilla and, on the other hand, by urban Kurdish radicalism, nourished as much by the region's socioeconomic conditions as by the guerrilla movement's refusal to yield to an exclusively political game.[7]

In Iraq, despite the repression of some insurrections between 1920 and 1945, the Kurdish population benefited from certain cultural rights that have been maintained to this day. Nevertheless, from the time of Mustafa Barzani's revolt in 1961, the real risk for the center and the Kurds was (and remains) linked to the political domain. Threatening the very existence of the Iraqi state on several occasions, the Kurdish movement took advantage of the war between Iran and Iraq to extend its influence. But the use of poison gas against the Kurds in 1988, conducted as part of the so-called "Anfal" operations, put a dramatic end to its success and it did not come into the limelight again until the end of the Gulf War of 1991.[8] The establishment of the "protection zone" allowed the Front of Kurdistan to establish its control over an important part of the Kurdish region and to organize elections there. Nevertheless, since then, hit by a double embargo, that of the UN on the whole of Iraq and that of Iraq on Kurdistan, this region has experienced a true politics of adjournment, made official by UN Security Council Resolution 688.

In Syria, which like Iraq is controlled by the Ba'ath Party (but the fraction that is hostile to that of Saddam Hussein), the Kurds' situation is different. Under the French mandate, the Kurdish intelligentsia, composed essentially of exiles from Turkey, enjoyed cultural rights. Still, after independence, the existence of the Kurds was progressively denied. Within the framework of the "Arab Belt" policy that aimed to arabize the region bordering Turkey, a segment of Kurds, said to number 300,000 today, was deprived of Syrian nationality. Hafez al-Assad's regime, which without recognizing cultural rights shifts the Kurdish problem to Turkey and Iraq by supporting, in varying degrees, the two countries' Kurdish opposition,[9] nevertheless manages to integrate formations of this minority into its political system. The regime which draws its support from the Alaouite minority thus uses this second minority group against the Sunni-Arab majority.[10]

In Iran the imperial regime, seriously threatened by the proclamation of the Azeri and Kurdish republics in 1946, did not deny the existence of a Kurdish entity that it considered as a "cousin" and as Aryan.[11] But it did not recognize any form of political or cultural autonomy. Thus, the regime born out of the Revolution struck up negotiations with the Kurdish opposition. But these were followed by a bloody civil war that put an end to the domination of the autonomist parties in the cities. This war was even easier for Teheran to win since it had become part of the other, more important war with Iraq. The resumption of negotiations after the death of Ayatollah Khomeini, was rewarded with the assassination of members of the Kurdish delegation, including the secretary general of the PDK-Iran in Vienna in 1989.[12]

In the USSR, after a "Red Kurdistan" republic was proclaimed in 1923 and suppressed in 1929 by Moscow, the Kurds were earmarked for Stalin's deportations. Although they subsequently enjoyed some cultural autonomy in Armenia, with *perestroika* they found themselves caught in the crossfire of ethnic conflicts, especially between Armenians and Azeris, and left the Caucasus region in great numbers. Their position in this conflict was determined by religion: Yezidi Kurds supported the Armenians; Moslem Kurds supported the Azeris.

Marginality and Minority: The Problem of Status

The Kurds are only one of numerous Third-World entities that have not achieved political sovereignty. Their case is thus in no way unique. Like the other analogous cases throughout the Third World, the Kurdish problem is linked, at its roots, to the legal and political status of ethnic, "macro-ethnic" and "national" groups without a state.[13] Theirs is an example of a new kind of nationalism, operating not within the framework of a colonial empire, but of modern states.[14] Following the categories elaborated by Hans Kohn and subsequently refined by Plamenatz, we can define it as "Oriental."[15] Nevertheless, it is distinguished from numerous other cases of the post-colonial Third World insofar as the Kurds are divided among several states whose relations with each other are often conflictual.

How are Kurds to be defined? As a minority? An entity that is marginal or marginalized? This somewhat blunt manner of putting the question immediately places us in a complex problematic, for the term "marginality" no less than "minority" raises certain difficulties when applied to the Kurdish situation. Legally and officially, a Kurd is a citizen of Iraq, Syria, Turkey, or Iran, and cannot, in this regard, be an object of discrimination. Thus, it is difficult to apply the concept of "marginality" to the Kurds. Likewise, these states often do not legally recognize the notion of "Moslem minorities." Moreover, demographically, Kurds are the majority in the regions they inhabit.

Yet, these two terms, ambiguous when taken separately, become more meaningful when they are put into an equation. Each validates the other, and they do so reciprocally. For the Kurds, legally citizens, thus not marginal, become such when taken as a group or a presupposed national category: as a member of a group, a Kurd is deprived of the possibility of enjoying a legal status equivalent to that of a member of the dominant ethnic or national group. From the demographic point of view, Kurds constitute a territorial majority; yet they form a minority in the etymological sense of the term, for they are excluded from "majority" status.[16] This *de jure* exclusion gives rise to their *de facto* marginalization in the countries where they live. We can easily observe the combination of these two statuses in several areas:

The Internal Political Domain

A Kurd can have a status equal to that of a Turk, Arab, or Persian if and when he renounces his Kurdishness and agrees to define himself as a Syrian, Iraqi, Turk, or Iranian.[17] Turkey has gone even farther in rejecting the assertion of Kurdish identity: M. E. Bozkurt, one of Mustafa Kemal's ministers, did not hesitate to declare that Kurds could have only a single right in the Republic of Turkey: that of being slaves.[18] Voluntary or forced recognition of the superiority of the dominant "nation" and individual assimilation then became the indispensable condition for breaking with the marginal status. But existence as a separate ethnic or national category signified the acceptance of marginality or, more often, illegality.[19]

The International Domain

The Kemalist Minister of Foreign Affairs described the Kurds (just as the other minorities) as "flies," and the states as "camels."[20] Kemal Atatürk, the founder of modern Turkey, declared that the rights of minorities were subordinate to those of nations that had already achieved statehood.[21] As for the permanence and legitimacy of the states, these were guaranteed by both the regional status quo and international law. The international system had two major consequences for the Kurds. Firstly, the territorial integrity of states has always been considered by international organizations as an incontestable principle.[22] The Kurds, therefore, had great difficulty in finding allies within the international system, even during the Cold War when playing the minority card could otherwise have been useful to them.[23] Secondly, each state could insist that the treatment of its minority was a purely internal affair.[24] Despite the theoretical "right of intervention" officially endorsed by UN Security Council Resolution 688, this view still remains dominant in international law.

The Economic Domain

Despite the mechanisms for redistribution and integration that are in place, the Kurdish regions of Iran, Iraq, and Turkey can be defined as internal colonies, furnishing resources but receiving little in return. 60% of Iraqi petroleum comes from Kurdish regions. Turkey, as the memoirs of some military dignitaries have revealed, has conducted a deliberate policy of preventing industrialization in the "risky" Kurdish area.[25] Before the launching of guerrilla warfare in 1984, which was followed by repressive measures that paralyzed economic life, the share of certain Kurdish cities in Turkey's industrial output was zero; from the Kurdish regions taken as a whole it did not exceed 5%.[26] Yet the principal hydraulic sources are found in the Kurdish region and feed the industry of the western regions. We can observe the same phenomenon of "under-development" in other areas, such as tourism, education, and health.[27]

The Historiographic Domain

In the majority of Middle Eastern countries, history is eschatological and by definition constitutes an affair of state. The principal task of the official historiography is to prove the continuity of a long, complex, but coherent process that leads, finally, to the establishment of the nation-state. Such a vision could only triumph by depriving ethnic minorities of their past.[28] In such an interpretation of history, the Kurds find themselves deprived of the right to exist as such, or are otherwise defined as elements that prevent history from attaining its objectives and accomplishing its mission. As a group claiming a political existence, the Kurds are thus characterized as "feudal," "reactionary," or as "religious fanatics"[29] (or even, in Iran, "red devils"). It is only through renouncing the demand to form a political entity that the Kurds, as individuals, can accede to history and to citizenship. To exclude oneself from history amounts to deliberate acceptance of an anachronistic position.[30] According to the official ideology of the state—Kemalist in Turkey, Ba'athist in Iraq—adhesion to the nation signifies adhesion to civilization: one cannot withdraw from one and not the other.

The theory of language and the Turkish thesis on history, which in large measure determined the vision of the Turkish university until the recent period, asserted a "Turkish" continuity with Anatolia.[31] Likewise, the thesis of Iraqi/Arab continuity from Babylon to Iraq (paradoxically, in parallel manner to Panarabism)[32] and of the "Arab Belt" in Syria, and that of Aryanness in Iran—all converge in reinterpreting history to exclude from it Kurds and all other minorities.

All these historical theses are intended, above all, to justify the state experiment as the culminating point of history. But they also imply a degradation of the condition of the minority. They are related to the process of assimilation,[33] presented as the sole means of ending marginality and avoiding the Kurd's humiliating condition. Assimilation was reinforced by the school, the banning of the Kurdish language and culture (in Syria and Turkey, and partially in Iran), deportations (in Turkey, between 1930 and 1938, and then from 1987 to the present; in Iraq, between 1975 and 1991), and special offers (financial benefits for those leaving Kurdish regions in Iraq). In this way, numerous assimilated Kurds were able to become true celebrities in the intellectual, artistic, indeed, political and—notably, in Turkey—economic spheres of those countries. But demographic numbers made the success of assimilation impossible for all but a small proportion of the Kurdish population.

The Kurdish Problem Between Doctrine and Reality

As has already been made clear, the Kurdish question does not arise in the context of a colonial empire, but rather, with the exception of Iran, within the framework of states born at the end of World War I or after the process of decolonization. The problem has emerged and evolved in a region that is a mosaic like those Balkans with which it provided the original theater of the "Eastern Question." Research on ethnic and religious affiliations in this region does not lend itself easily to comparisons with the Western world.[34] The problem has unique characteristics that make any comparison difficult. The fundamental data are quite different from those of the national problems encountered in the former USSR or Yugoslavia. Emerging within the framework of the Middle East, the issue has persisted through more than 70 years, not in a single state but four. It is set in the very heart of the Moslem world and touches no less than three cultural entities—Arab, Persian, and Turkish. This division led to the emergence of the Kurdish movement, and in itself constituted a disruptive element in inter state order, the post- World War I status quo. The problem subsequently unfolded in a setting without preestablished political or state structures or institutions, as in the former Yugloslav or Soviet republics. The restrictions placed on parliamentary competition also inevitably ensured the absence of legal representation from Kurdish political formations.[35] Under these conditions the Kurdish problem is perpetuated, above all, as an armed struggle, without adequate political processes being created that could serve as a bridge between the minority population and the central authorities. In contrast to the cases of the ex-Yugoslav and the ex-Soviet republics, civil or urban resistance has played a secondary role in the history of the Kurdish movement, subordinate to the armed struggle.

The Kurdish case also raises certain terminological difficulties: can the concepts of "nation" and "national" be used, uncritically, to define the groups and conflicts that emerge in this part of the globe? Or, in other words, can they be used without ideological presuppositions? Can the nation be considered as anterior to nationalism? Does it not need a foundational doctrine to gain legitimacy, and, then, reality? Is that not at the base of the institution called "nation" as a modern category whose legitimacy we should seek in the enterprise's success or failure, therefore, in social relations, rather than in theory, or discourse?[36]

Lacking the space to answer all these questions, suffice it to specify that the so-called national problem can only rarely be analyzed outside the social realm. Moreover, the evolution of the Kurdish problem cannot be seen in abstraction from history. Indeed, until the end of the Ottoman Empire, because of the role of Islam, the Kurds, while on the geographic periphery of the Empire, were, nevertheless, connected to the political and cultural center. They figured among the representatives of the dominant region and the Sublime Porte against the Christian communities. The Hamidian Brigades,[37] a veritable Kurdish *makhzen* formed at the end of the 19th century, officialized this role of guarantor-producer which the tribal chiefs used and abused on many occasions, including at the time of the extermination of the Armenians. This link with the center allowed the Kurds to enjoy both belonging to a specific territory and not being tied exclusively to it. In other words, the majority of Kurds found themselves on the same territory with undeniable benefits and advantages, while being able to move about without encountering economic, political, or cultural barriers in seeking access to the higher circles of the administration. Even the division between the two great empires, Ottoman and Persian, did not result in the imposition of rigid frontiers. Beyond that, fidelity to the Palace and to religion was the necessary and sufficient condition of the tacit contract binding the Kurds to the imperial state. Adhesion to an ideology, a nationalist one to boot, would not have been envisaged as part of the terms of such a contract.[38]

The end of empire, the emergence of various independence movements and especially state-oriented nationalisms that were victorious, in the short-term, at least, implied a deterioration of the Kurds' status: once an integral part of the center, they henceforth found themselves excluded. The state building process which began in the 1920s by itself transformed the Kurds into a minority in the etymological and legal sense of the term. As a new minority, they did not enjoy either internal autonomy or external protection, unlike the religious minorities of the past (the *millets*).[39]

There is no doubt that the ultimate objective of Kurdish nationalism, whatever the conjunctural variations of its discourse over the years, is to transform this status, in other words, to pass from the status of minor to that of legal majority.[40] But a minority nationalism cannot be viable when it is confined to the doctrinal level. In its development it is, indeed, constantly burdened by the states' foundational doctrines (in other words, the dominant nationalism) as well as its own. Nationalism, like any other ideology, can constitute itself into an element of legitimation and mobilization. But, legitimacy can only be understood as a process, always fragile, because the "symbolic haziness" at its source ceaselessly brings to it new terms and as it does so overthrows other nomenclatures.[41] Furthermore, the term "legitimation" should be used in the plural, for "legitimations can succeed one another and each time furnish new meanings to the sedimentary experiences of the collectivity in question."[42] The legitimacy conferred by the nationalist doctrine is no exception to this rule. Not only does the nationalist doctrine suffer from multiple paradoxes,[43] which can engender new mechanisms of legitimation, but in addition, in the majority of cases, it is only one of the parameters, alongside other forces that shape social relations, or the relations between the state and society (e.g., religion, distribution of resources, clientelism, and so much more). As a social fact, the so-called "national" problem is managed (or mismanaged) by, and in, the social domain. The strength of the nationalist doctrine as a source of legitimacy can increase and become dominant in this same social practice if the other mechanisms are deficient or if the regional context is dominated by violence. In other cases, when the state and the dominant group are strongly dependent upon their foundational doctrine, substituting it for other sources of legitimacy, the minority response can likewise be radicalized, sometimes even to the point of rejecting any basis of legitimacy other than their own nationalism.

The Kurdish problem allows us to observe the interaction and the limits of the social and of doctrine. The existence of a foundational doctrine that aims at the creation of a nation state has given it a nationalist dimension for more than 70 years (and this despite cultural, linguistic, and political divisions, among the Kurds). Kurdish nationalism, as an ideology, ends up creating mechanisms for organizing the Kurds and homogenizing mentalities, and, indeed, laying the foundation, here and there (notably in Iraq and Iran), for an important movement of cultural renewal. It ceaselessly sustains the myths of the construction of the Kurdish nation (e.g., the revolt of Kawa which marked the Newroz, i.e., the new day, in both senses of the word meaning "spring" and "new era"; the Medo-Kurdish continuity; and the Treaty of Sèvres of 1920). Its role is decisive in the invention and transformation of "Kurdish identity."

As we have already emphasized, the Kurdish problem occurs in a human mosaic on which the model of the nation-state can only be imposed with difficulty, where belonging is determined as much by religion and language as by the ethnic or, tribal, phenomenon. It is never reducible to the dimension of nation, that is, in any case, mostly hypothetical, a theoretical construction of the Westernized intelligentsia of the beginning of the century who bequeathed it to Kurdish, Marxist, Islamic, and even social democratic and liberal radicalisms.[44] Serving as a catalyst for the failure of this model in the Middle-East, minority nationalism hides within it other affiliations, sometimes trans-state or infra-state, other potential ethnic demands, and, indeed, other minorities. These have recourse to diverse modes of action and strategies: they can develop their own responses to the centers of power and to Kurdish nationalism in order to integrate themselves into the political system, and end their marginality, or, may even deploy specific forms of opposition, often radical, as in the case of the Alevi Kurds in Turkey.[45] Emigration, which in its turn is capable of creating new "marginalized" categories, can also provide a solution to the problems of these sub-minorities, as we see in the case of the Alevi Kurds of Maras in Turkey.[46]

Moreover, like its counterparts in the Middle-East, Kurdish nationalism is a doctrine of national construction, but unlike them, it cannot undertake this construction through legitimacy and coercion based on the state.[47] It can affirm its doctrinal purity at a discursive level. But the fact remains that it is confronted by a double reality—on the one hand, the dispersal of Kurds over many countries, and on the other, the very existence of the state, as a political, military, economic, and cultural center. This immediately gives the Kurdish problem a transnational character, but each country is a single state of undivided sovereignty so that the transborder element must deal simultaneously with the jurisdiction and sovereignty of more than one national state. This somewhat paradoxical situation leads to the notorious gap between the precepts and the practice of Kurdish movements in each country. The Kurdish movements are, then, obliged to manage this paradox, to combine the "national" and the "transnational," to navigate between the two series of mechanisms of legitimacy: those of the individual countries, of which minority nationalism is only one component, and those of the region, combining minority nationalism and regional clientelism which may include fidelity to the dream of an independent Kurdistan, loyalty towards a transborder ethnic group or/tribe, or to personified symbols,[48] or even privileged relations with a

Kurds: States, Marginality and Security

regional state, as was for a long time the case between Iran and the Iraqi PDK. This double or triple belonging naturally poses serious problems and reduces the chances for a unified Kurdish movement on a regional scale. But, at the same time, it makes it possible for Kurdish political actors to pass from one geographic context (national) to another (regional) and back, to try to utilize these, one against the other, in order to enlarge their room for maneuver, and to find additional sources of legitimacy in the one to be used in the other. The conflicted nature of the borders, which are disputed by states despite apparent acceptance of the *status quo*, was clearly revealed during the Iran-Iraq War (notably with regard to the control over the waters of Shatt-al-Arab) or during the latent Turko-Syrian conflict (with the status of the Sanjak of Alexandria rejecTed by Damascus), or again in Turko-Iraqnian relations (notably concerning the province of Kirkuk). This more or less openly declared series of conflicts only increased the freedom of action of the Kurdish movements in each state.

The Regional Dimension

The transborder situation defines, either through the regional *status quo* or through the parallel diplomacy that it engenders, the outer limit of the Kurdish movements' field of action. The regional *status quo* that remained effective for decades had its source in the weakness of the states: none was powerful enough or, above all, sufficiently legitimate to exert pressure on its neighbors. Moreover, for each one of them, the creation of states meant the construction of nation-states, legitimating only state-to-state relations. The status quo entailed the collective control of the minority players.

Parallel diplomacy, which became prevalent during the '70s and '90s, implied, in practice, the weakening of the burden of doctrine on the ruling elites of each of these countries, and a noticeable strengthening of the states, to an extent that allowed them to formulate regional ambitions. By this somewhat odd phrase, "parallel diplomacy," we mean the new rule that emerged on the Middle-Eastern diplomatic scene at the end of the '60s: the establishment of relations between an internationally recognized state and a minority movement (Kurdish), under the circumstances engaged in a struggle against its own state. Therefore, in place of interstate relations or in addition to them, parallel diplomacy "accredits" non-state players and allows states to circumvent the conventions of diplomacy. The trans-state elements able to evade the sovereign authority of a single state who had a regional field of action to begin with, become highly valued. The nation-state as a practical ideal is then threatened not only by the minority resisting assimilation but also by the regional ambitions of the states themselves. To the threat posed by the minority that resists assimilation are then added the regional ambitions of the state that uses it. In any case, as soon as one state attempts to legitimate the minority player of another country, the "limited sovereignty" of which Rémy Leveau speaks becomes a rule of the game to which it, too, must submit.[49]

In the Kurdish case, parallel diplomacy can be summed up in a formula that is too often verified to remain exclusively theoretical: utilization—sometimes manipulation—of Kurdish players by one regional capital against another.[50] The state concerned not only attempts, in this way, to displace the issue beyond its own borders, but even puts pressure on its neighbor to extract concessions in the settlement of the disputes between them, and, indeed, to enlarge its sphere of influence in the region by exploiting the Kurdish movement. Thus, the Kurdish problem passes beyond the framework of marginality within a single state and gains a regional dimension, becoming a security problem, as much for the states as for the Kurds themselves.

It would, certainly, be wrong to consider the Kurdish problem as a by-product of regional conflicts.[51] It must be acknowledged, nevertheless, that for at least two decades a very clear link has been observed between the rise of power of the Kurdish movements and the great regional crises. The increased violence in the area created a large playing field for the Kurdish movements by offering them the possibility of finding the necessary equipment as well as allies in the region. The Iranian Kurdish guerrilla movement, which was insignificant during the reign of the Shah, took advantage of the 1979 Revolution to spread out. Just as with the Iraqi Kurdish guerrilla, it increased its numbers and its efficiency during the Iran-Iraq War. The Kurdish guerrillas of Turkey first took up arms at the time of the Lebanese War in 1982 in the ranks of the Palestinian forces, before launching their operations in Turkish Kurdistan, as they also exploited the underlying tension between Turkey and Syria and the Gulf War. Nor will competition between Turkey and Iran—which is likely, as we already see some premonitory signs—fail to increase the commercial value of the region's Kurdish movements.

But this parallel diplomacy is a double-edged sword for the states. The opposing state can also have recourse to the same weapon. It creates the uncertain ground on which a multitude of states, non-state or trans-state political and military forces, which are often marginalized, such as the Palestinians, Armenians, Lebanese, and others, as well as the entire range of Kurdish political parties, of all origins and of all tendencies are engaged in conflict. In this field of the "minorities" ideas, means of communication, financial, and, probably, also, military resources circulate. The diaspora plays a part in that theatre insofar as it supplies resources as well as combatants, and allows the extension of the non-state "sovereignty" of the Kurdish formations to areas outside Kurdistan.[52]

Kurds: States, Marginality and Security

The point should be made that if this diaspora is becoming truly active, that is not due only to the humanitarian interest of the nongovernmental organizations or of certain sectors of the political classes in the West, but also to the fact that beyond a certain point, internationalization follows the regionalization of conflict.[53] The internationalization of the Kurdish problem is certainly not new. But the use that the two superpowers have made of it during the Cold War was carefully calculated.[54] It never became an important link in the chain of local conflicts in which they were involved on opposite sides. The end of the Cold War, only increased the autonomy of each regional player, under the apparent domination of America, pushing competition among the states to an extreme and thereby increasing the chances of internationalization of minority problems. There was no longer the balance of power between the blocs at the regional level and the constraints which that imposed. That meant that the Middle Eastern state, as a regional power, could acquire an increased autonomy, even if the international system clearly rejected irredentist claims as the Gulf War proved. But in such a situation, minority conflict could also acquire a new dynamism and become a threat to the international system, especially if the nature of the conflict is trans-state. Even so, by the same logic prohibiting all irredentism, any border change becomes a call to action for the international community. This may explain the accommodating attitude of the Security Council toward Baghdad on this matter in the aftermath of the Gulf War. Yet, paradoxically, although priority was given to safeguarding the unity of the existing state entities, the international community was led to concede, probably as a temporary measure, some recognition to the minority players. It is worth noting that the Americans, spurred on by the tragedy of April 1991 in Iraqi Kurdistan, in the aftermath of the Kurdish uprising, had to agree not only to the creation of so-called protection zones, but further, still, to shared administration with the Kurdish political parties. This sharing later gave way—notably after the recapture of the cities of Sulaymaniyeh and Erbil by the peshmergas—to the recognition of the Kurdistan Front's administration, which, in fact, by its governance, by the elections it organized, and the government it put in place, destroyed the sovereignty of Iraq.

Iraqi Kurdistan, where we find engaged not only the three countries of the region—Iran, Turkey, and Syria—but also the permanent members of the UN Security Council as well as the Iraqi, Iranian, and Turkish Kurdish players, is both a regional imbroglio and a field of experimentation for regional minority politics in which the Kurdish movements can compensate for their lack of power and legal recognition in their countries. However, that is often at the cost of manipulation which also becomes a rule of the game of parallel diplomacy. Taking into account the long-term risks of new confronta-

Hamit Bozarslan

tions, the development of this situation into a security problem is the price that each of the states involved pays for its inability to manage it by political and peaceful means.

Redistribution of Resources and Its Limits

If (or, perhaps, because) the states have failed in the Middle East in their enterprise of becoming nation-states, they have at least been able to maintain themselves; indeed, they have become powerful as territorial states. They have become effective machines, capable both of exerting an extended coercion and of proceeding to a redistribution of resources. Technological modernization and the security-mindedness of the states (that is due to the weakness of their internal support bases) have forced them to deploy increasingly sophisticated repressive mechanisms, but also to learn to manage the social, religious, and minority problems. The state can also, as is the case in Turkey (as well as in Iran), support certain ethnic claims (Zaza or Alevi, the one linguistic, the other based on religion), in other words, encourage, at the expense of its own unitarist doctrine, the invention of new ethnicities in order to bar the road to secession. It can, at the same time, encourage competition between the various Kurdish nationalist groups (Islamic and Marxist in Turkey and in Iraq) in order to have better control over the situation. Vast operations, sometimes even beyond the control of the political leaders (in Turkey via the counter-guerrilla, in Iraq via the "military command center of the northern provinces," etc.), allow them to create a delicate balance to maintain control in the Kurdish region. This may be backed up with emotional and logistic support for Kurds from the other countries (Iraqi Kurds in the Turkish case).

The insecurity of the minority population as well as the redistributive policies of the regime can give rise to dependence on the state. In this sense, David Laitin's observation on the ambiguities of the relations between the marginalized group and the center is realistic.[55] In a situation of total insecurity in which the members of the group risk losing everything, marginalized populations can turn to the state and look to it to exercise control. Thus Turkey's coup d'état of 12 September 1989, occurring in the midst of clashes between the two Kurdish groups, the KUK and the PKK, was widely supported by the Kurdish population. Likewise, as we see in modern-day Turkey, guerrilla activities supported by certain cities with a large Kurdish majority can provoke a feeling of insecurity in the cities with a mixed Turkish-Kurdish, or Sunni-Alevi population, thus giving the state additional trump cards. Nor do they fail to arouse the demand for increased state presence in the non-Kurdish cities. The attacks on civilians in a city like Istanbul have also produced the same effect.

Kurds: States, Marginality and Security

Along with political Islam, the Kurdish problem constitutes one of the key areas where the state finds itself in a position of manager. In this domain as in others, the state cannot provide, indeed, cannot envisage, a long-term solution and abandon coercion. But the cases are rare where violence succeeds in creating any other kinds of relationships between the Kurds and the state and other mechanisms for management and legitimation.[56] In fact, the states suffer as much if not more than the Kurdish movements from the gap between their foundational doctrines and their realities as territorial states. They often find themselves obliged in attempting to make the violence more effective and profitable, to proceed to a redistribution of resources among certain sectors of Kurdish society.[57] The nature of the resources that are distributed varies from country to country: they can be cultural, military, political or ethnic. In Iraq, where repression against the Kurds has been the most fierce, the state has recognized a Kurdish cultural sphere, which it has largely encouraged and utilized as a showcase; but at the same time it has reduced this to the role of simple accessory to the regime; in Iran, the government has also had recourse, for several years, to the promotion of Kurdish culture. Recently, Turkey recognized the existence of Kurds on its soil and opted for a more tolerant position toward publications in the Kurdish tongue. In Iraq, the government has recruited, among the tribal and non-tribal populations, subservient brigades that it arms and supports. In Turkey, the government also had recourse to more than 50,000 "Village Protectors" in effect ceding some of the sovereignty of the "nation" to the rural segments. In Syria, the chiefs of the Kurdish parties that were banned were, nevertheless, promoted to deputies; in Iraq, the fictional autonomy granted by Baghdad permitted a political promotion of Kurdish chiefs; in Turkey, the chiefs of certain tribes and brotherhoods were able, following the adoption of a multi-party system in 1946, to become deputies[58]. In Syria, the Kurds constitute a minority community that maintains privileged relationships with another minority, the Alaouites, against the Sunni majority. This policy enables the state to gain the loyal support of certain Kurdish segments, even during fierce repressions (as in Iraq from 1975 to 1989). Through these measures, the state succeeds in weakening Kurdish nationalism, either irredentist or autonomist, which, in the case of Turkey and Iraq, tends to become radicalized and to increase by the mobilization of urban populations that are more difficult to integrate in the same clientelist mechanisms.

Marginality and Violence

Paralleling the redistributive mechanisms of management, violence is both a basic fact of struggle and the principal means used by the state to neutralize it.

Hamit Bozarslan

As shown by the chemical bombardments and the numerous disappearances in Iraq, notably of the 8,000 members of the Barzani family,[59] the extremely bloody civil war in Iran or the coups d'état, the depopulation of villages and the massacres of civilians in Turkey, violence is one of the instruments the state uses to manage the Kurdish problem. At the same time, one of the Kurdish movement's traits is its capacity to regenerate the armed struggle, almost continuously over the past 70 years.

Armed struggle is as much inscribed in "community violence" as in "political violence," described by Michel Wieviorka as above all the "counterpart of a closed political system, of a weakness of institutional mechanisms for the treatment of social conflicts, an insufficiency of areas of negotiation."[60] Often, Kurdish opposition passes to a violent expression because the political space is reduced and incapable of treating this completely singular social fact of ethnic or national conflict, because the narrow structures of the nation-state are not able to create specific cultural and administrative forms for the minority, and finally because the group that straddles several international borders is denied any possibility of collective cultural or economic life. The perennial violent challenge to the center is, therefore, a price that the states must pay for having failed to create a political space in which other modes of action might prevail. Nevertheless, it also reflects the Kurdish movement's inability to invent other forms of expression and opposition. Indeed, after 70 years of revolts or insurrections, the Kurdish movement cannot point to any tangible gains.[61] Not only do the states command greater means of coercion, but they can also appeal to international law.[62]

The problem, therefore, is to know why at a given moment in the relations between the Kurds and the states, other means of managing conflict—even when they involve an enlarged redistribution in the form of incentives to collaborate, to leave Kurdish areas, or in some cases, to assimilate, no longer function or why they do not succeed at all in convincing the Kurds to accept compromise, either at an individual or collective level. In fact, in Iraq, these mechanisms have been, at the very least, suspended since the Kurdish regions' actual break with the center, and in Turkey they have difficulty in competing with the Kurdish contestation, which exerts tight control over the population, with the PKK performing numerous functions of state (including justice and tax collection), and are, in any event, incapable of checking the progress of the radical option. Why do the Kurds refuse assimilation, or, at least, integration, and why are they ready to pay a higher price than that of a status that implies subordination? Why are the states incapable of making them accept this?

The violent struggle against the center is explained by several factors that do not necessarily occur simultaneously. Each may account for a phase of the

Kurd-state relationship, then disappear completely or reemerge with greater force, under the impact of other elements.

The first of these factors largely brought about the initial phase of the Kurdish movement in the period 1920-1940. It can still, in certain cases, explain the rupture between the Kurds and the states even in our time: it is the incompatibility between the state's official doctrine and the specific interests of certain segments of Kurdish society. In fact, when a state resolves to apply its law to the letter, necessarily implying a centralizing program, as with the Kemalist regime in Turkey, the response of certain segments of Kurdish society, such as the tribes or brotherhoods, is radical, for the social and economic survival of these structures and the very functioning of their hierarchy depend on a minimal state presence and on the permeability of borders. The Kemalists' breaking their promises of an Islamic state and the abolition of the Caliphate in 1924 were also a factor in the Kurdish resistance at the beginning of the century, for they were perceived as deliberate destruction of the sole link between the Kurds and the Turks.[63] Similarly, there was an obvious incompatibility between the doctrinal bases of the Islamic Republic of Iran and the relatively egalitarian treatment that the monarchical system had accorded to the Kurds. The establishment of Shi'ism as a doctrine of state was not well received by Kurdish society, which is largely Sunni, and was probably as important a source of opposition as nationalism.[64]

The state can only overcome this challenge by renouncing the supra-social sovereignty which its doctrine confers on it. That means that it must open up to competition and redistribution areas of political and administrative life previously closed to minorities or offer them significant compensation for their continued exclusion. In fact, referring once again to the case of Turkey, the tranquility that the pluralist regime knew in that country from 1950 to, roughly speaking, the mid-'70s can be explained as much by the trauma of the repression of the years 1920-1940 as by the opening of the political field to competition from tribes and brotherhoods. Another way of dealing with the problem is to implement a thoroughgoing policy of repression. This, however, will not fail to provoke new waves of militant opposition, as both Iraqi and Turkish experience shows.

The entry of urban elements on the scene, for whom the quantity and quality of distributed goods is totally insufficient, constitutes the second factor in violent contestation. Urban youth, especially, cannot count on the redistributive mechanisms of the center, which are capable of integrating rural milieus and, in part, the leading citizens, but which condemn the youth themselves to a genuine marginalization.[65] Their entry on the scene beginning in the 1960s corresponds to a period when marginalization as a minority was accentuated by a process of marginalization as urbanized individuals or

Hamit Bozarslan

groups of uprooted peasants ("paysans dépaysannés").[66] Urbanization did not signify the end, but the breakup of rural solidarity groups, that were very difficult for the members to reconstitute.[67] Economic crisis, the difficulty of finding positions for the increasing numbers of young graduates, and the disarray due to the decline of the prestige of tribal structures and their value systems, all pushed this group onto the political scene. Its radicalization occurred in parallel manner to that of the worker and student organizations in the countries in question.[68] It is not at all surprising that the Kurdish movements born in the '60s and '70s leaned predominantly towards "Marxism," and called into question the states they perceived both as a "colonizing" force and as the "lackeys of American imperialism."[69] "Marxism," "the natural ally" of national or "nationalist" demands made it possible to put into place formidable machines for mobilization, allowing the newly marginal groups to create for themselves a social organization, the means of upward movement, the possibility of asserting themselves as political actors as well as of reproducing the traditional code of honor. "Marxism", in the Cold War context, also provided a language for the justification of violence. Thus, in Iran, Iraq, and Turkey, "Marxism" as the "universalism of the poor" almost became the prerogative of Kurdish oppositional groups who created either national or Kurdish Marxist organizations, some of which remain powerful.[70] Subsequently, in the 1980s, other, mainly Islamist organizations were also formed, but they had recourse to the same moulds.

In the process of urbanization, the nature and breadth and, indeed, the techniques of violence change. Some history may help to clarify the point. In the Ottoman and Persian Empires, recourse to violence or to coercion, particularly to rebellion and its repression, often resulted from the discontent of the periphery or the desire of the center to establish itself administratively and militarily in a more effective way. This was a matter of "primitive" violence, according to the classification of Charles Tilly.[71] From that point of view, it was written into a behavior code regulated by a tacit agreement that allowed a return, in the majority of cases, to the previous state of affairs. When such a return was not possible, the losing Kurdish chiefs were offered compensation, which explains why even when the Kurdish emirates were destroyed in the course of the 19th century, their chiefs were still honored by the Palace, and other forms of the tacit contract were set in place. This new agreement included substituting chiefs who were, often, of tribal origin for the former, quasi-autonomous *emirs*.[72]

Under the empires, the Kurdish periphery's violence and the center's coercion were exercised mainly in the countryside. Now if, in accordance with Ibn Khaldun's schema, the classical Middle Eastern state succeeded, even during the first half of the 20th century, in more or less controlling the cities but feared the countryside which was extremely difficult to rule, today it especially fears the cities, although it is still unable to control the countryside. This change can be explained by the fact that the entry of young people onto the political scene also radicalizes the other urban categories. It represents a considerable enlargement of the political space by the introduction of new elements as well as new relations of force between the center and the peripheral regions.

In fact, from this point of view, Kurdistan's situation is radically different from what it was about fifty years ago, when the urban population formed a small minority. In each of the countries that we are considering, the Kurdish population is now largely urbanized. The city of Erbil alone brings together a third of the Iraqi Kurd population. Diyarbakir, which barely had a population of 100,000 inhabitants about twenty years ago, is now close to 1 million. Dozens of other cities, small towns only a few decades ago, currently count hundreds of thousands of inhabitants. Young persons of less than 18 years make up more than half the population in all these cases put together. The youth as a group can thus become a driving force of mobilization and of social action. The movement from economic protest or the rejection of underdevelopment to nationalist challenge proper is, therefore, materially easier to effect.

The case of Kurdish opposition in Turkey is significant from this point of view. In the 1960s, it found expression through mass demonstrations in the majority of the Kurdish cities and demanded more infrastructure, more investments, etc. It constantly contrasted the progress that allowed mankind to discover the moon, while the Kurds continued to live "in the age of caves."[73] The only "nationalist" demands of the period were for radio (Turkey did not yet have television), newspapers, and education in Kurdish. Not only independence, but the demand for autonomy was still not on the agenda.

Ten years later, in the same country, the elections of 1977 resulted in the emergence of "Red municipalities," which, nevertheless, failed to put an end to the influence of traditional groups that they also used sometimes. That was the case not only in Diyarbakir, Lice, or Agri, traditionally known for being nationalist, but it was true also in Batman, where two Kurdish nationalist forces competed. Under the impetus, also, of televised broadcasts (an unintended consequence of the liberalization of the media and of solidarity with "our Palestinian brothers"[74]), the Kurdish cities experienced from 1989 to 1992 a veritable intifada, which could mobilize tens of thousands of persons in the majority of Kurdish cities, with widespread closing of shops, with funeral processions organized, especially for burials of PKK militants, sometimes violent clashes with the army, and, to be sure, in true Palestinian fashion, the symbolism of the stone.[75] A Social-Democrat deputy described this situation graphically: "Everybody is on the roofs, in the streets. Everybody

Hamit Bozarslan

is mobilized after each rumor. If you talk in percentages, you can say that 80% of these people only think about a single thing: the state of Kurdistan. It's all over."[76] The same phenomenon could also be seen elsewhere. In Iran, for example, in the elections of 1952, the PDK candidate received more than 80% of the votes. The same was true for the eve of the revolution in 1979 when the urban Kurdish populations boycotted in large numbers the referendums under Khomeini and voted massively for nationalist candidates. In Iraq, without achieving sole mastery of the Kurdish movement, the urban youth tried to distinguish itself from the traditional elites and became a driving force for the struggle from the '60s onward. While unable to put an end to the tribal or brotherhoods factor, here either, it has made a massive appearance on the scene since 1975 and has given rise to a multitude of organizations. The urban youth constituted the principal force of the guerrilla movement in that country between 1976 and 1988. In all three cases, movements born out of the youths' contestation shape the Kurdish political scene in our time.

A third factor explaining the passage to violent contestation is to be sought in the coercion exerted by the center. This is all the more significant in that in certain situations, one might logically have expected the state, in seeking to lower the cost of the crisis, to accept a certain integration of Kurdish radicalism the better to control it. In fact, by satisfying the minimum of Kurdish demands, the Iranian regime could have marginalized the radical Kurdish players, or else transformed them into allies during the war against Iraq. But, for numerous reasons, depending on the nature of the regime and the internal conflicts of its leaders, the radical tendency prevailed. Likewise, if the negotiations initiated by Talabani in 1984 had resulted in a new accord of autonomy, not only would Baghdad have gained an ally in the Iran-Iraq war, but it would, in addition, have divided the Kurdish movement and held even more cards. But the failure of this attempt pushed the UPK towards Iran and, above all, it permitted the Kurds, for the first time since 1975, to unite and create the Front of Kurdistan. In Turkey, the military authorities finally assumed the PKK discourse and conflated the Kurdish population with this party, thus conferring upon it the status of legitimate representative. This policy led to the contestation being officially dubbed "the 29th revolt of the Kurds," instead of just "the PKK guerrilla war," and served to justify the projects of "total war" and "partial mobilization."[77] In doing this, the state slid toward uncompromising positions and eliminated the possibility of any Kurdish representation other than by the PKK, which, was precisely, what it had been fighting.[78]

Now, coercion exerted by a center that refuses any compromise can result, through a series of perverse effects, in a breakdown of integrative mechanisms, even when the state is ready to develop them. The success of the center's strategy depends on numerous elements that it cannot always control. By way of example: much as coercion, combined with redistribution, has been successful in Iraq under the Ba'athist regime, in the sense that it has reduced the Kurdish movement's room for maneuver, it has failed in Turkey. In Iraq the degree of coercion, involving, alike, the use of gas, mass elimination of opponents and villagers considered dangerous, and, especially, a total control of the urban populations, made it impossible from 1988 onward to have recourse to violent contestation. Furthermore, the coercive measures at the state's disposal were applied over the whole of Iraq. In Turkey, the coercion failed to close off and neutralize Kurdistan completely for numerous reasons: political opposition from Turkish regions of the country that made the return to pluralism in 1983 inevitable, the military's incompetence in managing the economy, European pressure and its need for a better image with Western public opinion, the state's lack of an organizational capacity to encompass the whole of society, etc.. Certainly, the state indicated, at the same time, its readiness to make major investments in the Kurdish region, but the coercion that it exerted was, nevertheless, strong enough to provoke a military response which became very popular, and to devalue the importance of the redistribution of economic goods.[79] Seeking to understand the reason for the success of an organization as "blind" as the PKK, seeing its "mission through the perspective of bullets," Ömer Laçiner, editor of a Turkish Socialist journal, *Birikim*, reminds us first of the antipathy that the Kurdish population felt toward it before and just after the coup d'état of 1980. Here is what he concluded: "the sentiments and reactions that the practices of 12 September brought out in the population were such that they could make them forget the past. Even if the (Kurdish) population did not consider the PKK as their liberator, they could accept it as the interpreter of their feelings of an honor that had been sullied, of a consciousness of a rejected personality."[80] Ömer Laçiner is not the only one to offer this assessment. The majority of observers agree that in Turkey's case, coercion clearly produced perverse effects for the state and reinforced the Kurdish military option. Analyzing the repressive measures adopted by Ankara, Philip Robins arrives at the following conclusion:

> The measures appear to have helped politicize and then radicalize different constituencies of Kurdish people, particularly the young, who have been at the forefront of the demonstrations. This radicalization has also extended spatially from the border areas to some of the principal Kurdish towns. If the Kurdish community has indeed been radicalized and polarized by the repression, the Turkish state apparatus will have aided the cause of the PKK, which presumably used violence both in order to polarize the Kurdish community

Hamit Bozarslan

and to produce an indiscriminate backlash on the part of the Turkish military
authorities.[81]

The leaders of the PKK themselves do not hesitate to acknowledge their gratitude for the aid that Ankara brought them. Abdullah Öcalan, the head of the party, commenting on the pressure of the special units of the military forces which have a sorry reputation in the region, clarifies: "Even if we had given it our hardest try for fifty years, we couldn't have brought the city of Cizre over to our side."[82] And his brother Osman, the number three person in the movement, continues: "We owe our thanks to Turkey. We have won half of the city [of Cizre]. The other half was served to us on a silver platter."[83]

Finally, we may posit as a fourth factor, that the cultural, political, economic and other measures taken by the state to weaken violent contestation could be slow to take effect and already proved anachronistic at the time of their adoption.[84] By these measures, we mean the taming of ethnic contestation by allowing its participation in domains reserved for the dominant group, that is, a solution such as was found in Spain after Franco's death. In Spain the law on regional autonomy rendered the separatist option pointless, marginalizing it, even with the population concerned. Had it been adopted in 1984, and had it been more exhaustive and inclusive of certain other cultural rights, the plan to remove restrictions on the use of the Kurdish language in Turkey could have diminished the Kurdish challenge and given moral support to those Kurds who were opposed to armed struggle. Likewise, the SHP (Social Democratic Party) program proposed in 1990, which was forwarding-looking on numerous points (administrative cuts, decentralization, increased powers of locally elected officials, cultural rights), would have largely softened Kurdish resistance,[85] as would discussion of a "Basque-style solution," allowing a remapping of provinces and the notable increase in their autonomy.[86] In the event, none of these projects was realized and the Chief of Staff went so far as to forbid the very term "Basque" in the Turkish army. Similarly, Turgut Özal's proposals to decree an amnesty and to integrate Kurdish radicalism into political life only led to the marginalization of the president during the last months of his life.[87] As for the only real measure that was adopted, to wit, the abrogation of the oral interdiction of the Kurdish language, it came too late and it was too far down on the list of demands, because, in any event, the whole population spoke it anyway.

From "External" to "Internal" Violence

Several observers establish a quasi-automatic link between the absence or the precarious state of democracy in the states under discussion and the failure to resolve the Kurdish problem. Indeed, it seems evident that without a political solution to this major question, no democratic development can be envisaged.[88] The persistence of the military option seems, moreover, to reflect an even more fundamental fact: the impossibility of moving to a political solution. In fact, the Kurdish strategy toward the states that completely reject pluralism, whether political or ethnic, is also determined by its own inability to develop political forms of contestation. Quite evidently, the reliance on the military option alone can only be perpetuated at the expense of politics properly understood.

The state's repressive policy, often combined with an economic situation that is, to say the least, disastrous, is undoubtedly the principal element feeding the armed struggle, which, in its turn gives rise to other social or political violence. But this has other reasons, historical or cultural, as well, ranging from tribal tradition to the appropriation by the movements themselves of the practices of the most repressive states, such as Syria or Iraq. In effect, in the logic of the majority of Kurdish organizations, especially when they do not have the means to negotiate with the center in a "peaceful" way, military action is, clearly, imposed on society and seeks to secure the "Party" dominance over social relations. Without resorting to psychoanalytical arguments which should explain this violence in part, it would seem that we are dealing with a process that contains many elements of millenarianism. In fact, apart from the social support it manages to obtain, which is to some extent separate from its confrontations with the state as such this violence is exercised by militants who are not bound by the realities of the here and now.

Furthermore, combined with borrowed mechanisms, that is the Westernizing, Marxist, or Islamist ideology, Kurdish nationalist doctrine serves as a driving force not only for one, but for two types of programs: an external one, against the state, aiming, finally, to create a Kurdish state; and an internal one, aiming to transform Kurdish society. Unable to match the coercive means held by the state, the nationalist movement can also equip itself, in the process of violent contestation, with instruments of coercion that can be used in its own political domain. The armed struggle also gives rise to Kurd on Kurd violence, in other words, to a violence that the Kurdish players exercise outside the armed struggle, to assure themselves control over the population, or territory, or even over their own cadres. This violence which finds conventional justifications in the armed struggle ("in each armed struggle . . . such and such slips are inevitable;" "we need an iron discipline in order to face up to the enemy;" "you can't make an omelet without breaking eggs;" etc.) is naturally grafted onto that which opposes the Kurdish players to the state. But the objective is then no longer the realization of maximal or minimal demands by exploiting the capacity to do harm. Through the utilization of

Hamit Bozarslan

violence against the Kurds themselves, the Kurdish organizations seek to convince or compel the Kurds to engage in the struggle. Abdullah Öcalan, head of the PKK, explains this policy in the following manner: "above all, we need to lead people to believe that they need to be defended and to defend themselves."[89] This new form of violence aims to transform the social by the regimentation of society, by the imposition of so-called "revolutionary" taxes, or by a new socialization of the young people, by marginalization of the former elites, whether "collaborationist" or nationalist. It is the instrument that the national units use to set themselves up as sole players. Such violence calls to mind the combination of political violence and revolutionary action defined by M. Wieviorka.[90] It is detached from anti-state violence, for in aiming specifically at the Kurdish scene, it continues even when there are truces with the center.

This "internal" violence may also enable us to understand the surprising domination of "Marxism-Leninism" in the heart of the Kurdish formations of the '70s and '80s, indeed in our time. If "Marxist" ideology, such as revised and "corrected" by Stalin, can in no way explain the sociological *raison d'être* of the Kurdish movement, and especially the extent of the new wave of violent contestation since the '60s, it has, nevertheless, modified its discourse and the methods. It inculcates in it a "Messianic" message allowing the "revolutionary" youth to establish an avant-garde of a promised society and to imagine the end of the tunnel, transforming the "organization" into a source and executive arm of justice. It also makes new phases of the armed struggle conceivable. It can likewise permit the leaders of the politico-military organizations to gain an autonomy with regard to society, indeed with regard to their own organization,[91] to impose their hegemony on the whole of the Kurdish movement, in effect to demand the monopoly of legitimacy not in just one part of Kurdistan, but in its totality.[92] This hegemony can be explained especially by the cult of personality, yielding no place in certain respects to that of Kim Il Sung or of the Cuban "Lider Massimo."

Conclusion

In light of the above-mentioned elements, we can analyze the Kurdish problem from a double perspective, from a double system or sphere of affiliations:

—the sphere of the state: including the integration (or exclusion; often the two simultaneously) of the Kurds in the economic, political, and military system of each one of the countries in question. In this sphere, the state succeeds in limiting the impact of the Kurdish movement by using certain segments, notably the traditional elements, of Kurdish society. But its ability to integrate the Kurdish regions with the rest of the country and with the political system is threatened by the "politics from the bottom"[93] of the urban populations.

—the Kurdish regional sphere, open to intervention and penetration by numerous states, parties, and political forces, both Kurdish and non-Kurdish, allowing the nationalist movements to gloss over the marginality and lack of legal legitimacy from which they suffer in each of the countries, and to hold the trump cards against the state under whose jurisdiction they find themselves. Because it has difficulty in mastering the situation in this sphere, the Kurdish movement becomes an object of manipulation; but it also finds the possibility of asserting itself, thanks to this sphere, as a non-state player.

These two spheres are sometimes mutually exclusive, but more often than not they are complementary. It would, in fact, be difficult, for various reasons, to eliminate one of them and to create either only "nationals" of such and such a country or else individuals who would identify themselves exclusively with some Kurdish entity on a regional scale. The chances of permanently eliminating the tension that exists between the two are equally minimal. Nevertheless, we cannot exclude the possibility of a peaceful coexistence and combination of the two. The conditions for such a coexistence, would emphatically require the legalizing the Kurdish political forces, leading them to participate in the political and civic life and setting them up as a link between the citizen and the political domain. That is also necessary at the regional level. There is need for a new concept of the state other than that of the "nation-state," for a depoliticization of the "nation" (thus its separation from nationalism) and a reconsideration of those principles of contemporary international law that leave few alternatives between absolute sovereignty of the state entity and radical irredentism. It is, nevertheless, possible to envision the creation of cultural conditions, indeed, political circumstances, that would allow the Kurds to flourish as an entity, but still protect the existing borders of states. Only such arrangements would be capable of ending the situation of marginality and the minority status that together give rise to the Kurdish problem and transform it into a security problem.

Notes

1. Among the most important are those of Berzenci in Iraq and Simko in Iran (both holding strong, though with interruptions, until 1930), Cheikh Said (1925), Ararat (1930), and Dersim (1936-1938) in Turkey, Barzani in 1943 in Iraq, the one which resulted in the proclamation of the Republic of Mahabad in Iran in 1946, the one which began, once again, under the direction of Barzani

Hamit Bozarslan

in 1979 and 1980, and lastly, that of the PKK in Turkey since 1984.

2. Among whom are 4 million in Iraq, 6-7 million in Iran, 12 million in Turkey, according to the figures offered by Turgut Özal, President of the Republic (d. 1993), 1 million in Syria, more than 1 million in the former USSR, Lebanon, and the diaspora.

3. Statistics on the number of Alevis in Turkey are not available. It is estimated that they constitute between 20 and 25% of the country's total population.

4. A separation that dates from the 15th century, from the first division of the Middle East between the Ottoman Empire and Persia, Sunni and Shi'ite, respectively. They were dispersed among more states after World War I.

5. According to official figures, in nine years this war is said to have taken the lives of more than 11,000 persons, of whom "3144 were civilians, 2270 members of security forces, and 4517 separatist terrorists." In this figure must be included civilians killed by "unknowns." Still according to the official figures, the financial cost of the war from 1981 through 1993 amounted to 95 billion DM. Cf. Mehmet Sahin, "1993 un Kurdistan Panoramasi," Deng, no. 27, 1994, pp. 2-14.

6. The "social democratic" party, in power in coalition with the "liberal" DYP (Party of the Just Path), since the end of 1991.

7. A clandestine organization within the army created in the '60s, originally, to plan a response to an insurrectional situation, the Counter-Guerilla is responsible for combing the area for activists in Turkish Kurdistan.

8. These operations owe their title to the Quranic verse on "plunder." They are said to have been responsible for more than 180,000 casualties. For a part of the official Iraqi documents on these operations, see; Middle East Watch, *Genocide in Iraq: The Anfal Campaign against the Kurds*, New York, Washington, Los Angeles, Middle East Watch, 1993.

9. The Iraqi Kurdish experience went too far, both in democratization and in its ties with Turkey, which pushed Damascus to modify its position with regard to Iraqi Kurds.

10. Cf., among others, I. Cheriff Vanly, "The Kurds in Syria and Lebanon' in P. G. Kreyenbroek and St. Sperl, The Kurds: A Contemporary Overview, London and New York: Routledge, 1991, pp. 143-171.

11. The so-called Islamic regime followed the same line. Cf. Nouchine Yaveri, "Ethnies et ethnicité dans les manuels scolaires iraniens," in J.-P. Digard, *Le fait ethnique en Iran et en Afghanistan*, Paris, CNRS, 1988, pp. 247-265.

12. The successor to A. Ghassimlou, S. Scharafkendi, was assassinated as well, in 1992 in Berlin, by agents of the Iranian government.

13. For this notion, cf. O. Roy, "Ethnies et politiques en Asie centrale," *Revue du Monde Musulman et de la Méditerranée*, no. 59-60, 1991, pp. 17-36.

14. It is probably one of the first cases of this type of nationalism.

15. For a detailed analysis of the classification of Hans Kohn, cf. Louis L. Synder, *The Meaning of Nationalism*, Westport, Connecticut, Greenwood Press, 1977, 118-120. John Plamenatz, "Two Types of Nationalism" in E. Kamenka, *Nation-*

alism: *The Theory and Evolution of an Idea*, London, Edward Arnold, 1976, p. 30.

16. For a discussion on the relationship between marginality and minority, cf. P. George, *Géopolitique des minorités*, Paris, PUF, Que Sais-je? 1991.

17. Only the name "Turkey" refers explicitly to an ethnic group.

18. *Milliyet*, 1.5.1930.

19. There are Kurdish deputies in all these countries, but Kurdish political parties are forbidden in three of them. In Iraq, they are forbidden or subordinated to the authorities. In Turkey, S. Elçi, a minister of the government of Bülent Ecevit (1978-1979), was condemned to three years in prison following the 1980 coup d'état for having identified himself as a Kurd. According to the Constitution adopted in 1992, "the political parties cannot claim the existence in the Republic of Turkey's territory of any minorities based on a difference that is national or religious, cultural or denominational, racial or linguistic. They cannot use a language other than Turkish. . . . Neither can they remain indifferent to this kind of action led by others. Nevertheless, they can translate their statutes and their program into foreign languages other than those that are forbidden by law."

20. T. Rüstu, cited in "Note du Service de Renseignements sur le mouvement insurrectionnel kurde et les mesures militaires du gouvernement turc," 11.3.1925, AE E 311-3, vol. 10.10.1925-30.1.1929, pp. 141-144.

21. "Memorandum by H. Dobbs, High Commissioner for Iraq," 22.1.1926. Enclosure in Sir G. Clerck, Angora, 24.11.1926 (n. 621), FO E 6677/6677/44.

22. The United Nations preferred to preserve the territorial integrity of Iraq and adopted a "neutral" position immediately after the war against Sadam Hussein.

23. American aid to Barzani at the beginning of the 1970s, and Resolution 688 on humanitarian intervention, adopted by the United Nations to protect the Iraqi Kurds, nevertheless proves that the Kurdish problem cannot be completely isolated from major international balances of power.

24. The use of chemical weapons at Halabdja and Behdinan in 1988 was the saddest demonstration of this fact. Cf. Middle East Watch, *op. cit.* In 1931, a Turkish newspaper, *Vakit*, wrote: "The whole world knows it. We are far from the hatreds of race and color. We have found ourselves in the situation of needing to defend ourselves against those who betray us. Before judging whether anti-Semitism in Germany is in fact a defense need of this kind, it is up to the men who hold the destiny of one of the greatest peoples and one of the world's greatest states in their hands to express their opinion on this subject."(25.6.1931).

25. Cf., for example, C. Madanoglu, *Anilar*, 1911-1938, Çagdas Yayinlari, 1982.

26. In this sense, it would be difficult for us to analyze the Kurdish problem based on the model of class struggle. But it is evident that urbanization and improvement during the last two decades have only reproduced marginality in increasingly accelerated proportions. For the statistics on this, see Omer Tuku, "Kürdistan'da Türk Endüstrisi, Gelisim ve Sömürü, Istanbul, Doz Yayinlari,

Economy in Kurdistan, SOAS statement (London), 1991, 42 p.

27. Cf. Hamit Bozarslan, "Marginalité, Idéologie et Art: Notes sur la vie et l'oeuvre de Yilmaz Güney," CEMOTI, n. 9, pp. 27-40.

28. Turgut Özal, President of the Turkish Republic (d. 1993), divided Greek civilization into two parts: the first, Anatolian-Ionian, open, generous, scientific, tolerant, the cradle of civilization, naturally inherited by the Turks; the other, Athenian, incapable of creating a "scientific movement," "speculative," fanatic and paternalistic, male chauvinist, in fact, and, after all, "imperialistic," naturally inherited by Greece. See T. Özal, *La Turquie en Europe*, Paris, Plon 1988, pp. 51-54

29. This vocabulary, used by the Kemalist leaders as well as by the Baath Party, indeed, at one time by the regime of the Shah in Iran, bears a natural similarity to that of the Third International.

30. Özal defined the Armenian problem as an "anachronistic problem," op. cit., p. 164.

31. They went on to assert that all the world's languages and civilizations were Turkic.

32. Amatzia Baram, *Culture, History and Ideology in the Formation of Ba'athist Iraq*, 1968-1989, Oxford, St. Antony's College, 1991.

33. An etymological remark is in order: in fact, the national *minority*, as a concept, does not exist in the political culture of Islam, which considers non-Moslem communities, described by the term *millet*, exclusively as minorities, before their peaceful existence with the Moslem prince in the *dar-ul-islam*. Consequently, this word was used in Iran and Turkey to designate the notion of "nation." As for Iraq and Syria, they also chose a religious term, *umma*, to describe the nation.

34. Cf. Lucette Valensi, "La tour de Babel: les groupes de relations ethniques au Moyen-Orient et en Afrique du Nord," *Annales* ESC, no. 4, 1986, pp. 817-838.

35. Which permits diverse Kurdish organizations to set themselves upwell-versed in the Leninist teachings on the "worker party" as the historical representatives of the Kurdish nation. Iraqi Kurdistan is an exception.

36. For discussion of the nation, see E. Kedourie, *Nationalism*, London, Hutchinson, 1960; E. Kamenka, "Political nationalism" in E. Kamenka, *Nationalism: The Nature and Evolution of an Idea*, London, Edward Arnold, 1976; E. Gellner, *Nations et nationalisme*, Paris, Payot, 1989; B. Anderson, *Imagined Communities*, London, New York, Verso, 1991.

37. Cf. S. Duigid, "The Politics of Unity: Hamidian Policy in Eastern Anatolia," *Middle Eastern Studies*, no. 9-2, 1973, pp. 139-156.

38. Hans Kohn described the imperial system as "universalism at the top and the system of professional and local autonomy at the bottom," preventing the identification of the power-holding center with the nation, thus the emergence and domination of nationalism as a doctrine. Hans Kohn, *The Idea of Nationalism: A Study in Its Origins and Background*, New York, MacMillan, 1946, p. 85.

39. Cf. on this subject for a comparative point of view: Ghassan Salamé, "Minorité/Modernité: l'affaire kurde et au-delà" in E. Picard, *La question kurde*, Brussels, Complexe, 1991, pp. 135-151.

40. The slogan of the Kurdish parties of Iraq and Iran is: "democracy for Iraq (or Iran), autonomy for Kurdistan."

41. According to Jean Leca, legitimacy "flows from a symbolic vagueness that expresses a generalized and unconditional exchange where the solidarity and confidence (the 'pre-contractual' elements of social life) come to regulate the exchanges, the affronts, and the conflicts born out of the unequal access to the power and resources." J. Leca, "Sur la gouvernabilité," in J. Leca and R. Papioni, *Les démocraties sont-elles gouvernables?*, Paris, Economica, 1985, p. 19.

42. P. Berger and Th. Luckmann, La construction sociale de la réalité (transl from the American edition by P. Taminiaux), Paris, Meridien Klinckseck, 1986, p. 98.

43. Some of these paradoxes are raised by B. Anderson: 1. The objective modernity of nations to the historian's eye vs. their subjective antiquity in the eyes of nationalists. 2. The formal universality of nationality as a socio-cultural concept in the modern world everyone can, should, "have" a nationality, as he or she "has" a gender vs. the irremediable particularity of its concrete manifestations, such that, by definition, "Greek" nationality is sui generis. 3. The "political" power of nationalism vs. their philosophical poverty and even incoherence. In other words, unlike other "isms," nationalism has never produced its own great thinkers: no Hobbeses, Tocquevilles, Marxes or Webers. *Imagined Communities*, London and New York, Verso, 1991, p. 5.

44. This is notably the case in Turkey where the theme of "Kurdishness" serves as common denominator for the "Kurdish branches" (not officially recognized) of the Turkish political parties.

45. In that case, religion, crossing over linguistic boundaries, can play a decisive role in the formation of a new ethnicity. The same may be said concerning the Sunni populations of mixed towns. Cf. J.-F. Bayart, "La question alévie dans la Turquie moderne," in O. Carré (ed.), *L'Islam et l'Etat dans le monde d'aujourd'hui*, Paris, PUF, 1982.

46. This city was the setting for clashes between diverse radical groups in the 1970s. The massacres of 1979, perpetrated by the extreme right, officially caused more than 100 deaths among the Alevi population. They marked the collective memory of the city and led to a long series of departures that continue even to this day. The majority of Kurds asking for political asylum in Great Britain and in France are natives of that city.

47. Cf.Hamit Bozarslan, "Tribus, confréries et intellectuels: convergence des réponses kurdes au régime kémaliste," in S. Vaner (ed.), *Modernisation autoritaire en Turquie et en Iran*, Paris, l'Harmattan, 1991, pp. 61-80.

48. Political organizations can also become the center of a system of loyalty. Thus, for a long time the figure of Barzani transformed the Iranian PDK into a mother organization for all the other Kurdish formations.

49. Cf. R. Leveau, "A Moslem Population in France " in this volume.

Hamit Bozarslan

50. We can give numerous examples of this utilization: the Kurdish card became key throughout the long Iran-Iraq War during which each side supported, armed and equipped with logistic means, the Kurds of the adversary state. Syria played a determinant role in the formation of the Iraqi Kurdistan Front in 1987, among other things, to thwart Iraqi aid to Michel Aoun. Syria also helps (by logistic means, and probably also military means) the PKK in Turkey. Turkey itself played the card of the Iraqi Kurds against Baghdad before, during, and after the Gulf War. Ankara had a double objective: to obtain their collaboration against the PKK, and to begin an eventual modification of borders.

51. Cf. our article, "La régionalisation du problème kurde," in E. Picard (ed.), *La nouvelle dynamique du Moyen-Orient. Le monde arabe et la Turquie au tournant des années 90*, Paris, l'Harmattan, 1992, pp. 174-191.

52. The head of the PKK explained that his movement collected 50,000 DM in Europe, cf. his interviews with Yalçin Dogan, *Milliyet*, 22-25.4.1992.

53. Cf., among others, the proceedings of the International Conference of Paris, 14-15 Oct. 1989, *Les Kurdes: Droits de l'homme et identité culturelle*, Paris, Institut Kurde, 1991. This diaspora is also behind a lobby that has included such important figures as D. Mitterrand, Lord Avebury, B. Kouchner, E. Kennedy or P. Galbraith.

54. The USSR was behind the proclamation of the Kurdish Republic of Mahabad in Iran in 1946. Moscow's support was nevertheless lacking when it signed the economic accords with Teheran. Between 1971 and 1975, the United states, via Israel and Iran, supported the Kurds against Baghdad, which was closer than ever with Moscow. The ruling on the question of boundaries between Iran and Iraq in 1975 by the Accord of Algiers put an end to this support.

55. Cf. David D. Laitin, "Marginality: A Micro Perspective," (mimeo) and "A Formal Model of Marginality and Security" in this volume.

56. The Kurdish exodus of March 1991 to Iraqi Kurdistan constitutes, from this point of view, a first, not because Baghdad had not resorted to repression before this, notably by chemical weapons, but because almost the whole of the Kurdish population revolted against the regime on this occasion (most likely because, quite simply, it undervalued its hope for life), and transformed this revolt, via a mass exodus, into a plebicite. Likewise, it was also the first time that the totality of a population became the target of government attacks. The same phenomenon was produced in the south of the country, where the government also lost the entire Shi'ite population sections of which had in the past allowed it to maintain its domination. Even there a whole population became the target of army attacks.

57. For an analysis of this notion, cf. Jean Leca, "La démocratisation dans le monde arabe. Incertitude, vulnérabilité et légitimité: un essai de conceptualisation et quelques hypothèses," in G. Salamé (under the direction of), *Démocraties sans démocrates*, Paris, Fayard, 1994.

58. With the general elections in 1987, a large number of Kurdish nationalist deputies were able to enter the national Assembly. The 1991 elections permitted, on a large scale, the repetition of the same phenomenon. The Kurdish

nationalist party, the HEP, took more than 20 seats in the Assembly. Five of those whose parliamentary immunity was lifted are in prison today.

59. Cf. Middle East Watch, *op. cit.*

60. M. Wieviorka, *Sociétés et terrorisme*, Paris, Fayard, 1988, p. 463.

61. On this topic, cf. the critical article by Kendal Nezan, President of the Kurdish Institute of Paris, "Privés d'Etat, les Kurdes ne peuvent oublier les leçons de l'Histoire," *Le Monde diplomatique*, June 1991.

62. These factors may appear "minor," at first sight. Nevertheless, they explain the fate of almost all national disputes in the Third World: even though they are capable of maintaining themselves sometimes for decades, no movement of national liberation that is opposed to a state that was born out of decolonization or of a war of independence against a Western power has ever succeeded in achieving its ends. The only two exceptions that we know only confirm the rule: Bangladesh succeeded in proclaiming its independence because the "mother country" was far removed and because India intervened militarily. Eritrea formerly colonized by Italy achieved independence from an Ethiopia which was never colonized and which was itself undergoing a transition from Empire to nation-state.

63. Cf. Hamit Bozarslan, *Entre la 'umma et le nationalisme: l'Islam kurde au tournant du siècle*, Amsterdam, MERA, 1992.

64. The concessions made by the Iranian state to the Kurdish religious dignitary Sheik Izeddin Huseyni were not sufficient to defuse the Kurdish challenge.

65. This is also the case in the non-Kurdish parts of the countries in question. But the "underdevelopment" of the Kurdish regions diminishes even further the possibility of making advances in studies and especially devalues diplomas. Moreover, it is a rare youth who can study in the universities of the large cities.

66. This expression is borrowed from Farhad Khosrokhavar, *L'utopie sacrifiée: La sociologie de la Révolution iranienne*, Paris, FNSP, 1993.

67. The tribe and the religious brotherhood continue to be an important factor in policy making in Turkish Kurdistan. For about a decade, we have witnessed a retribalization of Kurdish political life in this country. They play a role that is not negligible in Iraq and Iran, even if in the former massive destruction of the countryside has weakened them.

68. Cf. for Turkey, Hamit Bozarslan, "Political Aspect of the Kurdish Question in Contemporary Turkey," in P. Kreyenbroek and S. Sperl (eds.), *The Kurds: A Contemporary Overview*, London, Kegan Paul, 1992, pp. 95-114.

69. According to a survey, the number of those who declared themselves Socialists in Turkey is currently 5%. This figure, however, reaches 14% in certain Kurdish cities. Cf. Taha Akyol, in *Milliyet*, 1.10.91.

70. One of the Kurdish parties, the PKK which is a dominant force in Turkish Kurdistan, considers itself the avant-garde of revolution in the Middle East and in the world. It aims to renew Marxism-Leninism. The same may be said for the Komeleh in Iran.

71. Charles Tilly, "War Making and state Making as Organised Crime," in P. Evans, D. Reuschemeyer, T. Skocpol (eds.), Bringing the Sate Back In, Cambridge, Cambridge University Press, 1985, p. 170.

Hamit Bozarslan

72. Concerning the Hamidian epoch (end of the 19th/beginning of the 20th century), one could at least describe these chiefs as "most favored lords," since the titles and honors graciously accorded to them by the Sultan were so numerous and important. Nevertheless, the expression loses its meaning for the subsequent periods and does not in itself explain either the violence or its forms, or the relations between the Kurds and the states. That does not mean, of course, that privileged relations between the state and certain tribes were nonexistent. To the contrary, even in the midst of the Kemalist period, where the state set up Jacobinism as a virtue, the center continued to have its allied tribes. But the status of "favored" disappeared as soon as it became a matter of the state's border security or when the center felt sufficiently strong to set itself outside this pragmatic game. Inversely, it could reemerge, as the Iraqi and Turkish cases show, as soon as the Kemalist state, just as the Iraqi state later did, preferred to depend on certain mechanisms of depoliticization and redistribution of resources—economic or educational—instead of creating a privileged Kurdish interlocutor.

73. Cf. M. E. Bozarslan, *Dogu'nun Sorunlari*, Ankara, Toplum Yayinlari, 1965, I. Besikçi, *Dogu Anadolu Mitinglerinin* Analizi, Istanbul, Yurt Yayinlari, 1992 (1st ed.: 1968).

74. Without wanting necessarily to extend the comparison, let us state precisely that just as in the occupied territories, two forces one Marxist (PKK), the other Islamist (Hezbollah) find themselves on the urban scene in Turkish Kurdistan. The Kurdish insurrection of March 1991 in Iraq is also called the "Kurdish intifada."

75. Cf. Çagdas Dernegi, *Güneydogu Çalisma Grubu, 9 Mart-9 Mayis Tarihleri Arasinda Güneydogu*, Istanbul, ÇGD, 1991.

76. *Milliyet*, 29.03.90.

77. For these documents, see *2000'e Dogru*, 4.10.1992.

78. As the writer Murat Belge remarks, "The PKK is outlawed, but it exists. A democratic Kurdish movement, one that defends liberties and is civilian, is largely outlawed and does not exist. Therefore, God help us." M. Belge, "Yasaklar ve Sonuçlari," *Cumhuriyet*, 3-9.4.1992.

79. Beginning in 1993, the state, moreover, on the pretext of the acts of sabotage by the PKK, halted all investment in Kurdish regions.

80. Ö. Laçiner, *Kürt Sorunu: Henüz Vakit Varken*, Istanbul, Birikim Yayinlari, 1991, p. 48.

81. P. Robins, *Turkey and the Middle East*, New York, Council on Foreign Relations: Published in North America for The Royal Institute of International Affairs, 1992, p. 33.

82. In R. Balli, *Kürt Dosyasi*, Istanbul, Cem Yayinlari, 1991, p. 252.

83. *Turkish Probe*, 13 July 1993.

84. As D. L. Horowitz observes: "There will generally not be the requisite determination to enact appropriate measures until ethnic conflict has already advanced to a dangerous level; out of that time the measures that are adequate are more

likely to be deflected or ineffective." D. L. Horowitz, *Ethnic Groups in Conflict*, Berkeley, Los Angeles, London, University of California Press, 1985.

85. It is fitting to mention, on the same score, the aborted program of democratization of the Demirel coalition, Cumhuriyet, 16.11.1991, 13-19.12.1991, etc.

86. Cf. notably "Demirel de Ilgilienmisti. Kürt Sorununa Bask Tipi çözüm," *2000'e Dogru*, 19.4.1992; Güneydogu'ya Model Arayislari. 'Kürtçe'ye özgürlük' . . . , *Nokta*, 3.6.1990.

87. These projects date to 1990-1991. Cf. "ANAP milletvekili Geylani'den Milliyet'e ilginç Açiklama: Özal PKK'ya Af Hazirliyor," *Milliyet*, 21.1.1991.

88. Cf. E. Picard, "Irak: Question cruciale de l'autonomie" in E. Picard (ed.), *La question kurde*. Brussels, Complexe, 1991.

89. Cited by Chris Kutschera. "Qui sont les combattants du PKK," *Les Cahiers de l'Orient*, no. 30, 1993, p. 61.

90. M. Wieviorka, *op. cit.*

91. Thus, certain military heads of the PKK are opposed to the decision of unilateral cease-fire taken by the lead of the organization, A. Öcalan, in 1993. The execution of about thirty army recruits on the order of one of them permitted the Turkish army to justify the renewed fighting in June 1993.

92. On the armed struggle, fratricidal struggles, and the social cost, cf. F. Karim, "La lutte armée entre le mythe et la réalité," in H. Hakim (under the direction of) *Les Kurdes par-delà l'exode*, Paris, l'Harmattan, 1992, pp. 106-123.

93. For this notion, cf. J.-F. Bayart, "Le politique par le bas en Afrique noire," Politique africaine, no. 1, 1984, pp. 53-83.

Chapter 5

JEWS AND PALESTINIANS:
FROM MARGIN TO CENTER AND BACK AGAIN?

Jonathan Boyarin

> I call 'politics as such' the prohibition of marginality that is im-
> plicit in the production of any explanation. From that point of
> view, the choice of particular binary oppositions . . . is no mere
> intellectual strategy. It is, in each case, the condition of the possi-
> bility for centralization (with appropriate apologies) and, corre-
> spondingly, marginalization.
> —Gayatri Chakravorti Spivak (1987:113)

The situation of the Israeli Jews and the Palestinian Arabs may be described as
a search for security for the former, and for both independence and security
for the latter. Certainly one of the major justifications of Zionism—that is,
both for the movement's territorial demands and for its claims to the loyalty
of Jews—has been its promise to achieve, once and for all, the collective security
of a group whose historical suffering is regarded as only slightly less unique
than its survival. Meanwhile, the Palestinians have created a deeply ingrained
national consciousness, through struggle against British colonialism, Zionist
encroachment, and the often deadly conditions of their own post-1948
diaspora. Perhaps because the Palestinian cause is so often depicted by its own
adherents as primarily a matter of freedom and honor, the current debate over
Palestinian national rights and the possibility of achieving peace through Israeli
territorial concessions tends to overlook the sheer physical insecurity of large
numbers of Palestinians.

Whatever the merits of the claims Israeli Jewish leaders make regarding
the necessary terms for their people's security, the insecurity of Israeli Jews is
certainly real. The persistent conflict—simultaneously Israeli-Palestinian and
Israeli-Arab—means that Israeli Jews live with the constant awareness not
only that they or their families may be victims of acts of terrorism that appear
entirely random and irrational to them, but that in any new war, their borders
may not once again hold. The insecurity of the Palestinians is of a different
order: that of stateless people, living under foreign occupation or at the

sufferance of suspicious "host" countries, subject according to their various situations to unpredictable curfew, arrest, travel ban, hunger, expulsion and bombardment.

The situation during the so-called Gulf War of 1991 dramatized this distinction. Israelis spent nearly a month huddled in "sealed rooms," waiting for rocket attacks from Iraq, only gradually coming to believe that those rockets would not be bearing chemical warheads. Though few of those rockets did significant damage, it was the first time since the establishment of the State of Israel that war had made its way inside the state. The demonic image of Palestinians held by many Israelis was deepened by vastly distorted reports of Palestinians "dancing on the rooftops" as the rockets from Iraq descended toward Israeli targets. Meanwhile, thousands of Palestinians from the Occupied Territories were barred from entering Israel to work, and thus providing their families with a minimum of economic security. In the aftermath of the war, thousands more Palestinians were expelled from Kuwait, fleeing to Jordan, where most of them remained in October 1992.

Both of these populations can plausibly be described as marginal, in complex ways that will be explored in this paper. Both are insecure, in the different ways I have just illustrated. That both are marginal and insecure and yet so different suggests the need for a critical interrogation of assumptions about marginality, centrality and security, and such an interrogation is the larger agenda of this paper.

Israel and Palestine at the Margins of Theory.

From the perspective of a world system centered in Europe, the history of Palestine as a marginal region may be said to begin with its incorporation into Alexander's Greece, and subsequently into the Roman Empire. Similarly, for modern European political theory, the model of a normal member of a secure and centralized polity is the Greek and then Roman citizen. Conquered peoples, according to the self-understanding of the early and expanding Roman Empire, were to be incorporated into the Roman hierarchy whether as slaves or as citizens, and their lands were to be incorporated into the Roman system of roads, aqueducts and bureaucratic administration. This was progress.

An administrative involvement with—such as that of an ancient tax official, or that of scholars drawing their authority from social science disciplines and metropolitan research foundations—certain populations which they define as "marginal" implies, whether in ancient Rome or in the contemporary United States, the confirmation of the centrality of those who express such concern. It seems wise, therefore, to start out with this reminder that centrality is always tenuous and in the long run always transient. Such populations will, of course, have their own opinions and expressions of their character, problems and interest, but they are far less likely to be cast in the interpretive framework of marginality.

Prior to that level of self-reflection, however, is the reminder that as much as we may broaden the concept, when we talk about "marginal populations" we are implicitly drawing a schematic picture. We are suggesting a spatial image of people who are disadvantaged by their geographical distance from some particular center of either population or power (usually both). The very metaphors of "margin" and "center," that is, are spatial, and are clearly derived from something like the Roman model, in which being an original inhabitant of the metropole implies greater privilege vis-à-vis those living at the edges of the polity. The very term "polity" expresses the link between residence in the home city and participation in group decisions. Furthermore, it is in the Roman tradition that the notion of the "citizen," again the city-dweller, who is in principle the political equal of all other male city dwellers. Though the city-state in Europe eventually grows into the nation-state, the close link between residence and birth at the center (especially of European empires) and political entitlement remains close.

Conversely, and especially if we think of the later, shrinking Roman Empire, the same example also suggests an implicit notion that the edges or margins are "wild," and hence those living there will be "insecure." Palestine was always a fractious province within that empire. Even though it was not always on the frontier, and even when the recurrent threat of violent revolt was relatively muted, a substantial portion of its Jewish residents stubbornly refused to adopt the modicum of civility expected of Roman subjects. That kind of "small-nation chauvinism" fed into a tradition of Roman, and eventually Christian, rhetoric viewing the Jews as benighted and irredeemably marginal, wherever they might live (D. Boyarin 1994). At the same time, Christianity—a spiritual messianism growing out of the contact between Roman universalism and Jewish sacred history—has made the sacred space of Palestine "central" to European consciousness for nearly two thousand years (Davies 1974).

Looking at the respective situations of the peoples claiming the land of Palestine today can suggest to us how slippery the notions of "centrality" and "marginality" have become. The conflict between Israeli Jews and Palestinian Arabs is still frequently ascribed to something called "tribalism," associated with the stereotype of Bedouin nomadic clannishness, and hence with the unsettled lands at the edge of civilization. Yet the region which forms the backdrop for their struggle is of major concern to those who participate as "central" actors in world affairs, and who when this paper was first drafted (September, 1991) were exerting great efforts to regularize and "civilize" these polities. In regard to the attention and the exercise of power they attract, Israeli Jews and Palestinian Arabs are thus unlike other marginal populations. Therefore the examples of Palestinian and Jewish experience seem appropriate for exploring the association of distance with danger, on one hand, and contemporary ideas of centralized nation-state "normality," on the other.

Rome is, of course, not only convenient as a common reference for academic analysts, but also frequently employed as a model of enlightened great-power administration. The phrases "pax Brittanica" and "pax Americana," illusory as they may or may not be, testify to the continued rhetorical effectiveness of the Roman model. Common rhetoric touting Israel as "the only democracy in the Middle East," underscores the legitimation of Israel as both a result and a pillar of those respective imperial burdens.

The repeated evocation of a word from the "dead" language Latin to indicate a beneficent, centralized universal administration reminds us of the importance of inserting a chronological dimension into our discussion of marginality and centrality. The notion of an all-encompassing "pax" remains intact through time as it migrates through space. As the series of "new Romes" and hence new barbarian hinterlands in the modern period suggests, the identities by which people are defined as marginal are chronotopically grounded, always located in space and time together (see J. Boyarin 1993).

Against this kind of reflection about the continued action of the past stands the rubric of "security." Within the framework of strategic or international relations thinking, the phrase implies an overwhelming focus on the current situation of various populations. This pragmatic discourse begins with the present and envisions certain controllable results within a mid-range future. It is true that current experiences of globalization in Western Europe and fragmentation in East and Central Europe have made security analysts less ready to assume that the geography upon which their scenarios are imagined is going to remain constant. But they still seem to frequently ignore how cultural authority, grounded in references to a living past, affords the power to mobilize certain populations and hence determine the outcome of events in ways that are not simply dependent on "the balance of power" or even on economic circumstances.

Considering issues of collective identity and security in the past—especially before the period when the nation-state model attained the ideological hegemony epitomized in the establishment of the United Nations—can increase our conceptual vocabulary. Remembering that ethnic nation-states have not always been seen as the best and "natural" guarantors of security may help us to imagine changes in the state system (Abu-Lughod 1989, Ashley 1989, McNeill 1986, Sahlins 1989, Tilly 1990). As the world's population grows increasingly dependent on a single, interlocking system (witness, for example, global warming and the twenty-four-hour electronic market), models from the past might even help us to imagine very different forms of polity. It may never be quite practical or desirable to think in terms of doing away with centers entirely. But it may be feasible, and certainly seems worth attempting, to question the assumption that order can only be maintained by the safeguarding of fixed, clear borders "at the margins," which seems to entail repeated violent conflicts to defend and reassert them.

But the relevance of the past for us is not limited to its heuristic value in helping us imagine ourselves. We need also to have a profound respect for the way narratives of the past can be used to create the unexamined certainty that there are no alternatives to a given state of affairs. In reference to marginal populations, one way such narratives actually help make populations marginal or legitimize their marginality is by defining them as wanderers. A clear example of this kind of intervention in the rhetoric of the Israeli-Palestinian conflict is the well-known book by Joan Peters, From Time Immemorial (1984), which purports to be an objective demonstration of the claim that far from being an "indigenous" population, most of the Arabs in Palestine arrived after the beginnings of Zionist immigration and development. The book has been bitterly attacked and some of its documentation thrown into question (Finkelstein 1988). Its relevance here, however, lies not so much in the accuracy or tendentiousness of its thesis, as in the fact that it virtually forces those interested in Palestinian rights to adopt the opposite stance—to emphasize a version of Palestinian history which regards the Palestinians as primordial dwellers on their land, and thus to reproduce a (second) version of key aspects of European Romantic nationalism in Palestine.

Joan Peters is clearly interested in justifying the Zionist claim to have fructified a barren and empty land, and to counter the Palestinian claim of dispossession. Relations between constructions of the past and present social patterns are not always as rationally transparent as they are in this example, but they are always, to varying degrees, socially productive rather than merely reflective. Thus both Israeli and Palestinian ideologists have often emphasized that the enemy is not autochthonous, not a "native," and hence has at best a secondary claim to the land. Doubtless it is true that throughout this century, continuing into the immediate present, Palestinian Arabs have been displaced to make room for Jewish newcomers. It seems clear as well that Arab rhetoric emphasizing that Jews "do not belong" in Palestine—rhetoric understood by those who indulged in it as consistent with the Third World-wide effort to be rid of European colonialism— has only served to confirm Jewish perception of Arab opposition to Zionism as a continuation of classic anti-Semitism, in which the rallying cry was always a variation of "the Jews don't belong here." It is an intriguing and hopeful sign that both the Palestine National Council as a body, and representative Palestinian intellectuals as individuals, have come to reject this attempt to marginalize the Jewish presence in Palestine.

In all of these cases, the issue of who came here "first" is agreed on as critical to determining who is properly here and thus "central," and who, therefore, must accept at best the tolerance ideally accorded those on the margins. Two lessons may be drawn from this kind of debate. The first is that parties in political and even violent dispute are nevertheless dependent on each other for the opposition which creates their identity. Both Zionists and Palestinian nationalists have depended on the figure of the other in creating the sense of their own group identity. Only if there are identifiable margins can there be centers. Thus, part of the process of nation and state building is in fact the production of marginal populations. The binary strategy of constructing centralizing identities tends to the formulation and imposition of rigid and mutually exclusive categories of difference. Groups which, for reasons of history, tradition or geography, cannot be clearly categorized require special attention—either projects aimed at integration, or constraints enforcing separation. Perhaps that is why the official categorization of Jews by the Israeli government includes the rather bizarre term "Anglo-Saxon Jews" (meaning, loosely, Jews from English-speaking countries), but not "Arab Jews." Blurred boundaries are a threat. In Israel there is little likelihood of confusing anyone called an Anglo-Saxon Jew with that mythical creature, a pureblooded Anglo-Saxon; but if Jews from Arab countries are allowed to be called Arab Jews, the carefully maintained and bitterly consequential distinction between Jews and Arabs as collectives might come into question.

Second, as suggested at the outset, there is a connection between the production of marginal populations by states and their production as academic "problems." Those of us concerned with the entirely legitimate problem of the security of marginal populations should also bear in mind that viewing marginality as inherently problematic, something which those who are marginal would be better off without, further reinforces the assumptions of centrality as normal and marginality as anomalous. Inevitably, the kind of work done by our research group has as much to do with the reproduction of our own, central "imagined communities" (Anderson 1983) as with an objective concern for the populations we are investigating. Of course this does not mean that the maintenance of Western neocolonial authority is an explicit goal of the participants. Yet the very social conventions of such an activity— the presumption of a possible and desirable objective description of a human problem suffered by others, the presumption that we are in the business of proposing recommended policies which might be acted upon by those who listen to us and are in a position to affect the situation of the sufferers—can

and power.

One of the memos drafted for the participants in this research group asked that we consider the question, "Does marginality imply a center?" It should be clear by now that talk of marginality certainly does imply a center. Again, as both the model of Rome and the sense of marginality as inherently problematic suggest, the idea of centrality is in turn closely linked to the conception of the normal. With regard to the form of marginality I examine here, the relevant norm is a system of ethnically homogeneous peoples contained within "their own" nation-states. As recent work by Paul Chilton has made clear, standard notions of national security rest on a "container metaphor:" those belonging to the state are kept safely inside, while those who constitute potential threats are kept outside at bay (Chilton 1989).

If the state is a container, then it seems likely that those identified as marginal peoples are in turn conceived as overflow or spillage, and hence expendable if not extremely dangerous. Indeed, a certain amount of excess available to be sacrificed—a tolerance for a given percentage of "waste"— might be implicit in the notion of normal system functioning here. It may or may not be helpful to marginal peoples if, as our common project implies, we create a map of marginality; but by all means we must beware of rationalizing, and thus helping to reproduce, their insecurity by quantifying it. Again, this does not mean that we are always defeated by our situation, or always acting selfishly even when we are speaking of the interest of others. It merely demands an awareness of the limitations and capabilities of our own conceptual apparatus, a persistent exercise, if you will, at the expansion of our peripheral vision.

Categories of marginality are not only always produced (but always unstable), and hence dependent on social or state practices of reinventing and reinforcing the borders. During the course of my recent fieldwork in Jerusalem, I participated in an event which clearly worked toward such an end—a day trip under the official sponsorship of the Department for Torah [i.e., Orthodox Jewish] Culture of the Culture Branch of the Jerusalem Municipality. Those who signed up for the tour were working-class, middle-aged and elderly religious Zionists—part of a political and religious sector which has become considerably more normative in Israel, despite being marginal to earlier pioneering Zionism. The tour was billed as a visit to the grave of the saintly Ari, a master of Jewish mysticism, in the city of Safed, on the occasion of the anniversary of his death. However, only the last hour or so was actually spent at the cemetery. The bulk of the day was devoted to a trek along the no-man's-land next to the Jordan River on the West Bank, and then to a surprise trip up to the Golan Heights. The first stop was at the remains of a synagogue near Jericho, which archaeologists have dated to the fifth or sixth century c.e. The guide, himself an Orthodox Jew and a former representative of the religious Zionist movement in the United States, stressed that the existence of this synagogue attested to the persistence of substantial and wealthy Jewish communities in Palestine centuries after the destruction of the Second Temple. All along the route, he pointed to sites of strategic significance in Israel's wars with Jordan and Syria: a valley through which terrorists had been able to reach Israel immediately after the 1967 war; the Golan, from which the Syrians had been able to take easy potshots at Israeli settlements below. Several of these observations were preceded by the disclaimer, "I don't want to talk about politics, but . . . " The implication was clear: but for our own good, we must keep these places in our control, and the Arabs don't deserve control of them in any case.

Given its official sponsorship, and the way the itinerary was redefined from a primarily religious and traditionalist objective toward a strategic tour of post-1967 boundaries of Israeli control, this tour—and especially the guide's performance—can be described as a state project of redefining centers and margins. The emphasis on the presence of the ancient synagogue worked to assert both the legitimacy of Jewish presence in the West Bank, and the length of time Jews had been a central population in ancient Palestine. The presence of our group was aimed both at asserting the normality of Jews traveling through the West Bank despite the intifada (this was most clear when we walked through a Palestinian resort area in order to get to the ancient synagogue), and to impress upon us a powerful (though not universally hegemonic) vision of Jewish domination in contemporary Palestine. The rhetorical denial that the guide's remarks were political clearly betrayed an obsession with the security of a central population, a worry that Jews as a nation are still not quite as central, as permanently established in this land as he would like them to be. The implication is that a tour guide in a secure and well-ordered state should be able to provide a relaxing and informative narrative free of the tensions and ambiguities of agonistic "politics," that politics is somehow inconsistent with normality and centrality. But alas, it was not to be. The entire tour functioned problematically as part of a massive and state-sponsored effort to effect a change from Jewish marginality to Jewish centrality.

This shift in the relations by which Jews as a collective are defined makes clear that while the binary opposition between centers and margins is stubbornly persistent, both the particular relations within which those values are ascribed to certain groups, and even the very ascription of centrality or marginality to a particular group, are subject to radical and unpredictable change. Generally, then, rather than assuming a simplistic model of one global

what 'central' populations are marginal populations to be defined?"

The historical marginality of Jewish communities grows out of their persistence as a distinct cultural group in many different cultural-social contexts. As I will discuss further below, that situation has been greatly exacerbated by the centralizing impulse of modern nationalism. Zionist Jews, therefore, are primarily working to end a situation of dispersed cultural marginality, seen as both unhealthy and inherently dangerous. The marginality of the Palestinians—indeed, to a large extent their very collective identity—grows on the other hand out of their situation as a colonized and overwhelmingly peasant population. Their statelessness can be attributed to their contingent marginality within the Arab world, the failure of their leadership to accept the U.N. partition plan of 1947, and the cynical way they have been treated as dispensable by the post-World War II great powers. Palestinian nationalists see themselves to a large extent as trying to overcome their marginality versus a persistent neo-imperialism which insists that they are expendable if not superfluous.

From a certain perspective, the history of the Palestinian-Israeli problem can be concisely described as directly related to the notion of centrality and marginality vis-à-vis states. In nineteenth-century Europe, the notion of centralized nation-state normality acquired hegemonic presence. A number of Jews, moved both by their own internalization of this notion and by external pressures coming from others obsessed with integrist nationalism, came to the Middle East to form at least a refuge and at best their own nation-state. In the process they helped to create a marginal population of stateless and generally landless Palestinians. The Palestinians' own collective identity, elaborated in the language of nationhood, derives in turn largely from their collective disaster.

This overall process has been repeated in miniature. Hundreds of thousands of citizens of the former Soviet Union, defined as Jews for diplomatic purposes if not necessarily by Jewish law, have left the former Soviet territories because of their presumed and created marginality there. They have been funnelled to Israel, and effectively barred from dispersing elsewhere. Once in Israel, some have settled in the Occupied Territories (including the expanded "Jerusalem") as part of the ongoing Zionist project of developing and expanding a Jewish center. Although there is a debate in Israel over the questionable Jewishness of some of these immigrants, no one with any authority in the responsible government ministries—absorption, housing, and so forth—seems to question their right to settle in Israel. On the contrary, they are welcomed as a contribution to the demographic and spatial struggle to assert an overwhelming majority Jewish presence in Israel and Palestine.

From Margin to Center and Back Again?

The Russian term used in Israel to designate a new immigrant to Israel is repatriant. On the most transparent ideological level, the term boldly makes the claim that these immigrants are coming home. It is intriguing that such cultural items as bank advertisements, written in Russian and aimed at attracting the business of these new immigrants, do not adopt the Hebrew term oleh. Oleh is a brilliant borrowing from Biblical culture, where it implied "going up" to sacrifice at the temple in Jerusalem at the time of the three annual festivals, and even today it has strong overtones of fulfillment of a joyous and sacred obligation. The term repatriant, on the other hand, remains within the framework of secular nationalism. Nevertheless, even more directly than oleh perhaps, it reinforces the notion that the "normal" place for a Jew to be is in Israel, the Jewish center, and that any Jew remaining in the Soviet Union is in a temporary and abnormal marginal situation. When used as a Russian word in Israel, it simultaneously reminds new Russian- speaking immigrants of the place where they have come from (because it is in their language), and reminds them that this is where they are "supposed" to be. Reminding immigrants in their native language that they have "returned" to their proper place is an acute example of how the subtle insistence that marginality is abnormal functions for the construction of the sense of a collective self.

At the same time, mentioning the Soviet Union in the 1990s is an effective caution against any argument that because ethnic/national identities are produced through cultural projects, they are therefore chimerical or subject to social engineering. Soviet nationalities policy represented an attempt to formalize and control ethnicity within a broader level of universal "citizenship." The resurgence of militant ethnic natonalism in the former Soviet Union, however, is not evidence that the problem is imperfect conformity to a universal secularist norm, but further evidence of the "anomalies" inherent in any attempt to rationalize the relations between state power and ethnicity. These anomalies—in the case of the Soviet Union, for example, the requirement that every nation have a homeland, and that no group without a homeland be recognized as a nation—are not a series of unfortunate exigencies to be addressed separately. Recognizing that they are part of the structure by which state authority is legitimated (ultimately without success in some cases) affords us another point of access for critique of the system which attempts to sustain itself at its margins (such as the Russian Empire appearing as the Union of Soviet Socialist Republics).

Complicating Diasporas

The common formula according to which the solution to the Jewish diaspora is presumed to have led to the creation of the Palestinian diaspora is certainly too simplistic. First of all, the Jewish diaspora—more precisely, the existence of Jewish populations outside the putative Jewish homeland—has not ended. Second of all, despite the disasters of modern Jewish history, it is not universally agreed that the dispersed nature of Jewish communities was a problem that required solution. As to the Palestinians, much of their political weakness before the disaster of 1948 stemmed from the dispersal of leading aristocratic families in cities such as Damascus and Beirut. While any thorough review of the historical complexities masked by the notions of Jewish and Palestinian homeland and diaspora approaches the scope of a life's work, a few chosen ironies should be useful here.

I will first deal with three Jewish situations: in the Russian Empire and the Soviet Union during the last two centuries; in France since World War II; and in contemporary Israel.

Jewish subjects of the Russian tsars suffered a number of legally-enforced disabilities. Most prominent among these, for the purposes of a discussion of marginal populations, was the geographical limitation of settlement rights. Indeed, there officially were no Jews in the Russian Empire until it expanded by swallowing eastern Poland in the partitions of 1772 and 1804, and the Jews in the East European parts of the empire were restricted to the provinces acquired through those partitions. Only a few Jews—those who managed to make their way into certain formal economic categories, and later on, those who managed to assimilate relatively well into Russian society and culture— were allowed to settle in the Russian interior. Jews were generally forbidden to own land, and under the infamous May Laws of 1881, thousands of Jews were forced off the countryside into existing urban communities (Mendelsohn 1970). This was a population inherited as a consequence of conquest, re-garded with distaste and mistrust by Russian nationalist conservatives and as a target for betterment projects by Russian liberals. Within a state defined by its loyalty to the Russian Orthodox church, and as a "middleman minority" between peasants, nobility and a weak capitalist industrial sector, Jews were a useful target of violent social unrest. In times of particular crisis, such as 1881 and the period leading up to the failed revolution of 1905, Jews were the victims of waves of pogroms throughout those portions of the empire where they maintained distinct communities. During World War I entire Jewish communities, regarded as a potential fifth column for the German enemy, were forcibly evacuated into the Russian interior.

It is largely this heritage of the Russian Empire that produced the Soviet Jewish "Exodus" (the loaded nature of that term should be obvious), even though the removal of formal legal discrimination against Jews was one of the first acts carried out in the name of the Russian Revolution. Ironically, one reason why the government of the Soviet Union was for so long reluctant to

From Margin to Center and Back Again?

permit this mass emigration was its desire to preserve the claim that Jews are not discriminated against in the Soviet Union. That is, the Soviet Union, as a radically secular "citizenist" state, was trying to contain its Jews, and thus to reinforce the illusion of shared centrality within the state.

In sharp contrast to the Jews of the former Soviet Union, Jews in France today constitute a marginal population that in many ways is well and securely integrated into the state. They are well represented not only in business, academic life and the liberal professions, but in politics as well. In some ways they might be regarded as the least marginal group we could apply the term to and still retain some distinctions between being marginal and being a minority.

Yet there are good reasons for considering them here. First, to an extent they have reconstituted themselves as marginal since the catastrophe of World War II and the arrival of hundreds of thousands of Jews from North Africa to France. Whereas French society, even more than that of the United States, has and to an extent continues to assume that immigrant groups should and want to assimilate as quickly as possible, the internal boundary mechanisms of French Jewry have in many ways been strengthened in the past decades. Second, despite their present relatively secure circumstances, Jews in France continue to experience a sense of marginality related not so much to present disabilities as to the "presence of the past," and a sense of possible danger in the future. Indeed, given a living history of murderous exclusion, isolated anti-Semitic incidents such as the desecration of a grave in the Jewish cemetery of Carpentras in 1990 acquire an enormously ominous weight. Third, and perhaps most important for my ultimate argument below, the "elite marginality" of many French Jewish intellectuals has produced or stimulated in turn some of the most creative Western thinking about collective identities vis-à-vis each other and vis-à-vis states. This creative marginal situation is epitomized in the annual Colloque des Intellectuels juifs de Language Française.

This intellectual vitality, and the attention it draws in wider French discourse, is in turn related to the presence of millions of much less articulate "marginal" people in France and in Europe generally today. Furthermore, I suspect it has helped to inspire a great deal of critical work on the problems of community, tradition and identity not necessarily done by Jews—such as Jean-Luc Nancy's, *La Communauté désouvrée*, (Nancy 1986, 1991) an attempt to synthesize the desire for community with the critique of totalizing discourses of identity. Nancy's critique of the equation of a happy community with sameness among all its members—in the terms of this paper, with happy community as shared centrality—helps make it clear that even when a group of people are successful and indeed feel secure (intellectually, financially, or demographically), by maintaining difference they may still be marginal. To argue otherwise is to presume tautologically that in order to be secure people have to be in the center, and anyone who is secure is therefore automatically in the center.

Where Jews in Eastern Europe struggled for centuries against structural discrimination, and Jews in France today operate within a remarkable but hardly guaranteed space of productive cultural tension, Jews in Israel are both actors and objects within a project of creating a new center. On one hand, that effort entails a redirection and revalorization of perennial themes in Jewish culture, such as attachment to the Land of Israel and the mutual responsibility of all Jews for each others' lives (sometimes, indeed, down to the most petty details). On the other, it involves dismantling an entire traditional cultural system based on the premise of divinely-ordained marginality. These two aspects combined in early Zionism to produce a powerful homogenizing urge—to make the new immigrants from vastly different backgrounds, with vastly different Jewish ideologies and practices, into similar secular "Israelis."

The category of "Oriental" Jews—technically referring to Jews from the Middle East, North Africa and India—arose in the context of this centralizing project. According to Israeli ideology and law, these people are the equals of the Ashkenazi (European-derived) Jews of Israel. Yet they are quite widely treated as a problematic population, and there are endless debates over whether their inferior situation is the result of active discrimination or cultural backwardness (Swirski 1989). Oriental Jews in Israel, to a large extent, represent the phenomenon of effective marginality "even" within the confines of a state ideology of inclusiveness. In fact, this collective designation lumping together people of such different backgrounds reflects a further ironic centralization technique—the production of binary distinctions "within" centers. Their anomalous situation—superior to those non-Jews officially recognized as Arabs, while in some ways inferior in "image" and opportunity to European (Russian) immigrants who are not even legally classified as Jews, can be compared to the situation of many of their parents and grandparents in North Africa, regarded as alien colonizers by local nationalist movements, and as Arab Jews by the colonial powers.

Oriental Jews—who for several years, at least until the arrival of the mass Soviet immigration, have constituted the majority of the Jews in Israel—present another kind of test case for the designation of a population as marginal: Can the majority of a state's population be marginal? This possibility has been suggested in the research group's discussions, but it really is a challenge to the notion of marginality, which seems grounded in the ideologies and to an extent the realities of American, French or British secularized citizenship.

If we do want to pursue seriously the proposition of marginal majorities, how are we to judge? Are there any forms of hierarchical discrimination which are not at the same time examples of the linked process of centralization and marginalization? To further complicate the issue, there is no reason to assume that people's structural situation will match how they say they "feel" vis-à-vis the state which claims their allegiance, or the state they or their parents were born in. Indeed, this glance at some of the nuances of Jewish marginality might as well end with a story which poignantly illustrates the frequent gap between ideologies of allegiance and a personal feeling of belonging. Several years ago a friend arrived at my home in New York and reported a conversation with a Jewish cab driver from the Soviet Union. She asked him whether he'd come directly to the States, or lived in Israel first. He told her he'd spent a few years in Israel. She asked where he felt his home was—the Soviet Union, Israel or America. He told her that Israel was his home. She asked why he hadn't stayed there, and he replied, "They don't like Russians there."

Whatever the weaknesses of the system of land tenure in Palestine may have been, whatever long-term preparations the Zionist movement may have made for the gradual takeover of Palestinian lands (Atran 1990), it is generally agreed that the "origins of the Palestinian refugee problem" are primarily located in the 1948 war and its aftermath, when, according to Benny Morris, "some 600,000-760,000 Palestinian Arabs became refugees and . . . remained refugees in the immediate postwar period" (Morris 1987:1). The controversy over the reasons for the Palestinian flight persists, and reactions to recent writing about that event vary widely. Thus, a Palestinian anthropologist has complained to me that Morris' recent book on the subject works far too hard in an unconvincing attempt to deny that there was an organized Zionist plan for the expulsion of the Palestinians. On the other hand, a liberal but politically uninvolved religious Israeli intellectual told me that his father had recently read the book, and added as a sad reflection, "It seems we really kicked the Palestinians out."

It is clear in any case that neither those who left in 1948 nor their descendants have been able to return to homes inside the pre-1967 borders of Israel. Furthermore, the Israeli conquest of the West Bank, Gaza and the Golan Heights in 1967 created a further wave of new refugees, and more crucially, a situation wherein the Palestinian residents of the occupied territories were marginalized vis-à-vis an increasingly aggressive military occupation by the Jewish nation-state.

Looking at the resulting situation in terms of a spatial model of marginality and centrality, three concentric "levels" of Palestinian marginality can be distinguished, not only by degree but also by quality of marginalization.

The first level constitutes Arab citizens of Israel. Their position has always been ambivalent, both toward the State of Israel and toward other Palestinian

Arabs. While officially they are fully-franchised Israeli citizens, in fact they are subject to a number of structural discriminations. They generally do not serve in the Israeli army, and therefore are not eligible for various benefits available to army veterans (i.e., to all male Israeli Jews except a minority of the extremely Orthodox, and to a large percentage of female Israeli Jews as well). More important, virtually all of the land inside Israel is still owned by the Jewish Agency, and it is virtually impossible for Israeli Arabs to buy land. An estimated 120 villages and smaller Arab settlements in the northern part of the country alone have never been officially recognized by the Israeli government. Such handicaps are, of course, in addition to the various forms of informal discrimination suffered by a distinctive cultural minority within a polity organized on the principle of integrist nationalism.

On the other hand, Israeli Arabs have been largely regarded with a good deal of suspicion and even resentment by other Palestinians—those who are living under Israeli occupation and/or those who in 1948 lost homes inside pre-1967 Israel. The relative security that went along with being a citizen of the Jewish state, and the ideological compromises entailed in maintaining homes within that state, made this population seem somehow "not really Palestinian." The events of the early 1990s—the intifada, with its appeal to unity among all Palestinians, and the Palestine National Council's recognition of the State of Israel—changed this situation considerably.

This shift was aptly summed up by a master of ceremonies at the annual convention of the United Holy Land Fund, the United States support group for al-Fatah, in the winter of 1989. Introducing an Arab member of the Israeli Knesset—someone who might have otherwise been regarded as having sold out thoroughly—the master of ceremonies referred to the speaker as being "min dakhel el dakhel," literally "from inside the inside." The phrase implied that if the audience wanted to claim that those "inside" (i.e., inside the territories) had a certain moral or ideological priority vis-à-vis Palestinians throughout the entire world, then even more so someone who was living and struggling "all the way" inside. He turned the notion that those who had stayed are unfairly privileged squarely on its head, revealing a strikingly complex conceptualization of political/historical geography on the part of the "marginal" population. These Palestinians are Israeli citizens, hence presumably less marginal vis-à-vis the state system in general than other, stateless Palestinians. Yet that very citizenship made them ideologically marginal vis-à-vis the "core" group of Palestinians struggling for self-determination, which is what necessitated the symbolic rescue effected by the phrase, "min dakhel el dakhel." In yet a further irony, the rescue itself rested on the point that these people were still living in the "Palestinian heartland," and hence could be thought of as holding the fort for their dispersed fellows.

From Margin to Center and Back Again?

Israeli Arabs remain, however, relatively invisible vis-à-vis Palestinians in the territories, even when they face similar problems such as land confiscation. In September 1991, the residents of a small "unrecognized" village called Ramya near the Israeli development town of Carmiel were fighting an order that they be evicted from land which they have lived on and farmed since before 1948. The case only got some publicity outside Israel because it unfolded at the same time as the debate over the release of $10 billion in U.S. loan guarantees for new Israeli Jewish housing.

The second level of Palestinian marginality consists of those in the occupied territories—not dakhel el dakhel, but still inside. It could be argued that the territories as a whole have been turned into a marginal region, since even Jewish settlers on the West Bank and Gaza are regarded very much as pioneers. But Palestinian residents of the occupied territories are kept marginal in much more material and less metaphorical ways. Aside from systematic and well-documented violations of the residents' human rights (B'tselem 1991), Palestinian workers have for years not been allowed to sleep within the Green Line marking the boundaries of pre-1967 Israel. Indeed, as that boundary is being erased for Jews by the frantic building of new settlements inside the territories, it has been reinforced for Palestinians by increased limitations on their movement in the context of the intifada and more recently the Gulf War. In addition to frequent curfews, Palestinians from the territories were subject to sporadic total banning from Israel around the time of the Gulf War. To a population which effectively constitutes a cheap colonial labor force, being prevented from getting to work was an economic disaster. Furthermore, a system of passes instituted early in 1991 remained in place until mid-1992. Not all Palestinians could afford them or were granted them, and thus many were effectively barred from entering Israel.

Here, too, there are of course internal differentiations. Many of the residents of the occupied territories are still considered refugees, have been living in refugee camps for over forty years and are relatively underprivileged vis-à-vis Palestinians who are "at home" in the occupied territories (this is especially true on the West Bank). This difference is most dramatically evident around Bethlehem, just a mile or two from the edge of the Jewish city of Jerusalem. On one side is the town of Beit Sahour, perhaps the richest Palestinian community anywhere in the occupied territories. On the other side is the refugee camp of Deheisha, where 8,000 people live on a hillside surrounded by a ten-foot fence, and enter and leave through a single turnstile. Nevertheless, Beit Sahour, like Deheisha, is subject to frequent curfews, as well as to arbitrary arrest and massive confiscation and destruction of goods as punishment for the townspeoples' refusal to pay taxes to the occupying authorities.

Jonathan Boyarin

At a third level, there are Palestinians dispersed throughout the Arab world—primarily in Syria, Jordan, Egypt and the Gulf states. Generally, the fate of these people, precarious as it may be, is not closely dependent on the situation or actions of their fellow Palestinians "inside," and thus they cannot be said to be strategically marginal vis-à-vis any Palestinian center. On the contrary, their situation can have an enormous effect on those inside. The clearest example of this is the disastrous loss of remittances sent back by Palestinians working in Kuwait. On the other hand, the situation of these Palestinians outside in Arab countries (especially Kuwait and other Gulf states) was affected negatively when the Palestine Liberation Organization, which works at the international diplomatic level to establish a Palestinian center of power, supported Iraq in the recent Gulf War (see Ashrawi 1991, Hulaileh 1991).

Ironically, Kuwait was itself the birthplace of the Palestine Liberation Organization (Baumgarten 1991). As the result of a move by the British to place former Palestinian civil servants in the infrastructure of newly-independent Kuwait, the bureaucratic class in Kuwait has been largely Palestinian for decades. These Palestinian immigrants long enjoyed relative freedom of speech and assembly, although they generally were denied Kuwaiti citizenship—a perfect recipe for the establishment of a new nationalist movement, with its own motivations, not always consistent with those of the people "inside."

Toward a New Articulation

The marginality of Palestinian intellectuals, like that of French Jews, has stimulated creative thinking about identity and politics. Thus Edward Said, a Palestinian living in a relatively privileged exile in the United States, has begun to articulate a model of a dispersed rather than statist nationalism (Said 1986). This work can be seen as a contribution to a larger attempt to imagine a model of power and polity beyond the dichotomization of center and periphery.

This larger attempt is not only carried out from the perspective of marginal ethnic groups. It has probably been most fully developed in feminist theory, where such ideas as normalcy, deviancy, center and identity have been closely interrogated, and where debates on the possibility and desirability of becoming more central versus working from the margins have been carried out in a sustained way (hooks 1984); Hartsock 1987; Butler 1990). Yet the elite discourse of feminist theory, like that of many Jewish or Palestinian critical intellectuals, fails to address adequately the problems of procreation, family and ethnicity—the problems of reproducing human life and sustaining cultural memory. It might be said that such critical positions, even when articulated by someone like Said or myself who are closely identified with a particular group, are consciously produced from these intellectual margins, and thus once again inevitably reproduce the binary distinction between margin and center.

At the same time, whatever his theoretical compunctions about the virtues of nationalism, Said is in active solidarity with a rather traditional "national liberation" movement aiming to establish a center for the suffering Palestinians. If there is an inconsistency between theory and practice here, Said is well aware of it. He recognizes that the model of a marginal people-hood based on ethics, kinship and cultural memory is less rather than more possible in our time.

Because exile, unlike nationalism, is fundamentally a discontinuous state of being, exiles are cut off from their roots, their land, their past. They generally do not have armies or states, although they are often in search of them. Exiles feel, therefore, an urgent need to reconstitute their broken lives, usually by choosing to see themselves as part of a triumphant ideology or a restored people. The crucial thing is that a state of exile free from this triumphant ideology—designed to reassemble an exile's broken history into a new whole—is virtually unbearable, and virtually impossible in today's world. Look at the fate of the Jews, the Palestinians and the Armenians. (Said 1984, 163)

The fate of the Jews and the Palestinians, considered together, may well lead us to question whether the best solution to the predicament of marginality is always a move toward the center. Here we have a case of two populations, both marginal with respect to global centers of both material power and cultural authority. Their respective situations function both to reinforce their internal sense of distinct identity, while the relation between the two groups themselves functions to reinforce their marginality and insecurity.

Ironically, one way this sense of insecurity is reproduced is through exaggerated notions each group has about the other's relative access to centers of power. Witness the idea, common to Palestinians and their supporters, that American Jews are "powerful" or "control the media." This notion, simplistic at best and reminiscent of anti-Semitic mythology at its worst, substitutes for a more profound understanding of both Jewish history and United States power politics. It thus blocks more effective Palestinian rhetoric and strategy, and helps to maintain Palestinian powerlessness. Fortunately again, some Palestinian activists and thinkers are attempting to redress this weakness with a greater attention to the Jewish situation.

Witness from the other side the idea, common to many Israelis and other Jews, that Palestinian territorial demands cannot be acceded to for security reasons, and furthermore are not legitimate because Palestinians are part of a

Jonathan Boyarin

massive (and therefore powerful) "Arab nation." The two notions are, of **149**
course, related: in this perception, Palestinians should be able to fit in elsewhere in the Arab world, and on the other hand, if they win independence,
their country will eventually be the staging ground for a united Arab effort to
uproot the Jews from Israel. An Israeli Arab householder in the small unrecognized village of Ramiya (see above), after repeating once again that all the
villagers want is to live in peace with their Jewish neighbors, summarized this
perception in a powerful metaphor: "They think we are wolves who will come
down from the mountains and kill their goats." Once again, the image of the
margin (whether economic, cultural or geographical) as a wild and dangerous
place reappears here.

This reminder that the problem of Palestinian marginality is not conven-
iently confined to the territories occupied by Israel since 1967 points out the
dilemma of an activist approach toward the resolution of the Israeli-Palestinian conflict. The program of "two states for two peoples"—establishing an
independent Palestinian state in all or most of the occupied territories, existing alongside an independent Israel—is the only proposal on the table which
promises to guarantee a modicum of both justice and security for Palestinian
Arabs and Israeli Jews. It was evidently not on the program of the latest "Pax
Americana," George Bush's "New World Order." It is certainly not on the
agenda of the Israeli government.

Furthermore, the slogan and program of "two states for two peoples"
explicitly accept and promote the binary and rigid division of the population
of Palestine into two separate peoples. Recognizing that this represents a
rhetorical choice does not mean, of course, that this division can be simply
"deconstructed" through criticism. As the example of the former Soviet
Union shows, the desire for ethnically-based statist independence has not
diminished on the part of "central" (i.e. Russian) or "marginal" (e.g. Armenian) populations. Nor—especially in the Middle East, a region where a
massive, deadly and debilitating arms buildup shows no immediate signs of
abating—would it seem feasible to attempt "marginality in one country."

Neither critical interrogation nor pragmatic activism should be abandoned. A measure of common good needs to be sought, grounded in the
realities of power politics and prevalent ethnocentrism. At the same time it is
necessary to think of ways, not to reduce the number of marginal individuals
or the degree of marginality, but rather to enhance security through the
cultivation of a creative marginality. The interrogation of the demand for a
unitary identity—evident as a state project in Israel, and as a rhetoric of
solidarity among Palestinians—is necessary both because that demand inter-
feres with the pragmatic political solution, and because it is integral to the

articulation of an alternative to a system of binaries which constantly reproduces threatened "marginal" populations.

Will we indefinitely continue to accept ancient Rome as our model of normative polity, security, centrality and marginality? Will we continue to assume that the problematic situation of populations culturally, socially or geographically removed from the loci of power is to be solved by drawing them closer to those centers? Is it possible to think rather that their ambiguous situation could serve as a resource for the transcendence of the cycle of reproduction of centers and margins, with the endemic violence and discrimination that structure entails?

The elaborate Washington ceremony in September 1993 surrounding the signature of the Statement of Principles binding the Israeli government and Arafat's Palestine Liberation Organization suggest that the model of great-power mediation still holds sway. The yawning gap between the statement's proposed timetable and the bloody, frustrating sequence of events in the ensuing months supplies ample evidence of the inadequacy of that model. Indeed, much of the difficulty in implementing the agreement stems from overconfident reliance on the centralizing authority of Shimon Peres and Yasser Arafat. Clearly the Israeli government only decided to deal openly with the P.L.O. at a time when that bureaucracy was at a weak and marginal position not only in the Arab world, but to a considerable extent among Palestinians as well. The limited rights and powers offered to Palestinians (in a confined portion of the occupied territories only!) under the Statement of Principles are too much for an enraged Israel right wing, and not nearly enough to summon loyalty from most Palestinians. Whether the current negotiations will in any way increase security for Israelis and Palestinians in the long run can only be determined in the long run.

What I have tried to suggest in this paper is not only that the marginal situations of both Jews and Palestinians are complex, contradictory, and fruitful as well as dangerous. The more consequential point is that the dilemma posed by Jewish and Palestinian demands for security and identity, currently structured as mutually exclusive, can only be reimagined as complimentary if the unstable binary opposition between competing and mutually exclusivist centers, or the inherently discriminatory distinction between center and margin, are overcome. The alternative is a more situational and personal concept of security (as psychological, material and not only military) and a formulation of identity as contingent, complimentary and multiple rather than fated, total and exclusive. I know that in this world, dominated as it still is by "the generative order of nationalism" (Portugali 1988), such a prescription is an inadequate answer to the demand for both security and justice. Yet it is useful as a reminder of the inherent limitations of statist-territorialist models linked to ethnic self-determination. Neither a simple embrace or return to the margins, nor the proliferation of new centers, is an adequate response to the situations and desires of Israeli Jews and Palestinians today.

Bibliography

Abu-Lughod, Janet. 1989. *Before European Hegemony*. New York: Oxford University Press.

————. n.d. "The Politics of Geography: Colonialism and Middle Eastern Geography."

Anderson, Benedict. 1983. *Imagined Communities: Reflections on the Spread of Nationalism*. London: Verso.

Ashforth, Adam. 1990. *The Politics of Official Discourse in Southern Africa*. New York: Oxford University Press.

Ashley, Richard. 1989. "Living on Border Lines: Man, Poststructuralism, and War." *In International/intertextual Relations: Postmodern Readings of World Politics*, ed. James Der Derian, ed. Michael J. Shapiro, 259-321. Lexington, MA: D.C. Heath and Company.

Ashrawi, Hanan Mikhail. 1991. "The Other Occupation: The Palestinian Response." In *Beyond the Storm: A Gulf Crisis Reader*, ed. Phyllis Bennis, ed. Michel Moushabeck, 191-98. Brooklyn: Olive Branch Press.

Atran, Scott. 1990. "The Surrogate Colonization of Palestine, 1917-1939." *American Ethnologist* 16(4):719-744

B'tselem. 1991. *Violations of Human Rights in the Occupied Territories 1990/1991*. Jerusalem. Bamyeh, Mohammed A. 1989. "Israel, Palestine, and Discursive Imagination: Notes on the Audible and the Inaudible in the Conflict." Paper Presented at the Modern Language Association Convention, Panel on "Imagining Israel and Palestine". Washington, DC.

Baumgarten, Helga. 1991. *Palastina: Befreiung in Den Staat*. Frankfurt am Main: Suhrkamp.

Bilgrami, Akeel. 1992. "What is a Muslim? Fundamental Commitment and Cultural Identity." *Critical Inquiry* 18(4):821-42.

Boyarin, Daniel. 1994. *A Radical Jew: Paul and the Politics of Identity*. Berkeley and Los Angeles: University of California Press.

Boyarin, Jonathan. 1991. "An Inquiry Into Inquiry and a Representation of Representations." *Sociological Forum* 6 (June):387-95.

————. 1993. "Space, Time and the Politics of Memory." In *Remapping Memory: The Politics of Timespace*. Ed. Jonathan Boyarin, 1-37. Minneapolis: University of Minnesota Press.

Butler, Judith. 1990. *Gender Trouble: Feminism and the Subversion of Identity*. New York: Routledge.

Chilton, Paul. 1989. "Containment and Beyond: Reformulations of Political Space." unpublished ms.

152   Clifford, James. 1988. "Identity in Mashpee." *In The Predicament of Culture: Twenti-eth-century Ethnography, Literature, and Art*, 277-346. Cambridge, MA: Harvard University Press.

Davies, W. D. 1974. *The Gospel and the Land: Early Christianity and Jewish Territorial Doctrine*. Berkeley and Los Angeles: University of California Press.

Dominguez, Virginia. 1990. *People as Subject, People as Object: Selfhood and People-hood in Contemporary Israel*. Madison: University of Wisconsin Press.

Finkelstein, Norman. 1988. "Disinformation and the Palestine Question: The Not-so-strange Case of Joan Peters' From Time Immemorial." In *Blaming the Victim: Spurious Scholarship and the Palestine Question*, ed. Edward W. Said and Christo-pher Hitchins, 33-69. New York: Verso.

Halperin, Jean, ed. George Levitte, ed. 1989. *La Question de l'etat: Colloque des Intellectuels juifs*. Paris: Denöel.

Hartsock, Nancy. 1987. "Rethinking Modernism: Minority Vs. Majority Theories." *Cultural Critique* 7:187-206.

Hooks, Bell. 1984. *Feminist Theory: From Margin to Center*. Boston: South End Press.

Hulaileh, Samir. 1991. "The Gulf Crisis and the Economy in the Occupied Territo-ries." In *Beyond the Storm: A Gulf Crisis Reader*, ed. Phyllis Bennis, ed. Michel Moushabeck, 199-204. Brooklyn: Olive Branch Press.

Levinas, Emmanuel. 1989. *The Levinas Reader*. Ed. Sean Hand. Cambridge, MA: Basil Blackwell.

McNeill, William B. 1986. *Polyethnicity and National Unity in World History*. Toronto: University of Toronto Press.

Mendelsohn, Ezra. 1970. *Class Struggle in the Pale*. Cambridge: Cambridge Univer-sity Press.

Morris, Benny. 1987. *The Birth of the Palestinian Refugee Problem*, 1947-1949. New York: Cambridge University Press.

Nancy, Jean-Luc. 1986. *La Communauté desouvrée*. Paris.

———. 1991. *The Inoperative Community*. Minneapolis: University of Minnesota Press.

Peters, Joan. 1984. *From Time Immemorial*. New York: Harper and Row.

Portugali, Yuval. 1988. "Nationalism, Social Theory and the Israeli/Palestinian Case." In *Nationalism, Self-Determination and Political Geography*, R. J. Johnston, David Knight, and Eleonore Kofman, 151-65. London: Croon Helm.

Sahlins, Peter. 1989. *Boundaries: The Making of France and Spain in the Pyrenees*. Berkeley and Los Angeles: University of California Press.

Said, Edward. 1984. "Reflections on Exile." *Granta* (13):157-72.

———. 1986. *After the Last Sky: Palestinian Lives*. New York: Pantheon.

Schnapper, Dominique Aron. 1991. "A Host Country of Immigrants That Does not Know Itself." *Diaspora* 1(3):?

Spivak, Gayatri Chakravorti. 1987. "Explanation and Culture: Marginalia." In *In Other Worlds: Essays in Cultural Politics*, 103-17. New York: Methuen.

Swirski, Shlomo. 1989. *Israel: The Oriental Majority*. Atlantic Highlands, NJ: Zed Books.

Jonathan Boyarin

Tilly, Charles. 1990. *Coercion, Capital and European States, 1990.* New York: Basil Blackwell.

————. 1991. "War and States in the Middle East." Working Papers of the Center for Studies of Social Change (112) (March).

Voegelin, Eric. 1956-87. *Order and History.* 5 Vols. Baton Rouge: Louisiana University Press.

Chapter 6

INDIGENOUS STRUGGLES AGAINST MARGINALITY IN LATIN AMERICA: BEYOND THE NATIONAL PHASE[1]

Charles R. Hale

Soon after the uprising began on January 1, 1994 it became clear that the Zapatista Army for National Liberation would present the Mexican government with a formidable challenge. Military conflict quickly gave way to a protracted and complex process of negotiation, but not before the Zapatistas had achieved intense (and generally sympathetic) international media attention and widespread public solidarity. Zapatista spokespeople communicated effectively to the international community, making the multi-leveled character of their demands known; they placed local grievances (e.g. racism, lack of access to land and credit) and national problems (e.g. an exclusionary and corrupt development model) in the context of global political-economic inequities epitomized by the recent approval of NAFTA. Regardless of the final outcome of negotiations over these demands, certain achievements soon were evident: the Zapatistas forced the government to abandon its initial objective of a military "solution"; equally important, the rebellion broke the spell of those who had touted President Salinas de Gortari as a political hero and had portrayed the Mexican economy as in the early stages of a neo-liberal "miracle." Some analysts have even argued that rebel presence provided the catalyst for the chain of events that resulted in the financial catastrophe of early 1995.[2]

Yet amid the surety about this political impact, a seemingly basic question about the uprising remains shrouded in controversy: who are the Zapatistas? More precisely, what is the role of people's culture and practice as Maya Indians in their opting to struggle, in the internal organization of their movement, in the formulation of their demands, and in other facets of the conflict? Consider three excerpts from recent writings, which contain highly disparate answers to these questions. The first is characteristic of mainstream print media editorials, which follow the *New York Times* in making Chiapas emblematic of the "other" Mexico:

While Mexico is rapidly making itself a modern state, by no means all of its people are equally well equipped for that transformation. The peasant uprising in the southernmost state of Chiapas is the old story of a revolt of the most neglected and isolated. . . . Chiapas has a large population of Maya Indians along with a history of Indian uprising that goes back three centuries . . . [3]

In a direct response to this "two Mexico" thesis, and drawing on extensive long-term research, anthropologist George Collier offers a starkly divergent view:

As [Indian migrants from the highlands] converged in rapidly shifting frontier settlements in the tropical forest, [they] shucked ethnic origin for generic peasant identities, diverse sects of Protestantism, and new forms of peasant organizing . . . In contrast to many analysts, I posit that [the Zapatista rebellion] is primarily a peasant rebellion . . . [4]

The point of Collier, journalist Alma Guillermoprieto (1994), and others who have taken this stance is not to deny that the Zapatistas are Indians, but rather, to insist that the rebels were motivated primarily by "generic peasant" not specifically "Indian" demands. Finally, the Pomo Indians of Mendicino county (California) sent an aid caravan to Chiapas with a rationale that is common in the outpouring of international solidarity for the Zapatistas:

It's the spirit of survival we want to share, to show that the Indian nations are aware their lands are the basis of their culture. . . . They say 15,000 Indians a year die there from lack of medicine. We can't sit by and deny them aid. This is from Indian nation to Indian nation. [5]

Can these three portrayals—spontaneous millenarian uprising, generic peasant rebellion, Indian struggle for sovereignty—be reconciled? If not, what is at stake in the divergence?

One dimension of this issue revolves around the basic premises commonly used to talk about identity, ethnicity, and Indian culture. A three-way complicity of state-centered ideologies, "ethnic" elites, and analysts of ethnicity has cemented in place the notion that ethnic identities are inherently bounded and unified by core cultural elements that all group members share. The result is a dichotomous analysis, which starts with an assertion about who Indians "are" and from this deduces an explanation for why they rebel, with the implicit assumption that the chain of logic would be radically different if the protagonists were not Indians. This reasoning is evident in the mainstream media portrayals, whose sympathy barely conceals contempt for the Indians' backwardness and hopeless incompatibility with modernity. Though the political inflection is reversed, the same reasoning underlies the third

Charles R. Hale

position: by definition Indians rebel to preserve identity, defend ancestral land, and achieve "national" sovereignty. Collier's highly sophisticated analysis, though in many ways a corrective to the other two, does not completely shake free from this dichotomous thinking. His analysis is predicated on a sharp distinction between "peasant" and "Indian" in the characterization of the protagonists' demands, and by implication, in their consciousness and daily political practice as well.[6] An alternative reading of his own evidence is that the uprising is not "primarily" peasant or indigenous, but resolutely *both* (and therefore, strictly speaking, neither).

These theoretical concerns, in turn, raise a more empirically grounded set of questions—the main focus of my analysis here. What accounts for the way that people articulate and deploy Indian identity, as they struggle to defend and advance their collective interests? If certain strategies can be predominantly associated with discrete historical periods, what explains the transition from one phase of struggle to the next? In regard to the current phase of struggle, what are its principal achievements, anticipated costs and unintended consequences? If an emergent phase is indeed on the horizon, how might it be characterized and what potential does it hold? My answers to these questions will strike a delicate balance, advancing a critique of essentialist premises in much analysis of indigenous politics, but tempered by the acknowledgement that, in the present historical moment, Indian leaders often deploy these very premises to represent their own cultures, formulate their strategies, and to unify people behind their cause. Similarly, I insist that indigenous movements have assigned sharply varying meanings to Indian identity in distinct historical moments, while carefully distinguishing this position from the reductive "instrumentalist" view, whereby identity is little more than an ensemble of cultural symbols manipulated to create a facade of collectivity that advances elite actors' particular interests.[7]

This analysis, in turn, will highlight a central contradiction that has plagued indigenous struggles against marginality in Latin America, at least since the 19th century rise of the nation-state. Generally oppressive and untrustworthy, the state has been a primary object of indigenous peoples' resistance; yet for a variety of reasons beginning with the extreme unevenness of this contest, key precepts of state and nation building have been incorporated into the demands, strategies and visions that indigenous people have chosen to follow. This ability to confront the nation-state on its own terms has become the key defining feature of indigenous struggles in the present moment. It has been the source of unprecedented strength and achievement, and increasingly, of serious liabilities as well. This argument brings the essay full circle, exploring the idea that the identity conundrum in the Chiapas uprising is symptomatic of an emergent moment, when indigenous struggles will be

Beyond the National Phase

less encumbered by precepts of the 19th century nation-state, better posi-
tioned to confront the post-national conditions of marginality that increasingly characterize their daily lives.

* * *

There is no better way to reveal the sophistry in the assumption that equates
the security of people and the security of their states than to examine this
equation from the perspective of the cultural margins. The critique is more
compelling still when these "margins" are associated with majority populations, as is the case with Indians in more than one Latin American country.
Viewed from the margins the entire repertoire of key discourses and practices
emanating from the state—citizenship, sovereignty, development, stability,
national unity—smack of hypocrisy; they become an arsenal of weapons
deployed to eliminate cultural difference and to preemptively neutralize the
resistance it entails. Moreover, these weapons of statecraft place indigenous
peoples in a double bind: to resist is to reinforce pervasive images of the
insubordinate primitive, to accommodate is to affirm a cultural logic that leads
to their own annihilation. The predicament rests on paired assumptions about
Indians deeply embedded in the collective political imaginary of dominant
culture elites throughout Latin America—noble and bloodthirsty savage,
redeemable citizen and inveterate outlaw, font of national identity and barrier
to the nation's progress—apparently contradictory but in effect sealing the case
for policies that keep Indians powerless (Adams 1990a; Burns 1980). The
stronger and more "secure" the state, the more efficacy these oppressive policies
can be expected to have.

Yet while indigenous peoples have suffered from some combination of
economic exploitation and political exclusion since colonial times, to emphasize continuity is to risk obscuring the great variation in these conditions and
in the character of indigenous resistance to them, across space and through
time.[8] It should be possible to associate this variation with distinct historical
phases, and to analyze the consequences associated with each. Because my
principal concern here is with the phase that emerged in the 1960s, I can only
make a gesture to the more distant past, leaving further elaboration and
substantiation for later. In brief, the colonial variant of this relationship was
distinguished by a profound disjuncture, such that the cultural and ideological precepts of indigenous resistance and those associated with colonial rule
shared only minimal common ground. This phase came to a close in the early
independence period, and the closure was consummated with the ascendancy
of liberal regimes in the late 19th century. Under liberal "modernization"
indigenous resistance persisted, but turned predominantly local, defensive,
and "everyday" rather than large-scale and frontal. Another clearly distinct

Charles R. Hale

phase of resistance emerged in the 1960s, marked by a dramatically new semantics and organizational politics of struggle. Speaking on behalf of increasingly well-organized constituencies, with political agendas of national scope, indigenous leaders came to formulate demands in a language that national elites would find threateningly familiar. Though still revolving around assertions of radical cultural difference and firmly rooted in claims of continuity from time immemorial, these demands now placed the entire arsenal of state-centered discourse to the service of indigenous struggles. Ironically, it was precisely this familiarity (i.e. *indigenous* sovereignty, nationhood, self-determination, etc.) that made dominant actors perceive these demands as so militant and unnegotiable.

The first section of this essay focuses on this post-1960 "national" phase of indigenous struggle, highlighting two closely related features that were crucial to its consummation. National indigenous movements appropriated the discourse of the nation-state to make their case; taking this step, in turn, constituted an explicit rejection of the most plausible alternative—to join forces with broader emancipatory (and equally "national") projects of the Left. The next section examines the quintessential demand of the national phase: indigenous rights to autonomy. I argue that demands for autonomy, though enormously appealing and powerful, from the outset have faced the twin barriers of repression and cooptation, which have seriously limited their success. These barriers, in turn, highlight the fundamental contradiction that plagues the national phase of indigenous struggle. Grounded in the precepts of state and nation building, demands for autonomy assign the state the dual role of adversary and arbiter, with the capacity both to rule out "unnegotiable" demands and make the rules for any concessions that do result. While much can be achieved within these parameters, with time the inherent limitations on this national struggle have grown increasingly apparent. The third section explores the proposition that, in part propelled by these limitations, an incipient shift is under way to "transnational" indigenous struggle. A key conducive condition of this shift, paradoxically, is the very success of national struggle. Increasingly, indigenous political discourse and action has begun to exert influence beyond indigenous peoples themselves, serving as a catalyst for diverse opposition movements. Once this happens, the fundamental rationale for national struggle—the drive to contest cultural oppression through collective rights defined in contraposition to the dominant culture—grows less compelling. A concluding section explores the possible contours and consequences of this emergent phase.

This analysis is also intended to provoke reflection on the dilemmas inherent in all struggles to overcome "marginality," as defined in this volume. How to gain full rights of participation in the dominant society, without submitting to an individualized notion of rights that undermines the potential power of identities grounded in radical cultural difference? How to build powerful strategies of collective action, without inadvertently affirming the deeply ingrained premises that associate cultural difference with exoticism, backwardness, millenarian militancy or other qualities deemed antithetical to the progress and prosperity of the nation? Most broadly, how to contest marginality, or even, mobilize marginality for emancipatory ends, without implicitly allowing the state, dominant actors and other adversaries to define the terms of struggle?

In regard to the emergent transnational phase of indigenous struggle, it will be possible only to suggest some defining characteristics and to raise critical questions. Do the "hybrid" identities that both motivate and emanate from the new strategies signal a means to avoid the no-win choice between exclusion and assimilation? Do they engender forms of resistance that affirm cultural difference without falling back on reductionist invocations of a unified oppositional subject? If so, what political consequences can be expected to follow? Because the Zapatista rebellion seems to fit the description of post-national indigenous struggle, it helps to bring these questions sharply into focus. In so doing, it also serves warning that the answers may well be sobering. Disparities in local class and power inequities are on the rise, the reconfigured alliance between a privatized state and multi-national capital implies no necessary "retreat" in the state's repressive apparatus nor in its willingness for recourse to repression. In these ways too Chiapas may be characteristic of the emergent transnational phase of indigenous struggle, of movements situated in a still largely indeterminate middle ground between a creative renewal of indigenous militancy with great transformative potential, and a contest against adversaries whose immense, yet decentered, power makes resistance harder than ever to consummate, and hegemony harder than ever to resist.

(1)

At the risk of redundancy, I want to disassociate my argument once again from any simplistic stage theory, which would portray one phase of indigenous struggle as abruptly stopping to give way to the next. Instead, I understand the process as additive. Strategies and underlying precepts gradually diversify, with an increasing accent on the new, eventually yielding a sharply distinct politics. The transition occurs in part because the protagonists develop a growing critical awareness of rigidities, contradictions or outright flaws in the prior framework, but this does not imply a sharp rupture or a renunciation of continuities with the past.[9] Indigenous peoples in Latin America initiated a new phase of this sort sometime in the 1960s, advancing a mode of struggle

Charles R. Hale

sharply distinguished from the past in both internal content and political impact.[10]

Although to my knowledge there is still no systematic explanation for the emergence of this national phase, its central features are easily discerned. During the 1960s indigenous organizations acquired a national political voice, that is, sufficient power and visibility to engage in political dialogue (or conflict) in the arena of national elites (Varese 1993). This capability, in turn, rested on the ascendance of an indigenous intelligentsia, well-educated and adept at communicating their message to diverse audiences of potential supporters (Stavenhagen 1992). Another key feature is the increasing prominence of international support networks—indigenous organizations of a transnational character, non-governmental organizations (NGOs) whose specific purpose is to support indigenous causes—and global shifts in funding priorities of these NGOs toward an increasing concern for the plight of indigenous people. Finally, the national phase is characterized by a common political discourse, which serves to unify indigenous struggles across the hemisphere. Though specifics vary, this discourse is invariably formulated in a national idiom, that is, resting on rights that the state would concede to Indian people, justified with language that runs closely parallel to the self-justificatory rhetoric of the state itself.

The primary alternative to national struggle, still common in the 1960s, was to join forces with transformative movements of the social democratic or revolutionary Left. In nearly every Latin American country with sizeable indigenous populations, there are prominent examples of Left movements, organizations, and political parties, in which indigenous peoples participated in significant numbers, generally under Mestizo or Ladino leadership. The ideologies and programs of these organizations vary widely, as do the specific contents of their analysis and practice with regard to indigenous peoples. At one pole are those whose leaders categorically deny the relevance of cultural difference, defining their struggles in strictly "objective" class terms. The archetype here is the Shining Path revolutionary party in Peru (Starn 1995), though many less extremist movements would fit this category as well. At the other pole (and with increasing frequency in the 1970s and '80s), are serious, if often convoluted, efforts to carve out a place for indigenous demands within a movement whose fundamental character remains unchanged. The telltale phrases in these cases are "secondary contradiction," and the "relative autonomy of culture," and a good example would be the evolving public analysis of the Guatemalan National Revolutionary movement, or URNG (Smith 1990). Irrespective of the variation among them, these Left projects share certain key precepts: class as the primary axis of inequity, capturing (and transforming) the state as the ultimate means to political ends, and the nation as ideological glue, the idiom through which the project is represented as being of and for the people.[11]

When Guillermo Bonfil Batalla (1981) wrote his now classic synthetic overview of Latin American indigenous movements in the late 1970s, he portrayed a still lively internal debate on the advisability of working within (or at least in alliance with) such Left projects. Though many issues were at stake in this debate, its crux was a tension between the allure of participation in movements that promised sweeping corrective transformations of the deep class inequities in Latin American societies, versus the profound irritation of having culturally specific demands postponed or belittled, of having to submit to the authority of leaders who paternalistically "spoke for" indigenous peoples, often prefacing the phrase with the telltale possessive "our." Since that time there has been a steady shift toward consolidation of the alternative position: national struggle epitomized by the demand for autonomy. Rather than attempt a comprehensive chronicle of this process I focus on one case—Nicaraguan cultural politics in the early 1980s. Conflict between the Sandinistas and the Miskitu Indians in Nicaragua is emblematic, because it came to symbolize the unraveling of hopes that a Left movement, after seizing state power, could overcome past deficiencies and address specific indigenous demands in a just and equitable manner. Disillusionment with the Sandinista revolution made the case for national indigenous struggle all the more compelling, portraying it as transcending ideology, applying irrespective of dominant culture divisions between Left and Right.

The Miskitu-Sandinista Conflict and Its Repercussions

Few issues have caused more division and acrimony within the Pan-American Indian movement than the Miskitu-Sandinista conflict in Nicaragua.[12] Within the American Indian Movement (AIM) the repercussions took an especially public form when two brothers, Russell and William Means, both historic leaders of AIM, announced their alignment with diametrically opposed positions;[13] in 1986 World Council of Indigenous Peoples president Clem Chartier took a strong stand in support of the Miskitu opposition, which generated enough resentment among Council members to have him removed from the post;[14] organizations that worked primarily with indigenous struggles and ones that had "solidarity with the revolution" as their primary objective often found themselves on contrary sides of the debate on U.S. foreign policy toward Nicaragua. Most analysts who wrote with authority on the topic were obliged—by the intensity of the conflict if not by our own ethics—to position ourselves as political actors. Some took up the cause of one side or the other with uncritical zeal—in this sense the analyses of Nietschmann (1985, 1989) and Jenkins Molieri (1986) are remarkably symmetrical. Others—myself included—criticized the Sandinistas but believed that reform from within the revolutionary process was necessary and possible.[15]

The problems underlying the conflict in Nicaragua were not new to anyone who had worked at the intersection of Left and indigenous politics in the Americas. Tensions with the Left had festered since the beginning of the indigenous movement's national phase, leading already to a few strong, influential proclamations that denounced dominant culture racism of both Left and Right, and insisted on indigenous autonomy (e.g. Reynaga 1970). Yet throughout the 1970s countervailing examples of apparently functional cooperation between the two could still be found, in the organizations themselves (e.g. the CRIC of Colombia) in solidarity initiatives (e.g. Declaration of Barbados [1971]), and most prominently, in the hopeful analyses of social scientists.[16] Those who wanted to make this argument often pointed to the example of the revolutionary movement in Guatemala, which was rapidly gaining strength in the late 1970s, and seemed to enjoy widespread support from Maya Indian peasants.[17]

Yet after the Sandinista movement successfully ousted the Somoza government power in 1979, Nicaragua became the litmus test. Among Left movements in Latin America the Sandinistas had earned a reputation as highly heterodox, pluralist, and creative, leading many to believe that the Nicaraguan revolution would find its way where others had stumbled. At first optimism on issues of cultural politics seemed warranted, as the Sandinistas recognized and worked closely with MISURASATA, a powerful organization representing the three indigenous peoples of the coastal region. In early 1981 when the conflict first flared up—with the Sandinista government otherwise strong, two other vibrant revolutionary movements in Central America, and the socialist alternative broadly perceived as plausible—skepticism could still be met with confident counter-analysis. Proponents of the Miskitu resistance portrayed MISURASATA as an organization with demands fully consistent with the hemispheric Indian movement, denounced Sandinista policies as preemptively repressive, and explained ties between Miskitu resistance fighters and U.S. government-sponsored aggression as a tactical alliance.[18] Sandinistas and their supporters, in contrast, characterized MISURASATA demands as intentionally provocative and openly separatist, all the more dangerous because Miskitu separatism fit so neatly within the imperial designs of the U.S. government.[19] As seemingly manageable tensions gave way to escalating armed conflict, Nicaraguan "exceptionalism" gave the analysis a very different inflection: if the Sandinistas could not overcome the legacy of racism on the Left, why expect that *anyone* could?

Beyond the National Phase

In retrospect, as the charged micro-political complexity fades into the background, a key defining feature of this conflict comes sharply into view. Both sides framed their own position, and sought to delegitimate their adversary, drawing on the same essential (and ultimately unnegotiable) premises of nationhood, territorial sovereignty, and self-determination.[20] However influential the ideals of socialism in Sandinista ideology, these were largely dispensable compared with the ideals of nationalism: as many analysts have observed, the Nicaraguan revolution was fundamentally a movement of *national* liberation.[21] Likewise, Miskitu leaders were deeply influenced by the now well-established discourse of the Pan-American Indian movement, which makes claims for indigenous peoples' rights based on their status as "nations within."[22] Such reasoning anchored the Miskitu struggle in a compelling legal-historical argument, helped to galvanize a grassroots response of near-utopian passion, and generated an impressive flow of international solidarity. However, these two parallel sets of claims left little space for negotiation: both defined their adversary as irredeemably misguided, and both rested on premises that the other summarily rejected. Armed conflict raged for three years under these conditions, with little hope of resolution.

*   *   *

One could of course argue that the Miskitu-Sandinista conflict was overdetermined by factors that do not generally come into play. Intense U.S.-orchestrated aggression against the Nicaraguan government, including extensive support for Miskitu armed resistance, after all, are not conditions that most indigenous movements can expect to enjoy when they confront intransigent states. Without U.S. backing, Miskitu resistance could not possibly have advanced as far as it did; if the movement had stalled, the great allure of national indigenous struggle could well have diminished accordingly. Yet to allow this line of argument redefine the issue—as many pro-Sandinista analysts did at the time—is to understate and obscure the many internal factors that contributed to the conflict. However definitive in the last analysis, U.S. intervention preyed on pre-existing fissures and blind spots in Sandinista ideology and practice, which had their analogs in every Left movement in Latin America.

These problems, quite apart from the incidence of external intervention, made the case for national indigenous struggle compelling. Racism within the Left, expressed as generic denigration of Indians and in a diminished importance assigned to cultural inequality, is one central irritant. Equally important, however, is the drive for cultural homogenization that characterizes Left variants of nationalism. Sandinista leaders generally displayed both, but tended to acknowledge and correct (at least rhetorically) the former, while leaving the latter unaddressed. It was the latter, in turn, that drove Miskitu

Charles R. Hale

most forcefully to embrace national struggle. In a setting where a "national liberation" movement had just produced such impressive achievements, the message was especially clear: national struggle, for those who belong, is the road to empowerment. If any doubts had remained, they were quickly dispelled by the explosive militancy of Miskitu townspeople's response to this message. While preemptive Sandinista repression may have pushed MISURASATA faster and further, the added impetus was hardly necessary.

As long as the conflict was framed in national terms, reconciliation remained nearly inconceivable. Sandinistas could and did address racism within the party, but it was much more difficult to step back from the assertion that the revolution was made to advance the interests of a unified national-popular subject. The Miskitu indigenous movement, in turn, found its stride with the invocation of national struggle. With external financial support, a compelling internationally legitimated discourse of rights, and immense grassroots support, leaders found no convincing rationale for compromise. The keyword around which their own position congealed, which came to epitomize the entire conflict, was "autonomy." This explained what Miskitu people were fighting for, and why the Sandinista government could not back down. The next section explores why autonomy achieves such centrality for indigenous movements, and examines the problems these movements confront, when autonomy becomes the primary focus of struggle.

(2)

Autonomy is the quintessential demand in the national phase of indigenous struggle. The specific contents are far from uniform across the dozens of cases where indigenous peoples have made this demand. Indeed the great variability in the details is surely one key to its widespread appeal: otherwise it might be difficult for a small, peripherally located people (e.g. Kuna of Panama) and a majority population such as the Maya of Guatemala both to find so much resonance in the same term. Yet despite this variability, the indigenous demand for autonomy does have important defining features: the claim to a discrete culture and identity as a people (*pueblo*), the designation of a physical territory that reinforces and derives from this collective identity, and the insistence on collective legal recognition, which inherently alters the standard presumption that the nation-state represents each citizen equally, *as an individual.*

The reasons that demands for autonomy have such power and efficacy among indigenous peoples are at least four-fold. In the first place, to demand autonomy is to register a forceful critique that sets the record straight. It reveals the hypocrisy of state discourses from "national security" to "social welfare," showing them to be generally predicated on assimilation to a single cultural standard, which at best assigns cultural oppression lower priority than other forms of inequality, and at worst delegitimates struggles for cultural rights altogether. The critique is more persuasive because it applies across the ideological spectrum, showing that the Left is just as capable of racism and assimilationist policies as the Right—as the Sandinista-Miskitu conflict allegedly demonstrated. Second, demands for autonomy lend strong support to efforts of identity formation, invoking a deep sense of boundedness and cultural difference, promising to demarcate and reconstitute the identities of peoples who have suffered and lost so much since the European invasion. Third, autonomy offers a means to address indigenous people's urgent material needs, without forcing a false choice between material satisfaction and cultural rights. The ubiquitous claims of spiritual ties to "Mother Earth" is an excellent example of this fusion—making the demand for an autonomous land base and the affirmation of indigenous spirituality one and the same. Finally, autonomy provides a common political language that links indigenous peoples throughout the hemisphere (and beyond). This common purpose across disparate experiences is empowering: a continent-wide movement of some 40 million indigenous peoples conveys a sense of efficacy and strength in numbers that isolated struggles could not. Moreover, this shared political objective helps to generate financial support from western governments, international agencies, and NGOs: rather than having to understand the complexities of each individual case, donors can proceed with reasonable surety that "autonomy" is a minimal, essential objective shared by them all.

It goes without saying that the practical and logistical details of autonomy are immensely easier to imagine when the indigenous group in question constitutes a small portion of the population, which claims a discrete, peripheral and relatively small territory as its homeland. The latter applies, for example, to the Kuna people of Panama, who have one of the most long-standing and successful autonomous governments in the Americas. They number about 35,000 in a total Panamanian population of two million, and the land they claim as their territory is located in a discrete, peripheral area of the country (Howe 1986a, 1991). The other extreme is the Maya of Guatemala, who even by conservative measures constitute a majority of the country's ten million people, and who are majority inhabitants in at least half the country's 22 administrative divisions.[23] These conditions blur the sharp rationale for autonomy, because the logistics become so complex, and because a well-organized Maya population could theoretically achieve even more ambitious ends through the well-established principle of majority rule. Yet it is testimony to the allure of autonomy that for the Maya too it has emerged as a galvanizing demand, which in turn is taken as a sign that the Maya movement has become a major force in national politics.[24]

Charles R. Hale

As compelling as the demand for autonomy may be, clear demonstrations of its efficacy as a political program are difficult to find. For this reason Nicaragua—one of the few places where autonomy was formally implemented—is again an important case to consider. The standoff between the Miskitu and the Sandinistas ended dramatically in late 1984. Sandinista leaders simultaneously announced their willingness to negotiate with Miskitu rebels and to grant autonomy to the coastal region. Although far from uniform or unilinear, the broad tendency of Miskitu opposition groups was to accept both offers. The region gradually returned to a tenuous peace, and by late 1987 the National Assembly had passed legislation to grant autonomy to the Atlantic Coast region. Readings of this negotiated transition to autonomy are nearly as contested as the conflict itself. Some have interpreted the outcome as evidence of the validity of the original claim: the Sandinista leadership underwent a learning process, and devised a political formula that (as their own slogan had it) "recognized cultural diversity as a means to forge national unity." The Nicaraguan case demonstrates, as Héctor Diaz Polanco (1991) has forcefully argued, that indigenous autonomy and national-popular revolution are compatible after all. Analysts of the opposing perspective denounced the Sandinista-backed autonomy law as little more than a Machiavellian plan for "administrative restructuring," which reaped political capital while ceding no real power.[25]

Although one could easily identify a middle ground between these two portrayals, here I simply want to focus on the fundamental concessions that had to occur before the process of negotiated settlement could proceed.[26] Of the three essential precepts of national indigenous struggle—nationhood, territorial sovereignty and self-determination—all were present in early MISURASATA documents, but none survived the negotiations intact. In the autonomy law approved by the National Assembly in September 1987, nationhood had been rendered as "ethnic communities," territorial sovereignty as "communal lands, waters and forests that have traditionally belonged to the communities," and self-determination as "participation" in a series of decision-making processes, "in accordance with national policies, plans and guidelines," within the framework of a "unitary state." While this examination of legal fine print far from exhausts the issue, it is revealing nonetheless. The claim that the autonomy law was mere rhetorical posturing faces abundant evidence to the contrary, the most persuasive of which, perhaps, is the continuing vigorous opposition by most Nicaraguan elites. However, the assertion that it demonstrates *even a theoretical* compatibility between the national-popular Left and indigenous struggles against marginality is strained at best. This assertion holds only if Indians completely concede the terrain of the national, a step that most movements would consider a fatal step backward.

Beyond the National Phase

When defined with expansive terms like self-determination and territorial sovereignty, demands for autonomy can rarely be expected to prosper. Dominant sectors, especially those connected directly with the state, are likely to conclude that "unnegotiable" principles have been threatened, and to respond with intransigence. This certainly was the case in Nicaragua, when Sandinista officials took Miskitu leaders' use of such terms as *prima facie* evidence that their true intentions were to separate a large swath of territory from Nicaragua and declare independence. The Sandinistas' first impulse was to crush the initiative militarily, and unfortunately, a similar response could be expected from most Latin American states. Given the brute realities in the configuration of political-military force in Latin America, indigenous movements have persisted in such confrontations only with considerable aid from a very powerful third party—as was the case for the Miskitu, and decades earlier, the Kuna.[27] Once such external aid is forthcoming, however, fears that autonomy is simply a veil for outright separatism take on greater plausibility and a self-fulfilling character. In short, expansive versions of the demand for autonomy, however justified in historical, ethical and legal terms, are set up to fail for the purely pragmatic reason that, for indigenous peoples, the ensuing conflict is so uneven and deadly.

Even if they are not ultimately successful, however, expansive versions of autonomy can be effective in creating openings, setting in motion a process of negotiation and compromise from which indigenous peoples can benefit considerably. Examples of successful implementation of some "compromise" version of autonomy are more common and more theoretically plausible. Typically, the key facilitating concessions that the indigenous movement must make include: to recognize the integrity of a single centrally constituted nation-state, the supreme authority of that state in key arenas such as the use of armed or coercive force, international affairs, and tax collection, and finally, a general subjugation of autonomy to interests of national security. This leaves important realms of rights on the negotiating table—the use and management of resources within the autonomous region, the exercise of local self-government, the administration of social services, and the codification and practice of customary law (*derecho conseuduinario*), to name a few. Such achievements are far from insignificant.

The problem in this case, however, is that once the initial (pragmatically necessary) concessions have been granted, the resulting arrangement is compatible with, if not directly beneficial to, the interests of the state. The sharpest edges of indigenous militancy are smoothed down, leaving indigenous leaders who have traded reluctant recognition of the state's fundamental authority for specific gains toward state endorsement of their rights to manage local affairs. Potential benefits of such an exchange notwithstanding, the grave

Charles R. Hale

danger is that indigenous leaders take on responsibility and public account- 169
ability for self-government, without the political-economic power to deliver
on the much heightened popular expectations generated by the new arrangement. Autonomy then becomes a recipe for corruption and factional disputes,
disillusionment and bitterness, and even the conclusion that "we cannot really
run our own affairs after all." This has been the main outcome to date in the
implementation of a compromise version of autonomy in Nicaragua. It also
helps to explain why "municipal autonomy," which granted Maya townships
a significant increased measure of local political control in Guatemala, was
introduced in 1985 by a centrist government as a tactic to advance counter-
insurgency objectives, and has at least partially served those ends.

More generally, these problems with autonomy are symptomatic of a
central predicament of indigenous marginality throughout Latin America.
Indigenous peoples are subjected to class exploitation and, in addition, to a
pervasive and powerful discourse that defines the terms of belonging within
the dominant society. This discourse explains indigenous people's exclusion
from society's benefits as a product of their own flawed culture, prescribes
disciplinary measures when their collective behavior turns threatening, and
ultimately, justifies their oppression. Except in extreme cases, this discourse
does extend an invitation to join the society and nation, but the terms are
costly. To belong, indigenous peoples must relinquish the potential power
that comes with specific cultural rights, and conform to the pursuit of
individual advancement within a hierarchical dominant society, confronting
political-economic inequity combined with the added stigma of proximity to
an Indian past. Yet the alternative path—to assert a distinctive collective
identity and associated cultural rights—can bring about unintended consequences that also have their costs. First, an assertion of cultural difference can
reinforce the dominant association of indigenous culture with backward-
looking primordialism, which precludes claims to rights associated with the
modernist ideals of citizenship and individual equality. Second, if demands
for autonomy rest on the same precepts as the discourse of nation-state
building, there will be a tendency to obscure inequities within the group, to
empower certain sectors who speak in the name of the collectivity, and silence
others. Finally, the prospects for broader alliances are apt to suffer: as long as
national precepts animate indigenous mobilization, success will accentuate
ethnic boundaries, thereby deepening the divide between indigenous peoples
and lower class members of the dominant culture.

At the heart of this predicament lies the binary framing of political
choices: indigenous people are forced to choose between collective and individual rights, between collective unity and the recognition of internal diversity, between ethnic and class solidarities. To demand autonomy is to accept

this very framing of the choices, to appropriate the basic precepts of nation building, and put them to the service of people who have always been excluded from its benefits. It is an audacious strategy, which in retrospect has worked remarkably well, but not without heavy costs. Indians are pitted against the state, yet virtually forced to use the state's discourse against itself, and even obliged to measure success by what the state will concede. However debilitating these costs, until recently indigenous peoples have been in no position to embark on the search for a new idiom of struggle. In the section that follows I suggest that we are entering a period when, in a gradual and preliminary way, this search has begun.

(3)

During the decade after the Sandinista-Miskitu conflict, the Left descended into a crisis of confidence and efficacy. The Sandinista electoral defeat of 1990 provided some of the more visible evidence of a much deeper shift under way: discussion of alternatives to market capitalism faded to a whisper, leaving the neo-liberal agenda to set the parameters for most serious political debate. The demise of Soviet bloc socialism powerfully contributed to this shift, less because these regimes had inspired genuine admiration than because they had helped, both materially and ideologically, to keep alternatives to capitalism possible to imagine.[28]

Bleak prospects for revolutionary transformation must not be confused, however, with political passivity. To the contrary, the 1980s witnessed a surge in grassroots activism of a different sort—revolving around a multiplicity of discrete identities, focused more on achieving diverse grassroots demands than seizing state power, eschewing large, hierarchical organizations in favor of local initiatives and situational alliances—what some have referred to as "new social movements."[29] Indigenous movements also gained strength steadily throughout the hemisphere, and though indigenous activism does not fit neatly with all the premises underlying the phrase "new social movements," it does run parallel to the broader trend. By the early 1990s evidence of indigenous organizations' dynamism could be found at every level, from community-based to transnational initiatives, often strongly encouraged and supported by external funding agencies.[30]

The anti-quincentenary campaign, which received ample funding mainly from European sources, exemplifies this new prominence. Controversy surrounding this campaign—especially evident in the Congress of Quetzaltenango (Xela), Guatemala in 1991—followed lines reminiscent of the Miskitu-Sandinista conflict, but with a completely different outcome. By that time the balance of power had been reversed: organizations of the Left actively sought an association with the indigenous movement to shore up their own

Charles R. Hale

legitimacy and power of persuasion. Over the course of a decade the question had changed fundamentally, from "should we join the Left?" to "should we allow them to join us?" This event, I suggest, both epitomized the consummation of "national" indigenous organizing, and contained seeds of the transition to a subsequent phase. It forms part of a process whereby indigenous militancy is transforming Left ideology and practice at their very roots.

Identity Politics in the Anti-Quincentenary Campaign[31]

Although conceived in part as a reaction against arrogant plans for a "quincentenary jubilee," the indigenous-led anti-quincentenary campaign soon had received more funding and public attention than the celebration itself. Campaign organizers recruited participants from throughout the Americas, moving beyond the confines of reactive politics, seizing the opportunity to advance longer term objectives: to reinforce transnational network of progressive organizations, catalyze local struggles, catch the attention of funding sources, and transmit the powerful message, "we have resisted for 500 years and we are stronger today than ever." After successful meetings in Colombia (1989) and Ecuador (1990), the initiative passed to Guatemala, where some 300 delegates converged for a week in late October 1991.

The choice of the 1991 conference site was significant for a number of reasons. Armed conflict in Guatemala had dragged on for 30 years and the guerrilla movement remained active, though much diminished in scope and influence. The Guatemala Armed Forces had "won" the war with methods of systematic state terror and repression approaching genocide, and in 1991 their political power remained determinant. Yet in 1985 the Armed Forces had formally returned the state to civilian hands, initiating a "democratic opening" that involved a significant reduction of internal political repression, a reintroduction of the trappings of electoral politics, and a much heightened official concern for Guatemala's international image. This helps to explain why state officials permitted the conference in the first place, even though it could be expected to give a platform to well-known opposition figures such as Rigoberta Menchú, provide a setting for dialogue among diverse organizations identified with progressive politics throughout the country, and indeed, to forge such ties across the hemisphere.

The choice of Guatemala as conference site also resonated with the reconfiguration of politics that occurred had since the "opening" of 1985. Among the diverse organizations that emerged to occupy and widen this political opening, by the early 1990s two principal tendencies had taken shape. One revolved around identities and political demands rooted directly in experiences of Left-aligned mobilization and state repression over the

Beyond the National Phase

previous decade (e.g. unions, peasant syndicates, organizations representing widows, families of the disappeared, refugees). Most of these sought to strike a balance between claims to ties with pre-existing Left initiatives, and emphasis on new identities, creative departures from old political molds. Including both indigenous and dominant culture (*ladino*) participants, these organizations distanced themselves from exclusively ethnic self-descriptions, and took on the generic identity *popular*. For organizations of the second tendency—which claimed the self-descriptive term *indígena*—the rupture with political models of the past decade was much more definitive, driven by an overriding focus on indigenous cultural rights, and a sharp critique of the Left's inability to address these issues. By 1991 key protagonists of the *indígena* stance had begun to speak of the Maya peoples' rights to autonomy, explicitly differentiating themselves from *populares*, who emphasized cross-ethnic class alliances focused on such issues as human rights, political reform, and material well-being for all Guatemalans. The Xela conference took on great significance, then, in its promise to promote dialogue across the *indígena-popular* divide. Rigoberta Menchú, the central figure of the conference, exemplified this promise; as a Maya woman who had been strongly associated with the revolutionary movement, she stood as proof that the central conference slogan—"indigenous and *popular* unity"—was within the reach of the anti-quincentenary campaign.[32]

Most analyses of the conference (my own included) have emphasized how elusive this "unity" turned out to be. Though numerous, complex and difficult to summarize, the issues in contention at the conference tended to follow the contours of the *indígena-popular* divide. *Populares* situated themselves within the realm of national-popular political aspirations, fusing anti-imperialism, class struggle and national liberation in a manner consistent with a long-standing Left/revolutionary tradition in Latin America. *Indígenas*, in contrast, made anti-colonialism their keyword, assigned priority to the struggle for autonomy against residual "colonialist" tendencies of both Left and Right, and insisted that the movement's identity be defined by features specific to Indian culture (e.g. pre-Conquest heritage, spirituality, relationship to the land). *Populares* generally controlled the conference, because they had achieved the majority in the organizing committee and in most country delegations. Many *indígenas* concluded the week-long activities feeling marginalized, without a voice, spoken for by others. Grumbling from the margins was rampant; more than once conflicts flared up, giving rise to urgent efforts of mediation to avert a major crisis.[33]

Yet even as they were outvoted and outmaneuvered in formal conference proceedings, in retrospect *indígenas* never lost the upper hand. In the first place, the very idea of a campaign grounded in "500 years of resistance"

Charles R. Hale

reinforced the primacy of *indígena* identity and struggle. Although non-Indians of most political colors in Latin America have found ways to put Indian symbols to the service of their own projects, the insistence on continuous resistance since 1492 makes such appropriation awkward and difficult to carry off. *Popular* discourse inevitably gravitates toward 19th century independence wars and nation building, thereby anchoring resistance in a time when Mestizos were political subjects in their own right. By privileging the "500 years" idea, including resistance against the "neo-colonial" nation-state, the campaign almost inevitably cede initiative to *indígenas*. More broadly, the fact that Left organizations assigned so much importance to the anti-quincentenary campaign, far from a sign of strength, signaled a crisis-ridden search for new sources of political legitimacy and dynamism. The outpouring of international NGO support for *indígena*-centered anti-quincentenary politics, as opposed, for example, to the traditional work of Left-aligned labor unions, political parties, or peasant leagues could only have driven home the urgency of this search. Quite literally, it began to pay to be Indian—or at least to take up *indígena* causes. In part this popularity can be attributed to shifts in external funding priorities, but a large part of the impetus also came from within: by the early 1990s *indígena* organizations were among the most effective and creative forms of oppositional politics in Latin America.[34]

While in the immediate aftermath of the conference it appeared that the *populares* had successfully "cashed in" on *indígena* dynamism, it soon became clear that the *popular* "victory" of Xela would be pyrrhic. Disgruntled *indígena* organizations withdrew from the anti-quincentenary campaign in protest, which threw it into financial and political crisis. Although some Indian leaders of international stature—most notably Menchú—remained identified with the campaign, their attempts to raise funds for the culminating meeting of 1992 confronted critique and competition from the opposing *indígena* tendency. Presented with contradictory claims to authenticity—who represents "true" indigenous interests?—potential funders backed away from the issue altogether. On a vote that split largely along *indígena-popular* lines, the Xela plenary had decided that the culminating conference would be held in Managua, Nicaragua. Many *indígena* organizations refused to participate because they viewed Managua as too strongly symbolic of the *popular* standpoint, and because they had become alienated from the campaign itself. They declared instead that for 1992, leaders should "concentrate on work at the grassroots." Especially compared to the previous year, the Managua conference of 1992 was lack-luster: It suffered from inadequate funding, the absence of many key participants, and an undertone of conflict that drained much of the excitement and momentum which had mounted over the past three years.

Beyond the National Phase

174 At one time projected to continue and build well beyond 1992, the "500 years campaign," without *indígena* support, quickly faded into insignificance.

A parallel process of change occurred at the level of grassroots organization and political strategy in many countries of the region. The case of Guatemala is illustrative. Until the Xela meeting of 1991, the distinction between *indígena* and *popular* organizations and their demands could be clearly identified and systematically documented (see e.g. Bastos and Camus 1992). This clarity dissipated in the months that followed, as disillusionment with the outcome in Xela began to reverberate. In at least one case a split ensued within a *popular* organization, reportedly provoked by one of the leaders who criticized the inadequate importance assigned to Maya cultural rights within the organization.[35] In addition, *popular* organizations began to take on positions more consonant with those of their *indígena* counterparts—explicitly confronting questions of indigenous rights within their organizations, even taking up the indigenous demand for autonomy.[36] Rigoberta Menchú, who had been deeply identified with the *populares*, increasingly sought to position herself as a bridge between the two, and shifted her own public discourse accordingly. Her receipt of the Nobel Peace Prize in 1992, an act steeped in political symbolism for the *indígena* cause, gave further impetus to this shift.[37]

* * *

If at the beginning of the 1980s indigenous movements still debated the question of their relationship to the Left, with *populares* representing one pole and national indigenous struggle the other, a decade later this debate showed clear signs of coming to a close. Through clumsy attempts to orchestrate the Xela conference to their advantage, *populares* dominated the proceedings, but this may actually have contributed to the already notable decline in their own efficacy. From that point on in Guatemala the debate took on new parameters: the specificity of indigenous organization and demands, rather than informing one possible alternative of struggle, moved toward the status of unquestioned premise for progressive initiatives. The same shift was already well under way in other key sites of indigenous struggle throughout Latin America, amounting to clear evidence that the national phase of indigenous struggle had been consummated.

At the same time, this very ascendancy has helped to open new terrain. Indigenous organizations have been able to revisit the question of cross-ethnic alliance, for example, no longer as alienated by the demand for unity around someone else's unnegotiable principles. The very meaning of "alliance" in these cases has been transformed, such that indigenous identity and cultural rights, rather than being subsumed within a broader project, offer orienting principles and strategies which non-Indians actively choose to follow. An early and still incomplete expression of this shift can be found in the anti-quincentenary campaign, when a broad cross-ethnic movement congealed around a specifically Indian issue; other analyses that portray Indian culture as broader political catalyst have come from Colombia, Ecuador, and Bolivia.[38] Although the national phase of indigenous struggle will surely predominate for some time to come, these changes suggest that a distinct phase of struggle may be on the horizon.

(4)

The mandate for national struggle has confronted indigenous peoples with a strategic dilemma: how to achieve demands of sufficient scope to eliminate the roots of indigenous marginality, yet moderate enough to assuage dominant sector fears of separatism? The more powerful and effective the expression of these national indigenous demands, the more acute the dilemma has grown. State repression is far from an idle threat in this equation: state elites perceive expansive national movements, epitomized by the demand for autonomy, as paramount to territorial dismemberment, and respond accordingly. But even apart from omnipresent threat of state repression, underlying the dilemma is a dichotomous choice: cultural difference and collective rights, whose logical extension is separation *versus* individual rights of citizenship, which paves the way for cultural homogeneity and assimilation. If indeed indigenous struggles are in the midst of a transition to an emergent phase, it will be defined fundamentally by a defiance of this dichotomy, which itself reiterates the cultural logic of nation-state building.

This emergent transnational phase of indigenous struggle can be contrasted to national struggle in at least four ways. First, the image of mutually exclusive building blocks of identity (e.g. peasant versus Indian, class versus ethnic) conceives each constituent group as having a discrete, bounded culture, and subordinates them all to the overarching unified cultural attributes of the nation. Transnational identities, by contrast, are apt to have blurred boundaries and hybrid or multiple affinities, which disrupt this ideal of a neat isomorphic order of national politics. Second, transnational indigenous demands move beyond the confines of the state-society dyad, whereby each constituent group juxtaposes its own interests to those of the state. Even indigenous autonomy, the quintessential demand of the national phase, would gradually be superseded, precisely because it rests so implicitly on the premises of this dyad. Demands for the state to allocate resources, recognize rights, and properly carry out stately responsibilities would remain important, but deemphasized in relation to other demands (local or transnational) which have the objective of sidestepping the state altogether. Third, the shift implies a defiance of national boundaries. Transnational identity politics are distinguished not by relations between entities that belong to a given nation (the appropriate term in this case is *inter*national), but rather, by identities and demands that render these very boundaries obsolete. A pan-American indigenous movement that promotes common cause between Aymara of Bolivia and Maya of Guatemala, for example, can easily remain within the *inter*national frame; an organization of Zapotec Indians that represents members in both Oaxaca and California, by contrast, has entered the realm of the transnational.[39] A final characteristic involves processes of representation. This involves, first, a heightened concern for processes by which such movements are represented to themselves and to the outside; and second, a transformed spacial and technological context in which this representation takes place. It is rare today for indigenous leaders to have not been deeply influenced by international travel and political interaction. Their repertoire of images, technological sophistication, and self-conscious deliberation in the formulation of political discourse has increased immensely, leading to forms of representation that move readily from local to global and back again. The state, once the unavoidably central interlocutor in these representational practices, is now often reduced to the role of incensed bystander.

All four factors are present to some degree in the Zapatista uprising, indeed, thinking about Chiapas has been influential in this preliminary delineation. A certain excitement for the Zapatistas' potential to open new paths for indigenous cultural politics, and subaltern politics more broadly, naturally follows. However, I also want these concluding lines to be cautionary, because the Mexican state seems poised to prevail in Chiapas, and more broadly, because the potential for creative renewal seems at least matched by the threat of a newly forged hegemony, degenerative fragmentation and *de facto* powerlessness. It is too early to do much more than raise serious questions of efficacy, to insist that the shift itself is still incipient and the consequences far from clear. Mexican cultural critic Carlos Monsiváis makes this final point eloquently in response to his own rhetorical question: "Is it possible to speak of a 'post-nationalism'?" He continues:

> . . . I say yes when I associate nationalism with the Mexican revolution, and consider how nationalism is deeply implicated with every oppressive government policy. My answer is negative when I take into account the crushing weight of inequality in the lives of Mexicans and Latin Americans, and think about the other role of nationalism, an internal language of the oppressed.[40]

National indigenous struggle does entail a powerful "internal language" that Indian peoples have fruitfully put to the service of their cause, and it persists at least in part because an equally effective alternative language has not yet emerged. Yet it would be seriously neglectful to gloss over the contradictions that national struggle has entailed, to obscure the rumblings of internal critique, and the changes under way. If the aim of the national phase of indigenous movements was to convert marginality into political advantage, transnational struggle seeks to displace the center-margin spacial metaphor altogether as a defining feature of politics. This strategy entails no guarantees, and there is much reason to expect that root causes of marginality would remain. Its potential lies in the promise to open alternative paths of struggle, allowing indigenous peoples to proceed according to political ideals more of their own making, less obliged to accept precepts fixed in place by the very forces that they most vigorously oppose.

Notes

1. Earlier versions of this chapter were presented at two meetings of the "Marginal Populations" Working Group, and I have benefitted much from discussions in those settings. In particular, my special thanks goes to Sam Nolutshungu, for insightful comments and encouragement in the preparation of this final version. Many of the ideas contained in this essay were worked out in the context of discussions and collaborative work with Stefano Varese and Carol A. Smith; thanks also to both of them.

2. See interview with Stanford anthropologist George Collier, summarized in the *Stanford Observer (Summarized in Stanford Observer,* Vol. 29, #3, p. 10.). Whether or not the causal link is that direct, there is no doubt that the international financial community views the continued existence of the Zapatistas as deeply inimical to Mexico's investment climate. Shockingly frank confirmation of these perceptions comes from a memo written by economist Riordan Roett, to the "Chase Manhattan Emerging Markets Group" (13 January 1995): "While Chiapas, in our opinion, does not pose a fundamental threat to Mexican political stability, it is perceived to be so by many in the investment community. The government will need to eliminate the Zapatistas to demonstrate their effective control of the national territory and of security policy."

3. From an editorial of the *Washington Post* (1/12/94).

4. This is a composite quotation from George Collier, "Perspective on Mexico: Rebellion Against Economic Exile," *Los angeles Times* editorial, 23 January 1994 and from Collier (1994: 7).

5. "Mendicino's Pomos Find their Tribal Voice" *San Francisco Chronicle*, 4/11/94.

6. Alma Guillermoprieto, whose analysis of Latin American culture and politics is generally superb, reveals her adherence to this dichotomous paradigm of ethnicity in the following passage:

> " . . . the first thing we learned [in our trip to the E.Z.L.N. stronghold] was that the new Zapatistas were not the most backward, or even the poorest, campesinos

of Chiapas—Maya tied to their exhausted small farms in the highlands by tradition and passivity—but rather, the innovators: adventurous frontiersmen and women who were convinced that they could make a new world.

The passage associates "Indianness" with being passive and tradition-bound, and implies that being an adventurous innovator somehow makes one less Indian. *New Yorker*, May 16, 1994, p. 52-53.

7. A sustained critique of this instrumentalist approach to ethnicity, in the context of a broader discussion of ethnicity theory, can be found in Hale (1994a, chapter 1).

8. Spacial variation within a given historical moment—an important facet of this topic—is unfortunately beyond the scope of discussion here.

9. This means of delimiting phases while avoiding the implication of stage theory is directly indebted to Stuart Hall's (1988) analysis of the two distinct "moments" of contemporary ethnic/racial politics in Britain and other parts of the West. My debt is also at the substantive level, in the sense that Hall's conception of these phases—"relations of representation" versus "burden of representation"—has influenced my own argument regarding the content of the national and transnational phases of indigenous struggle.

10. This is emphatically not to imply that "real" resistance did not occur previously, or conversely, that indigenous resistance before the national phase was somehow more genuine or culturally pure. To cite one of many examples, Irene Silverblatt's (1994) recent article eloquently demonstrates how, from the very onset of colonialism, native peoples actively created their identities as Indians through a contradictory process of resistance that included partial complicity with key precepts of colonial rule.

11. There is a prior moment in the history of the Latin American Left when nationalism was less important and variants of class-based internationalism held sway. For a theoretical statement that provides an essential starting point in the explanation of how Left projects became so firmly articulated with "national-popular" discourse, see Ernesto Laclau (1977).

12. A good gauge of this impact is the coverage of the conflict in *Akwesasne Notes*, a leading publication of North American Indian culture and politics. Although news on indigenous peoples of Latin America is sporadic in the publication, nearly every issue between 1981 and 1985 included coverage of Nicaragua. The focus of the articles was mainly supportive of the Miskitu resistance, but with considerable anguish and various attempts to give voice to the contrary stance. See, for example, a declaration by *Notes* editor John Mohawk (1982).

13. Although it is arguably the case that Russell Means abandoned the principles of AIM altogether through open alignment with the Reagan Administration and libertarian causes, his stance in support of the Miskitu opposition was not much more extreme than many Indian leaders took at the time. Moreover, the seeds of this position can be discerned in his famous declaration (1980). William Means remained a strong supporter of the Sandinistas, expressed mainly through the International Treaty Council, the international counter-part to AIM. See *Treaty*

14. For more information on this point, see Hale (1994a: 171-76 passim, and footnote 15).

15. See, for example, the account by Gordon (1991) of the closely related conflict between Afro-Nicaraguans (Creoles) and the revolution. This stance of critique from within was best expressed in the daily practice of such Miskitu leaders as Norman Bent, Amalia Dixon, and Jorge Matamoros.

16. See the "Plataforma política de CRIC" published in Bonfil (1981: 300-314). A good example of social science analysis that is sanguine about Left-indigenous cooperation is the collection of essays in Diaz Polanco (1985), and the work of Roxanne Dunbar Ortiz (e.g. 1984).

17. One example of many is the publication titled "Indian Guatemala: Path to Liberation" (Wheaton and Frank 1984). For a complete survey of these sources, see Smith et al. (1987).

18. See, for example, Wiggins (1981) and Nietschmann (1983, 1984).

19. See, for example, Jenkins Molieri (1986) and Dunbar Ortiz (1984).

20. Detailed substantiation of this point, with specific reference to the question of land rights, can be found in Hale (1994b),

21. This argument is stated in an especially forceful manner in Dunkerley (1990).

22. Many of the key theoretical texts supporting this conception of rights have come from North America, where the treaty experience gives the argument a strong legal-historical point of reference. See, for example, Manuel and Posluns (1974), and Deloria and Lytle (1984). George Manuel was the first president of the World Council of Indigenous Peoples (WCIP), which played a key role in promoting this perspective through yearly meetings of indigenous peoples from throughout the Americas. For an early history of the WCIP, see Sanders (1977).

23. Demographic data on the ethnic distribution of Guatemala's population can be found in Adams (1990b).

24. See COMG (1990, 1995) and especially Cojtí Cuxil (1994) for influential statements of "the specific rights of the Maya people" in which autonomy figures prominently as the organizing principle.

25. The quotation comes from MISURASATA (1985: 13); the argument is reiterated in Nietschmann (1989).

26. This paragraph draws directly on the more extensive analysis in Hale (1995).

27. For an interesting comparison of the similarities in these two cases, see Howe (1986b).

28. Emblematic is a recent cover of *NACLA*, one of the leading Left-oriented publication on Latin America in the United States, whose title reads "The Latin American Left: A Painful Rebirth" (Volume XXV, No. 5 1992). The articles contained therein, however, seem to convey more pain than rejuvenation.

29. The literature on this topic is enormous. For an overview see Escobar and Alvarez (1992).

30. During the 1980s the idea of indigenous rights and self-development went mainstream, gaining recognition in specially designated programs of USAID,

the World Bank, the European Community and most recently, a multilateral indigenous development fund endorsed by nearly every state in the Americas.

31. The paragraphs that follow summarize an argument presented in much more detail in Hale (1994c).

32. Menchú, though in exile since 1982, had gained great international notoriety mainly through the difussion of her testimony *I . . . Rigoberta Menchú*.
    The campaign to promote her candidacy for the Nobel Peace prize, granted a year later, was launched at the Xela conference.

33. I use the term *"indigenas"* here to refer specifically to the political position described in the preceding lines. I reserve the terms Indian and indigenous to refer more generally to a culture and identity, without specifying the associated political project. This distinction is important, in order to emphasize that Indians can and do opt for a range of political projects, not only *indígena* ones.

34. For a useful overview, see Albó (1991). A major exception to this trend, which Albó barely mentions, much less explains, is the highlands of Peru. There a majority Quechua Indian population has opted primarily for forms of political organization that do not emphasize *indígena* identity and cultural rights, and therefore depart sharply from the general pattern of national indigenous struggle. For an exploratory explanation for this divergence, see Degregori (1993).

35. The organization in question is the Coordinadora Nacional Indígena y Campesina (CONIC). The addition of "indígena" to the name stands in direct contrast to the organization from which the split occurred, the "Comité de Unidad Campesina" (CUC). A full account of these internal machinations has yet to be published.

36. *Majawil Q'ij*, a coalition of roughly ten organizations, represented the bulwark of the *popular* standpoint during the Xela conference. Three years later a discussion with a *Majawil* spokesperson in which I took part yielded a discourse that had merged with that of the *indígenas* on many important points.

37. For a recent statement characteristic of this convergence with the *indígena* stance, see Menchú (1992).

38. The argument to this effect in Colombia comes from Finji (1992); Suzana Sawyer has reported that in some cases mestizo peasants have looked to leaders of the indigenous organization CONAIE for leadership (1995 and personal communication); Albó (1987) and Rivera Cusicanqui (1986) make this argument for Bolivia. The most striking case in point, of course, is the present uprising in Chiapas.

39. See, for example, Kearney and Nagengast (1990) and Kearney (1991).

40. From a speech reprinted in *Uno Mas Uno* (From a speech reprinted in *La Jornada*, 6 June 1993), my translation.

Bibliography

Adams, Richard N.
  1990a Ethnic Images and Strategies in 1944. *In* C.A. Smith (ed.) *Guatemalan Indians and the State: 1540 to 1988*. Austin: University of Texas Press.

Charles R. Hale

1990b Algunas observaciones sobre el cambio étnico en Guatemala. *Anales Acaemdia de* 181
Geografía e Historia de Guatemala. LXIV, pp. 197-224.

Albó, Xavier

1991 El retorno del indio. *Revista Andina*, No. 2

Bastos, Santiago and Manuela Camus

1992 *Quebrando el Silencia.* Guatemala: FLACSO.

Bonfil Batalla, Guillermo

1981 *Utopía y Revolución.* Mexico: Editorial Nueva Imagen.

Burns, Bradford

1980 *The Poverty of Progress.* Berkeley: University of California Press.

Churchill, Ward (ed.)

1983 *Marxism and Native Americans.* Boston: South End Press.

Cojtí Cuxil, Demetrio

1994 Políticas para la Reivindicación de los Mayas de Hoy. Guatemala: Cholsamaj.

Collier, George

1995 *Basta! Land and the Zapatista Rebellion in Chiapas.* Oakland: Food First.

COMG

1990 Derechos Específicos del Pueblo Maya. Guatemala: COMG

1995 *Construyendo un Futuro para nuestro Pasado.* Guatemala: Cholsamaj.

Declaration of Barbados

1971 Published in: W. Dostal (ed.) *The Situation of the Indian in South America.* Geneva: WCIP (1972)

Degregori, Carlos Iván

1993 Identidad Etnica, Movimientos Sociales y Participación Política en el Perú. *In* Alberto Adrianzén et al. (eds.) *Democracia, etnicidad y violencia política en los países andinos.* Lima: IEP.

Deloria, Vine and C. Lytle

1984 *The Nations Within: The Past and Future of American Indian Sovereignty.* New York: Pantheon.

Díaz Polanco, Héctor

1985 La cuestión étnico-nacional. Mexico: Editorial Linea.

1991 *Autonomía de los pueblos indígenas.* Mexico: Siglo XXI.

Dunbar Ortiz, Roxanne

1984 Indians of the Americas. Human Rights and Self-Determination. New York: Praeger.

Dunkerley, James

1990 Reflections on the Nicaraguan Election. *New Left Review* 182: 33-51.

Escobar, Arturo and Sonia Alvarez (eds.)

1992 *The Making of Social Movements in Latin America.* Boulder: Westview.

Finji, María Teresa

1992 From Resistance to Social Movement: The Indigenous Authorities Movement in Colombia. *In* A. Escobar and S. Alvarez (eds.) *The Making of Social Movements in Latin America.* Boulder: Westview. pp. 112-133.

Gordon, Edmund T.

1991 Anthropology and Liberation. *In*: Faye Harrison (ed.) *Decolonizing Anthropology.* Washington D.C.: American Anthropological Association.

Guillermoprieto, Alma

182   1994 *New Yorker*. May 16, 1994, pp. 52-63.
Hale, Charles R.
1994a *Resistance and Contradiction: Miskitu Indians and the Nicaraguan State, 1894-1987* Stanford: Stanford University Press.
1994b Wan Tasbaya Dukiara: Contested notions of territorial rights in Miskitu history. In Jonathan Boyarin (ed.) Space, Time and the Politics of Memory. Minneapolis: Univ. of Minn. Press.
1994c Between Che Guevara and the Pachamama: Mestizos, Indians, and Identity Politics in the Anti-Quincentenary Campaign. *Critique of Anthropology*. 14(1): 9-39.
1995 De la militancia indígena a la conciencia multi-étnica: Los desafíos de la Autonomía en la Costa Atlántica de Nicaragua. *In* Stefano Varese (ed.) *Etnicidad y Derechos Indígenas* Quito: Abya Yala.
Hall, Stuart
1988 New Ethnicities. *In* Kobena Mercer (ed.) *Black Film, British Cinema*. ICA Documents #7, pp. 27-31.
Howe, James
1986a *The Kuna Gathering*. Austin: University of Texas Press.
1986b Native Rebellion and US Intervention in Central America. *Cultural Survival Quarterly*, 10(1): 59-65.
1991 An Ideological Triangle: The Struggle over San Blas Kuna Culture, 1915-1925 J. Sherzer and G. Urban (eds.) *Nation-States and Indians in Latin America*. Austin: University of Texas Press. pp. 19-52.
Jenkins Molieri, Jorge
1986 *El desafío indígena en Nicaragua: El caso de las Miskitu*. Mexico: Editorial Kantun
Kearney, Michael and Carole Nagengast
1990 Mixtec Ethnicity: Social Identity, Political Consciousness and Political Activism. *Latin American Research Review*. XXV(2): 61-91.
Kearney, Michael
1990 Borders and Boundaries of State and Self at the End of Empire. *Journal of Historical Sociology*. 4(1): 52-74.
Laclau, Ernesto
1977 *Politics and Ideology in Marxist Theory*. Verso: London.
Manuel, George and M. Posluns
1974 *The Fourth World: An Indian Reality*. Toronto: Collier Macmillian.
Means, Russell
1980 Fighting words on the future of the earth. *Mother Jones*, December, pp. 25-38.
Menchú, Rigoberta
1992 "El Tiempo de la Claridad" Entrevista por Felix Zurita, en la sección "Gente," publicación semanal de *Barricada* (Managua) (29 Oct. 1992).
MISURASATA
1985 Communique (September 13, 1985). Akwesasne Notes, Early Winter: 13.
Mohawk, John
1982 The possibilities of uniting Indians and the Left for Social Change in Nicaragua. *Cultural Survival Quarterly*. 6(1): 24-25.
Monsiváis, Carlos
1992 Speech reprinted in *La Jornada*, 6 June 1993.
Nietschmann, Bernard

Charles R. Hale

1983 Interview in Akwasasne Notes. Fall, pp. 6-8.

1984 Nicaragua's other war: Indian warriors vs Sandinistas. Coevolution Quarterly. Summer. pp. 41-7.

1985 Sandinismo y Lukanka India. Vuelta (Mexico) pp. 53-4.

1989 *The Unknown War*. New York: Freedom House.

Reynaga, Fausto

1970 *La revolución india*. Ediciones del Partido Indio de Bolivia. La Paz.

Rivera Cusicanqui, Silvia

1986 *Oprimidos pero no vencidos: Luchas del campesinado aymara y qhechwa de Bolivia, 1900-1980*. Ginebra: Naciones Unidas.

Sanders, Douglas

1977 Formation of the WCIP. IWGIA Document #29.

Sawyer, Suzana

1996 Marching to Nation across Ethnic Terrain: The 1992 Indian Mobilization in Lowland Ecuador. Forthcoming in *Latin American Perspectives*.

Silverblatt, Irene

1995 Becoming Indian in the Central Andes of Seventeenth-Century Peru. *In* G. Prakash (ed.) *After Colonialism*. Princeton: Princeton University Press.

Smith, Carol A.

1990 Conclusion: History and Revolution in Guatemala. *In* C.A. Smith (ed.) *Guatemalan Indians and the State: 1540 to 1988*. Austin: University of Texas Press.

Smith, Carol A. and Jeff Boyer

1987 Central America since 1979: Part 1. *Annual Review of Anthropology* 16:197-221.

Starn, Orin

1995 Maoism in the Andes: The Communist Party of Peru—Shinig Path and the Refusal of History. *Journal of Latin American Studies* 27(2): 399-422.

Stavenhagen, Rodolfo

1990 *The Ethnic Question: Conflicts, Development, Human Rights*. Geneva: United Nations University Press.

Varese, Stefano

1994 Globalización de la política indígena en América Latina. *Cuadernos Agrarios* 4(10): 9-23.

Wheaton, P. and L. Frank

1984 *Indian Guatemala: Path to Liberation*. Washington D.C.: EPICA.

Wiggins, Armstrong

1981 Colonialism and Revolution—Nicaraguan Sandinism and the Liberation of the Miskito, Sumu, and Rama Peoples: An Interview with Armstrong Wiggins. *Akwesasne Notes* 8(4): 4-15.

Chapter 7

ETHNIC BOUNDARIES, INDIGENOUS CATEGORIES AND STATE MANIPULATION: THE CIRCUMPOLAR NORTH

Alfred Darnell

Introduction

The fate of marginalized populations is intensely shaped by the interests and interventions of states. Frequently, their identification and conceptualization as a marginal people is predicated on one or more states' recognition of territorial or political-cultural boundaries associated with a given population. In Anthony Asiwaju's comparative study of inter-national borderlands, for example, he emphasizes the interaction of geographic and spatial isolation of borderland populations from mainstream national life with states' political, economic, and strategic concerns in creating and maintaining a population's marginality. Central to the processes Asiwaju highlights are the formal arrangements made by and between nation states on the geographic shape and character of their respective national boundaries. Populations located on or near national borders, especially borders that are contested in some fashion, are frequently confronted with issues of national affiliation, representation, and identity.

Boundaries and the difficulties that can emerge from their arbitrary character, though, are not only geographical. Borders that create or encapsulate marginalized populations also can be constructed along social and cultural dimensions. In such instances, populations that are clearly situated within a nation state can be "bounded" by *intra*-national policy making, which can lead to social and political segmentation and isolation within a particular national space.

In this chapter, I examine how states' administrative goals and actions in the circumpolar north[1] have functioned to constrain or bound the autonomy of indigenous peoples. Two aspects are of primary interest: (1) the effects of official definitions of indigenous peoples on ethnic boundaries and compositions are unavoidable; and (2) the impact of imposed western administrative infrastructures on the autonomy of indigenous peoples to control their own destinies. The first issue will be examined with respect to three prominent indigenous populations of the circumpolar north—Alaska Natives, Canadian Inuit, and Scandinavian Saami—which have been recognized and legitimized as distinct populations by their respective governments. Then, in order to explicate the dynamics of the state centered efforts to impose control over indigenous populations associated with the second aspect, I will concentrate on the United States' historical treatment of Alaska Natives.

My argument revolves around the position that the framework of administrative order into which indigenous people are brought is integral to a larger social and economic order in which their interests as a collectivity have no obvious place. In spite of stated intentions of state representatives, there are intentional and unintentional consequences that result in a teleology of incorporation or assimilation in the interventions of the state. Incorporation tends to be on the basis of stimulating economic relationships within indigenous communities or between them and the larger society. Such efforts can undermine indigenous peoples' ability to maintain their identity and autonomy or can impair their ability to incorporate with the majority on favorable terms.

A number of questions pertain to the circumstances circumpolar peoples find themselves in. How have government definitions affected the character of their ethnic boundaries? To what degree do governmental, formal terms correspond to the fraternal recognition within each population? Whose interests are best served by institutionalized definitions of each indigenous population? What are the effects of the way in which governments define ethnic membership on the size of their respective indigenous populations and their potential for growth? How are the autonomy, opportunities for self-determination, and the political-cultural security of these people affected by the criteria of membership used by governments in defining membership? And, what are the implications of formal legal definitions for the patrimony of circumpolar indigenous groups and the forms of political action they can engage in?

The creation and recreation of ethnic groups is frequently conceptualized as social boundaries forming around a single population to the exclusion of a second population. The process entails emphasizing social and cultural lines of differentiation between the groups and establishing social-cultural criteria that determine membership.[2] When examined at the level of society, it has been argued that state political processes are instrumental in this process because "the recognition and institutionalization of ethnicity in politics . . . *determines the boundaries* along which ethnic mobilization and/or conflict will occur by setting down the rules for political participation and political access".[3] It follows, that states are central actors in a process that defines and legitimates ethnic groups and the perviousness of their boundaries.[4] Clearly, the state must be considered a primary actor in establishing the salience of ethnic groups.

Much of the recent research on the relationship between the state and ethnic groups has concentrated on understanding emergent ethnic groups as a function of political organizations and processes.[5] Some scholars focus more on the contribution of states and state policies[6] while others center their attentions on scarce resources and competition itself.[7] These studies acknowledge the state's ability to shape the socio-political context or "[define] the framework for cultural pluralism"[8] in which ethnic identities emerge. But as Barkey and Parikh point out, "many aspects of state action are left unspecified" with regard to its effect on understanding the salience of ethnic boundaries.[9] Thus the political or institutional mechanisms by which states actually manipulate ethnic boundaries or how the standards states apply in defining a particular ethnic group can conflict with the terms applied by the ethnic group itself have not been well specified to date.

In order to approach these issues, this essay is divided into four parts. The first examines the importance of the state as a central actor in manipulating ethnic boundaries and orchestrating ethnic membership. Of interest is explaining how and why they engage in such actions. The second part examines the statutory definitions devised by states where the different indigenous groups reside and the historical progression of census figures of three indigenous groups. The objective is to observe shifting formal, institutionalized conceptions of population estimates of the different circumpolar indigenous populations before addressing their implications. The third part of the paper examines how state shaped formal-legal definitions have impacted on indigenous identities and options. Here I concentrate on the circumstances of Alaska's indigenous population. In the fourth and final segment, I conclude with a discussion of the implications of the limitations and types of constraints imposed on the three groups.

The Role of the State

States and state apparatuses in plural societies are faced with the dilemma of how to adequately maintain political and cultural order in all segments of the population. Indeed, from the point of view of the state, "at stake . . . [is] the demarcation of political alliances and coalitions, social movements, and interest groups, which may seek official recognition of their common identity."[10] In their attempts to assure political stability, states and actors representing the state operate under the influence of the dominant hegemonic order in ways that help reproduce its power structure and cultural and ideological features throughout society. Such interests are linked to societal expectations, since, as Park observed nearly a half-century ago, "[i]t is obvious that society . . . is concerned . . . with maintaining not merely a definite life program, but a manner, moral order, and style of life consistent with that conception."[11] In this sense, states are constantly engaged in state-building processes and are concerned with forming or reforming the character of society.

The state, though, is not necessarily acting exclusively on its own behalf. Rather, it may be acting according to the interests of dominant political or social segments of society. The polity and state apparatuses, then, can be thought of as representing, promoting, or protecting the views of the domi-nant population. However, given the plurality of interests involved and their shifting alignments as well as the peculiarities of bureaucratic motivations and practices, the accompanying processes can be inconsistent and even incoher-ent. The interests of minority groups, such as indigenous peoples, can often be neglected because the state and the polity are generally more responsive to better organized and better resourced interest groups within the dominant population—even when these operate in alliance with privileged elements within the indigenous group. The ability of minorities to control their own destinies can be significantly constrained as a result.

Definitions and recognition of racial ethnic boundaries is one fundamen-tal way in which states can manipulate minorities' autonomy and security. Until recently, for example, South Africa was a state in which policies were explicitly aimed at defining racial and ethnic boundaries. Government poli-cies historically were very effective in assuring ethnic and racial divisions within the black population as well as between blacks, coloreds and Indians.[12] In the years immediately prior to Mandela's ascendancy, policies of deraciali-zation seeking to incorporate coloreds and Indians "result[ed] in repre-sentation for coloreds and Indians in parliament on the basis of the intensification, not relaxation, of ethnic boundaries."[13] To avoid according individuals full equality on a color-blind one-person-one vote basis, it was essential for the state "to be able to identify individuals in ethnic terms."[14]

State policies do not have to be directed specifically at an ethnic or minority population, as they were in South Africa, to have an effect. In the United States, for example, the organization and shape of ethnic boundaries of Gypsies were greatly affected by government welfare policies in the 1930s and 40s even though they were not directed specifically at the Gypsy popula-tion. Beverly Nagel (1986) has observed that federal policies in the United States were integral to drawing disparate Gypsy groups under one umbrella organization because "government policy, by allocating funds to corporate groups, directly influenced the level and nature of ethnic activity pursued by

Gypsies. These policies simultaneously encouraged the formation of a corporate group with quasi-political aims and the shift in ethnic boundaries to a
more inclusive level."[15] A similar, though less direct, effect was experienced by
Gypsies in Great Britain during the 1960s. The British government decentral-
ized decision making over certain land use issues, including designation of
camping areas, which conferred more authority to local governments over
these matters. Previously disassociated Gypsy groups found it in their interests
to form a larger national alliance in order to confront the difficulties brought
on by changes in policy.[16]

A state or its representatives, then, can employ actions designed to maximize the political security of its positions vis-a-vis forces that could conceivably lessen its influence in a region of the country or segment of the
population. The processes of defining populations and of enumeration are
rational strategies that can meet this objective because "methods of classifying
and measuring the size of population groups" allow the state to influence or
"direct the flow of . . . 'preferments' and . . . spur various allegiances and
antagonisms throughout the population." Indeed, "numbers are not absolute"
and will vary by policy decisions[17] so the mere presence or "absence of
numbers may . . . be telling"[18] and can be manipulated to fit particular
interests of the state at different times.[19]

Among nations that touch on the arctic circle, states have been and
continue to be engaged in managing indigenous populations so as to ensure
political stability in northern regions with concentrated populations of indigenous people. Demands by indigenous peoples for political, cultural, and
economic autonomy over territorial and water rights in the circumpolar north
present challenges to regional political-legal superiority and security of northern circumpolar nations.[20]

The United States, Canada, and Norway, for example, each have been
concerned with regulating and integrating the social and political activities of
their respective northern indigenous populations in order to control or facilitate a socio-political climate conducive to political order and economic development. The process of managing these populations has frequently included
providing them with social services, financial, educational, and cultural support different and unique from those offered the dominant populations. Such
programs result in economic and political stress on states and their apparatus
because of economic and political costs to maintaining them. In addition,
indigenous groups have made legal claims for land ownership that have
resulted in significant title transfers to indigenous groups. For example, the
Alaska Native Claims Settlement Act of 1971 provided the Alaska Natives
with title to 40 million acres of land and Canada recently agreed to set aside
740,000 square miles of the Northwest Territories as a new Territory to be

called Nunavut (Inuit for "homeland"). No Scandinavian country has offered such significant territorial rewards to the Saami, but Norway granted constitutional guarantees of special protection for its cultural minorities with the Saami population particularly in mind.

Even though aboriginal groups are being compensated for infringements on their indigenous land use and their political-cultural rights they are not without potential costs to their autonomy. Steve Cornell, for example, warns that in the case of American Indians such incorporation speaks more to "the political relationships that link [indigenous groups] to the larger system, whether those relationships are responsive to group concerns or not."[21] But, incorporation and the theoretical autonomy that accompanies it does not relieve the state of a vested interest in limiting the size and influence of each population. There remains an interest to protect states' dominance in each region and over each population. In Alaska and Canada, for example, even though indigenous groups constitute a distinct minority of the total population, they are a significant majority in the northern rural regions. Saami also are a significant constituency in rural districts of Scandinavia, comprising up to 75 per cent of the population in some communities.[22] Consequently, even though circumpolar minorities are small in number relative to entire national populations, their regional concentrations potentially make them influential political voices.

Two mechanisms that have been adopted by the United State, Canada, and Norway to facilitate order and control over indigenous groups have been to (1) constrain the definitional character of ethnic boundaries, thus containing the size of the populations, and (2) create and impose administrative structures on indigenous peoples that are compatible with western forms of governance. In the first instance, one particularly prominent method that has been consciously employed by states historically to determine ethnic boundaries and affiliation uses formal and/or legal stipulations of individuals' ethnicity or race according to blood quotients. Or in less controversial terms, a person's ethnic ancestry is used to assign his/her primary ethnic identity. As recently as 1920 the United States government relied on blood quotients to define African-American and American Indian racial categories in the US. Census.[23] While the practice has stopped with respect to treatment of African-Americans by the federal government,[24] assigning membership to ethnic or racial groups according to blood quotients continues to be a standard approach in policy circles in order to identify Alaska Natives and American Indians in the United States.[25]

Blood quotients, kinship lineages, language use, or some combination of these criteria are applied to individuals in Canada and Scandinavia when assessing governmental recognition of individuals' indigenous birthrights.

Alfred Darnell

Even though blood lines are not always explicitly identified as the definitive measure, they remain an integral feature of formal-legal recognition of indigenous populations in these countries.

In the second instance, the act of naming groups and the definition of their boundaries and of criteria of belonging responds to an administrative requirement and logic that often conflicts with the felt needs of the people affected. The overriding bureaucratic imperative in these instances is to delimit an administrative problem—to specify, to fix in time and space, and to bound it. Even though they are establishing the limits of "only" a category the effect in practice can be the same as physically constraining a population. In the Alaska case, for example, the federal government imposed western and capitalist corporate structures and forms of governance on the Native population that are not very compatible with the communal lifestyles or collective patrimonies that characterize the majority of Alaska Native communities.

Because these populations are perceived as anomalous there is an underlying desire to bring them into conformity with the administrative order. But in doing so bureaucrats rely on seemingly "objective" notions of identity that are in fact historically contingent and inconsistently applied. Built into administrative definitions are "primordialist" views of ethnicity which highlight biology or those aspects of culture more closely tied to descent that can resonate with indigenous peoples' own views. Let me turn now to the definitions and enumerations of the three circumpolar groups and their variability over time.

Definitions and Demographics

Historically, identifying and measuring the populations of Alaska Natives, Canadian Inuit and Scandinavian Saami has been a highly variable and politicized process. It has given rise to inconsistent and imprecise estimates for the total numbers for these indigenous populations and the changes they have undergone over the last 90 years. In each instance though, these indigenous groups constitute the largest minority population of each region or country.[26] Let us look at each group separately.

Scandinavian Saami

Estimates of the total Saami population in Fennoscandia[27] are probably less reliable and more variable than for Alaska Natives or Canadian Inuit. Finland, Norway, and Sweden each identify Saami according to different criteria and each have varied their forms of identification over time. For example, three current estimates of the Saami population in Fennoscandia as a whole place their numbers between 34,000 and 50,000. Knapp puts the population at approximately 34,000 in 1970,[28] while Aikio concludes there are up to 40,000 Lappish speakers in 1988,[29] and Keskitalo (1981) and Lundgren (1987) identify the largest number with 50,000.[30] It is important to note that the critical variable here is not growth in population over time because the figure Keskitalo arrives at precedes those of Lundgren and Aikio by a significant number of years. Rather, fluctuations appear to be a function of changing politically or socially contrived definitions of ethnic categories.

The population figures also vary within each country. The total number of Saami in Finland has been identified as ranging from 3800 to 5800, in Norway from 30 to 40 thousand and in Sweden between 15,000 and 17,000.[31] Measures from each country are complicated by inconsistent enumerating practices and their reliance on different criteria for determining Saami membership. In Finland, for example, systematic government attempts to measure the number of Saami did not begin until 1970 when they were included as a distinct category on the national census. At that time, membership was determined by language criteria rather than familial heritage or self identification.[32]

Under the language guideline an individual's ethnic identity is determined by calculations made according to criteria established under the Finnish Statute on the Saami Delegation which "defines a member of the Saami as a person who himself or of whose parents or grandparents at least one has, in accordance with the population statistics of 1962, learnt the Saami language as the first language."[33] Using language, and more importantly an individual's first language, as the defining feature for determining ethnic identity is problematic because, obviously, it imposes a significant constraint on any individual who does not speak a Saami dialect or have parents and/or grandparents who used Lappish as their first language. Even if a person can trace their lineage clearly to a Saami heritage, it does not count in the eyes of the government if the first language is not Saami in origin within one generation. This policy also excludes the possibility of learning the language at a later date in order to qualify as having a Saami heritage and identity.

An additional problem with this strategy of enumeration is the impact of researchers' perceptions. For example, Keskitalo asserts that four-fifths of Saami in Finland speak the dialects of Central and Northern Saami[34] while M. Aikio clearly implies a much smaller proportion, less than half, use a Saami dialect to any great extent.[35] Interpretation of language use can lead to some interesting problems, one of which was well documented in a 19th century census in northern Norway. In this particular census one individual's ethnic identity changed three times during a twenty six year period: from Saami to Finnish (but speaking Norwegian) and finally to Finnish and speaking Saami.[36] The fluidity of the ethnic boundary in this instance was attributed

Alfred Darnell

less to changes in the individual's circumstances than to biases of the enumerator.[37]

A consequence of using language as the basis of measurement is to increase the likelihood of a shrinking Saami population in Finland and Sweden, where similar criteria have been applied. In the Vuotso Region of Finland, for example, the use of Saami language has declined dramatically. In 1910 over 60 per cent of all age groups and 75 per cent of those over 50 among Saami used Lappish as their primary language. By 1930 these percentages of Saami language usage were half of the 1910 figures and by 1950 they had been reduced to a fraction of the 1930 statistics: less than 30 per cent of those more than 30 years old and less than 1 per cent of those under 20 used Saami as a primary language. In 1970, no individual with a Saami heritage and under 40 years use Lappish as their first language and less than 20 percent of them used Saami language to one degree or another.[38] Consequently, in this region of Finland, it will take but one more generation from 1970 for the children to be excluded from being able to officially identify themselves as Saami.

Currently in Norway the basis of measurement is not the same as in Finland or Sweden. In the 1970 Norwegian census special attention was paid to identifying individuals with a Saami heritage. In this census, Saami heritage was determined according to self response on questions concerning language usage and ethnic identification. As a result, researchers in Norway felt confident in concluding that the lives of 40,000 individuals "[were] affected [one way or another] by Lappish ancestry."[39] The 1970 census, however, is the first time that language was not the primary criteria in Norway. Censuses carried out from the mid-1800s by churches and the state generally used language usage as the primary determinant when reporting their statistics. In essence, then, figures over time are highly variable and not necessarily consistent with those of more recent censuses.

Canadian Inuit

The Inuit of Canada are not a large proportion of Canada's population. In 1981, for example they constituted only 1 per cent of the total population, as shown in Table 1. Although, when Inuit are included with American Indians and Metis the total indigenous population of Canada makes up nearly three per cent of the total population in 1981. Inuit, also, are not widely distributed throughout Canada. Rather, when concentrating on populations of Territories or Provinces, we can see Inuit are found to comprise a significant proportion the population in only the Northwest Territories. There they make up 34.6 per cent of the population. However, these numbers are largely concentrated in the northern portions of the Territory where Nunavut will be created.

The Circumpolar North

Table 7.1 Indigenous Population of Canada, 1871-1981

Province	1871			1881			1891			1901			1911			1921		
	# of Indians	# of Inuit	Total Pop.	# of Indians	# of Inuit	Total Pop.	# of Indians	# of Inuit	Total Pop.	# of Indians	# of Inuit	Total Pop.	# of Indians	# of Inuit	Total Pop.	# of Indians	# of Inuit	Total Pop.
Prince Edward Ils.	323		94021	281		108891	314		109708	258		103259	248		93728	235		88615
Nova Scotia	1666		387800	2125		440572	2076		450396	1629		459574	1915		492338	2048		523837
New Brunswick	1404		285594	1401		321233	1521		321263	1465		331120	1541		351889	1331		387876
Quebec	6988		1191516	7515		1359027	13361		1488535	10142		164808	9993		2005776	11566		2360510
Ontario	12978		1620851	15235		1926922	17915		2114321	24674		2182947	23044		2527292	26436		2933662
British Columbia	23000		36247	25661		49459	34202		98173	28949		178657	20134		392480	22377		524582
Manitoba			25228			62260			152506	16277		255211	7876		461394	13869		610118
Saskatchewan			25228			62260			152506			91279	11718		492432	12914		757510
Alberta												73022	11630		374295	14577		588454
Yukon										3322		27219	1489		8512	1390		4157
Northwest Territory			48000			56446				14921		20129	15904		6507	3873		8163
Totals	102358		3689257	108547		4324810	120638		4833239	147941		5371315	105492		7206643	110596		8787949
% of Total	2.8			2.5			2.5			2.4			1.5			1.3		

Table 7.1 Indigenous Population of Canada, 1871-1981

Province	1931			1941			1951			1961			1971			1981		
	# of Indians	# of Inuit	Total Pop.	# of Indians	# of Inuit	Total Pop.	# of Indians	# of Inuit	Total Pop.	# of Indians	# of Inuit	Total Pop.	# of Indians	# of Inuit	Total Pop.	# of Indians	# of Inuit	Total Pop.
Prince Edward Ils.	233		88038	258		95047	257		98	363		105			112	595	30	123
Nova Scotia	2191		512849	2063		577962	2717		643	3834		737			789	7665	130	847
New Brunswick	1685		408219	1939		457401	2255		516	3629		598			635	5510	5	696
Quebec	12312	1159	2874662	11863	1778	3331882	14631	1958	4056	23043		5259		3800	6028	47520	4875	6438
Ontario	30368		3431683	30336		3787655	37370		4567	47260		6236		800	7703	108965	1095	8625
British Columbia	24599		694263	24875		817861	28478		1165	40990		1629			2185		515	2744
Manitoba	15417	62	700139	15473		729744	21024		777	2778		922			988	66050	230	1026
Saskatchewan	15268		921785	13384		895992	22250		832	27672		925			926	59055	145	968
Alberta	15258	3	731605	12565		796169	21163		940	22738		1332			1628	71540	510	2238
Yukon	1543	85	4230	1508		4914	1533		09	2142		14			18	3950	95	23
Northwest Territory	4046	4670	9316	4052	5404	12028	3838	6822	16	5235	11500	23		13500	35	10520	15910	46
Totals	122920	5979	10376786	118316	7205	11506655	155874	9733	14001	204796	11500	18238	257619	17550	21568	466070	25390	24343
% of Total	1.2	0.05		1.0	0.06		1.1	0.06		1.1	0.06		1.2	0.08		1.9	1.0	

The dependability of the figures for the Northwest Territories, however, are problematic. It is not likely that the Inuit population increased by over 100 per cent between 1951 and 1971. While not as great, this increase is mirrored in figures for the Indian population which show strong shifts that belie continuity in measuring and reliability. The changes are more likely the result of censuses that have been incomplete counts because there are indications that the criteria to assess ethnic background varied over the years.[40]

There are several striking features of how indigenous peoples have been counted in Canada. First, even though they have been counted regularly since 1871 provinces did not uniformly count either Inuit or American Indians. Significantly, with the exception of Ontario, those provinces with the greatest numbers of Inuit and Indians did not individually enumerate Indians until after 1941 and Inuit until 1981. Prior to 1981 the pattern was to identify indigenous peoples as either "Indian" or as indigenous and not to report statistics for Inuit. In contrast the Northwest Territories, which has the greatest proportion of Inuit of the different territories, began to selectively identify Inuit continuously from the 1931 census. Four other Territories or Provinces also identified Inuit in 1931, but they did not resume the practice until 1981.

Second, the absence of population statistics for Inuit and American Indians of Canada essentially undermines their existence as a constituency whose interests need representation. If numbers are strictly impressionistic or non-existent, then these indigenous peoples can remain invisible to the rest of the polity. Given the relatively low numbers of whites who resided in the Northwest Territories, for example, to have indigenous peoples publicly outnumbering them could have proved awkward in term of whose voices were regarded more seriously.

Alaska Natives

Alaska Natives, like Saami and Canadian Inuit, are a distinct minority in Alaska as a whole even though they maintain a clear majority in certain regions of the state. As can be seen in Table 2 they comprised only 15 per cent of the total Alaska population in 1990. In many rural communities, however, they constitute over 90 per cent of the population.[41] The process of identifying Natives for census purposes is significantly different than that used in Finland and Sweden, they simply rely on self identification. But like Canada, historically the indigenous population in Alaska was not differentiated according to the different tribes or ethnic groups until the 1970 census. Consequently, Aleuts, American Indians, and Eskimo were all categorized together. The Census Bureau began to draw rough distinctions between the different groups and

Year	Total Pop.	Natives			Non-Natives			Ratio of Native to Non-Native
		No. of Persons	% of Total	% Change	No. of Persons	% of Total	% Change	
1900	63582	29536	46.4	—	34056	53.6	—	.767
1910	64356	25331	39.4	-14.2	39025	60.6	14.6	.649
1920	55035	26558	48.3	4.8	28478	51.7	-27.0	.933
1930	59278	29983	50.6	12.9	28295	49.4	2.9	1.140
1940	72524	32458	44.8	8.3	40066	55.2	36.8	.810
1950	128643	33863	26.3	4.3	94780	73.7	136.6	.357
1960	226167	43081	19.0	27.8	183086	81.0	93.2	.235
1970	300382	50654	16.9	17.6	249729	83.1	36.4	.205
1980	401851	64103	16.0	27.6	337748	84.0	35.2	.190
1990	550043	85698	15.6	33.7	464345	83.4	37.5	.185

finally established clear divisions among different Eskimo, Indians, and Aleuts by the 1980 census.

The statistics in Table 2 show that prior to 1890 Alaska's non-Native population accounted for just less than 21 per cent of the region's total population while Alaska's indigenous population made up the remaining 79 per cent.[42] But by 1900 the Native population had shrunk to just 46 per cent of the total population. This is because of increases in the non-indigenous population due to the Alaska Gold Rush and an expanding fishing industry that attracted thousands of new residents. For the next thirty-five to forty-five years the number of Natives as a percent of the total regional population hovered around the same mark, with a low of 39 per cent of the total population in 1910 and a high of nearly 51 per cent in 1930.

During World War II and the immediate post war years, however, Alaska experienced an influx of non-Natives so great that by 1950 the Native population comprised only 26 per cent of the total population. During the next twenty years, with the completion of land and marine highways to Alaska, the percentage of Natives in the total population slowly declined to 16 per cent. This figure changed very little between 1970 and 1980, which can be explained by two factors: First, the fertility rate of Natives has been

The Circumpolar North

increasing which, when combined with a slowing expansion of the non-Native population between 1970 and 1980, aided in maintaining similar proportions. Second, and more importantly, the Alaska Native Claims Settlement Act of 1971, provided a financial and material incentive to identify one's self as a Native. It is likely people who qualified as a Native under the stipulations of ANCSA identified themselves as a Native even though previously they had not acknowledged their Indian, Eskimo or Aleut heritage.

In each of these cases, the definitions used to establish population sizes have been historically variable. Efforts to establish continuity at given points in time have resulted in variability over time and standards that tend to minimize the size of indigenous groups. Even though governments have come to acknowledge the existence and legitimacy of indigenous groups over time, they also strive to minimalize and marginalize their existence by imposing significant constraints on membership.

There are several implications for indigenous peoples with regard to the limitations states impose on criteria for enumerating. First, the size of an indigenous constituency and the need or desirability of being responsive to that group is influenced by the manner in which they are counted. If a group is made statistically insignificant in size or eliminated all together, then the likelihood of having their interests represented is greatly reduced. This issue is particularly salient with regard to different Native American tribes in the United States attempting to gain formal federal recognition even though they have not existed as a legitimate category for decades and sometimes centuries. Second, the definitions arrived at by census takers are also problematic because they establish and enforce criteria that are not necessarily commensurate with the manner in which indigenous groups determine membership. In Alaska, Finland, and Sweden census takers apply a much more rigid set of criteria than the indigenous groups, thus excluding potential members from official recognition and limiting the size of the constituency.

In sum, because these populations are perceived as anomalous there is an underlying desire to bring them into conformity with the administrative order. In doing so bureaucrats rely on seemingly "objective" notions of identity. Built into administrators' perceptions are prevailing views among indigenous peoples which have maintained a remarkable continuity over the centuries, thus favoring "primordialist" views of ethnicity.

Creating Administrative Order: An Alaskan Example

Central government control over the circumpolar north developed in the United States, Canada, and Norway over a relatively long period of time. The incorporation of the indigenous populations in these regions into the dominant social structure has developed at an even slower pace. Like other state-building endeavors, historically the task that lay before the different governments has been to create an administrative and political environment which was conducive to developing and populating the region. An integral part of this process has been to distinguish indigenous from non-indigenous groups in order to more effectively manage or avoid conflict between the two populations.[43] The state has been forceful in establishing this distinction by legislating ethnic group membership. While other methods have existed, this is perhaps the most visible and most political in character.

The use of legislation to define Alaska Natives and their status vis-à-vis other groups has been widely relied upon by the federal government since the region was acquired from Russia in 1867 and has been a source of lively debate over indigenous rights over the last twenty-five years.[44] For Alaska Natives two periods stand out during their 125 years under federal domination: the first twenty-five years of United States ownership of Alaska and the statutory stipulations from the Alaska Native Claims Settlement Act of 1971.

Problems of categorizing and defining Alaska's indigenous population began with the Treaty of Cession of 1867, which passed ownership of Alaska from Russia to the United States, and continue today. A distinction is made in the treaty between "'uncivilized tribes' and the other 'inhabitants of the ceded territory'." Uncivilized peoples "were to be 'subject to such laws and regulations as the United States may . . . adopt in regard to aboriginal tribes of the country'" while other residents would enjoy "'all the rights, advantages and immunities of citizens of the United States'." This created confusion over whether all peoples indigenous to the region were to be categorized as uncivilized or if some portion might be considered civilized.[45] The relationship of civilized versus non-civilized peoples to the federal government was held to be different in the treaty.

The distinctions between civilized and barbarian/savage and between Christian and heathen has been observed by Benedict Anderson[46] and George Fredrickson[47] as an important tool for categorizing indigenous peoples in early colonial enterprises. In the course of establishing settlements in North America early perceptions of Native American's were typically influenced by a heritage that had previously believed that:

> some men were so wild and uncouth that they wandered in forests and had no society of any kind. This category of ultra-barbarians, or pure savages, who allegedly lived more like beasts than men, seemed to many Europeans of the sixteenth and seventeenth centuries appropriate for peoples like the Cape "Hottentots" or the North American, Caribbean, and Brazilian Indians, who were commonly thought to be wilderness nomads utterly devoid of religion or culture.[48]

The Circumpolar North

Even though attitudes may have become more enlightened toward the end of the nineteenth century, similar views continued to be held toward peoples indigenous to the contiguous States and were visibly applied to categorizing and understanding the peoples indigenous to Alaska. In one of the first government reports on conditions in the new territory the dominant criteria used by the investigator in assessing the circumstances of the native peoples was the extent to which they had been "raised from barbarism" and whether they could be categorized according to "one of [two] classes . . . the Christian Aleuts . . . [or] the Indians occupying all the rest of the inhabited country."[49] Even though some whites had considered large segments of the indigenous population to be civilized and Christian, Elliot could not "recognize the claim to-day; they have worn off what little Christianity they may have possessed."[50] He concluded his assessment of Alaska's indigenous population by observing that:

> the Eskimo race and immediate derivatives are quite amiable in their barbarism. . . . [and] we can only consider the present condition of the Indians of Alaska as that of savages, and beyond the power of the Government or of the church to change for the better.[51]

Nearly forty years after Elliot's visit to Alaska, attitudes toward the indigenous people had changed but not dramatically. For example, in Congressional Hearings before the Committee on Territories in 1912, the testimony of Bishop Rowe of Alaska and the comments of the committee's Chairman reflect prevalent attitudes toward Alaska's indigenous peoples. In response to the desirability of creating reservations in Alaska, Bishop Rowe stated that he did not think the natives would feel sad or be dispirited by being confined because "They are all children" who "of course . . . feel as children do."[52] During the same hearings, Congressman Henry D. Flood, of Virginia, in commenting on the government's responsibility to educate the indigenous population labeled the natives of Alaska as "half-dead people," which was responded to with general laughter.[53]

The Treaty of Cession, the Organic Act of 1884, and related acts passed through 1900[54] had significant ramifications for Alaska Natives because avenues for development by non-indigenous people were encouraged at the expense of indigenous rights and forms of livelihood. In short, the manner in which indigenous groups were defined and conceptualized limited and constrained their rights in relation to developers interested in extracting natural resources. Even though each of the Acts contained provisions designed to protect Natives' land use rights, at the same time they established principles detrimental to Natives' access to the land. "It was generally assumed that these acts equated Native possession with non-Native possession and entitled

Alaska Natives only to land which was in their individual and actual use and occupancy."[55] The notion that Native land use extended over huge tracts of land that were not physically occupied was not acknowledged; nor was the fact that patterns of use extended over generations. Even today this principle is not widely recognized or accepted by non-indigenous people involved in these policy making processes.[56] As a result, the Organic Act of 1884 functioned as a guide for non-Natives in general and the government in particular in the expropriation of land for generations to come.

Although Natives' rights were reputedly protected, the lack of clarity in the law combined with a disregard for Native land rights resulted in problems for Natives early in their relations with non-Natives. By the late 1800s reports were arriving in Washington D.C. of whites' indifference to Native land use rights, which significantly restricted Natives' access to land for subsistence. For example, a Special Agent to the Treasury Department noted in an 1895 report:

> [I]t is true that foreigners are brought from San Francisco to fish the streams of Alaska and that they actually look upon the streams and fish as their own. The unfortunate native Aleuts ... are hustled out of the way of these Mediterranean fishermen with scant ceremony, and forbidden to fish in their native streams.[57]

The perceptions of whites toward Alaska's indigenous population during the first twenty-five years of U.S. control over Alaska remained prevalent in federal and Territorial approaches to Alaska Natives through the 1960s. They basically viewed the Native population as a second class citizenry which was not entitled to equal rights with non-indigenous peoples. The 1960s and the discovery of oil reserves in northern Alaska, however, provided a catalyst for redefining the social location of the Native population, a position eventually encapsulated in the Alaska Native Claims Settlement Act of 1971 (ANCSA).

Besides depriving Alaska Natives of any further legal claims to aboriginal land rights or use,[58] ANCSA gave the Aleuts, Eskimos, and Indians of Alaska compensation for the invasion of their aboriginal lands and for the loss of any livelihood they suffered as a result of the infusion of "Western" technology, populace, and culture into their world.[59] The Act was unprecedented in its magnitude. Over forty million acres of land and nearly one billion dollars were divided among the different Native groups and communities. Title to the land and the cash were given to twelve Native owned regional corporations and over two-hundred Native village corporations which were created explicitly to manage the land and money. The former were structured as profit-making ventures and the latter as not-for-profit organizations.

The Circumpolar North

ANCSA can be viewed as a major administrative accomplishment from the point of view of the federal government. Three strong reasons stand out. First, it established physical criteria for determining Native status, thus defining a relative concrete boundary around indigenous peoples of Alaska. Second, it imposed a western corporate structure on the indigenous peoples to manage the financial and land awarded to the population, thus channeling the form of economic activities they can engage in into western, profit driven standards. Third, the Act was a major step by the federal government in releasing itself from its federal stewardship over Alaska's indigenous population.

In the first instance, the Act established a blood quotient as a primary determinant for identifying individuals who could qualify as Alaska Native:

> "Native" means a citizen of the Unites States who is a person of one-fourth degree or more Alaska Indian . . . Eskimo, or Aleut blood, or combination thereof.[60]

One consequence of the standard is that it created a formal, physical boundary around Natives that is difficult for an individual or a group to manipulate according to their own interests. In addition, Native status had to be formally acknowledged by Native communities by listing all entitled individuals as of December 1971 on formally established village rolls. All people born after 1971 would not benefit directly from the Settlement. A result of this provision is that it is one of the few points on which all Natives agree: Natives born after 1971 should be formally recognized and acknowledged by the Act. As one Native resident of interior Alaska stated, "I feel very strongly about the children that were not entitled to go on from 1971 . . . well, were not entitled to any shares. Should stay open should not be closed at all (sic)."[61]

A central problem that has resulted from this shortcoming is a growing sense that there are different classes of Natives within a given community. The comments of a Native resident of the Aleutians are telling on this point:

> The other problem that I, you know, I'd like to speak on is that, and you said it's been brought up throughout the state, is after 1971 the (sic), you're no longer an Aleut or an Indian or an Eskimo. You're just—that's it according to the Act. You have to be born and enrolled by 1971. There's no provision in it, after that date set up for children born after that time (sic).[62]

In the second instance, the ANCSA established formal [legal] institutions through which Native interests would be represented and administered. Technically, they were profit and not-for-profit corporations established to manage the money and land received from the settlement, but they also stand as

Alfred Darnell

formal media through which the state can interact with the indigenous
population. Third, and finally, ANCSA provided the federal government with an avenue ultimately to free itself of responsibility for the welfare of the indigenous population. The financial settlement and the creation of the corporate structure were clearly intended as the means by which Native self sufficiency in the modern economy would be realized. Many Natives believe the corporate structure set up to deal with the settlement is itself antithetical to Native culture and society and that it is working to break down traditional norms and social arrangements. One Athabascan Indian explained:

> Another thing about the land claim and the village selection, because of the land claim I think it restricted the land use to many of our people. I know that currently people can't trap, hunt, fish or even pick berries anywhere because they have this fear of trespassing on another person's property or another village selection in this area, or the regional [corporation's] selection. And I hate to see that when you cross the borderline of another village, they say you can't park your car here or get into our lake because you're not a stockholder of our village, although we're so close to one another. It shouldn't be that way. It should be open too.[63]

By establishing these administrative structures, the Native population was necessarily marginalized along several different lines: (1) the alienating effects of formal criteria of who can be officially considered Native on their social and cultural patrimony; (2) the imposition of corporate structures on every Native community that are culturally and economically assimilationist; and (3) the constraints on sovereignty Natives can legally and legitimately exercise in Native villages.[64] These concerns highlight and reinforce the boundaries encompassing the Native population by fueling political-cultural differences between and among the indigenous and non-indigenous populations.

In the third instance, Alaska Natives have, in recent years, come to be concerned with the degree of autonomy from State and Federal laws that village governments can exercise. With ANCSA the Federal government has attempted to disassociate itself from the traditional patrimonial relationship to Alaska Natives—a relationship other peoples indigenous to the United States continue to experience. The terms of ANCSA make the federal government less inclined to become involved in issues debated by Natives and the State than it was prior to 1971. Adding to this controversy is the Federal government's unwillingness to extend to Native communities provisions of the Indian Reorganization Act that would enable them to incorporate under Federal law, rather than under State municipal laws.[65] In short, the conjunction of many Native communities' attempts to maximize their autonomy and of the Federal government's apparent reduced responsibility toward Alaska's

Natives has resulted in State-Native conflict over which government will be the final authority in Native communities—the Federal or the State governments.

A fundamental aspect of this conflict is over the degree of autonomy Native communities will be permitted to exercise in determining the forms of legal and social organization in their communities. The state of Alaska, for example has been attempting to increase its political, institutional and formal legal control over all rural communities. One of the ways this has been done has been to pressure villages to incorporate under State municipal laws. If villages do not incorporate a wide range of State services and resources are not made available, and since the Federal government is less inclined to become involved, villages that do not comply with the system find it more difficult to acquire money and other resources.

If a village elects to incorporate under State laws, then resources are more easily obtained, but the State gains influence that it otherwise would not have. Villages that incorporate under State municipal codes possess a more rigid formal legal structure than villages incorporated under the Federal government[66] or those which have not incorporated at all. A village that incorporates under State laws must maintain elected councils with a standard number of members, a specific number of officers, a minimum number of days in session, minutes of all meetings, and a commitment to meeting community responsibilities, such as sanitary improvement, law enforcement, or fire protection.[67] Such institutions are not necessarily incompatible with traditional social institutions or norms, but their formality and the resources which must be invested in them often are. What is problematic for many Native communities is that such laws and regulations provide avenues through which the State can exert control over community affairs, because failure of a village to meet the legal requirements of the municipal codes can lead to significant economic and political penalties.

By defining and categorizing Alaska Natives and the organizational structure of their communities the federal (and State) government has created a social and political infra-structure with rigid parameters on the options before the indigenous population. Whatever preferences Alaska Natives may identify in their attempts to contend with the circumstances they are confronted by are determined, in part, by the available set of choices defined by the structures imposed on their communities. Such constraints necessarily marginalize preferences that do not fit within the rubric of the states "acceptable" parameters of action. There are those, of course, who would argue that even though the structures and definitions are shaped by the state, within these social and political arrangement Alaska's Native population has a fair degree of autonomy in decision making. The paradox of this independence, though, is that by adopting the new systems and definitions, the Native population is increasingly integrated into the dominant social order.

Anton Hoem has argued similar problems are beginning to confront the Saami in Norway. Even though being Saami entitles individuals and groups to special educational and economic considerations, their long term patrimony of Saami may be problematic. Constitutional recognition and definition of the Saami population has made them increasingly acceptable to the wider population and more easily integrated into the dominant society because education programs promote bilingualism and biculturalism among Saami but not Norwegians.[68] As a result, Saami are expected to engage in western economic practices and interact with Norwegians according to the terms of the dominant population rather than the other way around.

The circumstances of Canada's circumpolar indigenous groups are evolving toward a somewhat different direction. The degree of autonomy Canadian Inuit are about to achieve is far greater than either Alaska Natives or Scandinavian Saami will ever experience. However, as the Canadian Territory of Nunavut develops, it will have to establish a governing structure commensurate with the rest of Canada as well as an economic base that will enable the Territory to be self-sufficient and interact with the rest of the country. Integration, will for all intents, be necessary because the rest of Canada will probably not adapt to Nunavut.

The institutions devised by states for indigenous peoples—even those which seek to offer compensation for past violation of rights—tend to subordinate indigenous people to social processes and procedures which divide them and create marginal elements within their ranks. The settlement accepted by Alaska's Native population illuminate some of these pitfalls, issues that could easily confront Canadian Inuit as they set out establish greater degrees of autonomy in the Canadian north. Saami in contrast will probably never be the benefactors of economic or territorial concessions on the scale of Alaska's or Canada's indigenous peoples. However, because of other political solutions to their cultural patrimony, they too face serious problems associated with controlling the social and political forces that will affect the future of their populations.

Conclusions

In the opening pages of this chapter I posited the argument that indigenous peoples in the circumpolar north were being subjected to states' efforts to establish administrative order in the north that was not well integrated with indigenous peoples' cultural or social interests. There exists, I suggested, "a teleology of incorporation or assimilation" that essentially has undermined circumpolar peoples' abilities to maintain sufficient autonomy over their lives to influence or control the terms of integration with the larger society. This is not to say states are intentionally setting out to destroy or consume indigenous peoples, rather they are deeply concerned with facilitating social and political environments that are conducive to western economic development and stability. When dealing with indigenous groups, though, states have asserted administrative order in ways compatible with their own cultural and bureaucratic world views. Establishing western categories and structures in the north have been two significant strategies they have adopted.

The creation of clearly discernible ethnic boundaries for indigenous groups has been an objective of states' policies across the three cases. In so doing, the state has determined membership according to its interests by creating relatively rigid criteria for the distribution of entitlements. Blood quotients and language use are concrete and largely inflexible measures.

Even though official government recognition has greatly legitimated the existence and rights of indigenous groups, the processes of enumeration have resulted in the subordination of indigenous political and cultural interests to those of the state. The state has been able to determine definitions and provisions of what constitutes an ethnic group which in turn determines the size in indigenous constituencies and who has access to select entitlements. Such a strategy essentially devalues and marginalizes the political, cultural, or economic interests of the indigenous populations in relation to those of the dominant polity. Indeed, the state is essentially able to "map" the ethnic composition of the society according to its own needs.[69]

Even though government actions have been supportive of aboriginal populations in recent decades by offering constitutionally guaranteed entitlements and financial benefits, they do not mean that indigenous political, economic, or cultural interests are adequately represented or that their political stability is ensured. On the contrary, state strategies have facilitated incorporating Alaska Natives, Canadian Inuit, and Norwegian Saami into their respective dominant political systems according to the terms set by the state. Consequently, there remain significant threats to their respective cultures, problems of an accelerating marginalization of their indigenous life-styles, and efforts to assimilate them into a dominant social order. In short, the political and cultural security of the indigenous peoples of the circumpolar north is threatened because the terms of their existence, along with their political autonomy, and future political capacities have been defined according to categories and conceptions that are reflective of the states' interests.

It is evident, though, that over the centuries complete incorporation of circumpolar peoples has not occurred and is not likely to occur in the foreseeable future. Consequently, the participation of these peoples as equal and full citizens in plural societies will be impeded unless they surrender their cultural and social autonomy along with control over their lands to the majority society. In effect, unless they succumb to assimilationist forces, circumpolar peoples will be suspended between being a part of and outside of the dominant society and continually at risk. Indeed, it is in this tension that we find the main site of insecurity and marginality for indigenous peoples.

It would be imperious to advocate preservation of indigenous cultures because of their antiquity. To do so would be to adopt a paternalistic, museum-like ideology that denies the evolving nature of societies. Rather, the presumption here is that indigenous people should have the opportunity to shape their own social, political, and cultural securities or destinies. In this regard, the issue is not merely the persistence of what remains of their ancient ways of life, but whether incorporation and distinctness can coexist with the majority without being subjected to the coercion and exploitation that has so often happened in the past. The challenge here is for the relationship between states and indigenous peoples, and those of the circumpolar north in particular, to be guided by reciprocal accommodation and advantage that can lead to progress for indigenous peoples that is compatible with their interests, preferences, and collective patrimony.

Acknowledgments

The research reported here was supported in part by a Spencer Foundation Small Grant and a Vanderbilt Summer Research Grant to Alfred Darnell. I appreciate the comments and assistance of Sam Nolutshungu, Sue Hinze, Anthony Asiwaju, Frank Darnell, Emily Rosenberg, and the members of SSRC's Marginal Populations Working Group in writing this paper.

Notes

1. Circumpolar north refers to those regions that touch on the arctic circle. Use of circumpolar as an adjective, such as circumpolar peoples, alludes to those indigenous populations whose traditional lands touch on the arctic circle.
2. Barth 1969.
3. Nagel 1986: 98.
4. Nagel 1986; Olzak 1985; Olzak and Nagel 1986; Brass 1985.
5. Nagel 1986: 97; Young 1976.
6. Brass 1985; Greenwood 1985; Young 1976, 1985; See 1987; Ziontz 1985.
7. Nagel 1986; Nagel and Olzak 1986; Despres 1975; Ragin 1979.
8. Young 1976: 67.
9. Barkey and Parikh 1990: 543.
10. Starr 1987: 44.

11. Park 1950: 115.
12. Adam 1971; James 1986.
13. James 1986: 141.
14. James 1986: 141.
15. B. Nagel 1986: 80.
16. B. Nagel 1986: 85.
17. Starr 1987: 35; see also Petersen (1987: 229) who argues that "keeping track of the population's ethnic composition" in United States varies according to "pressures from Congress or the public."
18. Alonso and Starr, 1987, pp. 2-3.
19. Petersen 1987.
20. Korsmo 1988.
21. Cornell 1989: 88.
22. von Bonsdorf, et al. 1974: 17.
23. Lee 1993.
24. The use of blood quotients to define racial identities at the State level has not ceased in the U.S.
25. Thornton 1987; "Alaska Native Claims Settlement Act of 1971, Section 3b".
26. Although in Canada this is true only if one includes Native Americans along with Inuit when discussing indigenous peoples.
27. The region of Scandinavia occupied by Saami in Norway, Sweden and Finland "is collectively known as Fennoscandia" (Korsmo 1988).
28. Knapp 1991: Table 3.
29. S. Aikio 1989: 45.
30. There do not appear to be radical shifts in population occurring during the last 50 years although it has shown noticeable increase. In particular, Knapp reports the total Saami population in 1930 as approximately 27,000 (1991: Table 3).
31. Mathiesen 1990; Lundgren 1987; Broms 1988; Keskitalo 1981; Thomasson 1978.
32. von Bonsdorf, et al. 1974: 15.
33. Footnoted in Broms 1988: 301.
34. Keskitalo 1981: 3.
35. M. Aikio 1989.
36. Torp 1990: 81.
37. Torp 1990.
38. M. Aikio 1989: 56.
39. Vilhelm Aubert quoted in Mathiesen 1990: 7.
40. The Canadian Yearbook does not report systematically the different strategies used. However, a footnote to the 1951 statistics reports that figures "include all persons with a paternal ancestor of Indian race, many of whom have long been assimilated and have lost their identity as Indians" (Canadian Yearbook 1955: 155.)
41. ISER Data Base.
42. The percents reported here were calculated from figures compiled and estimated in Armstrong (1977: 136).

Alfred Darnell

43. Managing conflict has been accomplished in recent decades by compensating **209** indigenous groups for lost aboriginal land rights and land use and attempts to reinforce deteriorating cultural heritages.
44. Case 1984.
45. Case 1984: 6.
46. Anderson 1984: 21.
47. Fredrickson 1981: 21-37.
48. Fredrickson 1981: 9.
49. Elliot 1875: 20.
50. Elliot 1875: 20.
51. Elliot 1875: 26-27.
52. U.S. Congress, House of Representatives, Committee on the Territories, Statement of Bishop Peter T. Rowe of Alaska, 1912: 14.
53. U.S. Congress, House of Representatives, Committee on the Territories, 1912: 19.
54. Besides the Organic Act of 1884 there were the Homestead Act of 1898, the Act of March 3, 1881, sec. 14, 26 Stat. 1095, and the Act of June 6, 1900, sec 217, 31 Stat. 330 (Case, 1984: 6, ff. 52).
55. Case 1984: 6.
56. One of the best illustrations of how land use extends over large expanses of land and extends over generations is Brody's account, in *Maps and Dreams* (1981), of the economy and land use among the Beaver Indians of northwest British Columbia.
57. U.S. Department of Treasury 1898: 409.
58. "Alaska Native Claims Settlement Act" Section 2 (e), 1971.
59. The first paragraph of ANCSA emphasizes this as a primary objective of the Act.
60. "Alaska Native Claims Settlement Act," Section 3 (b), 1971: 2.
61. Comments of Mildred T. Jonathan, Alaska Native Review Commission, Village Meetings, Vol. 8, 1984: 76.
62. Comments of Kathy Grimnes, Alaska Native Review Commission, Village Meetings, Vol. 36, 1984: 77.
63. Statement of Betty Thomas-Denny, Alaska Native Review Commission, Village Meetings Vol 8, 1984: 41.
64. Berger 1985; Garber 1984; Alaska Native Review Commission Transcripts 1983-85; Federal/State Tribal Relations Task Force Hearing Transcripts 1984-1985; Report of the Governor's Task Force on Federal-State-Tribal Relations 1986.
65. A large number of Native villages, since the early 1980s, have been trying to incorporate under the Indian Reorganization Act because Federal constraints under such an arrangement are considerably less than those under State municipal laws. Some villages have even been trying to rescind their municipal incorporation in order to reorganize under Federal laws.
66. Darnell 1984: 56-58.
67. Alaska Statutes, 1972, "Title 29: Municipal Government".
68. Personal interview with Anton Hoem, University of Oslo, July 2, 1991.
69. Starr 1987: 44.

Adam, Heribert. 1971. *Modernizing Racial Domination: The Dynamics of South African Politics. Berkeley.* The University of California Press.

Aikio, Marjut (1989). "Language Loss and Ethnicity among the Sami." In *Social Change and Space: Indigenous Nations and Ethnic Communities in Canada and Finland* edited by Ludger Muller-Wille. Minor in Northern Studies Program, Department of Geography McGill University.

Aikio, Samuli (1989). "Sami in Finland: Legal Status of a Small Linguist Minority." In *Social Change and Space: Indigenous Nations and Ethnic Communities in Canada and Finland* edited by Ludger Muller-Wille. Minor in Northern Studies Program, Department of Geography McGill University.

Alonso, William and Paul Starr (1987). "Introduction." In *The Politics of Numbers,* edited by William Alonso and Paul Starr. New York: Russell Sage Foundation.

Alaska Native Review Commission. 1983-1984. Hearing testimony collected by the Alaska Native Review Commission. Vols.1-64. Anchorage, Alaska: Inuit Circumpolar Conference.

Anderson, Benedict. 1983. *Imagined Communities: Reflections on the Origin and Spread of Nationalism.* London: Verso.

Barkey, Karen and Sunita Parikh. 1991. "Comparative Perspectives on the State." *Annual Review of Sociology* 17:523-49.

Barth, Fredrik. 1969. "Introduction." *In Ethnic Groups and Boundaries.* Edited by Fredrik Barth. The Little, Brown Series in Anthropology, Boston: Little, Brown, and Company.

Berger, Thomas R. 1985. *Village Journey: The Report of the Alaska Native Review Commission.* New York: Hill and Wang.

von Bonsdorff, Camilla, Johan Fellman, and Thord Lewin (1974). "Demographic Studies on the Inari Lapps in Finland with Special Reference to their Genealogy." *Arctic Medical Research Report* 6:13-35.

Broms, Bengt (1988). "Identity and Equality: Co-existence of Separate Sovereignties in the Same Territory." *Nordic Journal of International Law,* Special Issue on "The Small Nations of the North."

Case, David. 1984. *Alaska Natives and American Laws.* The University of Alaska Press.

Cohen, Abner. 1975. *Two Dimensional Man: An Essay on the Anthropology of Power and Symbolism in Complex Societies.* Berkeley: University of California Press.

Cohen, Anthony P. 1975. *The Management of Myths: The Politics of Legitimation in a Newfoundland Community.* Newfoundland Social and Economic Studies No. 14, Institute of Social and Economic Research, Memorial University of Newfoundland.

Cornell, S. 1988. *The Return of the Native.* Oxford: Oxford University Press.

Despres, Leo, ed. 1975. *Ethnicity and Resource Competition in Plural Societies.* The Hague: Mouton Publishers.

Elliott Henry W., Special Agent, Treasury Department. 1875. *A Report Upon the Conditions of Affairs in the Territory of Alaska.* U.S. Department of Treasury. Washington, D.C.: Government Printing Office.

Alfred Darnell

Ervin, Alexander. 1976. "The Emergence of Native Alaskan Political Capacity, 1955-71." *Musk Ox* 19.

Fredrickson, George M. 1981. *White Supremacy: A Comparative Study in American and South African History.* Oxford: Oxford University Press.

Garber, Bart K. 1984. Memorandum to Thomas R. Berger, Alaska Native Review Commission. From Bart Garber's personal files.

Hechter, Michael. 1985. "Internal Colonialism Revisited." In *New Nationalisms of the Developed West.* Edited by E. A. Tiryakian and R. Rogowski. Boston: Allen & Unwin.

————. 1975. *Internal Colonialism: The Celtic Fringe in British National Development. 1536-1966.* Berkeley: University of California Press.

Horowitz, Donald L. 1985. *Ethnic Groups in Conflict.* Berkeley: The University of California Press.

Hunter, Guy. 1962. *The New Societies of Tropical Africa.* London: Oxford University Press.

Institute of Social and Economic Research (ISER). 1984. Data Base, Institute of Social and Economic Research, University of Alaska, Anchorage, Alaska.

Issacs, H. 1975. "Basic Group Identity: The Idols of the Tribe." In *Ethnicity.* Edited by N. Glazer and D. P. Moynihan. Cambridge: Harvard University Press.

Keskitalo, Alf Isak (1981). "The Sami People in Finland, Norway and Sweden." In *Education of Samis* edited by Asta Pietila. Information Bulletin of the National Board of General Education Research Development Bureau. Helsinki: Government Printing Office.

Knapp, Gunnar (1991). "The Population of the Circumpolar North. " Unpublished paper, Institute of Social and Economic Research, University of Alaska—Anchorage.

Korsmo, Fae L. (1988). "Nordic Security and the Saami Minority: Territorial Rights in Northern Fennoscandia." *Human Rights Quarterly* 10:509-24.

Lee, Sharon (1993). "Racial Classification in the U.S. Census: 1890- 1990." *Ethnic and Racial Studies* 16:1:75-94.

Lundgren, Jan O. (1987). "The Nordkalotten Circumpolar Region and the Sami: A Review of Geographic and Development Characteristics." In *Arctic Policy* edited by M. A. Stenback. Centre for Northern Studies and Research in Conjunction with the Inuit Circumpolar Conference and the Eben Hobson Chair. McGill University: Centre for Northern Studies and Research.

Lustick, Ian. 1980. *Arabs in the Jewish State: A Study in Control of a Minority Population.* Austin: University of Texas Press.

Mathiesen, Per (1990). "Ethnicity as Pattern: Past and Present." *Acta Borealia,* pages 5-13.

Nagel, Beverly. 1986. "Gypsies in the United States and Great Britain: Ethnic Boundaries and Political Mobilization." In *Competitive Ethnic Relations,* edited by Susan Olzak and Joane Nagel. Orlando: Academic Press.

Nagel, Joane. 1986. "The Political Construction of Ethnicity." In *Competitive Ethnic Relations.* Edited by Susan Olzak and Joane Nagel. Orlando, Florida: Academic Press.

212 Nagel, Joane. 1984. "The Political Construction of Ethnicity." Unpublished paper presented at the Workshop on Race and Ethnicity in the United States, Center for the Study of Industrial Societies, University of Chicago.

Nagel, Joane and Susan Olzak. 1982. "Ethnic Mobilization in New and Old States: An Extension of the Competition Model." *Social Problems* 30: 127-43.

Nielson, Francois. 1985. "Toward a Theory of Ethnic Solidarity in Modern Societies." *American Sociological Review* 50(April):133-49.

Nielson, François. 1980. "The Flemish Movement in Belgium after World War II: A Dynamic Analysis." *American Sociological Review* 45(February):76-94.

Olzak, Susan. 1983. "Contemporary Ethnic Mobilization." *Annual Review of Sociology* 9:355-74.

Olzak, Susan and Joane Nagel, eds. 1986. *Competitive Ethnic Relations.* Orlando, Florida: Academic Press.

Petersen, William. 1987. "Politics and the Measurement of Ethnicity." In *The Politics of Numbers,* edited by William Alonso and Paul Starr. New York: Russell Sage Foundation.

Ragin, Charles. 1986. "The Impact of Celtic Nationalism on Class Politics." In *Competitive Ethnic Relations.* Edited by Susan Olzak and Joane Nagel. Orlando, Florida: Academic Press.

See, K. O. 1986. *First World Nationalism.* Chicago: University of Chicago Press.

Starr, Paul. 1987. "The Sociology of Official Statistics." In *The Politics of Numbers,* edited by William Alonso and Paul Starr. New York: Russell Sage Foundation.

Thomasson, Lars. 1978. "Swedish Government Policies on the Lapps." *Current Sweden,* No. 180, January 1978. Published by the Swedish Institute, Stockholm.

Torp, Eivind. 1990. "Information about Information: Relating Different Historical Sources to One Another." *Acta Borealia* 2:81-85.

Young, Crawford. 1976. *The Politics of Cultural Pluralism.* Madison: The University of Wisconsin Press.

Ziontz, Alvin J. 1985. "Recent Government Attitudes Toward Indian Tribal Autonomy and Separation in the United States." In *Ethnic Groups and the State.* Edited by Paul Brass. Totowa, N.J.: Barnes and Noble Books.

Alfred Darnell

Chapter 8

MARGINS WITHIN MARGINS: HOMELESSNESS AMONG AFRICAN-AMERICAN MEN

Kim Hopper

Among the more distinctive features of contemporary homelessness in the U.S. is the ease with which this spectacle has been assimilated. In the space of a decade, scenes that had been absent from cityscapes for half a century reappeared, and then quickly replicated themselves across the country. From Los Angeles to Phoenix to Houston to Atlanta, up to Washington, D.C. and New York, and back across to Chicago, Santa Barbara and Seattle: unauthorized shanty settlements, or "squatments,"[1] wrote themselves into the new annals of poverty. In their vitality, size and seeming permanence, they rivaled makeshifts last seen during the Great Depression. Typically, they took shape in piecemeal fashion, allowing nearby residents (if there were any) time to adapt. Official recognition of their presence was gradual, the delay a kind of grace period of tolerance. When it did come, shock (even sympathy) soon gave way to irritation and offense. Boundaries had been breached; traditional lines of demarcation no longer held; interstitial invisibility had become harder to come by. Even New York seemed to have lost its distinctive capacity, in the celebrated formulation of E.B. White, "to absorb anything that comes along without inflicting the event on its inhabitants."[2]

What were first alien, even sympathetic, sights quickly became merely nagging reminders of all that urban civilization was supposed to negate: reckless disregard for public safety and sanitation, haphazard construction, unembarrassed display of practices properly kept private, accumulations of waste. This is the world of Tompkins Square Park depicted in DeLillo's novel *Mao II*, set in present-day New York:

> It was something you come upon and then stop in your tracks. A tent city. Huts and shacks . . . blue plastic sheeting covering the lean-tos and the networks of boxes and shipping containers that people lived in. A refugee camp or the rattiest edge of some dusty township. . . . There were bodies shrouded on benches, bedding set out to dry on the fence of the children's pool. And the makeshift shelters draped in blue, the boxhuts, the charcoal

stoves and shaving mirrors, smoke rising from fires set in oildrums. It was a world apart but powerfully here . . .[3]

These are images—refugee camps, tent cities, shanty-towns—that Americans associate with the Third World. Indeed, so potent was this association, and so dissonant the notion that they might be homegrown, that for a while the *New York Times* took to referring to these and similar tableaux as "the New Calcutta" (in an editorial series that began 15 July 1987). The trope caught on, and a report from the New York State Senate later followed suit.

Such places soon came to signify in ways that went far beyond their survival value, however inventive that original achievement may have been. In the eyes of some observers, they were no more than symbolic tokens of impending urban "disorder" on a par with such behavioral "pollutants" as panhandling. Others found justifiable reason for celebrating the lumpen artistry embodied in some of these street projects, wrested out of waste spaces and discarded materials in the precarious margins of the city. By a strange alchemy, their homeless proprietors—people with no property except that they scavenge—had turned these outlaw spaces into places of order, respite, even hope.[4] Still others found the making of rude communities of the otherwise disaffiliated.[5] Nor could their de facto contribution to the informal housing stock be discounted. Although it appears in a novel, DeLillo's colorful inventory of homemade housing at Tompkins Square is no fiction. At the time of the 1990 Census, scores of people were bedded down nightly within the confines of that park. However one chose to construe what they represented, their strangely doubled character—familiar yet "out-of-place"—was undeniable. DeLillo again: "a world apart but powerfully here." Not even a comma demarcates this margin.

Arguably of a piece with this larger assimilation of homelessness has been the erasure of the element of race.[6] With few exceptions, the presence of disproportionate numbers of African-Americans among the homeless poor has occasioned no more than glancing notice. Not, it turns out, that this is a novel omission in the history of homelessness. This time, however, the strain not to see what was plainly there took real effort. This chapter is about the marginalization of black homeless men, historically and present-day, in both the literal and literary worlds. It is meant as a twofold corrective: first, to restore the missing story of homeless black men to the annals of homelessness; and second, to reconstruct the linkages between black homelessness and the more durable realities of race and poverty. Even if one allows for lapses in the record and biases in observers past, on the scale seen today, it is still the case that this particular marginality is of relatively recent vintage and not something that previous investigators simply missed.

Kim Hopper

In a volume treating global structures of dispossession, it may appear a bit anomalous to include a chapter devoted to African-American homelessness. This is not, after all, the homelessness of forced exile, of peripatetic stateless peoples, or of transnational displacement and seizure (Bozarslan, this volume). Still, global forces do figure in the production of domestic homelessness and certain distinctions of marginality do apply, in particular, the structural restrictions placed on full participation in social life (Nolutshungu, this volume). The social opprobrium entailed and physical hardships endured are well known, much-documented features of homelessness. Others—the arduous thankless work that coping with sustained homelessness requires, the loneliness, the loss of privacy, the political disenfranchisement—are less commonly noted.[7]

For the most part, homeless men and women in the U.S. today are marginalized in a liminal fashion, caught betwixt and between for the duration of a condition—being openly without a place of one's own—that may be transient, episodic or relatively permanent. Early reviews were impressed by the extent to which contemporary homelessness threatened to become a captive state; more recent work stresses its transitory nature. Some sense of both scale and turnover may be had from recent studies of shelter occupancy over time in Philadelphia and New York: 3 percent of the population in each city made use of public shelters, over a three year period in Philadelphia, and a five year period in New York. Converted to annual rates of shelter use for each city's poor population, this becomes 4.7 percent for Philadelphia and 6 percent for New York. Nor, to judge from comparable analyses of other shelter systems, are these rates unusual.[8]

There is no denying the damage that homelessness does, especially when part of a "synergism of plagues" in depressed urban areas.[9] The toll in morbidity and mortality is invariably elevated, in ways we are only now beginning to measure with some precision: a careful analysis of deaths among a large cohort of homeless adults in Philadelphia over a four-year period found their age-adjusted mortality rate to be three and a half times that of the city's general population.[10] Homeless men and women are beset by the usual diseases of poverty, especially functional disabilities and chronic disorders, made more pernicious by the state-specific stresses and isolation of street and shelter life. Homeless people are harried by resurgent old afflictions (like tuberculosis), by lethal new ones (like HIV-related illnesses), and by infectious agents that have put novel twists on their virulence (like drug-resistant TB strains). Alcohol, drug abuse and mental health problems are especially common, and often intertwined. However one deciphers the causal relationship

Homelessness Among African-American Men

between homelessness and psychiatric disorder, the added toll taken by home-lessness itself is clear—from the demoralization long documented among shelter dwellers, to the deterioration in mental state observed over time, to the difficulties of getting appropriate care in supportive surrounds, to the perva-sive loss of rights on the street.[11]

Harm is one thing; its social registration, quite another. For margins to have political meaning, they must be acknowledged. Strictly speaking, in the U.S. being poor is a status conferred in the process of being assisted. Not absolute privation, but a degree of relative deprivation sanctioned as socially untenable (the "poverty threshold") is the definitive determination. This doesn't mean that unrecognized suffering is without social meaning or utility. But it does mean that hardship must undergo not only a process of discovery but one of translation and validation before it becomes a public charge. The process by which certain forms of distress escape the domain of private burden to become recognized as collective responsibilities is fundamental to the politics of marginality, as well as the welfare state.[12] Like the operations of "administrative" reason discussed elsewhere in this volume by Darnell and Asiwaju, how the metes and bounds of legitimate need are drawn—what counts as homelessness?—will determine the potential size and duration of claims against the state by marginal groups.

It follows that the official definition of homelessness[13] has a certain face validity that, as ethnographic fact, is bound to be respected. It also follows that any account that sticks exclusively to official records will yield a seriously distorted picture. Like the acts the state defines as crime, the condition it defines as homelessness is instructive not only in its own right,[14] but also as an index of the political dimensions of categorical need. And like the taxed exchanges it defines as the economy, the official field of action is only part of a larger one.

Some Limitations in the Literature

Anthropologists are taught to search out signature traces of meaning, utility and power in cultural beliefs and behavior. Values, customs and daily routines must not only be carefully documented, they must be situated as well. If there is a core article of faith to the discipline, it is that the intelligibility of practice can only be grasped in relation to context. Context not only lends vivid local color, it provides the necessary field of boundaries and contingencies, framing constraints and insistent pressures, within which daily lives, choices and identities take shape. In the present instance, attending to context means placing overt homelessness within the larger transformation of American cities that has occurred within the past two decades. It is this transformation,

Kim Hopper

especially in its economic and demographic dimensions, that makes for the distinctive marginality of young African-American men. I have in mind not only the consolidation of a service-based labor market with its polarized wage structure, the persistent rise of female-headed households, and the new strains on extended kin, but also the restructuring of urban space into increasingly segregated residential zones, contested public places, ever more costly housing stock. Especially important in this regard are global forces and flows that are reshaping local markets and habitats, while at the same time creating new spaces and amalgamations where the usual categories of distinction no longer apply.[15]

Because it is African-American homeless men with whom we deal here, this discussion must also be placed within the enduring legacy of racism in this country. And here we encounter the first of what will prove a number of sub-marginalizations in this account. In recent years, coming to terms with black homelessness has been relegated to a minor sideshow of the larger (and largely segregated) debates about "the underclass." If these are "usually disguised battles about race,"[16] they are also tacit expressions of the subordination of poverty to color. An enduring example of the symbolic transformation of marginality noted at the outset of this chapter, the consignment of the bulk of discussion of single black male poverty to the underclass debate illustrates what happens when perceptions of menace outweigh pathos.[17]

As an anthropologist, too, I should take special note of the limitations in the ethnographic record that bears upon African-American homelessness. With the development of longitudinal studies of homelessness, it has become clear that far from being a terminal status (as was true of skid row men a quarter-century ago), contemporary homelessness is increasingly an episodic or recurrent circumstance. "Residential instability" is the more encompassing framework[18] and attention to the routine, everyday strategies of survival practiced in poor neighborhoods is essential. Given their overrepresentation in urban homeless populations, members of black households should be of particular interest. Yet, with a handful of notable exceptions,[19] American urban ethnographers in the 1980s tended to ignore the community and kinship contexts of African-American "ghetto" life. Consequently, much about recurring patterns of improvised (e.g., temporarily "doubled-up") residence or overt homelessness among this group, despite its prominence in contemporary debates on poverty, remains unknown. Contemporary discussion of the role of informal support, kinship especially, in staving off (or coping with) homelessness is noticeably the poorer as a result. And this account of the dynamics of homelessness among black American males suffers in consequence.

Homelessness Among African-American Men

Historically, the decisive features of vagrancy that catapult it onto the stage of public awareness and action are scale and visibility.[20] Once noticeable in sufficient numbers, homeless men have customarily been treated as a threat to be contained, whether because they openly challenged the work ethic, implicitly mocked the family and the claims of kinship, or were read as portents of more insidious social disorder. In cities, vagrancy typically becomes a social problem when too many footloose men, unable to "give good account" of themselves, make nuisances of themselves instead—through the sheer spectacle of their presence or the insistence of their begging.

Being at risk of homelessness is first and foremost a function of persisting poverty and uncertain employment. On this account, black men would seem to be ripe candidates. But practicing homelessness is another story. Scale and visibility for black men on the road have meant a host of obstacles, not least among which was rank discrimination at the hands of both police and proprietors catering to homeless men. Concealment was among the necessary skills of those who did take to the road, a fact that hobbles attempts to reconstruct that ill-recorded history. But in recounting the story of homelessness among African-American men, the narrator confronts not one, but two kinds of invisibility. The first, lasting roughly from the Reconstruction Era (late 1860s) to the 1970s, is empirical. In police station and shelter records, in tables assembled by research studies, and in memoirs of road life, when they are mentioned at all, black men are a tiny (if distinctive) minority. That absence, we will see, is hardly uniform and ends abruptly, at any rate, with the Great Depression. It resumes with a postwar skid row literature that endorsed as conventional wisdom the notion that black homelessness was extremely rare, when its own empirical accounts tell a different story. The second kind of invisibility, from the 1970s to the present, is something else. In this period, while the numbers of black men on the road, in the shelters and on the streets have steadily grown, their representation in the public discourse of homelessness remains erratic at best, a passing mention as a rule.

The earliest link between African-Americans and homelessness was forged by punishment, not poverty. Colonial poor laws treated the wandering poor as suspect, possibly dangerous, a potential drain on local funds. They shared a symbolic kinship with the slave. "[B]oth were perceived as set apart from the rest of society and unlikely to labor unless they were forced to do so;" vagrancy codes frequently included "recalcitrant or runaway servants or slaves" among their target class.[21] Hence, the original New York City "House of Correction, Workhouse and Poorhouse" (1734) was not only a place where the terminally ill were nursed, deserted children put up, and the luckless and friendless quartered; it was also where runaway slaves were jailed.[22] That symbolic kinship persisted into the early 1800s: street begging was becoming a growing nuisance, so the city charged four officers with detaining "for examination all vagrants, Negroes, common prostitutes, and other persons whom they suspect have not gained a legal settlement."[23]

For the most part, though, African-American men are conspicuous by their absence in standard accounts of American homelessness. In the antebellum period, only in major urban areas like Philadelphia, where blacks accounted for as much as half of the arrested vagrants, was their presence notable. Even in the surge of tramping that followed the Civil War, in most regions they appear to have been markedly inconspicuous. Black men constituted less than 1 percent of the "tramp census" conducted by McCook in the late 19th century, made up only 2 percent of turn-of-the-century tramp cohorts in Chicago and Minneapolis, and were all but invisible in Progressive era accounts of lodging houses and road life.[24]

This apparent absence makes more sense if we look at the style of homelessness that prevailed from the 1870s to the 1920s. "Tramping" was a way of paying tribute to the necessity of work while doing so (at least in part) on one's own terms. For all but the dissolute, it was a young man's game, and a risky one at that. One survived on the road by one's wits, trusting to the hospitality of strangers, scavenging when necessary, dodging the police, hoping for a stint of (usually dirty) work at the end. Black men were at a decided disadvantage on all four counts. Not surprisingly, much of the little we know of African-Americans on the road in the late 19th and early 20th centuries comes from police records. DuBois noted in *The Philadelphia Negro* (1899) that blacks were overrepresented in that city's vagrancy arrest rolls. Over ten percent of Washington, D.C.'s police station house lodgers from 1891-95 appear to have been black ("nonwhite"); the same is true of vagrancy arrests in Omaha from 1887-1913 and charity lodging house occupants in Philadelphia in 1905; fully a third of Kansas City's transients in that era were reportedly black.[25] Frazier devoted a chapter of *The Negro Family in the United States* (1939) to the lifeways of those "roving men and homeless women" who took to the road following emancipation and whose ranks had increased significantly in the 1920s. After reviewing an impressive range of records, memoirs and reports, one historian concludes not only that blacks were well represented among tramping workers in the post-Civil War period, but also that the "egalitarian nature of the [tramping] culture" (in contrast to the increasingly segregated nature of American society at large) made road life especially attractive to them.[26] But if the racial divide was relaxed among (at least some) homeless men on the road, the same cannot be said of the establishments catering to them, where strict discrimination remained the rule. In Chicago,

Homelessness Among African-American Men

for example, where the impact of black migration from the South was especially strong, the city's free-wheeling "hobohemia" restricted homeless black men to segregated "colored men's hotels;" other establishments simply referred newly arrived homeless migrants to the Urban League.[27]

During the Great Depression of the 1930s black homelessness grew substantially. By the winter of 1932-33, nearly a quarter of the "homeless transients" served in Philadelphia were black, as were 10 percent of Chicago's shelter men. Across the country, between 7 and 12 percent of the local caseloads of "unattached" men (the contemporary term for homeless) assisted through the federal Transient Relief Program were black. Such percentages may be misleading, for black men on the move during the Depression took pains to avoid relief centers because of what they experienced as the thin line between transiency (a social status) and vagrancy (a civil offense punishable by a term in jail or the workhouse).[28] As one black migrant worker recalled: "When I was hoboing I was in jail two-thirds of the time."[29]

In Depression-era New York, black homeless men were nearly a decade younger than their white counterparts on average. They traveled more, left home earlier, had less schooling, had been unemployed longer and were in better health (probably reflecting their age). Black homeless men were also more likely to be married and less likely to be native New Yorkers. Although they comprised only 5 percent of the adult male population in the city, they made up 15 percent of the public shelter clientele in June 1931, owing in part to the scarcity of private facilities for black homeless men. Of 125 men arrested on vagrancy charges over a 30-day period and referred for casework to a new "Mendicancy Project" at the workhouse on Welfare Island, 9 percent were black. In western New York State, blacks made up fully a fifth of "landsmen [i.e., non-seamen] transients" in Buffalo and outnumbered whites among native-born homeless men in Lackawanna. Black men were similarly overrepresented in Pittsburgh, though not in Washington, D.C. or (apparently) in Houston. For the most part, an unpublished report by Nels Anderson concluded, such men "were generally left to their own devices to seek shelter in private homes or to sleep out."[30] One of Anderson's sources fleshes out the picture of how such men fared at the time:

> The Negro drifter on New York City is not given to living in 'jungle' [i.e., hobo] camps. He prefers to get his food by 'sponging' from friends, begging, or doing odd chores of a few hours' duration. For sleeping quarters during warm weather he finds shelter on the docks of the East River, on the Harlem River water-front between 126 Street and 150 Street, in empty rooms, lofts and basements in Harlem, in the subway stations along the Lenox Avenue line, or perhaps he rides the subway or elevated trains a few hours. During the winter of 1930-31 some of them live in an improvised shelter in a

wreckage pile on Park Avenue between 133 Street and 134 Street. In colder months of the year they often prevail upon friends or acquaintances to let them sleep in an unoccupied basement or loft. Charity organizations in Harlem take care of a daily average of about 130. . . . On even the coldest nights some can be found sleeping on the benches . . . [31]

Relief rolls and case registers are thus unreliable gauges with which to take the measure of African-American homelessness during the Depression. For in addition to these official "transients" were "many more highly mobile solitary men and women [who] without the aid of relief ma[d]e their living by both lawful and unlawful means . . ."[32]

Warfare has few peers when it comes to full employment programs, particularly for men whom the market has relinquished (Nolutshungu, this volume). The black homeless man joined the exodus from relief rolls that the wartime economy spurred in the early 1940s. This exodus effectively trans-formed "hobohemia" from a reservoir of casual labor into "skid row," a repository of the unemployable "where the impoverished, the disesteemed, and the powerless [could] take refuge and find comfort."[33] Postwar scholars paid scant heed to African-American men who, despite their poverty and recurrent joblessness, did not show up in great numbers on skid row thanks largely to timeworn informal, kin- and neighborhood-based networks of support that sustained newly migrating refugees from the American south.[34] Not only were the bonds of extended kinship among African-American families resilient, but its boundaries proved elastic as well. It was not unusual for boarders, for example, to be included as family; "adopted relatives" were common. Outside the family proper, mutual aid societies, storefront churches, and "improvement associations" played crucial roles.[35] The redun-dancy of such "backup" resources proved vitally important to the self-suffi-ciency of newly transplanted communities—a fact noted as early as Reconstruction days—and largely explains why, in the face of substantial and persisting need, migrant African-Americans maintained a lower profile than northern-born blacks in the postwar welfare rolls.[36]

Nonetheless, close studies did reveal a stubborn African-American pres-ence on skid rows that rivaled Depression figures.[37] Nearly 20 percent of incarcerated inebriates in Rochester were black in the mid-fifties. Black men made up 22.3 percent of the "skid row case load" in New York City in 1955, a percentage thought to be increasing in the early 1960s, when the city's "nonwhite" population stood at 14.7 percent of the total. In the late 1950s, one-ninth of Chicago's estimated 12,000 skid row men were black, most residing in segregated districts or facilities. Two-fifths of the men showing up for a free breakfast at a Philadelphia church hostel in 1964 were black; half of them had some housing, but 39 percent had just come from sleeping in

Homelessness Among African-American Men

all-night theaters. In the mid-1960s, researchers from Columbia University's Bureau of Applied Social Science consistently found that a substantial minority (29 percent) of Bowery men were black and that some traditional skid row institutions catered to them. Curiously, the only notice given that fact in the definitive volume on the Columbia project was the near-throwaway comment that the Bowery was "probably 'darker' than most skid rows in northern cities." Color-blindness seems the only explanation for researchers impressed by "the underrepresentation of blacks" on skid row.[38]

At that time, too, "the remnant of a skid row" could still be discerned along 125th St. But more interesting for our purposes here is the report by a graduate student on the Columbia project that makeshift accommodations (such as the practice of men living in basements as building superintendent "helpers") were commonplace in Harlem at that time.[39] This observation, and others like it made elsewhere, convinced some analysts that the relative invisibility of black men on postwar skid rows was more a problem of misclassification than one of missing men.

Missing Men or Hidden Homeless?

These analysts argued that searching for black "skid rows" was misguided. Investigators would be better served by searching instead for "skid row-like men" (addiction coupled with extreme poverty) among the "ranks of the more amorphous destitute residents of the slums."[40] Such men proved easy to find. Yet the differences between makeshift residential arrangements in the black community and formal institutionalized homelessness are as profound as the similarities.

In the early 'seventies on the South Side of Chicago, for example, men who readily met the criteria of "skid row-like" could regularly be found hanging out on street corners. Their panhandling and "bottle gang" drinking distinguished them from other "respectable" men with whom they shared the corner. For "wineheads," food and shelter paled in urgency next to the necessity of procuring another "taste." On occasion, they would walk the streets all night, or snatch brief periods of sleep in parked cars. Some took on seasonal work; others traded sex for room and board.[41] But relatively few showed up on Chicago's skid row.

Similar observations were made about unattached black men living in New York City's single-room-occupancy (SRO) hotels in the late 1960s and early 1970s, just before that stock began its precipitous decline.[42] Once again, although sharing some afflictions (notably poverty and addiction) and practices (gang-drinking), the men living in such dwellings were clearly thought by their chroniclers and their contemporaries to be different from ("a social cut above") their counterparts on the Bowery.[43] The SRO was an "alternative" to skid row, a place where truly "homeless people . . . [occasionally] wander[ed] [in to] use the hotel bathrooms, especially the bathtubs, to sleep in."[44]

There is a difference worth preserving between a mode of subsistence that manages exigency through careful husbanding (or, for that matter, reckless exploitation) of indigenous resources, and one that is forced to petition the grudging bounty of the state. These are not ink-tight categories. As Nels Anderson observed 50 years ago, strategies of survival do not denote distinct "types" of homeless men.[45] Many of those showing up for shelter, for example, do so only after having exhausted the resources of kin and family. Still, I want to insist again on the utility of distinguishing between the invisible poor struggling to get by and the officially homeless.

Racial discrimination remains the rule in many Bowery flophouses today, whose older residents are still predominantly white. But a different picture prevails in both the public shelters and the missions. As the haunt of elderly white men, the Bowery was already in decline by the early 1970s. Before the decade was out, new recruits totally transformed the place. Between 1966 and 1976, the proportion of the annual caseload at the Men's Shelter made up of first-time users rose from 28 to 48 percent. These "new arrivals" were much younger than their predecessors, half were black, and they were likely to leave within months of their arrival (skid row men typically had left in a pine box). By the early 1980s, at least two-thirds of regular shelter users were African-American.[46]

African-Americans Among Today's Homeless Poor

Estimating the number of homeless Americans—even supposing one can agree on the definition of the term and the relevant time period—remains an exercise bristling with difficulties. Estimates vary widely. In 1990, the Census Bureau enumerated 228,621 "homeless" Americans on a given night, though it was unusually diligent in noting that the operational definition of "homeless" and rules of enumeration made the count less than exhaustive. Point-in-time counts, however, underestimate the extent of an intermittent condition. A recent study that interviewed housed respondents by telephone in a nationwide random sample offers a corrective: within the period 1985-90, 3.1 percent of respondents—5.7 million adults and (corrected to include children) over 7 million Americans all told—had been homeless at some point.[47]

Whatever the precise dimensions, researchers throughout the 1980s consistently found that black males were overrepresented among local homeless populations. Fully 41 percent of the 1990 Census Bureau "S-Night" count of residents in shelters were African-American, as were 39 percent on those found on the streets and in abandoned buildings. The proportion of blacks among homeless Vietnam Era Veterans is three times that found among general Vietnam Era Veterans. A recent review of 60 studies conducted during the 1980s found that, on average, 44 percent of the researched homeless populations were black.[48]

As its clientele has changed, so have the institutions of skid row. Formerly a seedy retirement community, playing host to "old men drunk and sober,"[49] public shelters perform a dual service today: seeing to the immediate needs of those who show up at their doors and providing respite to families who would otherwise shoulder their support. In some areas, urban shelters have taken over functions formerly performed by extended kin, fictive and real. In some poor minority neighborhoods of New York City, for example, shelters function as "community bedrooms," partially

> remov[ing] the burden of caring for individuals whose presence adds an extraordinary strain on the viability of these embattled households—either because they can no longer contribute to the income of the household, or because of their behavior and special needs.[50]

Elsewhere, a certain developmental logic may be discerned as well. In a study set in Boston and spanning twenty years, Peter Hainer describes how "transience" can work in African-American households of the inner city. Periods of residential instability are understandably common among young black men. Their "naturally" disruptive tendencies test even the flexibly configured confines of hospitality normally accorded kith and kin. And so, for a while, they

> live a kind of vagabonding existence with age mates . . . [who] support and help each other, as they live 'on the street,' often as 'homeless' people in abandoned buildings, in low rent apartments with their 'brothers,' or moving in and out of various family apartments.[51]

Their families practice an economy of makeshifts, ejecting (or passing on) these men in the interest of domestic stability and peace. At that time, public shelters were beginning to function not only as places of rough sanctuary but as flourishing nodes of informal exchange—as "institution[s] of trade, sustenance and even transient community for the sometimes working poor."[52] Young black men found a ready substitute home.

Accounting for the New Homelessness Among African-American Men

The factors that account for the rise of homelessness among black males are the same ones that explain persisting poverty in that population—and then

"Postmodern poverty in America" is still distinctively weighted by color:
the proportion of blacks living under the official poverty line[53] is three times
that of whites (28 vs. 8.8 percent); nearly half of all black children reside in
poor households, a figure four times that for white children. More seriously,
38 percent of black children remain poor for at least 6 years, a rate more than
seven times that of white children. Among African-Americans, too, income
divisions have widened. Residential segregation, long a unique feature imposed
upon black American communities, shows little sign of receding; segregation
in schooling has increased. Intermarriage rates between African-Americans and
other racial/ethnic groups remain anomalously low. So firmly embedded is the
racial divide in U.S. society that a book on race in the early 1990s borrowed a
phrase from the Kerner Commission report of 1968—"separate and unequal"—for its subtitle.[54]

Why should extreme poverty in the last decade increasingly take the form
of homelessness among young males, especially in light of the robust legacy of
the black extended family? Some clues are provided by the few published
accounts that have examined the linkage between race and homelessness
explicitly.[55] A study in Ohio found that, compared to whites, black respondents were younger, had somewhat better educations, were more likely to be
Vietnam Veterans, were longer-term local residents and more recently homeless, and were "more likely to move in and out of homeless conditions." Like
the pattern in African-American poverty generally, recurrent homelessness
tended to be less "event-driven" and more a matter of "reshuffling." A Detroit
study found that African-Americans were more likely than whites to have
sustained ties with relatives, to have been in alcohol or drug detoxification
units, in jail or prison, but less likely to have a psychiatric history.[56] Thought
frequently to be resorting to makeshift alternatives with friends and families,
blacks nonetheless accounted for 31 percent of a Birmingham sample; in a
neighboring city, disinclination to make use of local missions means that
blacks are overrepresented on the street. Racial and ethnic differences were less
clear in Chicago, where both black and Hispanic families were "more likely
[than whites] to subsidize their dependent adult members."

Work and kinship remain critical gauges of the risk of homelessness. In
some regions, decades-old trends in segmented labor markets have been
exacerbated by the growth of the informal sector and influx of new immigrants, who compete for cheap housing and menial jobs in service and
"downgraded manufacturing" sectors.[57] Single males especially are subject to
a growing scarcity of affordable housing and cutbacks in income maintenance
programs for the unattached and/or disabled poor. Lately, too, a cultural turn
has re-emerged in the guise of the "underclass" debate—that ghetto residents

Homelessness Among African-American Men

are beset not only by "concentrated" poverty but by singularly disabling cultural deficits as well. All four topics are addressed below.

Trends in the Labor Market

In the past quarter century, for young black males especially, rates of unemployment, underemployment, and long-term joblessness have dramatically risen; they have been especially severe for those who lack appropriate adequate skills and/or adequate schooling. Since the mid-1970s, too, the earnings of young black males relative to whites have steadily deteriorated, across all education groups.[58] In the central cities, the picture is even bleaker. If one included discouraged and involuntary part-time workers, nearly a quarter of black males were jobless in the first quarter of 1992, twice the rate of white men.[59]

Economists may debate the relative weights of reputed causes of the dismal employment prospects of the black worker, but few doubt the severity or the tenacity of the trend. When the percentage of black men of prime laboring age who are idle leaps fivefold—from 6.8 to 32.7 percent—from 1963-65 to 1985-1987,[60] that trend is difficult to ignore. Proposed explanatory factors range from changes in the supply of workers (skills, wage expectations, acceptable work) in local and global settings, to the effects of plant relocation or closure, to changing demands on workers within industries or occupations (tending toward both high-end "information-processing" and low-end work in service or downgraded manufacturing), to the competing lure of "underground" or other "nonwork" sources of income, to the continuing preference of employers for non-black workers.[61] In none of these scenarios, can the enabling hand of government in shaping the postwar job and housing markets be ignored.

Whatever the relevance of such factors in the specific instance, demand for labor is the critical dependent variable. Tight local labor markets substantially improve the employment picture for inner city black men, especially those with poor education. When demand for workers is there, the percent of blacks working goes up, average earnings increase, and poverty rates decline.[62] Such results support survey findings of a still strong work ethic in minority neighborhoods; they animate advocates of a full employment policy, too, despite the dismal history of efforts to implement it.[63]

Exactly how and where to stimulate demand remains a vexed issue. Take, for example, the findings grouped under the "spatial mismatch" hypothesis. Twenty-five years ago, John Kain first argued that the "postwar dispersal" of jobs to the suburbs, coupled with persisting (if not worsening) patterns of residential segregation, meant that black employment prospects, already handicapped by employer discrimination and poor education, could well deteriorate.[64] Studies of cities undergoing deindustrialization have shown that job displacement and job elimination occurred much earlier and more severely for African-American blue-collar workers. But was race or space at fault? Ironically, black gains in manufacturing in the industrial north during the immediate postwar period meant that they were disproportionately employed in industries that have stagnated or declined since then. Whether they were autoworkers in Detroit, steel workers on the South Side and West Side of Chicago, production workers in Philadelphia, or blue collar operatives in New York City, the effect was the same; only the scale of plant closures and lost jobs varied. Outside of the rustbelt, "deproletarianization" was not so widespread and played less of a role in the economic fortunes of blacks in the 1970s. Still, four cities in the industrial north accounted for 35 percent of ghetto poor in 1980; by then, however, other factors were at work as well.[65]

Spatial mismatch theorists will need to reckon with the fact that the converse (proximity to jobs) has not historically made much difference to black employment rates. Additional longitudinal research is also needed that will attend more closely to the motivation and behavior of both workers and employers, and turn a critical eye on the captivity effects of concentrated ghetto poverty.[66]

Prolonged periods of enforced idleness can hardly promote attachment to the labor force. In a culture that places a high premium on work for males, damage to both self-esteem and the regard of others surely follow. As Luther, a newsstand attendant in Chicago puts it: "A man without things to do is not a man."[67] Nor are legitimate "nonwork" sources of income any refuge for able-bodied men of working age. Unemployment benefits reach a smaller proportion of the jobless than at any time in the last twenty years. State-administered "general assistance" programs were eroded by inflation and cut back by governments throughout the 1980s; they were further slashed in the early 1990s. In not a single one of 44 metropolitan areas were maximum monthly G.A. benefits sufficient to meet fair market rent for an efficiency apartment.[68]

All of which serves to make it increasingly unlikely that jobless young black males—those who comprise the largest proportion of the single homeless population—will be able to meet their responsibilities in contributing to shared household expenses. Kinship may be elastic but its patience is sorely tested by time and trouble.

Changes in the Black Extended Family

Kinship has historically provided the first line of defense against misfortune and the bedrock of social security. In times of turmoil, loss, relocation and adaptation to new forms of work, kin ties provide the indispensable connections to obligated others—"diffuse, enduring solidarity"[69]—that enable people to carry on. Its resources are myriad; its claims may be contested but are difficult to ignore; local and geographically dispersed members may be brought into play; even long dormant ties can prove available in times of trouble. But maintaining kinship takes work, and that crucial labor is typically performed (and regulated) by women.[70]

As discussed earlier, bondage imposed singular difficulties upon African-American families, difficulties that did not end with Emancipation. Still, the celebrated legacy of the black family is one of resiliency and innovation. Its "flexibility and strength" not only "anchored" the Great Migration north,[71] but continue to distinguish present-day black communities. If details of slave family culture remain to be clarified; if, in their zeal to correct a portrait of black family life as little more than a "tangle of pathology," some analysts have underplayed the toil, trouble and strain inherent in managing extended households; if too little attention has been paid to the uneven ledgers of reciprocity in practice and the difficulties of extracting oneself from over-demanding networks—if, in short, too much has been made of the contrivances of kinship and too little of their costs, still, their record of support is strong.[72] Especially germane here is the buffer of subsistence extended to kin, real and fictive,[73] through earnings and resource pooling.

What most strains the ties that bind are not the normal processes of economic growth, but the dislocations that arise from irregular or suddenly interrupted employment.[74] In the 1970s, the viability of such households suffered severe setbacks, setbacks which have doubtless worsened since then. Between 1969 and 1979, the prevalence of extended households among the urban jobless or marginally employed increased by 24 percent (from 17 to 21 percent); among blacks, the increase was 44 percent (from 18 to 26 percent).[75] At the same time, if one sets aside public "transfer payments," their pooled ability to raise household income above poverty level was nearly halved. In 1969, 30 percent of extended household heads earned sufficient income to lift them above the poverty line; but an additional 39 percent of such households were kept out of poverty by the combined effect of other family earnings and the contributions of non-family household members. In 1979, by contrast, even fewer extended households (24 percent) avoided poverty through the earnings of their heads; and just over another fifth (22.5 percent) were held above poverty by ancillary earnings and non-family contributions.[76]

This "precipitous decline in the antipoverty effectiveness"[77] of the informal resources of extended households contributed to a substantial growth in the population at risk of displacement and homelessness. For a while, a series of makeshift accommodations, "reshuffling" the burden of support, may have

Kim Hopper

sufficed to keep frank homelessness at bay. But faced with a renewed on-slaught on its carrying capacity from both the market and the state[78] in the 1980s, even families renowned for their tenacity and resourcefulness in the face of adversity were bound to be courting exhaustion. To judge from shelter demographics, a good number of the single men they put up (and who were later to show up in the shelters) came with a serious drug or alcohol problem, suffered from a severe psychiatric disorder, or confronted the re-entry problems of an ex-offender—none of which can have eased the burden on kin.[79]

Housing

Highway construction, mortgage guarantees, revisions in the tax code to allow write-offs for property taxes and mortgage interest, assessment practices biased against urban areas, all bear witness to the heavy hand of the federal government in the postwar suburban housing boom in the United States. Race as well as geography has been at work. Housing development in the last 50 years betrays the actions of a government "anxious to use its power and resources for the social control of racial minorities." Its abiding legacy has been a pattern of residential segregation so tenacious as to earn the appellation "American apartheid."[80]

Affordability and habitability in the dwellings of the urban poor have suffered in consequence. In the past 20 years, the rental housing gap—the number of available and affordable units relative to the need—has widened appreciably.[81] Nationwide, an estimated 5.1 million very low income households are classified by HUD as having "worst case housing needs." That is, their incomes are below 50 percent of the area median, and they pay at least half their income on housing, or live in severely substandard dwellings, or both. As a rule, federal housing subsidies fail to offset affordability difficulties for poor families, fewer than a fifth of whom live in subsidized units. Nearly two-thirds of welfare households live in unsubsidized housing and pay over half of their income for the privilege; a third of this housing is "substandard." Blacks are much more likely than whites to live in physically deficient or overcrowded dwellings, and nearly three-quarters of poor black households pay more than 30 percent of income for housing.[82]

A more meaningful reckoning is provided by the measure "shelter poverty." This refers to the situation of households who, having met their housing costs, are unable to satisfy non-housing needs at a minimal level of adequacy. By this standard, approximately half of all black households were shelter poor in the period 1972-1991, a rate typically 20 percentage points higher than that of all households. Although blacks account for only 11% of all households, they make up 19% of shelter-poor households.[83]

The precarious housing situation of poor households has obvious bearing on their capacity to offer assistance to others. More directly pertinent to the housing options of young black men is the fate of low-cost residential hotels, which had provided housing of last resort for people whose habits and incomes complicated the business of making ends meet. In the 1970s, fueled by gentrification and urban "revitalization" movements, that stock was virtually depleted in many urban areas. Nationwide, an early estimate placed the loss of units of "one and two rooms lacking facilities" during the 1970s at more than a million, or 47 percent of the total. Subsequent studies have generally confirmed this estimate, detailing the loss in specific cities.[84]

In New York City, the trends for housing, residential hotels and, in the last decade, shelters are telling. Between 1978 and 1987, low-rent units declined by 26 percent; vacancies in that range fell by 72 percent. At the same time, the pool of poor renters increased slightly during the same period and income polarization intensified. Stock losses and inflation coupled to reduce the supply of housing affordable by households on public assistance by 60 percent. Notwithstanding modest gains in the last two decades, compared to whites, black renter households are still five times as likely to be occupying dilapidated units, three times as likely to be overcrowded, and more than twice as likely to be living in physically inadequate conditions. In the late 1980s, signs of owner disinvestment (the withdrawal of essential services, failure to pay taxes, or defaulting on mortgage payments) could be discerned in one of every six rental properties; these are concentrated in poor neighborhoods with high proportions of African-American and Latino residents.[85] Options for poor single people in the city have narrowed considerably. Fully 63 percent of low-cost residential hotel units were lost (to conversions, abandonment, demolition) from 1975 to 1981. On the heels of that loss, the number of municipal shelters for single persons in the city has grown dramatically, from a single Bowery-based intake center in 1979 to two dozen facilities scattered throughout four boroughs. Nightly census topped 10,000 in the late 1980s.[86]

Such indicators confirm that the city's housing shortage persists, that affordability problems have worsened, and that the burden of housing distress falls disproportionately on poor and nonwhite groups. With no little irony, some analysts took to referring to shelters as the public housing initiative for the poor in the 1980s.

Culture

As noted earlier, serious research on African-American communities in the U.S. was interrupted in the early 1970s in the wake of the bitter dispute over the "culture of poverty." The exceptions that subsequently appeared were, for the most part, corrective in nature, bent on countering the image of the dysfunctional black family. By default, power to define the terms of the renewed debate in the early 1980s was ceded to conservative scholars. The debate has been lately rejoined, fueled by free-wheeling comments on under-class culture, blunt calls for rectifying "the moral environment of the poor," and forays into the new politics of dependency.[87] With respect to homelessness, the issues have generally taken shape more narrowly around three questions: whether shelter providers should insist upon behavioral quid-pro-quos from their guests in exchange for a bed for the night; to what extent homeless persons' adaptations to the street or to the routine of shelters themselves disable them for more settled living; and how addiction is to be dealt with.

A brief word about the term "culture," if only to stress that cultures are not the symbolic equivalent of straitjackets. They provide—not tight, hyper-coherent programs for action and thought—but rather "tool kits" of images, frames, competencies, world-views, from which people assemble heuristic "strategies of action."[88] These stores of images and explanatory constructs, of reasons for doing and compulsions to do, are subject to continuous editing and correction in the daily round of activity. Even for matters that go to the heart of American culture—the recurring ones here are kinship, marriage, work, initiative, dependency, dealings with the state, harmful habits—mean-ings are not fixed but unsettled, contested by any number of stakeholders.

Few observers deny that some of the poor (at least some of the time) "hold values and take actions far outside the mainstream," that for some these can become characteristic patterns, and that such behavior adds to the injuries and exacerbates the captivity of ghetto life. But how best to interpret such behavior, how tightly it is coupled to present-day contextual variables, how long it persists in the absence of its generative conditions, where critical loci of control lie—these remain hotly disputed. As was the case in the culture of poverty debate, the most divisive issue remains that of "self-perpetuation"—the extent to which "some cultural traits may take on a life of their of own for a period of time and thereby become a constraining or liberating factor" in the lives of those who bear them.[89]

For social scientists if not moralists, it is a root axiom of faith that patterned behavior, however aberrant or self-defeating, "makes sense" once the limits and pressures of the determining context are read carefully. Much hinges on the execution of that reading. It can be done intelligently, as when economists struggle to imagine the incentive structure and adult models confronted by young black men; it can also be done in a way that borders on caricature, with culture invoked as an explanation of itself.[90] But even if one ignores the uneven talents of analysts, five problems continue to plague the invocation of culture in underclass discourse:

How distinctive are portrayals of present-day black "underclass" culture? Although much is made in today's debate of the "social isolation" of contemporary ghetto culture, ethnographic accounts of its predecessor in the postwar period offer not contrasting cases, but familiar ones: co-existing but hardly commingling communities, divided along class lines.[91] Hyperbolic, contradictory images of human agency badly hobble the discussion. In accounts hedged against victim-blaming, ghetto dwellers appear largely as victims, buffeted by macro-economic and micro-cultural forces only dimly within their ken and far outside their control. Adaptation is largely unconscious, an abstract operation imputed from without. Alternatively, ghetto dwellers appear as adepts schooled in the art of cultural resistance. Instead of "adapting" to unyielding circumstance, an oppositional culture develops in response: rich, innovative and defiant. Often downplayed in such accounts are the tragic costs of such defiance, recognition that refusal may serve to perpetuate the structure of exclusion.[92] Anomalies in the ethnographic record abound, making dubious the notion of a consistent African-American "value-set." Consider the competing versions of young black fatherhood offered by Anderson and Sullivan: the first sees it in terms of "sex codes" (chiefly, "the peer-group ethic of 'hit and run' "); the second, using a comparative design that varied configurations of class, ethnicity and social ecology, identifies a dominant pattern of quietly honored paternity among young black fathers.[93] Striking differences appear in accounts of schooling, too.[94] Unresolved measurement issues have emerged as hypotheses have become more refined. Classification and causal inference remain vexed problems, whether one is describing neighborhoods and developing indices for tracking changes over time, or demonstrating the strength and direction of alleged effects on the carrying capacity of households.[95] Finally, to turn from the object of inquiry to the inquiring subject is to confront some uncomfortable and much-denied points of kinship. Distancing maneuvers have long made their appearance in the annals of homelessness.[96] For the most part, such maneuvers have had the effect of masking those implicit connections between the world of the observer and that of the observed. Hochschild has argued that certain features of what passes for "underclass" life cannot be set aside as merely strange, menacing or pitiable. To the contrary: the discipline and work ethic of the drug trade, the wiles devoted to outwitting government regulations, the taste for pain-numbing pastimes, all make their practitioners "not only inhabitants of an alien culture or innocent victims of the capitalist juggernaut . . . [but] in an exaggerated and distorted way, us."[97]

Kim Hopper

In summary, then, the verdict is still out and likely to be mixed on the roles of culture advanced so far. That said, it would be foolhardy to ignore the evidence for specific strands of that argument. In some ghetto communities, paternal and avuncular embodiments of responsibility (and hence "respectability") are in scarce supply. Absent males (and, with them, foregone connections to work) mean that informal sanctions of antisocial behavior and effective means of countering it are often gone as well; disciplinary responsibility shifts to female heads of households. In some regions, a linguistic divide has opened between whites and blacks, compounded by further misunderstandings rooted in non-verbal aspects of communication (gestures of deference, indices of respect, face saving maneuvers); both contribute to those missed cues between boss and employee that interfere with job prospects. Even if endemic drug use may be interpreted as part of a culture of "repudiation" that does not negate the additional damage done to self, family and neighborhood by the trade itself.[98] To the extent that any of these factors works further mischief with one's chances in the job market or jinxes one's welcome at home, it increases the risk of homelessness.

Black Male Homelessness in the 1980s: A Hypothesis

Owing to a confluence of factors—structural, familial and individual—homelessness among black men rose markedly in the 1980s. Labor and housing markets grew progressively more hostile to men of low skill and modest means. Ghetto neighborhoods reeling under the impact of concentrated poverty saw commercial investments decline, public services cut back, and sectors of a physical landscape reduced to ruins. Extended households found it progressively more difficult to make ends meet, as non-family member earnings and government benefits both declined in value. When focus shifts from the material base to informal governance, other factors become salient. With the social regulatory function of work degraded and the disciplinary function formerly played by old males (employed or retired) attenuated, the burden of informal control shifts progressively to the shoulders of women. One of the most effective sanctions they wield is ejection from the household. The upshot: when market losses in affordable housing and decent work are coupled with the mounting strains on extended families, feminization of familial discipline, the growth in the drug trade and continued failures of community-based mental health services, homelessness among black men is an all but foregone conclusion.

Although absent or long severed family ties figure in the histories of some of the homeless poor, for many others—and especially, it appears, for those whose homelessness is local and episodic—such ties are not only maintained, but spell the difference (sometimes recurrently) between a berth amid kin or friends and a cot among strangers. Far from suffering from "a pathology of connectedness,"[99] these men avoid homelessness and/or "exit" from it periodically thanks largely to the resiliency of such networks. As was the case with their forebears in the late 1930s, it is the generosity of extended households in the 1980s that impresses.

But even obligations anchored by kinship have their limits. Tolerating demanding or overcrowded situations is easier if one can expect them to be short-lived. If, that is, viable alternatives to doubling up exist. A local surplus of affordable housing was essential to the fluid reshuffling of residential arrangements that earlier analysts of the African-American extended family saw as vital to its elastic ability to expand and contract as need and discipline required.[100] In many cities in the 1980s, the accommodating inefficiencies in the formal housing market that made it possible for the informal kin-based system to operate in this fashion have virtually disappeared. It seems reasonable to conclude that this loss of housing, however disreputable it may have been, badly hedged the options of circulating family members. Whatever "slack" remained in household carrying capacity was soon exhausted.

Even if one supposes that disruptiveness could be contained, men are still at higher risk of homelessness. For should hardship persist in extended households, eventually a kind of triaging may be instituted. As declining resources make it impossible to meet the needs of all, the circle of kin is more stringently drawn; those better able to fend for themselves are expected to do so.[101] For good reason, triaging is gender-biased. Differences in expectations of independence on the part of men and women persist in the larger (sub-)cultural sphere(s). Women are more valued and versatile as household members. Until recently at least, they were less prone to disabling drug or alcohol use.[102] More to the point here, women do the work of kinship; their investment in the social capital of family ties—and thus their expected return—is greater and more durable than that of men.[103] It is surely stronger than that of young men, many of whom have yet to secure the foothold in the labor market that would enable them to perform as "responsible" (and hence, "respectable") members of the family. By the same token (reliability of female kin, instability of male livelihood), marital prospects may be viewed by young black women as decidedly bleak. For these and related reasons, then, a lengthy sojourn with family immediately precedes the homelessness of women far more often than it does with men.[104]

But neither can it be said that men are immune to the nagging claims of kinship.[105] Pride bristles at prolonged dependency when one has little with which to reciprocate. Under such circumstances, leaving a sorely strapped household and seeking public shelter may be a way of repaying hospitality.

Kim Hopper

Given a scarcity of market units and severe pressure on informal resources, the appeal of non-market alternatives grows. Military service was one such option, although it came at the cost of a heavy commitment. By the mid-1970s, another had surfaced. Absent any change in the operating rules of the institution itself but concurrent with a decline in its traditional clientele, functional patterns of use in public shelters began to shift dramatically in that decade. From a terminal station for elderly, poor and friendless white men, the shelters became way stations for young black men in flux—a modern, relatively unstructured version of the 19th century police station houses for tramps.

The upshot is a pattern of intermittent official homelessness (staying in the shelters or on the street) that can make drawing strict distinctions between housed and "houseless" poverty quite vexing—a confusion evident in the following press account: "Although he described himself as homeless when he was arrested Monday, friends and neighbors at his parents' house . . . said yesterday that he had been living there off and on recently." Over half of New York City shelter residents report that they make use of the system on a part-time or occasional basis; if only one in seven residents currently considers the shelter "home," nearly a third do so from time to time.[106]

Conclusion

". . . solidarity is only gesturing when it involves no sacrifice."[107]

This chapter concludes on a perhaps reckless note of optimism, taking as its point of departure two visions of solidarity as embodied in the mythic tale of Philoctetes.[108]

In Sophocles's original play, Philoctetes leads a miserable life, castaway by his shipmates on the uninhabited island of Lemnos. A foul, festering snake-bite had left him to "moan and howl incessantly" (ln. 8) to the point where his company had become intolerable. He himself readily admits that he is "not an easy cargo" (ln. 475). His life in exile is one of toil, loneliness, and bouts of searing pain, relieved only by the fleeting kindness of an accidental tourist:

> What do my visitors do? Talk kindly to me,
> Give me a little charity, food maybe,
> Or bits of clothing, but, if I mention it,
> A passage home—no; anything but that. (ll. 307-310)

Only because it turns out that the warring Greeks who had marooned him need the bow of Heracles with which he had been entrusted, and only through the intercession of the god himself, is Philoctetes persuaded to leave the island

and join the army besieging Troy. There, he is also promised, he may find relief at the hands of Asclepius, father of heroic medicine. But note: his decade-long ordeal holds no intrinsic lesson. His exile ends not because he has been healed but because his newly appraised utility outweighs the liability of his noxious foot. Duty gets the better of his bitter pride.

Contrast Derek Walcott's reimagined version of the story in *Omeros*, set in the present day Caribbean. In the opening pages, a crew of fishermen gets ready to set to sea, leaving ashore another Philoctete, disabled by his wound, "still unhealed" and an unquenchable source of pain. While the others farm the sea, Philoctete tends his garden and idles, passing most of his hours in the "No Pain" cafe. Its proprietor, Ma Kilman, treats his ruined shin (torn on a rusty anchor) with vaseline and rum. His wound at first seems the stigmata of his imported race's chains, the preternatural patience it requires a lesson to others in enduring those sorrows which, "like stones . . . never melt" (p. 241). But Ma Kilman's skills go beyond the palliative; she is *obeah* as well as publican. Her search for a cure leads her to an unknown weed, brought (like the mythic source of Philoctete's wound) from across the sea centuries earlier. The weed's pull is homeopathic: "its power rooted in bitterness;" its odor redolent of Philoctete's own "putrescent shin." In the end, a potion brewed from the weed, sea water and sulphur does the trick; "the wound has found her own cure" (p. 248). As the tale ends, Philoctete is set to "return"—not to war—but to stand godfather for Helen's soon-to-be-born child. And the narrator, musing on the irony of the cure and reviewing his own stone sorrows, concludes with a glimpse of the healing power of even this transplanted language, a tongue still stained by its provenance in captivity.

The two images of exclusion relate to the subject at hand as history and hope. In the first, homelessness takes shape as a kind of domestic exile, a sentence levied for a "crime" (becoming an intolerable burden) beyond one's own control. Solidarity is conditioned upon utility; one's return to the fold awaits the emergence of requisite demand and necessary instrumentalities. This is essentially the lesson of the last two great waves of homelessness in the U.S., in the 'teens and 'thirties. In each case, mass homelessness was resolved by the surge in demand for labor by an economy mobilizing for war. Absent such abnormal periods, a quiet kind of disregard has been the rule. When scale and visibility intensify, the response is much like those close margins with which we began—the ramshackle settlement of homeless people in Tompkins Square. What reigns is not solidarity but exhibition, at least to the point at which civic patience breaks down, alleviated by the uncertain charity of passers-by.

In the later account, narrator and protagonist a different color, solidarity is conditioned upon and expressed in the key of kinship. From the place accorded and forbearance extended to the crippled Philoctete, to the homeo-pathic power of the curative weed, to the guardian role Philoctete assumes upon his return, to the metonymic lesson the narrator plays upon at the end ("what else might it cure?"), the thrummed chord is connectedness not division. Most apposite here, perhaps, is the flexibility that embraces departures from the norm that do arise and persist. Accommodation is not simply a matter of including the otherwise marginal, but of reworking what it means to belong in the process.

If African-American men are to avoid homelessness, more than the operative myths must change. "Official" homelessness could be lessened by raising the entry "fee" to public shelters (the toll taken in indignity or compulsory toil) by imposing stringent documentation requirements on applicants, or by enforcing restrictive stay rules. Such measures reduce demand through deterrence, providing the semblance of improvement by forcing the evidence into hiding. What other options present themselves today? Not many. Homelessness won't be solved by a sudden surge in demand for labor—some domestic equivalent of war—though that would surely help. With the defeat of the Clinton administration's economic "stimulus" package in late 1993, the moment for a large-scale revival of a WPA-style public employment has come and gone. Without substantial improvement in the living circumstances of extended households, thresholds of tolerance there are unlikely to rise; one hopeful sign may be found in still provisional ethnographic reports that recruitment of new crack users may be subsiding in some areas as the full force of its destructive effects sinks home. Despite the currency of epidemiological tropes these days, official homelessness is not a disease, awaiting the development of some specific remedy to neutralize it. The better comparison is to unemployment: informal means of coping with it or compensating for it are manifold, but only by replacing the jobs that have been lost is it "solved". Likewise, provision of substitute "homes" will mean facing questions of livelihood as well as housing.

In any event, an observation of Hochchild's, made with reference to the American dilemma of race, may apply with special force to the knotted union of race and extreme poverty at issue here. High-minded professions of a commitment to reform aside, any serious effort to resolve the problem is sure to "entail much more fundamental change than the nation had bargained for."[109]

Notes

1. Anthony Leeds coined the word to refer to Latin American settlements that were "not docketed in the city registries either as individual houses or as aggregates of houses, or places" ("The Concept of the 'Culture of Poverty,' " in

238   E. Leacock, ed. *The Culture of Poverty: A Critique.* New York: Simon and Shuster, 1971, p. 237).

2. As cited by Kenneth Jackson "The Capital of Capitalism," in A. Sutcliffe, ed. *Metropolis: 1890-1940.* London: Alexandrine Press, 1984, p. 348.

3. *Mao II,* New York: Penguin, 1991, p. 149.

4. It is this remarkable achievement that Diana Balmori and Margaret Morton chronicle in their spare and thoughtful book, *Transitory Gardens, Uprooted Lives,* New Haven: Yale University Press, 1993.

5. For one, extant only a few years, see J. Lardner, "Shantytown," *The New Yorker,* 1 July 1991, 67-76.

6. Lucy White's article, "Representing 'The Real Deal,' " *University of Miami Law Review* 45: 271-313 (1990-91) is essential reading.

7. On exile, see B. Breytenbach, "The Long March from Hearth to Heart," *Social Research,* 58:69-83, 1991. On gypsies, see J.C. Berland and M. T. Salo, eds., "Peripatetic Peoples," Special issue of *Nomadic Peoples* 21/22, December 1986. On the work entailed in coping with homelessness, see E. Liebow, *Tell Them Who I Am.* New York: Free Press, 1993; and L. Eighner, *Travels With Lizbeth.* New York: St. Martin's, 1993. In the U.S., voting rights of homeless adults are still contested, though when brought to court (e.g., *Pitts v. Black*, 608 F. Supp. 696 (S.D. N.Y. 1984)), barriers to registration have been overturned.

8. See D. P. Culhane, P., Dejowski, E.F., Ibañez, J., Needham, E., and Macchia, I., "Public Shelter Admission Rates in Philadelphia and New York City: The Implications for Turnover for Sheltered Homeless Counts," *Housing Policy Debate* 5:107-140, 1994. Available figures from jurisdictions in six additional states confirm that such rates are unremarkable; between 4.4 and 13 percent of the local poor made use of public shelter annually in the early 1990s. See M. Burt, "Commentary" (on Culhane et al.), Housing Policy Debate 5:141-152. 1994.

9. R. Wallace, "A Synergism of Plagues: Planned Shrinkages, Contagious Housing Destruction and AIDS in the Bronx," *Environmental Research* 47:1-33, 1989.

10. Injuries and heart disease were the leading causes, followed by "ill-defined conditions," poisoning and liver disease. The first and last two causes are thought be associated with substance abuse, but even homeless persons with no substance abuse problems in this study died at three times the rate of their non-homeless counterparts. See J.R. Hibbs, L. Benner, L. Klugman, et al. "Mortality in a Cohort of Homeless Adults in Philadelphia," *New England Journal of Medicine,*331:304-309.

11. For studies of health problems, see W.R. Breakey, P. J. Fischer, M. Kramer, et al. "Health and Mental Health Problems of Homeless Men and Women in Balti-more," *Journal of the American Medical Association,* 262:1352-1357, 1989; P. W. Brickner, L.K. Scharer, B. Conanan, M. Savarese and B.C. Scanlan, eds. *Under the Safety Net,* New York: W.W. Norton, 1990; K. Brudney, K. and J. Dobkin, "Resurgent Tuberculosis in New York City," *American Review of Respiratory Disease,* 144:745-749, 1991; L. Gelberg, L.S. Linn, R.P. Usatine, M.H. Smith,

"Health, Homelessness, and Poverty," *Archives of Internal Medicine*, 150:2325-
2330., 1990.

12. See D. Stone, *The Disabled State*. Philadelphia: Temple University, 1984; A. Gutman, ed. *Democracy and the Welfare State*. Princeton: Princeton University 1988; M. Weir, A.S. Orloff, and T. Skocpol, T., *The Politics of Social Policy in the United States*, Princeton: Princeton University, 1988.

13. By "homelessness" I have in mind the prevailing definition of "not having customary and regular access to a conventional dwelling" (P. H. Rossi, *Down and Out in America*, Chicago: University of Chicago Press, 1989, p. 10). Governmental bureaucracies usually construe this to mean only those living in shelters or on the street. For my purposes here, resort to such makeshifts as "doubling-up" will be viewed as *alternatives* to "overt homelessness"—another modality of marginality, perhaps—even though they may clearly be characterized by the same "residential instability" that some researchers (including myself) see as the core dynamic of homelessness. The reason for that distinction should become clearer as the account unfolds.

14. Whatever misgivings native members of the culture at large may have about the biases in that definition. If given expression or plumbed in targeted inquiry, these too may become grist for the ethnographic mill.

15. S. Sassen, for one, has called upon anthropologists to explore new "analytic borderlands" that are neglected in conventional accounts of the global city—in particular, the situation of the "amalgamated other." Typically represented as a devalued, downgraded space in the dominant economic account of the global city, this is the terrain of the recent immigrant community, of the black ghetto, and increasingly of the old manufacturing district. In the extreme, it becomes the space of the "underclass," harboring menace, burden and decay. But it is from such precincts that the huge ranks of invisible workers—predominantly women, immigrants and people of color, usually working at night—who make up the low-waged infrastructure of the corporate economy are drawn. See Cities in a *World Economy*. New York: Pine Forge/Sage, 1993.

16. Jennifer Hochschild, "The Politics of the Estranged Poor," Ethics 101:560-578, 1991, p. 561 n.3.

17. M. Katz, *The Undeserving Poor*, New York: Pantheon, 1989, pp. 185-86.

18. As M. Sosin, I. Piliavin, and H. Westerfelt suggested in "Toward a Longitudinal Analysis of Homelessness," *Journal of Social Issues*, 46:157-174, 1990.

19. J. MacLeod, *Ain't No Makin' It.*, Boulder: Westview. 1987; B. Williams, *Upscaling Downtown*, Ithaca: Cornell University Press, 1988; M. Sullivan, *Getting Paid: Youth, Crime and Work in the Inner City*, Ithaca: Cornell University Press, 1989; L.M. Burton, "Teenage Childbearing as an Alternative Life-Course Strategy in Multigeneration Black Families," *Human Nature*, 1:123-143, 1990; M. Fine, *Framing Dropouts*, Albany: State University of New York Press.1991; P. Hainer, "Sharing Kith and Kin: A Study of Kinship Behavior, An Approach to Explanation". Ph.D. Dissertation, Brandeis University, 1991.

240 20. An earlier version of this history appeared in K. Hopper, "Two Kinds of Invisibility," in R.R. Jennings, ed. *The Status of Black Men in America*, Lawrence, Ks.: National Council of African-American Men, 1994.

21. K. Kusmer, "The Underclass: Tramps and Vagrants in American Society, 1865-1930," Ph.D. Dissertation, University of Chicago, 1980, p. 27.

22. M.L. Booth, *History of the City of New York*. New York: W.R.C. Clark and Meeker, 1859, p. 347.

23. N. Anderson, *The Homeless in New York City*. New York: Welfare Council, 1934, p. 5.

24. P. F. Clement, "The Transformation of the Wandering Poor in Nineteenth-Century Philadelphia," in E.H. Monkkonen, ed. *Walking to Work: Tramps in America, 1790-1935*, Lincoln: University of Nebraska, 1984, pp. 56-84; K. Kusmer, "The Underclass in Historical Perspective," in R. Beard, ed, *On Being Homeless: Historical Perspectives*. New York: Museum for the City of New York, 1987, pp. 20-31. A.W. Solenberger, One Thousand Homeless Men. New York: Russell Sage, 1911, pp. 216, 306; C.B. Barnes, *The Homeless Man*, New York: unpublished ms. 1914, p. 41; P. T. Ringenbach, *Tramps and Reformers, 1873-1916*, Westport, CT: Greenwood, 1973: 60, 70-71; E.Monkkonen, "Introduction" and "Regional Dimensions of Tramping," in E.H. Monkkonen, ed. 1984, pp. 1-17, 189-211; J. C. Schneider, "Tramping Workers, 1890-1920: A Subcultural View," in E. H. Monkkonen, ed. 1984, pp. 212-234.

25. Monkkonen 1984, p.14; Schneider 1984, p.213-215; Kusmer 1987:22; L.U. Blumberg, T. F. Shipley and S. F. Barsky, *Liquor and Poverty*, New Brunswick: Rutgers Center of Alcohol Studies, 1978, p.123.

26. K. Kusmer, "The Underclass: Tramps and Vagrants in American Society, 1865-1930," Ph.D. Dissertation, University of Chicago, 1980,p.225. The reasons behind mobility of the two groups were strikingly different, however. For white men, tramping often meant a means of escape from (even defiance of) the new regime of industrial work. Much more than a reflexive response to unemployment, tramping was "a clear indication of worker discontent" (K. Kusmer, "Conceptualizing Social History: Homeless Men in America, 1865-1940, as a Case Study," in *Reconstructing American Literary and Historical Studies*, G.H. Lenz, H. Keil, and S. Bröck-Sellah, eds. New York: St. Martin's, 1990, p. 101). Barred from industrial employment and "reduced to peonage" by a new sharecropping system that left them but one remove from slavery, blacks were motivated by a different impulse. "The tendency of blacks to join the underclass [of tramps] must thus be viewed as part of a much larger spectrum of rebellion against their economic and political repression in the South. . . . In the immediate aftermath of slavery, freedom of movement per se seemed especially important to a race that had been denied geographic mobility during the long centuries of bondage" (Kusmer 1980, p. 223; cf. J. Jones, The Dispossessed. New York, Basic, 1993, especially her discussion of "shifting"). Even when they secured industrial—say, in Chicago's meatpacking firms—"[c]hanging jobs . . . constituted an extension of migration itself, with movement remaining a meta-

Kim Hopper

phor for freedom" (J.R. Grossman, *Land of Hope*, Chicago: University of **241** Chicago, 1989, p. 197).

27. N. Anderson, *The Hobo*, Chicago: University of Chicago, 1923, p. 8; E. F. Frazier, *The Negro Family in Chicago*, Chicago: University of Chicago, 1932, p. 118; Grossman 1989, p.134.

28. Anderson 1934:134; E. H. Sutherland and H. J. Locke, *Twenty Thousand Homeless Men*. Chicago: Lipincott, 1936, pp.38, 42; J. N. Webb, *The Transient Unemployed*, Washington: WPA, 1935, p.33; J. M. Crouse, *The Homeless Transient in the Great Depression, New York State, 1929-1941*, Albany: State University of New York, 1986, p. 9.

29. S. Turkel, *Hard Times*. New York: Avon, 1970, pp. 56-60. His account also corroborates earlier ones in noting that the color line tended to fade among men sharing the hardships of road life, but William Peery's closely documented memoir of that time raises questions about the extent to which wandering men shed their prejudices (Black Fire. New York: New Press, 1994, pp. 89-129)

30. 1934, pp. 138-140, 135. Citations for other figures in the paragraph are: M. Aaron, *Report of the Mendicancy Project*, 18 June, 1935; H.J.P. Schubert, *Twenty Thousand Transients*, Buffalo: Emergency Relief Bureau, 1935; D. A. Clarke, "Men on Relief in Lackawanna, N.Y., 1934-1935," University of Buffalo Studies 14(4):67-119, 1937.

31. Louis LeCount, as cited in Anderson 1934, p. 135.

32. E. F. Frazier, *The Negro Family in the United States. Chicago: University of Chicago, 1939*, p. 285.

33. K. A. Lovald, "From Hobohemia to Skid Row," Ph.D. Dissertation, University of Minnesota, 1960, p. 449.

34. The literature here is immense, and is increasingly attentive to differences in the move north depending upon conditions in the cities settled. Ken Kusmer's recent review is a authoritative guide ("African Americans in the City since World War II," *Journal of Urban History* 21:458-504, 1995). A rich cross-section of urban case studies may be found in J. W, Trotter, ed. *The Great Migration in Historical Perspective*, Bloomington: Indiana University, 1991.

35. Grossman 1989, pp.133ff; Jones 1993; J. Borchert, *Alley Life in Washington*, Chicago: University of Illinois, 1980, pp. 81-82; J.W. Trotter, "Blacks in the Urban North," in M. Katz, ed. *The "Underclass" Debate*, Princeton: Princeton University, 1993, p.78;

36. W. J. Wilson, *The Truly Disadvantaged*. Chicago: University of Chicago, 1987, pp. 177-178.

37. Figures in this paragraph are taken from: D. J. Pittman and T. W. Gordon, *Revolving Door: A Study of the Chronic Police Case Inebriate*, New York: Free Press, 1958; H. Bigart, "Grim Problems of the Bowery Complicate Clean-Up Drive," *New York Times*, 20 November 1961, pp. 1, 36.1961; B. Levinson, "The Homeless Man: A Psychological Enigma," Mental Hygiene 47:590-600, 1963 and "A Comparative Study of Northern and Southern Negro Homeless Men," *Journal of Negro Education*, 35:144-150, 1966; G. G. Kean, "A Comparative Study of Negro and White Homeless Men", Ph.D. Dissertation, Yeshiva Uni-

versity, 1965; D. Bogue, *Skid Row in American Cities*, Chicago: University of Chicago, 1963, pp. 106-108; C. Hoch and R. A. Slayton, *New Homeless and Old*. Philadelphia: Temple University Press, 1989, pp. 98-99; J.F. Rooney, "Race Relations in Skid Row." Unpublished manuscript, 1969; H. M. Bahr and T. Caplow, *Old Men Drunk and Sober.*, New York: New York University, 1973, Table 2-1; p. 35.

38. H. M. Bahr, *Skid Row; An Introduction to Disaffiliation*, New York: Oxford, p. 105. Working in Philadelphia and New York, James Rooney was a notable exception; so were Blumberg et al. (1978).

39. G. Nash, *The Habitats of Homeless Men in Manhattan*, New York: Columbia University, Bureau of Applied Social Science, 1964, p. D-26ff.

40. Blumberg et al., 1978, p.175.

41. E. Anderson, *A Place on the Corner.*, Chicago: University of Chicago, 1978.

42. For a strikingly detailed portrayal of day-to-day life in one such hotel in the twilight year before its wholesale renovation, see R. Hamburger, *All the Lonely People.*, New York: Ticknor & Fields, 1983.

43. J. H. Shapiro, Communities of the Alone. New York, Association Press, 1971, p. 24. Although as a class of tenants, uptown "SRO -type population" represents "the chronically disabled residual" of what had been, in pre-war days, a much more heterogeneous group of Bowery residents (ibid. p. 150).

44. H. A. Siegel, *Outposts of the Forgotten.*, Totowa, N.J.: Transaction Books, pp. xix-xxi, 65.

45. Anderson 1934:151-52.

46. C. Cohen and J. Sokolovsky, *Old Men of the Bowery*, New York: Guilford, 1989; A. Bonner, Jerry McAuley and His Mission, rev.ed. *Neptune*, N. J.: Loizeaux Brothers, 1990; Vera Institute of Justice, *Report to the Office of Family and Adult Services*, New York, 1977 and *First Time Users of Men's Shelter Services*, New York, 1980; S. Crystal and M. Goldstein, *New Arrivals: First-Time Shelter Clients*, New York: Human Resources Administration, 1982; S. Crystal, M. Goldstein and R. Levitt, *Chronic and Situational Dependency*, New York: Human Resources Administration, 1982.

47. C. M. Taeuber, ed. *Enumerating Homeless Persons: Methods and Data Needs*, Washington, D.C.:U.S. Bureau of the Census, 1991; B. G. Link, E. Susser, A. Stueve, et al., "Lifetime and Five-Year Prevalence of Homelessness in the United States," American Journal of Public Health 84:1907-1912, 1994. As noted above (p. 215), local studies of shelter turnover in Philadelphia, New York City and elsewhere have corroborated that result .

48. D. F. Barrett, I. Anolik, I., and F. H. Abramson, "The 1990 Census Shelter and Street Night Enumeration," Paper presented at the Annual Meeting of the American Statistical Association, Boston, August 1992; R. Rosenheck, P. Gallup, C. Leda et al. *Reaching Out Across America*, West Haven, CT: Department of Veterans Affairs Medical Center, 1989, Table 5-5; A.B. Shlay and P. Rossi, "Social Science Research and Contemporary Studies of Homelessness," *Annual Review of Sociology*, 18:135, 1992.

49. Bahr and Caplow 1973.

50. K. Gounis, "The Domestication of Urban Marginality.," Ph.D. Dissertation, Columbia University, 1993.

51. P. Hainer, Sharing Kith and Kin . . . pp. 223-224. Compare Randy, a 15-year-old in a Southern town, whose mother is "somewhere up north": "Presently he stays with his father. . . . . He says he doesn't usually get along with his father, and when that happens he goes to live with his grandmother across the street. 'When I get tired of staying with my grandmama, or when she puts me out, I go stay with my sister. Sometimes I go to my brother's house; other times to my friend's house. His mother lets me stay there whenever I want to.' " (T. R. Kennedy, *You Gotta Deal With It*, New York: Oxford, 1980, p. 34.)

52. K. Hopper, E. Susser, S. Conover, "Economies of Markeshift: Homelessness and Deindustrialization in New York City," *Urban Anthropology*, 14:183-236, 1985, p. 221.

53. Census Bureau figures used in calculating such rates are notoriously unreliable for adult black males. In the 1990 census, official estimates of the undercount of African Americans range from 4.4 to 5.7 percent, depending upon the method used; the comparable figures for the general population are 1.6 to 1.8 percent (Hogan and Robinson 1993). Use of household data from the Current Population Survey is even more hazardous: the March 1986 CPS is thought to have missed from 18 to 20 percent of black men age 16 and higher (Panel on Census Requirements in the Year 2000 and Beyond 1993: 15n).

54. J. Jones, *The Dispossesed*, New York: Basic, 1992, p. 270; I.V. Sawhill, "Young Children and Families," in H. J. Aaron and C. I. Schultze, eds. *Setting Domestic Priorities*, Washington, D.C.: Brookings Institution, 1992, p. 156; D. S Massey and N.A. Denton, *American Apartheid*, Cambridge: Harvard University, 1993; G. Orfield, *The Growth of Segregation in American Schools*, Alexandria: National School Boards Association, 1993; *New York Times*, 25 September 1992:A12; R. Sanjek, "Intermarriage and the Future of Races in the United States," in S. Gregory and R. Sanjek, eds. *Everyone's Business: The Politics of Race and Identity*. New Brunswick: Rutgers University Press. 1995; A. Hacker, *Two Nations*, New York: Random House, 1992.

55. Figures in this paragraph are from: R. J.First, D. Roth, and B. D. Arewa, "Homelessness: Understanding the Dimensions for Minorities," *Social Work*, 33:120-124, 1988; M.J. Bane, "Household Composition and Poverty," in S. H. Danziger and W.H. Weinberg, eds. *Fighting Poverty*, Cambridge: Harvard University, 1986, pp. 209-231; R. L. Douglass and B. J. Hodgkins, "Racial Differences Regarding Shelter and Housing in a Sample of the Urban Elderly Homeless," in S. M. Keigher, ed. *Housing Risks and Homelessness among the Urban Elderly*, New York: Haworth, 1991; M. LaGrory, F.J., Ritchey, T. O'Donoghue, and J. Mullin, "Homelessness in Alabama," in J.A. Momeni, ed., *Homelessness in the United States*, Westport: Greenwood, 1989; J. Wilson, D.M. McCallum, and J.M. Bolland, "The Magnitude and Demographics of Homelessness in Huntsville." Tuscaloosa: University of Alabama, 1991; Rossi, 1989, p. 125.

Homelessness Among African-American Men

244   56.   Evidence on differences in rates of psychiatric disorders is inconsistent, however, with most studies reporting no differences in the prevalence of severe mental illness among homeless persons by ethnicity (R. C. Tessler and D. L. Dennis, A Synthesis of NIMH-Funded Research Concerning Persons Who Are Homeless and Mentally Ill. Rockville: NIMH, 1989; M.J. Robertson, "The Prevalence of Mental Disorder Among Homeless People," in R. Jahiel, ed. *Homelessness*. *Baltimore*: Johns Hopkins, 1992, p. 123; C. S. North and E. M. Smith, "Comparison of White and Nonwhite Homeless Men and Women," *Social Work*, 39:639-647, 1994. Local differences and methodological disorder probably explain the lack of regularity.

57.   S. Sassen, *The Mobility of Labor and Capital*, New York: Cambridge, 1988; *and* "The Informal Economy," in J. H. Mollenkopf and M. Castells, eds. *Dual City: Restructuring New York*, New York: Russell Sage, 1991, pp. 78-102.

58.   J. F. Kasarda, "Urban Industrial Transition and the Underclass," *Annals of the American Academy of Political and Social Science*, 501:26-47, 1989; D. T. Lichter, Racial Differences in Underemployment in American Cities," *American Journal of Sociology*, 93:771-792, 1988; P. Moss and C. Tilly, *Why Black Men are Doing Worse in the Labor Market.*, New York: Social Science Research Council, 1991.

59.   B. J. Tidwell and M. L. Jackson, *Perils of Neglect: Black Employment in the Nineties*, Washington, D.C.: National Urban League, 1992. This figure is deflated owing to the number of black men behind bars—blacks constitute 46% of all state/federal correctional inmates as of June 1991, a rate nearly four times their representation in the general population (U.S. Census Bureau, Poverty in the U.S. 1991. P60, #181, August, 1992)—or in the armed services or school (Moss and Tilly 1991, pp. 77-80). A decade earlier, "fully one-third of inner-city black [men were] jobless, unable to find full-time jobs, or unable to earn enough money to raise themselves significantly above the poverty threshold" (Lichter 1988, p. 789).

60.   C. Jencks, *Rethinking Social Policy*, Cambridge: Harvard University, 1992, Table 5.3.

61.   Figures from: Sassen 1988:Ch. 5; Moss and Tilly 1991; Jencks 1992; M. L. Blackburn, D. Bloom and R.B. Freeman, "The Declining Economic Position of Less Skilled American Men," in G. Burtless, ed., *A Future of Lousy Jobs*? Washington, D.C.: Brookings Institution, 1990; J. Kirschenman and K. M. Neckerman, 'We'd Love to Hire Them, But . . . ' " in C. Jencks and P. Peterson, eds., *The Urban Underclass*, Washington, D.C. Brookings Institution, 1991; R. M. Fernandez, "A Review of 'Why Black Men are Doing Worse in the Labor Market," Paper prepared for the SSRC Conference, "The Urban Underclass: Perspectives from the Social Sciences," Ann Arbor, June 8-10, 1992.

62.   R. Freeman, "Employment and Earnings of Disadvantaged Young Men in a Labor Shortage Economy," in Jencks and Peterson, 1991, pp. 103-121; P. Osterman, "Gains from Growth?" in ibid., pp. 121-134.

63.   M. Tienda and H. Stier, "Joblessness and Shiftlessness," in Jencks and Peterson, eds. 1991, pp. 135-54; M. Weir, *Politics and Jobs*, Princeton: Princeton University, 1992.

64. J. Kain, "Housing Segregation, Negro Employment, and Metropolitan Decentralization," *Quarterly Journal of Economics*, 82:175-197, 1968.
65. T. J. Sugrue, "The Structures of Urban Poverty," in Katz, ed. 1993, pp.85-117. 1993; L.J.D. Wacquant and W. J. Wilson, "The Cost of Racial and Class Exclusion in the Inner City," *Annals of the American Academy of Political and Social Science*, 501:8-25, 1989; L.J.D. Wacquant, "The Ghetto, the State, and the New Capitalist Economy," *Dissent*, 36 (Fall): 508-520, 1989; Kasarda 1989; M. Stern, "Poverty and Family Composition Since 1940," in Katz, ed. 1993, pp. 224-226; P. A. Jargowsky and M. J. Bane, "Ghetto Poverty in the United States, 1970-1980," in Jencks and Peterson, eds. 1991, p.254. In New York City, it was the relative loss of jobs in personal services that hit native blacks hardest, while their concentration in public sector offered some shielding; see T. Bailey and R. Waldinger, "The Changing Ethnic/Racial Division of Labor," in J. H. Mollenkopf and M. Castells, eds. Dual City. New York: Russell Sage, pp. 43-78.
66. Kusmer 1995; Fernandez 1992.
67. M. Duneier, *Slim's Table*, Chicago: University of Chicago, 1992, p. 35.
68. *New York Times*, 2 December 1990:A1; Shapiro, I., M. Sheft, L. Summer, et al., *The States and the Poor. I and II*. Washington, D.C. and Albany: Center on Budget and Policy Priorities and Center for the Study of the States, 1991, 1993; S. Hauser, Jobless, Penniless and Often Homeless. New York: Center on Social Welfare Policy and Law, 1994; P. A. Leonard and E.B. Lazere, *The Low-Income Housing Crisis in 44 Major Metropolitan Areas.*, Washington, D.C.: Center for Budget and Policy Priorities, 1992, p. 43.
69. D. M.Schneider, *American Kinship.*, Englewood-Cliffs: Prentice-Hall, 1968.
70. Micaela di Leonardo coined the term "the work of kinship" (*The Varieties of Ethnic Experience*, Ithaca: Cornell University, 1984, pp. 194ff), and it is apt here. The centrality of women in that work and the extraordinary burden it can mean is clear in historical accounts of textile workers (T. Hareven, *Family Time and Industrial Time*, New York: Cambridge, 1982, esp. pp. 105ff), as well as in contemporary portraits of Italian-American (di Leonardo 1984), Japanese-American (S.J. Yanagisako, *Transforming the Past*, Stanford: Stanford University Press, 1985), and African-American families (C. Stack, *All Our Kin*, New York: Harper and Row, 1974; C. Stack, *Call to Home*, New York: Basic, 1996. J. Aschenbrenner, *Lifelines*, New York: Holt, Rinehart and Winston, 1975; E. P. Martin and J. M. Martin, The Black Extended Family. Chicago: University of Chicago, 1978; Williams 1988; Burton 1990). The point I am trying to make, critical to an understanding later of "social capital," is that kinship cannot be entered into the subsistence equation simply as a bankable asset. Its circuits of obligation and reciprocity require proper maintenance and cultivation (cf. P. Bourdieu, *In Other Words*, Stanford: Stanford University, 1990, p. 96).
71. Grossman 1989, pp. 106-107.
72. S. Gudeman, "Herbert Gutman's The Black Family in Slavery and Freedom, 1750-1925: An Anthropologist's View," Social Science History 3 (3&4):56-65, 1979; Aschenbrenner 1975, p. 118; Martin and Martin 1978, p.111; D. E. Belle,

"The Impact of Poverty on Social Networks and Supports," *Marriage and Family Review*, 5:89-103,1983; Stack 1974, p. 33.

73. Fictive kinship originally designated the practice of "binding unrelated slave adults to one another and thereby infusing these groups with conceptions of reciprocity and obligation that had initially flowed from kin obligations" (H. Gutman, Power and Culture. New York: The New Press, 1987. pp. 365-366. It has since been applied to non-slave cultures and maintains pride of place among the innovations of African-American households today (e.g., Hainer 1991).

74. N. J. Smelser and S. Halpern, "The Historical Triangulation of Family, Economy, and Education," in *Turning Points, Historical and Sociological Essays on the Family*, Supplement, *American Journal of Sociology* 84:S288-S315, 1984.

75. Stern 1993.

76. Calculated from figures in Stern's Table 7.7. Separate data for income source are not reported for black households.

77. Ibid., p. 244.

78. Adjusted for inflation, the value of AFDC benefits declined by 42 percent between 1970 and 1991 (Committee on Ways and Means, 1991 Green Book. Washington, D.C.: GPO, 1991, p. 605.

79. J. Baumohl and R. Huebner, "Alcohol and Other Drug Problems Among the Homeless," *Housing Policy Debate*, 2:837-865, 1991; D. A. Snow and L. Anderson, *Down on Their Luck*, Berkeley: University of California, 1993, pp.259-261; D. Dennis, I. S. Levine, and F. C. Osher, "The Physical and Mental Health Status of Homeless Adults," *Housing Policy Debate*, 2:815-835, 1991. Not only do serious alcohol- and drug-use make for difficulties in maintaining one's hold on rented housing; they are also the source of much friction and grief in the informal economy of friends and family. In this connection, it is instructive that the best research indicates that such problems commonly began before the first bout of homelessness (Baumohl and Huebner 1991, p. 844). Snow and Anderson, while acknowledging that family resources may be exhausted by some homeless men, also argue that for the majority of their informants, "family relationships appeared to be nonexistent, weak, or, at best, highly ambivalent." Most came from families that were ill-equipped economically to offer much support (1993, p. 265). For another argument on the role of abandonment, in many forms, in the genesis of the homelessness of single men, see P. Marin, "The Prejudice Against Men," The Nation, 8 July 1991, pp. 46-50.

80. K. T. Jackson, *Crabgrass Frontier*, New York: Oxford, 1985, p. 191, 219ff.; Massey and Denton 1993.

81. In 1970, the number of low rent units was roughly equal to the number of low income renters (6.8 and 6.4 million, respectively). In 1989, the supply of such units had shrunken to 5.5 million while the need for them had grown to 9.6 million (E.B. Lazere, Leonard, P.A., Dolbeare, C.N., and Zigas, B. *The Low Income Housing Crisis Continues*, Washington, D.C.: Center on Budget and Policy Priorities and Low Income Housing Information Service. 1991:4-5).

82. Ibid., pp. 4,8, 63-64; J. Alker and C. Dolbeare. The Closing Door. Washington, D.C.: National Coalition for the Homeless, 1990.

83. M. Stone, *Shelter Poverty*, Philadelphia: Temple University, 1993, p. 147-150. **247**
84. C. B. Green, "Housing Single Low-Income People," Paper prepared for Sterling Forest Conference, October 1-2, 1982; Hoch and Slayton 1988:Ch. 9; J. Blau, *The Visible Poor*, New York: Oxford, 1992, p.75; M. Burt, *Over the Edge*, New York: Russell Sage, 1992, pp. 33-34.
85. P. Weitzman, *Worlds Apart: Housing, Race/Ethnicity and Income*, in New York City, 1978-1987. New York: Community Service Society, 1989; V. Bach and S.Y. West, *Housing on the Block.*, New York: Community Service Society, 1993.
86. P. Kasinitz, "Gentrification and Homelessness," *Urban and Social Change Review*, 17:9-14, 1984; Human Resources Administration, *Monthly Shelter Reports*, New York, 1993.
87. Wilson 1987:4-19; J. Schwartz, "The Moral Environment of the Poor," *The Public Interest*, 103:21-37, 1991; L. Mead, *The New Politics of Dependency*, New York: Basic Books, 1992.
88. A. Swidler, "Culture in Action," *American Sociological Review*, 51:273-286, 1986.
89. J. Hochschild, "The Politics of the Estranged Poor," Ethics 101:560-78, 1991, p. 565; Wilson 1987, p. 138.
90. Contrast Mercer Sullivan's detailed developmental portrait of the "social ecology" of three different neighborhoods housing black, Hispanic and white teenagers, *Getting Paid* (Ithaca: Cornell University,1989) with Mead 1992, p. 148: "Evidently, the worldview of blacks makes them uniquely prone to the attitudes contrary to work, and thus vulnerable to poverty and dependency."
91. U. Hannerz, Soulside. New York: Columbia University, 1969; K. Newman, "Culture and Structure in *The Truly Disadvantaged*," City & Society 6:3-25, 1992. Intriguingly, so does one of the few studies of white underclass culture at that time, J. Howell, *Hard Living on Clay Street*, Garden City: Anchor, 1973.
92. Compare Massey and Denton 1993:165ff. with P. Bourdieu and L. Wacquant, *An Invitation to Reflexive Sociology*, Chicago: University of Chicago 1992, p. 80.
93. E. Anderson, "Sex Codes and Family Life among Poor Inner-City Youths," *Annals of the American Academy of Political and Social Science* 501: 59-78, 1989; M. Sullivan, "Absent Fathers in the Inner City," *Annals of the American Academy of Political and Social Science* 501: 48-58.
94. Contrast Fine 1991 and J. U. Ogbu, The Consequences of the American Caste System," in U. Neisser, ed. *The School Achievement of Minority Children*, Hillsdale: L. Erlbaum, pp.19-56; with MacLeod 1987.
95. M.A. Gephart, "Neighborhoods and Communities in Concentrated Poverty," *Items* (Social Science Research Council) 43(4):84-92, 1989:87; M. Tienda, "Poor People and Poor Places: Deciphering Neighborhood Effects on Poverty Outcomes," in J. Huber, ed. Macro-Micro Linkages in Sociology. Newbury Park: Sage, 1991, pp. 244-262.
96. K. Hopper, "A Poor Apart," *Social Research*, 58:107-132, 1991.
97. Hochschild 1991, p.573. Cf. E. Currie, *Reckoning*, New York: Hill and Wang, 1993, p. 143f; and C.H. Nightingale, *On the Edge*, New York: Basic, pp. 135-165.

98. Currie 1993, p. 11. Many of these points are illustrated in a series of ongoing ethnographic studies of drugs and crime in minority communities. The studies span three decades and cover eight neighborhoods in six American studies. They seek to illuminate the role of "changes in the social relationships and interactions between groups of people than ensued when neighborhoods 'hardened' social and economically" (J. Fagan, "Crime, Drugs and Neighborhood Change." Background Memorandum Prepared for the SSRC Policy Conference on Persistent Urban Poverty, November 9-10, Washington, D.C. 1993:1). From material available so far, a consistent picture emerges of both lost work and ties to work (both economic opportunities and the people who mediated access to those opportunities); disrupted intergenerational relationships and, with them, the decline of traditional sources of social control; the growing legitimation and institutionalization of the drug trade in the absence of licit employment alternatives and strong social sanctions; and the interdependence of ghetto drug trade with other areas of the city that promises to sustain it even in the face of declining local demand.

99. H. M. Bahr, "Introduction" to J. Momeni, ed. 1989, pp. xx-xxi.

100. See especially Stack 1974, p.61 (that kin live in proximity to one another is key to their effectiveness in mutual aid networks); and Hainer 1991, p. 297 (housing surplus must exist to accommodate changing family rosters and preserve family unity as "a movable feast").

101. Carol Stack, as cited in J. Hochschild, "Equal Opportunity and the Estranged Poor," *Annals of the American Academy of Political and Social Science*, 501:143-55,1989, p. 149.

102. Psychiatric hospitalization and victimization, however, figure more highly in their pre-homeless careers. The rise of crack cocaine may have already weakened some of these sex differences by the time they were reported (Burt 1992, pp. 111-116). If journalistic accounts are borne out, the subsequent increase in virtually abandoned kids, a kind of forced fosterage, has placed great strains on black grandmothers.

103. In this connection, an early observation by S. Crystal merits note. In examining intake assessments of a 1982-83 cohort of shelter applicants in New York, he found that the women were more than twice as likely as the men (7.4 percent vs. 2.8 percent) to have had institutional or foster care placements as the "*principal* living arrangement in which they grew up" ("Homeless Men and Homeless Women," *Urban and Social Change Review*, 17(2):2-6, 1984), p. 4; emph. orig.). Many more, Crystal adds, had spent at least part of their childhood in such settings.

104. Liebow, 1993, pp. 81-82. For African-American women, the hardship associated with "multiple family occupancy" and domestic violence appear to be the most common precipitants of homelessness (N. Milburn and A. D'Ercole, Homeless Women: Moving Toward a Comprehensive Model," *American Psychologist*, 46:1161-1169, 1991). In New York, black mothers with children applying for emergency shelter report not a dearth of family ties, but a shortage of kin with the capacity to put them up, usually because they had already relied upon such

kin for a place to live or help with rent in the previous year (M. B. Shinn, J. Knickman, B. Weitzman, "Homeless Women: Moving Toward a Comprehensive Model," American Psychologist 46:1161-1169, 1991).

105. I draw here on my own ethnographic work in New York City from 1979 to 1984, on interviews with applicants for shelter in Westchester County in 1992-1994, and on Gounis' ethnography (1993).

106. *New York Times*, 11 January 1989, p.B3; E. L. Struening and L. Pittman, Characteristics of Residents of the New York City Shelter System, Summer 1987. New York: Epidemiology of Mental Disorders Department, New York State Psychiatric Institute, 1987.

107. M. Douglas, *How Institutions Think*, Syracuse: Syracuse University, 1986, p. 4.

108. Sophocles, Philoctetes. trans. E.F. Watling. New York: Penguin, 1953; D. Walcott, Omeros. New York: Farrar, Straus and Giroux, 1990. I want to thank Kostas Gounis for bringing the original Greek version to my attention.

109. J. Hochschild, *The New American Dilemma*, New Haven: Yale University, 1984, p. 18.

Chapter 9

PUBLIC POLICY FOR OVERCOMING MARGINALIZATION: BORDERLANDS IN AFRICA, NORTH AMERICA AND WESTERN EUROPE

Anthony Asiwaju

Classical diplomatic methods alone cannot be successfully used in solving border problems in Africa. There should be a focus on the citizens inhabiting the border as the real instruments of transborder cooperation in independent African states. There would be problems at the borders as long as border citizens are neglected in policy measures designed for cooperation between adjacent states on the management of their borders . . . (Codjo Sodokin, as cited by Metoho Mehunnu, "Nigeria-Bénin Transborder Cooperation," *National Concord*, Lagos, May 5, 1988, p. 3)

We live dangerously here in Laredo. We are subject to floods, droughts, the Mexican government and the United States government. (An elderly ex-City Attorney of Laredo, Texas, U.S.A., quoted in J. W. Sloan and J. P. West [1976], p. 463)

One aim of transfrontier co-operation is to abolish divisive elements in frontier areas—to overcome the frontier . . . Nowhere are the arguments in favour of abolishing national sovereignty and all its obstructive effects more obvious than they are in the frontier areas of neighboring states . . . Thus it is in the frontier areas that the demand for common, transfrontier solutions first finds its more concrete expression . . . There is no need to do away with frontiers altogether, or to abolish national sovereignty; an effort must simply be made to heal the wounds of history and enable people in frontier areas to live and work together peaceably (sic) . . . Viktor von Malchus ([1975], p. 9)

The Problem

"Borderlands" refers to what has been aptly defined as "sub-national areas whose economic and social life is directly and significantly affected by proximity to an international boundary."[1] Since such localities are, more often than not, areas of coherent cultures, borderlands are also generally partitioned homelands of distinct ethnic groups. While the various parts may be viewed and treated in the contexts of the particular national states in which they have been located, the real hallmark of partitioned culture areas is in the status of the inhabitants as "transborder peoples." In his seminal comparative perspective study of the Mexican-Americans, Myron Weiner has identified three main types: those, like the Arabs of North Africa and the Middle East, who "constitute a majority in each of the countries in which they live;" those—like the French, the Germans, the Somali, the Irish, the Turks, the Greeks, the Chinese, the Indians, the Bangladeshi, the Nepali, and the Mexican-Americans—each of whom "constitutes a majority in one country, but spills across the borders into neighboring countries where it is a minority;" and, finally, those like the Catalans and Basques in Spain and France, the Kurds in Iraq and Iran, the Armenians in Turkey and the former Soviet Union, the Baluchi in Pakistan, Iran, and Afghanistan, who "constitute a minority in each of the states in which they live and can claim no country of their own."[2]

The categorization of borderland communities as marginal populations derives from certain geographical, political, strategic, economic and social indicators arising basically from locations across particular inter-sovereignty boundaries. Geographically, not only are such locations physically in the peripheries or margins of the national territories; spatial distance and remoteness from core areas, typical of most borderland locations, ensure a certain degree of separation from mainstream national life.

Politically, transborder people are at inherent disadvantage vis-à-vis other subnational communities. Whether as part of a majority or minority group in the country of their residence, the loyalty of borderland residents tends to be doubted by national authorities. At best, when the situation is one of familiar-type ambivalence, due largely to the proximity of a foreign state and the weakening of national stereotypes, borderlanders are simply distrusted. Where—as in the cases of the Somali and the Irish—there is an irredentism, or,—as in the cases of the Basques and the Kurds—there is separatism, borderlands become targets of counter nationalist campaigns. In borderlands, fundamental human rights are flagrantly disregarded when, as almost always, these are viewed as opposed to nationalistically determined interests of the central authorities. For instance, while movements across inter-sovereignty borders are officially restricted, such movements are generally claimed as part and parcel of both the fundamental human and "national" rights of borderland residents. Such claims are based on the local peoples' views of the areas as coherent and indivisible homelands in spite of the presence, and separation functions of externally imposed international boundaries.

Straddled by international boundaries and sandwiched between the sovereign states, vivisected communities astride international boundaries suffer

Anthony Asiwaju

exceptionally from an unusual convergence on their homelands of both domestic and international laws as well as the operation of the multiplicity of state security agencies created to enforce the borders at their backyards. Borders tend to criminalize local border citizenry. Both as contraband staging centers and as asylums for smugglers and other criminal offenders, borderlanders are prone to be drawn into disrepute. In many parts of the nation-state world where, as in Africa, the majority are simple rural folk, the borderlands populace suffers violations and abuse as much from the fugitive offenders as from the police authorities, both controlled from outside the border regions. While borderlanders must stand at the receiving end of adverse effects of the nationally controlled legislation and enforcement procedures, their views are never taken into account in the formulation and implementation of border policies, regardless of obvious consequences and implications for local community life.

The strategic indicators of borderlanders' inherent disadvantage are equally demonstrable. Borderlanders are, for example, exceptionally vulnerable to adverse effects of national and international crises. In their unique locations in and around entry and exit points into and from particular national territories, borderland communities (where they themselves are not directly involved) bear the brunt of the passage of refugees, escaping from civil wars or related internal disturbances, and armed aggressors operating from outside. Portions of ethnic homelands on one side of an international boundary also often get used as training grounds and launching pads for dissidents operating against government forces on the other side. The problems of insecurity are especially well illustrated by the several contemporary African cases of border conflicts, civil wars and alien expulsion orders. In these situations, so well illustrated by the ongoing civil war in Somalia, where particular vivisected ethnic groups are themselves the victims of national and international crises, the exceptional nature of borderlands' vulnerability and insecurity is especially easy to observe.

The political and strategic dimensions of borderland disadvantage have their socio-economic consequences and implications. Due partly to the mistrust of national peripheries and partly to their vulnerability, economic development of borderlands is, as a matter of policy, neglected by those in charge of the machines of state. Focusing on this aspect of the problem, Professor Orianne of the Catholic University of Louvain said it for all borderlands when, in a specific reference to local authorities in European border regions, he observed that "frontier areas are, by definition, at a disadvantage as compared with others because, to a certain degree, they have their backs turned to the wall."[3] According to Orianne, their handicap is three-fold: usually, they are further away from the center (capital or regional center); their most favorable trading area is largely abroad; some of the local authorities who have to cooperate with them are in another country.

The inherent economic disadvantage of "backs turned to the wall" have been underscored in the theoretical literature.[4] Walter Christaller and August Lösch, leading German scholars whose writings dominated the debate of location theory and its relevance to an understanding of the nature of borderlands in Europe in the inter-war years tended to regard border regions as "disadvantaged areas because of barriers to international trade and the threat of military invasion."[5] In Christaller's consideration, border regions were fragile because international boundaries "artificially fragment complementary economic regions."[6] Lösch considered it the "characteristic of national frontiers to hamper the crossing of boundaries by market areas, to create new gaps in market networks where none existed, and to discourage industries from settling near a boundary, where they often would have a market in one direction only."[7]

Location theorists recognize that regions on stable borders can and do give rise to certain advantages.[8] For example, the distribution of certain "central goods" such as concerts and dining, is not necessarily impeded by the border and may, in fact, be facilitated by inducements offered by complementary regions that extend far into the neighboring country. It is, in fact, argued that border regions benefit enormously from transfrontier investment made for the express purpose of avoiding customs duties. Concrete examples of such border industries include branches of Swiss businesses established in limitrophe German border regions or the maquiladoras on the Mexican side of the U.S.-Mexico border, owned and run by business interests based in the neighboring USA.

Indeed, as has been noted by Niles Hansen, small-scale national states, such as Switzerland, Holland, and Luxembourg or Benin, the Gambia and Botswana have attributes of border regions or borderlands, but they are also known to have turned these features into advantage to achieve relative prosperity.[9]

Nevertheless, the overall picture of border regions presented in location theory literature is that they are structurally "disadvantaged." This point is especially elaborated by Gendarme, the leading French Growth Pole theorist. He has argued rather persuasively that "the main consequence of a political frontier is to check the spread effects of a development pole."[10] He has called attention to the phenomenon of inherent inequality of levels of development on both sides of any given international boundary. Drawing his empirical data from the history and contemporary experience of areas of France limitrophe to Germany up to 1945, Gendarme explained that there is a "fortress mentality: that has led to stagnation since industrialists tend to refrain from investing in "threatened areas."

Anthony Asiwaju

The state-centric development strategies adopted by many a national authority acting on the basis of these theoretical assumptions has resulted in observably sharp dichotomies between core and peripheries with regard to infrastructural facilities. Because of the assumption of border areas as "militarily threatened areas," borderlands are deliberately avoided not only in decisions to locate industries; they are also left out of the planning and development of roads and railways as well as standard educational and medical facilities. Accordingly, as the African situation shows, borderlands are generally the most depressed sub-national areas economically and socially. They are, for the most part, areas of sharp discontinuities of the national transportation and communication networks. These normally peter out in the direction of international boundaries. This and other discriminatory treatment generally have the counterproductive effect of alienating rather than integrating national peripheries with the centers.

The marginalizing effects of international boundaries on borderlands go beyond the fragmentation of economic planning regions. Coherent culture areas are also balkanized, leaving each of the resultant bits and pieces inherently unable to organize its own security and well-being, without having to interact with other parts structurally cut off through enforced placement in other jurisdictional spheres.[11]

This strictly human dimension of marginality and insecurity in borderlands involves, among other issues, forced separation of families and kinsmen. The different fractions often become victims of the parallel integration and socialization processes put in place by governments on the different sides of the border. While the overall objectives of such parallel "assimilation" policies was to produce sufficiently distinct national characters, the divisive effects on local cultures manifest themselves best in Europe, North America, with special reference to the U.S.-Mexico border, and most parts of Africa, where borderlands represent areas of different official languages and cultures, and contrasting political, legal, administrative and economic systems.

Typologies of Borderlands and Borderland Communities

Borderlands and borderlands communities are known to vary widely across the nation-state world. The observable variations are experienced not only from place to place (including sector to sector on particular borders) but also from time to time in the same place. There is also the problem of differentiation within particular local communities along lines of distinct interests such as those based on occupation, profession, kinship and class. There is a challenge to efforts, such as the one undertaken in this essay, aimed at discussing borderlands communities as unified entities. While several scholars (Gross

1973; Strassoldo 1989; Momoh 1989) have attempted the classification, perhaps the most comprehensive is the one contained in a recent publication by Oscar J. Martinez, the renowned comparative historian of the U.S.-Mexico borderlands (Martinez 1994).[12]

Martinez recognizes four main categories of borderlands based on the ideal-type borders and border regimes. First is the "alienated borderlands." This is identified with borders that are "functionally closed, and [where] cross-border interaction is totally or nearly totally absent." As Martinez has further explained, the relation between states on the different sides of "closed" borders that define "alienated borderlands" are marked by "tension." Inhabitants of "alienated borderlands" on the one and the other sides of closed borders are forced to relate to each other as "strangers" even when, as nearly always, they are members of the same basic culture or even kinship groups.

Concrete examples of "closed" borders and "alienated borderlands" included those of former Communist states in Europe via-à-vis themselves and, more importantly, between each of them and limitrophe capitalist Western European countries. Examples of "closed" borders and "alienated borderlands" still include the border and borderlands between North and South Korea. In "alienated borderlands," the question of insecurity of the borderland communities as marginal populations is posed exceptionally boldly. In such border areas, fundamental human rights have no meaning whatsoever. The only meaningful rights are those of the sovereign states based on might.

The second and third categories of borderlands in Martinez's schema are the "co-existent" and "inter-dependent" borderlands. The difference is one of degree, not of type, since the hallmark of the border in each situation is that it is stable, though palpably more so in the "interdependent" than in "co-existent" borderlands. In both cases, too, the border is relatively "open," allowing for the development of binational interaction, more limited in the "co-existent" than "interdependent" borderlands where, for reasons of greater stability of the borders, increased cross-border interaction is a function of a significant degree of "economic and social complementarity." While citizens of "co-existent" borderlands are assisted to "develop closer relationships," "interdependent" borderlanders can even "carry on friendly and co-operative relationships." Living examples of "co-existent" and "interdependent" borderlands and borderlanders are to be found across most of the borders of ex-colonial national states in North America, Latin America, Asia and Africa. While the "coexistent" is the dominant type in Africa, Asia and Latin America (including the U.S.-Mexico border), the "interdependent" category is best exemplified by the U.S.-Canada border.

The fourth category in the schema worked out by Martinez is the "integrated borderlands' where the stability of the border can be described as "strong and permanent." According to Martinez, this is the situation in which the "economies of the limitrophe countries are functionally merged and there is unrestricted movement of people and goods across the boundary." In this kind of situation, Martinez would conclude, "borderlanders perceive themselves as members of one social system."

As is to be expected, concrete examples of integrated borderlands are concentrated in Western Europe, cradle of the nation-state and its border problematics, where, for reasons of the old age of states, the stability of the borders may be described as "strong and stable" and where, as post-1945 developments can easily be used to show, limitrophe national economies have been virtually completely integrated within the framework of a single regional organization. In such situations, characterized by a total commitment on the part of governments and peoples to the policy of transborder cooperation, borderlanders become living witnesses of the positive impact of public policy aimed at remedying a marginalization that had resulted from centuries of the evolutionary history of the classical nation-state and the barrier function of its borders.

There is a historical perspective to the quadruple classification of borderlands. Raimondo Strassoldo underscored this when he argued that "a comparison between the African, American and European border situations seems to correspond to the three general models or ideal types, which can be arranged in a comparative-evolutionary scale, referring to three different stages of (state) societal development."[13] He labeled the three phases, respectively, as "nation-building," "co-existence" and "integration." The characteristics of the first phase, that of "nation-building," may be said to approximate to borderland features that fall between the brackets of what Martinez classified as "alienated" and "co-existent" borderlands, while the "co-existence" and "integration" phases in Strassoldo's evolutionary scale may be said to be productive of situations which Martinez has categorized as "interdependent" and "integrated" borderlands respectively.

In Strassoldo's view, the phase of "nation-building" is manifest in nation-states of relatively recent origin, such as are found in Africa, Asia and Latin America. Former satellite Communist states in Eastern Europe , most of which owed their origin to the outcome of the Two World Wars (most especially the post-1945 Cold War), also have borders and borderlands characteristics of the "nation-building" stage of state societal development. As Strassoldo correctly observed, nation-states at this stage "have the paramount problems of internal integration, which also means a "hardening" of their boundaries."[14] At this stage, the national states tend to guard their boundaries jealously vis-à-vis neighboring states to ensure necessary differentiation from outside. The implications for border areas generally include forced fragmentation for pre-existing cultural homogeneities with the different fractions forced "to develop along divergent paths" and to "nurture different loyalties, languages, values and economies" in accordance to the dictates of the limitrophe sovereign authorities under whose different jurisdictions the fractions of the pre-existing homogeneities have been placed.

The "co-existence" phase in Strassoldo's comparative-evolutionary scale is one in which neighboring states may be said to have "achieved some satisfactory degree of . . . internal integration" and self-confidence, leading to relative stability of their borders and the evolution, therefore, of what Martinez has categorized as "co-existent" and/or "interdependent" borderlands. The U.S.-Canada and the U.S.-Mexico borderlands, already used to illustrate Martinez's "interdependent" and "co-existent" ideal types respectively, may be reckoned in varying degrees as features of Strassoldo's "co-existence" phase of evolutionary development. There is no problem whatsoever in recognizing Martinez's "integrative borderlands" as the feature of the most advanced stage in Strassoldo's evolutionary scale, that of "integration," exemplified by Western Europe since 1945.

Public Policy Concerns: An Overview

Indeed, given the nature of borderlanders as "transborder peoples" and the nature of borderlands as inherently internationalized localities, there are perhaps no other human situations that so compel the need for public policy intervention at both national and, more importantly, international levels. The international level of public policy design is underscored by Orianne when he observes that "if . . . , in other fields, international cooperation may simply be useful or desirable, there [i.e., in borderlands] it is an absolute necessity."[15]

But critical as international cooperation is to the resolution of borderlands problems, it depends on the stability of the states concerned. A state torn by civil war or other forms of internal strife may not be able to negotiate an international cooperation agreement, especially one focusing on the factor of shared borders and borderlands. Post-war Europe has been in the forefront of other regions of the world in matters relating to regional integration and transborder cooperation. This is a clear demonstration of the extent to which genuine commitment to the cause of democracy, advocacy for human rights and the concomitant humanization of the machinery of states constitute the conditions for success of public policy for overcoming the problems of marginality and insecurity of borderlands.

Since the problem of borderland communities is basically one of homelands with "backs turned to the wall," the principal objective of public policy has to be the removal of the barrier effects of the wall, if not the wall itself. In other words, public policy must be aimed not only at solving problems of transborder cooperation but also at promoting equitable and accelerated development. Experts distinguish between three main categories of the problems that public policy must seek to solve if transborder cooperation is to be achieved. These have been categorized as the exogenous, the general and the specific.[16] Exogenous problems are those of world-wide, continental, sub-continental or national origins, which tend to hamper the development, as it were, of the ideal-type frontierless society at the various levels.

With particular reference to the generally adverse effects on border relations, examples include the fanning of "negative," as opposed to "practical or utilitarian" nationalism;[17] apathy among the generality of the population of the countries of a given region or sub-region of the world; inflationary trends in the national economies of a whole region or sub-region; defective currency systems, giving rise to serious asymmetry of relations between national currencies and accompanying distortions in the exchange rates; a lack of commitment to regional or sub-regional solidarity; and a chronic absence of a catholic perception of problems on the part of decision makers, especially at national levels. While these problems do not affect borderlands directly, their solution creates the right type of conditions and environment that facilitate effective tackling of problems more directly connected with transborder relations.

General border problems, on the other hand, are those liable to prevent the integration of states in particular regions or sub-regions of the world. They include currency disparities; differences in educational systems and qualifications; divergent socialization processes giving rise to national characteristics of substantially different hues; differences in political, administrative, legal systems and practices; and differences in economic systems. These problems are most easily observed along borders in Europe, Western and Southern Africa, as well as in North America and Mexico, where culturally contrastive sovereign entities are in juxtaposition.[18]

Specific border problems, the third main category of obstacles, which have to be cleared to achieve transborder cooperation, are such as have developed in the course of the history of particular borders and borderlands. They relate to regional and town planning; local administration; infrastructural facilities; environment; culture; community health; and emergency relief and disaster management. In borderlands situations, there is no better approach to the solution of these problems than by way of a transborder cooperation policy.

The specific aims and functions of the policy are concerned with healing the wounds imposed on the borderlands by the history of the nation-states; harmonizing regional planning policies of limitrophe states where they impinge on one another; harnessing the economic potentials of borderlands through sound regional development programs; and improving infrastructure to ensure and facilitate cross-border movement of persons and goods, thus bringing about more equitable living conditions for borderland inhabitants of affected areas.[19]

Other aims and functions are to achieve necessary coordination of measures intended for joint management of the environment and related transborder natural resources; harmonize cultural policies through joint scientific research programs and institution-building as well as youth fellowships and sports; stimulate intermunicipal cooperation on such matters as provision of hospitals, waste disposal and recreation; and finally, contribute to the overall achievement of socio-economic, if not political, integration of concerned regions of the world.

Regional Case Studies

Given the multiple levels—global, regional (continental), sub-regional, national and sub-national—at which border problems are encountered, projects (i.e., policy decisions and implementation strategies, including relevant organizations and institutions) for the diminution—if not complete demolition—of the border as barrier or "wall" have to be examined also at the various levels. However, since the fullness of application and the effectiveness of the efforts must be expected to vary according to the type of borderlands and the corresponding level of development of state societies in focus, the rest of this essay is devoted to the discussion of actual development in Africa, North America and Western Europe in that order of position in Strassoldo's "comparative-evolutionary scale." In doing so, however, our emphasis is more on past achievements than future projections: the essay is, for example, less concerned with future developments in the North American Free Trade Area (NAFTA) and European Union than with the history and analysis of transborder cooperation at local level in the areas.

Africa: Transborder Cooperation in "Nation Building" Contexts

Compared with the cases in Western Europe, homeland of the nation-state, North America, where the United States of America successfully fought a war of liberation against Great Britain from 1776 to 1783 to become the world's oldest ex-colonial territory to attain a sovereign status, national states and international boundaries in Africa are indisputably of relatively recent origin.

Given the continuous nature of the evolution—be this from nations to states, as in the case of the classical "nation-states" of Western Europe; or from states to nations, as in the case of the "state-nations " in the mostly ex-colonial parts of the rest of the world where the modern states are successors of former European colonies[20]—it is not surprising that, in spite of over three decades of the history of most independent states in Africa and the much longer history of their boundaries, border and borderlands manifestations in the continent are still typically those of the nation-building phase of the evolutionary history.

Outside the five African Island states of Madagascar, Cape Verde, Seychelles, Mauritius, and Sao Tomé and Principé, there are, in mainland Africa, forty-seven independent states sharing a total of one hundred and three international boundaries of widely varying lengths and physical types. For most scholars, who regard as "artificial" all boundaries other than those made up of geographical or natural features such as rivers, hills, mountains and valleys, Africa has been a choice region of the world. This is because only 26% of the borders in the continent are based on geographical features (i.e., the so-called "natural frontiers"), the remaining 74% being shared alignments based on astronomical and mathematical lines.

However, as we have argued elsewhere,[21] all are "artificial boundaries" for as long as the state-centric objective for which they are created is for them to function as effective lines of demarcation and separation between the limitrophe sovereign states. Though generally ill-defined and, for the most part, inadequately demarcated, the borders in Africa, as elsewhere, are known to have been drawn and subsequently enforced without much regard to coherent culture areas and natural planning regions straddled and consequently fragmented by the various boundary alignments.[22]

Arising from several factors, including the contradiction in having to enforce the borders in spite of their generally indeterminate character and the usual rivalry between limitrophe states on the exploitation of valuable transborder natural resources, relations across Africa's international boundaries are typically those of actual and potential conflicts, too numerous and too well known to warrant being listed in this paper.[23]

While most African borders may be classified as "open," in the sense that they can be crossed subject to possession of a valid traveling document, "closed" and sometimes "Berlin Wall" borders are encountered in a number of places and on a number of occasions. Witness, for example, the high security fencing along the Togo-Ghana border in the heart of the Economic Community of West African States (ECOWAS) and, before the dismantling of apartheid, land mines and an electric fence along South Africa's border with Mozambique. The two-year official closure of Nigeria's borders vis-à-vis all her neighbors from 24 April 1984 to 1 March 1986 illustrated familiar episodes of normally "open borders" being ordered to be closed on the basis of unilateral decisions of governments of individual states. Thus, the borderland categories in Africa may be said to range from the "alienated" for the worst and "interdependent" for the best.

In this type of situation, characterized by a strong sense of attachments on the part of the states to the notion of territorial sovereignty, transborder cooperation policy is necessarily at its very rudimentary stage of development. While the grassroot realities of sovereignty-perforating factors of shared environment, transborder natural and cultural resources, and the vibrant regional networks of informal social and economic transactions continue to beckon at and compel the policy, the sovereignty-sensitive states have, in general, continued to respond within the framework of international organizations whose rules guarantee their sovereign status as corporate members. Whether in the context of the Organization of African Unity (OAU), or sub-regional organizations such as the Economic Community of Western African States (ECOWAS), the Economic Community of Central African States (ECCAS), and Southern African Development Coordination Conference (SADCC), behavior of African states, severally and collectively, is indicative of a general wish to practice solidarity but without the corresponding readiness to sacrifice sovereignty. The result is that, despite public declarations and pronouncements in favor of regional integration and, by implication, transborder cooperation between limitrophe African states, the prevalence of a strong sense of attachment to the notion of sovereignty on the part of member-states has continued to work against actual policy implementation.

Important decisions of the OAU since its inception in 1963, relevant to the issue of boundaries, leave one in no doubt whatsoever that the basic policy concern was more for the sovereignty of individual member-sates than commitment to the cause of regional solidarity and, by implication, transborder cooperation. Take, for example, the provision of Paragraph 3 of Article III of the OAU Charter whereby "the member-states solemnly affirmed and declared their adherence to the principle of respect for the sovereignty and territorial integrity of each State."

The Cairo Declaration of 1964 advanced the position of territorial sovereignty of the member-states when, in addition to reaffirming "the strict respect by all Member States . . . for the principles laid down in Paragraph 3 of Article III of the OAU Charter," the Summit "solemnly declares that all member-states pledge themselves to respect the borders existing on their achievement of national independence," thus bringing Africa in line with the *Uttis Possidetis* position of Latin American states. Although certain member-states with irredentist claims against their neighbors, notably Somalia and Morocco, took exception to this OAU policy stand, it is these decisions that have, by and large, continued to determine the attitude of OAU as a body to territorial and border disputes and conflicts within and between member-

eration for peace and unity of the continent, it has been allowed to evolve in a way that has tended to progressively cast the borders more in the mold of ramparts than in the image of bridges between states.

That this position has not changed in any substantial manner is proved by the trend of the discussion and decisions of the 1991 OAU Summit in Abuja: while the Heads of Sate and Government found it easy to ceremoniously append their signatures to the African Economic Community Treaty, based on the familiar assumption of the Sovereign status of member-states, the preparatory Meeting of the Council of Ministers which preceded the Summit, was unable to agree to recommend a resuscitated proposal, first made by Nigeria in 1981, for the establishment of an OAU Boundary Commission. The Commission was intended as a specialized border problem-solving insti-tution that would work not only to settle the ever-increasing disputes and conflicts peacefully, but also systematically to promote transborder coopera-tion between member-states.

At a sub-regional level, as the case of ECOWAS demonstrates, provisions of the treaty and related protocols regarding free movement of the Commu-nity citizens, and trade liberalizations are continuing to be rendered ineffec-tive by the border-enforcement agencies of member-states, staffed for the most part by poorly trained, ill-motivated, inadequately paid and corrupt officials. The view of borderlanders, that these border-enforcement agencies are a menace, is widespread in West Africa where, as in most Nigerian border regions, the popular demand is that they should be removed.[24]

At the national level the picture can hardly be expected to differ from what it is at the international level. However, as the case of Nigeria may be made to show, there have been, in recent years some positive indications of a preparedness to work out some definite institutional frameworks for transbor-der cooperation policy-making and implementation vis-à-vis each of Nigeria's neighbors. This local initiative seemed to have grown from the larger border policy reconsideration which lead to the proposal for an OAU Boundary Commission, which Nigeria first submitted to the 37th Meeting of the Ministerial Council in Nairobi in 1981.

While the OAU vacillated, Nigeria went ahead to establish its own National Boundary Commission with a permanent Secretariat. Formally inaugurated on 20th July 1988, on the basis of Decree No. 38 of 17th December 1987, the Commission was aptly described as one of the most imaginative of border problem-solving mechanisms to be put in place in any independent African state.[25]

With jurisdiction over both the international and internal boundaries of the nation, the Commission's responsibility included settlement of disputes,

264   prevention of conflict, confidence building through transborder cooperation endeavors, border region development and border policy coordination. The ultimate aim was a transborder cooperation agreement on the model of the European Outline Convention on Transborder Cooperation Between Territorial Authorities or communities.[26] The Commission was also formally committed to the policy of "compensatory" accelerated development of border regions.

While the perspective of the special development focus on the borderlands was national to begin with, the Commission was fully aware of transborder planning and development as the ultimate. Since the foremost development problems of the areas are inaccessibility and welfare, the planning focus in the early stages was on development of access roads, rural electrification as well as rural health and educational facilities. In cooperation with the "gateway" states and local governments, the federal government was to share the cost of the program of accelerated development, including the identification as well as the projected planning and development of model border towns and villages.

In its first four years, from 1988 to 1992, the National Boundary Commission left the Nigerian public and the wider international community in no doubt of the seriousness of Nigerian government's commitment to the creation of a cooperative rather than a conflictual border regime in Nigeria and between Nigeria and each of its neighbors. With regard to the international boundaries, which constitute our focus in this essay, the Commission actively organized and successfully hosted a series of bilateral consultative workshops with each of the limitrophe countries: Benin in 1988; Niger in 1989; Cameroon in May 1992; and Equatorial Guinea November 1992.[27]

Apart from these transborder cooperation workshop series, the Commission also initiated and undertook confidence-building missions to the respective proximate countries.[28] Federal Ministers and parastatals with duties and responsibilities which impinged on the function of the borders as well as states and local governments of the Federation which abut directly on any of the international boundaries were continuously sensitized to the need to reflect a reorientation in line with the national government's new determination to turn the nation's borders vis-à-vis neighboring countries from a prevalent posture of barrier to new roles as bridges between Nigeria and adjacent countries.[29]

Needless to say, these programs inaugurated a new era of intensive but positive interactions. The reactions of neighboring countries to Nigeria's initiative were positive, though these seemed to have varied from the rating of "very high" for, say, Benin, Niger, and Equatorial Guinea to just "high" for Cameroon and Chad. The morale of borderlands would appear to have risen

Anthony Asiwaju

considerably due to locally noticeable effects of the new Nigerian initiative. One major morale booster in the borderlands was the unprecedented interest shown by the national and sub-national authorities in the welfare of border populations and positive development of the areas.[30] Although actual achievements in border infrastructural development have varied widely between laudable concrete achievements along the border with the Republic of Niger and a state of virtual abandonment along the western and eastern borders with Benin and Cameroon, all border communities were given a feel of a new concern by the federal, state and local governments.

Of particular importance has been the phenomenal increase in the initiative and drive on the part of Nigerian border state governments, formally sanctioned by the federal government, to establish cooperative working relationships with counterpart territorial authorities in respective limitrophe countries. A growing practice of formalized cooperative linkages was especially noticeable along the Nigeria-Niger border where—within the framework of the Nigeria-Niger Joint Commission on Cooperation (based in Niamey)—the pioneering initiatives have been mounted by the Sokoto state government vis-à-vis the adjacent Nigérien *départements* of Dosso and Tahoua; and Katsina state government vis-à-vis the neighboring Nigerien *départements* of Maradi and Zinder. Similar exchanges took place across other international boundaries of Nigeria, notably the western border with Benin as follow-up to the Nigeria-Benin Transborder Cooperation Workshop of 1988.

Exchanges of visits occurred between Nigerian "gateway" state governors and their counterparts in Niger, Benin and, to some extent, Cameroon, in addition to a series of joint tours of border areas by Nigeria's Minister of Internal Affairs and his counterparts in the limitrophe countries. The initiative, begun on the Nigeria-Benin border, in February 1986, was extended to the border with Niger in 1991 as follow-up to a relevant recommendation of the Nigeria-Niger Transborder Cooperation Workshop in Kano in 1989. Similar arrangements were initiated for the borders with Cameroon and Equatorial Guinea, following the Transborder Cooperation Workshops between Nigeria and these two countries in May and November 1992, respectively.

Nigeria's decision to systematically promote transborder cooperation with proximate neighbors in the late 1980s and early 1990s was facilitated by a wider context of inter-related foreign and domestic policy initiatives being taken at the same time. On the foreign policy front, for example, there was a rededication to the cause of regional and sub-regional integration in Africa, as evidenced by the huge investments of human and material resources to projects of the OAU and ECOWAS, notably the African Economic Community Treaty opened to signature at Abuja in 1991, the ECOWAS Peace

Monitoring Unit (ECOMOG) in war-torn Liberia since the late 1980s and the ECOWAS Revised Treaty approved at the Accra summit in 1993. On the domestic front, there were bold initiatives aimed at ushering in democracy, public accountability and respect for fundamental human rights.

The progress made in Nigeria has, however, been typically fragile and ephemeral. For a familiar combination of factors, often characteristic of national states at the nation-building stage of development, the course of transborder cooperation policy has been disrupted. The factors in question have included political uncertainty, regime instability, policy discontinuity, negative nationalism and economic crisis. In Nigeria, the failure of General Babangida's administration to install a democratically elected government in August 1993 and the change of political regime in November 1993, which ushered in the present military administration of General Sanni Abacha, have typically led to a drastic policy review with adverse consequences for the transborder cooperation policy promotion of the preceding military regime.

In particular, the renewal of the border conflict with Cameroon, following the movement of Nigerian troops and military equipment on the Bakassi peninsula, a strategic location within a wider oil-rich coastal and maritime border area long disputed by the two countries, in December 1993 has since negated whatever the gains of the confidence-building measures that have been mounted since 1991. Such measures have included the special mission to Cameroon by the National Boundary Commission, led by the Honorable Minister of External Affairs in his capacity as the Chairman of the Commission's Technical Committee on International Boundaries in 1991, the Nigeria-Cameroon Transborder Cooperation Workshop of 1992; the series of bilateral meetings of the Nigeria-Cameroon Joint Committee of Experts on Border Issues, created in 1991 to work out strategies for the demarcation of the entire boundary; and the preparations for a Joint Border Tour by the Ministers of the Interior of the two countries on the model of the successful exercises on the borders with the Republic of Benin and Niger in 1986 through 1991. One other potential casualty of the 1993/94 militarization of the border conflict with Cameroon was the Gulf of Guinea Commission, proposed by Nigeria and agreed by Cameroon in 1991. The commission was to embrace such other maritime states as Equatorial Guinea, Gabon, Sao Tomé and Principé and was to operate on the model of the Lake Chad Basin Commission. The Commission was to facilitate the demarcations of all the maritime boundaries as well as evolve peaceful strategies for joint and equitable exploration and exploitation of such sensitive transborder natural resources as hydro-carbon deposits and fisheries and manage incidental environmental problems.

Anthony Asiwaju

Both Nigeria and Cameroon have done well to prevent the border conflict from escalating into war; but the path of peaceful dialogue, which characterized the years preceding November 1993, has been effectively replaced by the alternative path of aggressive nationalism, expressed first in terms of military mobilization and now litigation following Cameroon's decision to take the matter to the International Court of Justice at the Hague for adjudication. Apart from its immediate adverse effects on Nigeria-Cameroon border relations, the conflict with Cameroon has also understandably opened Nigeria and her transborder cooperation policy initiative to wide-spread suspicion of her neighbors and their allies in the wider international community.

Besides, the deepening political and economic crises in Nigeria and neighboring countries have made border issues to go down the scale of priority of the decision-makers. In Nigeria, it is perhaps as a proof of this current loss of interest of government in borders and borderlands concerns that one must view the observable vacillation, if not outright irresponsiveness, to the several requests which the Republic of Benin has made for the signing of the Transborder Cooperation Treaty Between the Federal Republic of Nigeria and the Republic of Benin. Based on the workshop conclusions of 1988 and engrossed in 1992, the draft Treaty was approved for signature by the Nigerian Head of State since February 1993. In this circumstance, work on the draft treaties with Niger, Cameroon and Equatorial Guinea, begun by the National Boundary Commission Secretariat following the Workshops of 1989 and 1992, has been discontinued. As with transborder cooperation, the initial enthusiasm for border region development has waned on the general complaint of lack of funds.

In the face of all these adverse developments, the boundaries and borderlands have remained virtually abandoned to the mercies of clandestine cross-border business operators and the mostly corrupt border-enforcement officials both of whom are best regarded as partners in the common exploitation of the ever expanding "second economy" as this has flourished and continued to flourish across Nigeria's international boundaries. The real empowerment and demarginalization of borderland communities in Africa, as the Nigerian case has been made to show, may have to await the full establishment of democracy and the realization of the culture of respect for fundamental human rights.

North America: Transborder Cooperation in a "Coexistence" Phase

North America is substantially different from Africa, not just because the borders there are much older but that they are remarkably few and more stable.

Unlike mainland Africa, which is divided into close to fifty independent states sharing, among them, 103 boundaries, there are in North America only three sovereign states: Canada, the United States of America and Mexico sharing among them the two longest trans-continental international boundaries—the U.S.-Canada border of over five thousand miles and the U.S.-Mexico of close to two thousand, each running from the Atlantic coast in the east to the Pacific in the West.

While the U.S.-Canada border has resulted from the opposing position of the United States and Canada in the American War of Independence of 1776 to 1783, the U.S.-Mexico frontierline was negotiated in the aftermath of the U.S.-Mexico War of 1846, which led to the annexation of Northern Mexican provinces and their incorporation into what have since become the States of California, New Mexico, Arizona and Texas in the southwestern United States.

The borderlands focused on in this case study, the nearly two-thousand mile-long border between the United States and Mexico, derive their abiding fascination for scholars from an unrivaled position as the longest "corridor of land in the world where North meets South."[31] Along this border, the leading "First World" post-industrial society is in direct contact with a typical industrializing "Third World" country. The asymmetry is also one between a truly giant-size and incomparably technologically sophisticated economy, that of the U.S. to the north, and the relatively small and technologically less developed Mexican economy to the south. These exceptionally sharp contrasts have been further emphasized by the fact of the border as a line of demarcation between the Anglo-American and the Latin American world; between Common Law and Civil Law tradition, between a federalist and a centralist state.[32]

But while, at one level, the aforementioned features of asymmetry may and should be considered as part and parcel of the indicators on the border in terms of its typical role as a "separator," other equally potent data point to the other side of the border paradox, that of its role as "integrator." Of these features, there is perhaps none as crucial to the U.S.-Mexico case study as its attribute as the most urbanized in the world. The ten twin cities: San Diego/Tijuana, Calexico/Mexicali, Yuma/San Luis, Nogales/Nogales, Douglas/Agua Praeta, El Paso/Ciudad Juarez, Del Rio/Ciudad Acuna, Eagle Pass/Piedras Negras, Laredo/Nuevo Laredo, McAlen/Reymosa, and Brownsville/Matamoros—rank as the most renowned twin sets of "transfrontier metropolis" anywhere.[33]

The binational cities merely symptomize other fundamental undercurrents of interpenetration across the border. The patterns of interdigitation noticeable in the spatial responses between the twin cities as poles of mutual attraction were created and subsequently regularly fueled by a combination of factors which Lawrence Herzog has correctly listed to include "historical and territorial linkages, cycles of migration and family ties, economically motivated cross-boundary travel, and reciprocal environmental processes."[34] From the borderlands viewpoint in this essay, there is perhaps no other more important single factor of interpenetration across the U.S.-Mexico border than the fact of the American side as a natural and unbroken extension of the predominantly Mexican culture area to the south.

But in spite of the observable fact of interpenetration and its natural and, indeed, compelling attraction for transborder cooperation, the choice of policy by the governments of the U.S. and Mexico is that based on the extremely sovereignty-conscious principle of "co-existence." Both in Washington, D.C. and Mexico City, as well as in the headquarters of the limitrophe U.S. and Mexican state governments and administrations, the preference is for a view of the border as "separator," and not the "integrator" that is strongly suggested by borderlands grassroots realities of what has been aptly referred to as "perforated sovereignties."[35]

Thus, in spite of such formal transborder cooperation organizations as the U.S.-Mexico Trade commission (created in 1965) or, more significantly, the U.S.-Mexico Commission for Border Development and Friendship, formed the following year, international relations across the U.S. border with Mexico normally proceed on the basis of the provisions of familiar-type international legal instruments such as treaties and agreements that are often reached during summits of the Presidents or in the context of interparliamentary conferences that take place across the border. However, with a possible exception of the International Boundary and Water Commission (IBWC), the oldest U.S.-Mexico binationally structured transborder cooperative institution created in 1889, most of the other formal cooperative arrangements, so crucial to borderlands interests, have fallen victim to the usual diplomatic inertia.[36] Unfortunately, while the IBWC has recorded outstanding successes in the exercise of its mandate focused on water resources management, the Commission's mandate now stands in urgent need of a substantial expansion if its functions are to cover borderland communities' wider areas of concern.

Even at the national and sub-national levels, borderlands interests continue to suffer utter neglect. Within the United States, for example, formal structures such as the National Governors Association, National Association of State Developmental Agencies and even the Southwest Border Regional Commission "reflect state, not border, interests."[37] In the authoritative words of Ellwyn Stoddard, the foremost U.S.-Mexico borderlands scholar,

> On balance, border peoples are poverty-prone, and politically impotent. It
> is unlikely that their miseries, low on state priorities, would be spearheaded

in the search for national support for state problems. It is even more unlikely that any national attempts to solve border problems would take serious account of local desires.[38]

It is against this "perception along the border that bureaucrats in the two capital cities (and the regional centers) are out of touch, disinterested or not under-standing of border matters"[39] that one must understand the fall back on informal arrangements as the most effective way at the disposal of officials of municipal authorities operating in each of the "transfrontier metropoles" on the U.S.-Mexican border.

In view of the numerous studies that have been done on the subject of "informal policy making in U.S.-Mexico border cities"[40] there is no need for this essay to be concerned with the details. Suffice it to state that the focus, naturally, is on such subjects of contact usually reported between sister-city officials; they are, as to be expected, matters of critical importance to the border localities, but overlooked or even outlawed by legislatures and bu-reaucracies in the national capitals and regional centers on either side. These issues, significantly, have been listed to include public safety, social festivities, information and equipment exchange, public health, physical development, public interest in business and commerce, public education and recreation, tourism and agriculture.[41]

As we have noted in our introductory discussion on the nature, aim and functions of transborder cooperation policy, the issues of informal policy-making along the U.S.-Mexico border are basically the same as the one which transborder cooperation policy entails. What formal transborder cooperation policy seeks to achieve is the removal of the fundamental weakness in "infor-mal policy making," namely, its vulnerability to negative sanctions and veto by national and sub-national authorities, the latter including, in the case under study, such limitrophe U.S. and Mexican states as California and Baja California Norte or Texas and Chihuahua, respectively. Through an arrange-ment, which enables the national and sub-national authorities to formally approve the initiatives of border local officials, "informal policy making" is transformed into transborder cooperation policy.

It is not yet clear what the impact of NAFTA would be on this develop-ment. Signed by the three Heads of State in 1992 and ratified by the three national legislatures—Canada, United States and Mexico—in 1993, this 2000 page trinational agreement has created, in the words of two experts, "the world's largest common market by eliminating most barriers to the free flow of goods and services between the three North American nations over a fifteen-year period."[42] The fact of its conception as an experiment and the definition of its goal as the creation of a free trade area, not regional integra-

Anthony Asiwaju

tion, underscores the status of the borders and borderlands in North America as essentially "interdependent" in the case of the U.S. and Canada and "co-existent" in that of the U.S. and Mexico under focus.

The much sharper contrasts between the U.S. and Mexico, in terms not only of the levels of technological and economic development but also socio-cultural dispositions, have dictated the significantly more prolonged negotiations over NAFTA than was known of the preceding U.S.-Canada Free Trade Agreement executed in 1987.

Typically statist in perspective, NAFTA makes little or no explicit reference to the community needs and concerns of the "transborder peoples" of North America, as represented by Mexicans and Mexican-Americans and the surviving Indian populations astride the U.S.-Mexican border. The numerous studies which have evaluated the trinational agreement since its coming into effect in 1993 have characteristically focused more on the implications for the national economies than the effects on the local peoples in the adjoining border regions. With particular reference to the U.S. and Mexico, scholarly evaluations of NAFTA have been dominated by economists and political scientists whose concentrations have been on such basically establishment questions as immigration, employment, environment, crimes and criminalization.[43] As always, the essentially humanistic concerns must await the usually delayed responses of experts in the anthropology, sociology and contemporary history of the U.S.-Mexico border and borderlands.

Nonetheless, NAFTA may be seen as offering an unprecedented opportunity for initiating and advancing the process for the formalization of transborder cooperation policy across the U.S.-Mexico border. it can be explored and exploited as the legal framework within which local community leaders, especially those in charge of the binational municipal authorities, to persuade the border states and ultimately the national governments to pursue supplementary agreements similar to those permitted and actively encouraged within the framework of the now famous European Outline Convention on Transfrontier Cooperation Between Territorial Communities or Authorities.[44]

A precedence for a supplementary agreement on "transfrontier cooperation between territorial communities or authorities" across the U.S.-Mexico border, based on NAFTA, can be found in NAFTA-related trinational agreements on the environment.[45] A similar suggestion for labor is implied in a U.S. criticism of the Bush administration "for not including in the NAFTA proposal protection of U.S. workers threatened to lose their jobs as a result of the shift of work to Mexico."[46] Hopefully, the current trend of liberalization of the Mexican economy, which has facilitated the successful negotiation of NAFTA in the first instance, would be matched by a similar liberalization of

Mexican politics. For it is full democratization, accompanied by a decentralization of the Mexican administration, that can bring about developments in Mexico in line with the U.S. where, in law and practice, the federal States and their constituent counties enjoy a high degree of independence of action, including the initiative to enter into agreements with foreign jurisdictions such as those in limitrophe countries. It is in the light of this possibility for accelerating the pace of economic and political liberalization on both sides of the U.S.-Mexico border and ultimate policy coordination, including a systematic transborder cooperation in planning and development, that NAFTA can be of significance for the demarginalization of the U.S.-Mexico borderlands.

Western Europe: The "Integration" Model

With a history that is usually dated to the Treaty of Westphalia, which ended the Thirty Years War of 1618 to 1648, the nation-states of Western Europe are not only the oldest in the world; by reason of their world-wide imperialist expansion, first into the Americas and Asia in the 17th and 18th centuries and then into Africa in the last quarter of the 19th century, the nation-states of Western Europe—notably Britain, France, Portugal, Spain, Holland, Germany and Italy in that order of importance—were also the creators of national states elsewhere in the world in which most of such states are successors of the former European colonies.

As Strassoldo has observed, since "it was in Western Europe that nationalstates were first invented, it is only natural that it was also there that they first matured and, hopefully, decayed."[47] The most advanced on the "comparative-evolutionary scale," the "integration" phase has been idealized as one in which

> Neighbouring (states) are steered towards ever higher degrees of integration, of mutual interpenetration, of merging. States are willing to "devolve" their powers and surrender their sovereignty to higher and wider level societal organization. At their borders, what were walls and barriers evolve into doors, bridges and junctions; and these, in turn, may evolve into new centers of the overall supra-system.[48]

The borderlands category that has been found to correspond to this most advanced stage of border evolutionary history is the "integrated" on Martinez's classificatory system or a combination of the "civilized" and the "periphery" in Felix Gross. Shared international boundaries are very stable and permanent: cooperation, not conflict, is the hallmark of international relations across borders at this evolutionary phase; the limitrophe economies are functionally merged and there is so much freedom of cross-border move-

ment of persons and goods that "borderlanders perceive themselves as members of the societal system."[49]

Borders and borderlands in Western Europe approximate to this ideal type, thanks to the success story of the post-1945 regional integration endeavors and the associated commitment to transborder cooperation policy. These developments have resulted in the conversion of the old Europe of the nation-states into today's post-war Europe of the region and the people. From the point of view of the security of marginal populations, therefore, Western Europe provides the most appropriate environment in which to examine the actual operation of transborder cooperation policy at its best, the public policy category that we have considered the most relevant instrument for dealing with the twin-problems of marginality and insecurity as they manifest in a typical population, that of residents of national peripheries.

These truly phenomenal developments in post-war Western Europe have generated such an avalanche of recent literature by scholars and public policy analysts[50] that only a synthesis or summary needs to be attempted in this essay. While many of the available studies and publications have been devoted to the discussion of the more dramatic issue of regional integration and, in particular, the history, politics and organizational structure of the European Economic Community, far less attention appears to have been paid to relevant aspects of the literature as it relates to the more critical, if not explosive, territorial question posed by the "barrier" functions and "wall" effects of the classical nation-states boundaries and the painstaking enterprise for a transborder cooperation policy design as was undertaken within the institutional framework of the Council of Europe founded in 1949.[51] This feat, of successfully steering Europe in the direction of an ultimate adoption of an transborder cooperation policy, was achieved by the Council through the European Outline Convention on Transborder Cooperation between Territorial Communities or Authorities which was opened for the signatures of member-states in Madrid in 1980 and, by 1984, had been fully ratified by all of them, including centralist France.[52]

The Council of Europe was able to achieve this spectacular policy architecture through an active collaboration not only with the European Economic Community (EEC) and other related international organizations, notably, the Organization for Economic Cooperation and Development (OECD) which, in addition to the regular member-states of the EEC and Council of Europe, embraced the United States of America and Canada. In evolving transborder cooperation policy for Europe, the Council of Europe also had to be engaged in active consultation with a myriad of governmental and non-governmental organizations operating at the levels of the individual nation-state and their sub-regional groupings. A particularly unique and extremely influential contribution to the work of the Council of Europe in this regard was the animating role of organizations that came to be put in place by the various European borderlands communities themselves.

Unlike their predecessors in pre-war Europe or their contemporaries elsewhere, notably in North America and Africa, who still have to endure situations that range from "interdependent" to "alienated" categories of borderlands, post-war European borderlands have been enormously assisted by a new political process. This was based not only on a massive sense of rejection of the notion of negative nationalism which Europeans have come to associate with frequent outbreaks of wars in their sub-continent. The new political process was also a rededication to the multiple causes and values of democracy, fundamental human rights including the rights to social-economic development and full political participation hitherto denied the neglected and down-trodden. Consequently, post-war European borderlanders were able to organize themselves into active associations through which they succeeded in drawing the attention of a new breed of public policy makers to their well-known but hitherto nationalistically ignored problems of marginality and insecurity occasioned by their status as residents of national peripheries.

In the case of Western Europe, then, there are active organizations at all the important levels (global, regional, sub-regional, national, sub-national and the strictly local), which effectively operated to counteract what we have already referred to as the exogenous, general and specific problems or obstacles in the way of a transborder cooperation policy.

With regard to the Council of Europe, nothing illustrates its complete dedication to the cause of transfrontier cooperation in the sub-region more than the incontrovertible evidence of the involvement of virtually all its organizations.

Of special significance has been the role of such Council of Europe's institutions as the European Conference of Ministers Responsible for Regional Planning and, more especially, the Conference of Local and Regional Authorities (CLRAE) made up of representatives of "districts," "cantons," "kreise," "landër," "counties," "départements," "provinces," or "regions," depending on the structures and categories of regional or local authorities in use in the member-states concerned.[53] CLRAE should be considered the model of a body, the only such body in any continent or region of the world, which officially represents local and sub-national authorities across several international boundaries in their relations to an international institution. Because of obvious closeness to the grassroots, including particularly borderland grassroots, CLRAE became the most effective advocate of borderland views and perspectives vis-à-vis the other organs of the Council of Europe.

Anthony Asiwaju

where the Council's particular preoccupations with transborder cooperation policy promotion coincided with such EEC's related concerns. One example was the EEC's relatively recent formulation of a regional policy in the course of which the special problems posed by European "frontier regions," much earlier realized by the Council of Europe in Strasbourg and long placed on the agenda of the Council, came into full awareness of EEC in Brussels.[54] It is for similar reasons that the Council of Europe found an ally in OECD. Following the adoption by the Organization's Council in 1974 of the "principles for avoidance of environmental pollution in frontier areas" and the "recommendation that all member-states should observe these in their environmental policies," the coincidence with Council of Europe's concerns with transborder cooperation became quite evident.

Then, there are the vital supportive roles of non-governmental organizations, notably, the Council of European Municipalities (CEM), the Association of Twin Cities, the Working Group of European Frontier Regions, the Permanent Conference of the Chambers of Commerce of the EEC, and, above all, the academic and research communities based in several European universities and research institutions including, particularly, the Institute of European Studies of the University of Brussels, the University Institute of European Studies in Geneva, the European University Institute in Florence and the Institute of International Sociology in Gorizia.[55]

Immediately below the international organizations assisting in the evolution of a Transborder Cooperation Policy for Europe are sectoral organizations grouping two or more limitrophe European states together. This included the BENELUX, an economic union of Belgium, Netherlands and Luxembourg, formed during the Second World War; the Nordic Council, founded on the basis of the 1962 Treaty of Helsinki, which became the pioneer of transborder cooperation between the Nordic countries; the German-Dutch Regional Planning Commission, and so on. The important point about all these and other small-scale groupings of neighboring states in Europe is that each was actively engaged in highly productive projects that demonstrated the socio-economic benefits of regional integration through active and systematic transborder cooperation in planning and development.

Finally, the promotion of transborder cooperation policy by the Council of Europe enjoyed active and sustained support of grassroots-level organizations of the borderland communities themselves. The examples are too many to be listed here. Suffice it simply to note that they were found throughout the entire area of the membership of the Council. Key examples include the *Euregio* rooted in a movement which began in about 1954 and embraced the adjacent borderlands of the Federal Republic of Germany and the Netherlands in the Middle Rhine; the Conference of the Upper Rhine Valley; the Regio Basiliense, which is concerned with the demarginalization and planned development of the trinational metropolis of Basel spread across the Franco-German-Swiss borders in the lower Rhine; the Committee for the Promotion of Alpine Region Cooperation; and finally, the Association of European Border Regions. With a virile liaison office in Strasbourg, the Association of European Border Regions was able to circulate information to relevant organs and institutions of the Council of Europe also based there.

The European Outline convention of Transborder Cooperation between Territorial Authorities or Communities which, as we have noted, approximated to the formal adoption of a transborder cooperation policy by Western Europe, occupied a position in a long process that has involved intensive and extensive consultative activities that have enjoyed sustained input and support of all and sundry. Of special significance here has been the highly successful outcome of the first two in the series of the European Symposia on Frontier Regions hosted by the Council of Europe in 1972 and 1975.[56] The massive documentation which resulted from these programs has helped in providing the basis and overall framework not only for the formulation of the Outline Convention but also the relative ease with which it was ratified and since systematically implemented.[57] The point in this essay is that the adoption of a transborder cooperation policy by Europe has substantially reduced, even it if has not completely eliminated, the problem of marginality and insecurity of European borderlanders who once ranked, as their African and North American contemporaries still do, as typical examples of marginal populations.

The suggestion here is not that all is now perfectly well with the borders and borderlands communities in Europe. As has been pointed out in a recent case study of the Dutch-German border, in spite of the thirty years success story of the European Cooperation which culminated in the Maastricht and Schengen Agreements and the formal inauguration of the European Union in 1993,

> . . . (T)he road to a fully fledged political and economic union along the lines of a federated "United States of Europe" will not be easy. Resistance towards the Maastricht Agreements, the British-German row over monetary policy, persistent ideologies of national sovereignty and frequent mistrust of the EC bureaucracy in Brussels suggest that a closer dialogue between citizens, communities, regions and nation-states will be needed to maintain the pace of European integration.[58]

Apart from the need for maintaining the momentum of transborder cooperation at the local level, to ensure the ultimate abolition of the internal boundaries of the European Union, there is also the problem about the final

not been facilitated by the challenges posed by the democratic revolutions in communist Europe in 1989-90, the reunification of Germany, the dissolution of the U.S.S.R. and mounting pressures for the expansion of the European Union to include former communist European states. Wherever the external frontiers of the Union is placed, the problems of marginalization of transborder peoples, being currently solved through the adoption of a dynamic transborder cooperation between current member states, would be recreated unless the policy of cooperation is also adopted for the external boundaries of the Union. This underscores the correctness of an expert opinion, expressed quite early in the contemporary history of transborder cooperation policy in Europe, that the policy of cross-border cooperation has no sense if it is limited merely to countries within the European Community, which have begun to integrate. It was, therefore, strongly recommended that the policy "must be extended to other countries, too, whether or not they belong to the EEC, whether or not they belong to the Council of Europe."[59]

The pace of development in Europe has been maintained, thanks to the entrenchment of a democratic political culture which has enabled the transborder communities to be directly and actively involved in the promotion of transborder cooperation activities. Comparative perspective studies of North America, Africa and Latin America[60] are increasingly being undertaken to draw attention of public policy makers to possible lessons in the European historical experience.

Conclusion

Borderlands have always been recognized as ideal laboratories in which one may undertake a comparative measurement of state performance because, there, the interactions between limitrophe states in terms of the localized impact of their policies (domestic and foreign) are as clearly seen as they would have been if such interactions have had to be placed under a microscope.[61] The African, American and European case histories attempted in this essay would appear to have borne out this established fact.

Borders and borderlands present the image of a typical paradox. As Strassoldo has put it in his characteristically poetic style, the "ambiguities" are easily seen in the fact that

> [Borders] divide and unite, bind the interior and link with the exterior, [they] are barriers and junctions, walls and doors, organs of defense and attack. Frontier areas (borderlands) can be managed as to maximize either of such

functions. They can be militarized, as bulwarks against neighbors, or made into areas of peaceful interchange.[62]

This offer of a choice between one of two policy alternatives was underscored long ago by Lord Curzon when, in his famous Romanes Lecture at Oxford in 1906, he uttered the statement that has since become an axiom that "frontiers [borders] are the razor's edge on which hang suspended the modern issues of war or peace, of life or death to nations."[63]

From the point of view of the Project on Security of Marginal Populations and this particular essay on public policy for overcoming marginalization as manifested in the borderlands of Africa, North America and Western Europe, the preferred choice is quite clear: it is cooperation, not conflict; peace, not war; life, not death. Our emphasis on the history of Europe as the ideal type has been guided by the ease with which the consequences of the alternatives are demonstrated to the rest of the relatively less experienced parts of the wider world of the nation-state.

While the pre-1945 era, embracing the "nation-building" and "co-existence" phases of border and borderland evolutionary history, was characterized by continuous wars which ended with the most catastrophic case of the Second World War, the post-1945 period, which marked the phase of "integration" and "integrated borderlands," have been specially marked by a dedication to the twin causes of regional integration and transborder cooperation.

As the Western European case has shown, there is only one choice of public policy open for overcoming the problem of insecurity of borderlanders as marginal populations: it is transborder cooperation along lines of its development in post-war Western Europe. The correctness of that choice has been proved not only by the vital contribution it has made towards the achievement of the European community but also the multiplier effect on wider Europe as evidenced in the physical tearing down of the Berlin Wall in the wake of the democratic revolutions of 1989-90 that have since turned the entire sub-continent, if not the world at large, in a general direction of a new world "without frontiers"; and, if with frontiers, then frontiers with a human face.

Notes

1. A. Hansen, *The Border economy: Regional Development in the Southwest* (Austin: University of Texas Press, 1981), p. 19.
2. M. Weiner, "Transborder Peoples," in C. Walker, ed., *Mexican Americans in Comparative Perspective* (Washington D.C.: The Urban Institute, 1985), p. 130-31.

Anthony Asiwaju

3. P. Orianne, *Study of the Difficulties in European Co-operation Between Local* *Authorities and Ways of Resolving Them* (Report to Council of Europe Committee on Co-operation in Municipal and Regional Matters, 1973), p. 4.

4. The discussion of theories relevant to borderlands as economic regions draws heavily from Hansen, chapter 2.

5. Hansen, p. 22.

6. Ibid.

7. Ibid.

8. Ibid., p. 25.

9. Ibid., p. 19.

10. Ibid, pp. 27 ff.

11. For sample studies of "partitioned" or "transborder" peoples, see A. I. Asiwaju, *Western Yorubaland Under European Rule, 1889-1945: A Comparative Analysis of French and British Colonialism* (London: Longman, 1976); A. I. Asiwaju, ed., *Partitioned Africans: Ethnic Relations Across Africa's International Boundaries, 1884-1984* (New York: St. Martin's Press, 1985); Johnson (1976); G. Handerson, R. Lebrow and j. Stoessinger (eds.), *Divided Nations in a Divided World* (New York: McKay, 1974); M. Weiner, "Transborder Peoples," in C. Walker, ed., *Mexican Americans in Comparative Perspective* (Washington D.C.: The Urban Institute, 1985); and P. Sahlin, *Boundaries: The Making of France and Spain in the Pyrenees* (Berkeley, University of California Press, 1989).

12. Gross, F., "Registering and Ranking of Tension Areas" in R. Strassoldo (ed.), *Boundaries and Regions* (Trieste, LINT, 1973) 317-328; Strassoldo, R., "Border Studies in Europe" in Asiwaju and Adeniy; (eds.) 1989; Momoh, C.S., "A Critique of Borderlands Theories" in Asiwaju and Adeniy; (eds.) op. cit.; and Martinez, O. J., "The Dynamics of Border Interaction: New Approaches to Border Analaysis" in C. H. Schofield (ed.) *Global Boundaries* (London: Routledge, 1994).

13. R. Strassoldo and G. D. Zotti, "Border Studies: The State of the Art in Europe," in Asiwaju and Adeniyi, eds., *Borderlands in Africa: A Multidisciplinary and Comparative Focus on Nigeria and West Africa* (Lagos: University of Lagos Press, 1985), p. 389.

14. Ibid.

15. Orianne, p. 5.

16. V. Von Malchus, *The Co-operation of European Frontier Regions* (Basic Report to the First European Symposium on Frontier Regions), 1972, Section VI, pp. 51-58.

17. This distinction between "negative" and "utilitarian" nationalism is owed to Strassoldo (1989), p. 391.

18. For interesting case studies, see Sahlin (1989), Asiwaju (1976), and J. W. House, *Frontier on the Rio Grande* (Oxford: Oxford University Press, 1982).

19. A more elaborate discussion of shared borderlands as bridgeheads for regional integration is attempted in A. I. Asiwaju, *Artificial Boundaries* (Lagos: University of Lagos Press Inaugural Lecture Series, 1984).

Overcoming Marginalization

280　20. This categorization of national states into "nation-states" and "state-nations" is owed to A. Smith, *Nationalism*, 1971.

21. For further reference, see Asiwaju, 1984.

22. See Asiwaju, 1985.

23. For studies of African boundary conflicts, see S. Touval, *The Boundary Politics of Independent Africa* (Cambridge, MA: Harvard University Press, 1972); G. Widstrand, ed., *African Boundary Problems* (Uppsala: Nordiska Afrika Institutet, 1969); I. W. Zartman, "The Politics of Boundaries in North and West Africa," *Journal of Africa History*, vol. III, no. 2, 1965, pp. 150-73; J. B. Boyd, Jr. "African Boundary Conflict: An Empirical Study," *African Studies Review*, vol. XXII, no. 3, 1979, pp. 3, 1-15.

24. This information is based on the data collected in the course of an official tour of border regions in Lagos, Ogun and Oyo States of Nigeria, undertaken in 1991 by the writer in his then capacity as Commissioner of the Nigeria National Boundary Commission, based in Lagos.

25. A. I. Asiwaju, "National Boundary Commissions as Problem-Solving Institutions: Preliminary Research Notes on Nigeria, Niger and Mali," In Grundy-Warr, C., ed., *International Boundaries and Boundary Conflict Resolutions* (London: Archives Press, 1990) and Asiwaju, *Artificial Boundaries/Les Frontieres Artificielles* (New York: Civiletis International, 1990).

26. See text in European Treaty Series No. 106.

27. A. I. Asiwaju and B. M. Barkindo, eds. *The Nigerian-Niger Transborder Cooperation: Proceedings of a Bilateral Workshop, Kano, July 1989.* (Lagos: Malthouse Press for the National Boundary Commission, Lagos, 1993) and A. I. Asiwaju and O. J. Igue, eds., *The Nigeria-Benin Transborder Cooperation: Proceedings of a Bilateral Workshop, May 1988* (University of Lagos Press for the National Boundary Commission, 1994).

28. A. I. Asiwaju, "Promoting Shared Borders as Bridgeheads for Regional Integration in Africa: The Nigerian Experience vis-a-vis Limitrope Countries," Paper Presented to a Regional Meeting of Experts on Regional Integration in West Africa, Cotonou, 6-9 May, 1993).

29. ibid.

30. A. I. Asiwaju, *Border Region Development: Proceedings of the National Planning Conference on the Development of Nigerian Border Regions. Lagos. August 10-12, 1989.* (National Boundary Commission, Lagos, 1993).

31. L. A. Herzog, *Where North Meets South: Cities, Space and Politics in the U.S.-Mexico Border* (Austin: Centre for Mexican American Studies, 1990), p. 258.

32. Comparative studies of the U.S.-Mexico borderlands include J. Price, "Mexican and Canadian Border Comparisons" in W. R. Stoddard, R. L. Nostrand and J. P. West (eds.) *Borderlands Sourcebook: A Guide to the Literature on Northern Mexico and the American Southwest* (Oklahoma: University of Oklahoma Press, 1982); Asiwaju 1983; and O. J. Martinez, ed., *Across Boundaries: Transborder Interaction in Comparative Perspective* (El Paso: Texas Western Press, 1986).

33. Herzog, 1990, is the most detailed and most up-to-date study of the twin-cities.

34. ibid.

Anthony Asiwaju

35. This concept ("perforated sovereignties") is borrowed from I.D. Duchacek, D. **281** Latonche and G. Stevenson (eds.) *Perforated Sovereignties and International Relations: Trans-Sovereign Contacts of Subnational Governments* (New York: Greenwood Press, 1988).
36. Herzog, op. cit. p. 256.
37. E. R. Stoddard, "Problem-Solving Along the U.S.-Mexico Border: A United States View," in Martinez, *Across Boundaries: Transborder Interaction in Comparative Perspective*, 1986, p. 67.
38. Stoddard, as cited in Herzog (1990), p. 256.
39. Ibid.
40. For sample studies of informal policy making on the U.S.-Mexico border cities, see J. W. Sloan and J. P. West, "Community Integration and Policies Among Elites in Two Border Cities: Los Dos Laredos," *Journal of Inter-American Studies and World Affairs*, Vol. 18, 1976, pp. 451-74; J. W. Sloan and J. P. West, "The Role of Informal Policy Making in the U.S.-Mexico Border Cities," *Social Science Quarterly*, Vol. 58, no. 2, 1977, pp. 170-82; W. W. D'Antonio and W. H. Form, *Influentials in the Two Border Cities: A Study in Community Decision-Making in El Paso and Ciudad Juarez* (Notre Dame: University of Notre Dame Press, 1965); and E. R. Stoddard, *Functional dimension of Informal Border Networks* (El Paso: Centre for Inter-American and Border Studies, "Border Perspectives" Series No. 8, 1984).
41. Sloan and West (1977), p. 275.
42. J. B. Pick, and S. Stephenson Glade, "The NAFTA Agreement and Labor Force Projections: Implications for the Border Region," *Journal of Borderlands Studies* 1: 69-99, 1994.
43. S. L. Mumme, "An Environmental Agenda for North America: Post-NAFTA," *North American Outlook, Vol. 4 No. 3 (Extract in Transboundary Resources Report or TR Report*, published by the International Transboundary Resources Centre of the University of New Mexico School of Law, Vol. 8, No. 3, 1-3, 1994; *TR Report*, "The North American Environment: Opportunities for Trinational Cooperation by Canada, the United States and Mexico: A colloquium sponsored by the North American Institute, Santa Fe, Feb. 12-14, 1993, 1-7; J. T. Brannon and D. D. James, "Cometh the NAFTA, Whither the Maquiladoras? Reflections on the Future of Industrialization in Northern Mexico," *Journal of Borderland Studies*, Vol. IX, No. 2; Pick and Stephenson-Glade, 1994.
44. Council of Europe, Strasbourg, *Explanatory Report on the European Outline Convention on Transfrontier Cooperation Between Territorial Communities or Authorities* (49 pages), 1980; N. Hansen, "European Transboundary Cooperation and its Relevance for the United States-Mexico Border," *Journal of the American Planning Association*, 49 (Summer), 334-336, 1983.
45. Mumme, 1994.
46. Pick and Stephenson-Glade, 1994.
47. Strassoldo (1989), p. 391.
48. Ibid.
49. Martinez (1991).

50. Sample studies of Regional Integration and, especially, Transborder Cooperation in Europe include R. Strassoldo and G.D. Zotti (eds.) *Cooperation and Conflict in Border Areas* (Milano: Frances Angeli, 1982); B. De Marchi and A. M. Blileau, eds., *Boundaries and Minorities in Western Europe* (Milano: Franco Angeli Editore, 1982); M. Anderson, ed., *Frontier Regions in Western Europe* (Special Issue of *West European Politics* Vol. 5, no. 4, Frank Cass, London, 1982; R. Strassoldo, *Frontier Regions: Analytical Study* (Background Paper for European Conference of Ministers Responsible for Regional Planning, 2nd Session, La Grande Motte, 25-27 September, 1973); and P. Romus, ed., *Les Regions Frontalières à L'Heure du Marché Commun* (Colloque Organisé les 27 et 28 Novembre 1969 par L'Institut d'Etudes Européennes, Université Libre de Bruxelles), Presse Universitaire de Bruxelles.

51. Founded in 1949, Council of Europe was among the very first regional organizations to be created immediately after the Second World War. It brought together 21 democratic countries of Western Europe , including all the European Common Market countries. Its objectives, significantly, were to work for closer European unity; protect democracy and human rights; and improve living conditions. Its headquarters are based in Strasbourg, France.

52. The efforts of the Council have been richly demonstrated. Apart from the several policy and official position papers submitted by functionaries of the Council of Europe for the consideration of its various organs (see, e.g., Doc. 3228 Report on the First European Symposium on Frontier Regions; Doc. 3807 Report on the Conclusions of the Second European Symposium on Frontier Regions; and Doc. MCL-35(82) 4-E Conference of European Ministers Responsible for Local Government, Lugeno 1982: "The State of Transfrontier cooperation Between Territorial Communities or Authorities"), there are several specialized studies commissioned and published by the Council of Europe on the subject of Transborder Cooperation. They include V. Von Malchus, *The Co-operation of European Frontier Regions* (Basic Report to the First European Symposium on Frontier Regions, 1972); Von Malchus, *The Co-operation of European Frontier Regions: State of the Question and Recent Development* (Basic Report to the Second European Symposium on Frontier Regions, Council of Europe, 1973); Strassoldo, 1975; J. M. Quintin, *European Co-operation in Frontier Regions*, Background Paper for the European Conference of Ministers Responsible for Regional Planning (2nd Session), La Grande Motte, 25-27 September 1973); J. André, *Planning and Infrastructure in Frontier Regions* (Report of the author as Director-General of the Société Provinciale d'Industrialisation LIEGE, Belgium, to the First European Symposium on Frontier Regions, 1972); P. Pernthalier, "Methods and Models for Regional Planning in Frontier Regions" (Report to the Second European Symposium on Frontier Regions, 1975); Orianne, 1973; and A. Partl, "The Institutional Development of Transfrontier Co-operation: Achievements and Prospects—Implementation of the European Outline Convention on Transfrontier Co-operation Between Territorial Communities or Authorities," Contribution to the 3rd

53. See Von Malchus, 1975, pp. 18-20.
54. Ibid.
55. Evidence of research support by European University institutions for Transborder Cooperation is to be found in a series of vital publications by scholars in such establishments as ISIG (Institute of International Sociology in Gorizia, Italy) and Institute of European Studies of the University of Brussels (see note 46 for sample titles).
56. Sample titles of studies commissioned by the Council of Europe have already been included in note 50, above.
57. For an assessment, see Partl, 1984.
58. J. W. Scott, "The Institutionalization of Transboundary Cooperation in Europe: Recent Development on the Dutch-German Border," *Journal of Borderlands Studies* Vol. viii, No. 1, 39-66.
59. J. M. Quitin, *European Cooperation in Frontier Region* (Strasbourg: Council of Europe, 1973), p. 41
60. N. Hansen (1983), "European Transboundary Cooperation and Its Relevance for the United States—Mexico Border," *Journal of the American Planning Association*, 49 (Summer); and L. Llambi, "The Venezuela-Columbia Borderlands: A Regional and Historical Perspective," *Journal of Borderlands Studies*, Vol. IV, No. 1, 1989, pp. 1-38 and Asiwaju, 1984.
61. The recognition of borderlands as "laboratories" is indicated in J. R. V. Prescott, *Boundaries and Frontiers* (London: Allen and Unwin, 1978); Strassoldo and Zotti, 1982; Asiwaju, 1976; and Sahlin, 1989.
62. Strassoldo (1989), p. 393.
63. Lord Curzon, *Frontiers*. Romanes Lectures, Oxford, 1907, p. 11.

Conclusion

Sam C. Nolutshungu

We began with the state-people relationship as it applies to international security. One particular variant of it predominates in the studies that make up this book, namely that of state-and-nation involving state-nations and nation-states, where the "nation" is the criterion and ideal of collective existence and the state is legitimated as its embodiment and servitor. This is the context where assimilation and rejection occur in ways most relevant to the study of marginality. In these closing pages we offer a few brief comments on this relationship in the two institutional spheres of nation-state formation and democracy that are absolutely central to modern politics. We underline the fact that the development of this relationship is inherently contradictory—or dialectical—and suggest that, as such, it invites analytical and theoretical attention to popular *political action* (as distinct from state practice)—its forms, its options and its theaters—as an appropriate focus of international security studies.

The main aim of this book is to draw attention to international security as a problem for persons, or groups of people, within states—deliberately, and distinctly shifting the focus from *states* viewed in the abstract as ends in themselves or as, in some way, total representatives of the security interests of the people who live under them. In the attempt to uncover the interests of persons in international security it links the "international" to other, no less pressing, every day forms of insecurity with states.

People suffer insecurity within states because of the way states are configured and run at various, distinguishable but interdependent levels—social economic, political and cultural. The insecurity is rooted in the internal history of diverse peoples and communities brought together within states. Yet, the conditions for many groups discussed here are comparable across countries and sometimes reflect a shared history across state boundaries. That is clearly so with the East European Roma and with the indigenous peoples of other continents with whom their leaders increasingly associate themselves. Often conditions of a group or similar groups deteriorate not in one but in several countries at once. Xenophobic responses toward certain groups—both those who have traditionally been used as scapegoats for social and economic ills and new immigrants—become, as it were, contagious as in the current resurgence of antisemitism and racism across the European Community.

International political developments provoke or aggravate internal crises within states and change the relationships among groups, the power balances within states produce vast changes in ideology and the schemes of legitimation in ways that have far-reaching effects on the security of groups. The end of the Cold War shrank the Soviet Empire and left many ethnic Russians orphaned throughout the newly independent states (as well as making ethnic minorities associated with some of those states less secure within Russia). Its impact on the European state order has brought about marked changes of attitude towards immigrants, refugees and minorities of non-European descent.[1] The Gulf War of 1991, underlined and made worse the insecurity of minorities in that region and in Iraq, especially. The changing global economic order has been catalytic to profound challenges to the cohesion of what previously appeared to be well integrated societies from Algeria to Mexico. It has also had a clear impact on the capacities of economies to absorb peripheral communities and of states to integrate and protect marginal groups. As a result, certain on vulnerable categories within societies in many, different, countries at vastly contrasted levels of development have been reduced to indigence and homelessness.

The attempts by leaders of insecure groups to gain assurance for themselves or their populations often create conditions that generate new insecure populations or new forms of insecurity as several contemporary tragedies, most notably those of Rwanda, Bosnia and Burundi, illustrate. Despite the outrage provoked by such extreme situations, international responses are typically tardy, inadequate, opportunistic, and unpredictable. Indeed, the existence of a relevant *international* security problem in such cases is often contested: international security" shrinks into its narrower—for many people, truer"—meaning of *our* (national) security" in international affairs.

International responses, whether motivated by humanitarian concern or seeking to maintain order and secure favorable power distributions, seldom produce entirely satisfactory or lasting solutions to the problem of insecurity, whether it presents itself primarily as a domestic phenomenon or connects directly to relations between states. Nor do they have the institutional and financial basis for following through with the construction of stable, lasting security arrangements within states and regions.

The sources of insecurity are numerous and diverse, and so are the groups that suffer it. Within states people might aspire to some durable political arrangements that reduce the severity of the problem if they cannot entirely eliminate it but at the international level, and for those forms of insecurity that are predominantly international, it seems almost impossible, even in principle, to envisage an appropriate institutional and normative order: short of what many people regard as utopian solutions of the world government type.

Even traditional conception of international security fails to define a universal interest in international security even among states whatever its pretensions to that effect may be, from time to time. A broader concept that embraces human groups in all their diversity of situation is even less likely to do so. But like the former, it still suggests a plausible ideal. We may put the matter somewhat differently: if "international security" as a shared objective is worth pursuing as an interest of states, it is even more worthwhile as a condition of the well-being of real individuals and groups. This book has tried to show the compelling character of that need with respect to a particular category of people within states: marginal populations whose particular concerns are generally under-represented in the activity of states. Their insecurity, it has been argued is integrally related to their marginality.

A double objective is served by this approach : the need is underlined for a more critical accounting of who, exactly, is made secure by various policies and arrangements, and who is left out and why; and, poignant illustration is provided of the various ways in which, and the reasons why, different sections of populations in a diversity of geographic and historical settings are excluded from the purview of security as pursued by states and, in some cases, actually rendered more vulnerable by their efforts to achieve it. The various contributions high-light the centrality of the state-people relation and insist on treating it as inherently problematic in any construction of international security responsive to the needs of people and appropriate to the realities of our time. What is required is more than a simple opposition of people and states, yielding, as it might, a modish preference for non-state things against state-centric ones, or even a moody but unrealistic categoric choice of one over the other. The relationship demands a more subtle attitude sensitive to its ambiguity and complexity. The conflicts of interest that produce insecurity may occur between states, or between groups of people and states, but they also occur among non-state actors with states playing no independent causative role, as when, e.g., they are enfeebled to the point of non-existence by civil conflict or, rendered irrelevant by their very inability to deliver security. Examples of such moments may be found in the histories of several contemporary conflicts: in Chad, Liberia and Somalia.

Nevertheless, the state does have a privileged role and it is the recognition of its centrality that makes this collective work a political study despite the diversity of the contributors from a disciplinary standpoint. International security is pre-eminently the business of states. It is the classic site of raison d'etat: providing (or coordinating the collective work of) security against

Conclusion

external danger is essential to the moral justification of the state and states do, indeed, play a special role in it. Ordinary citizens do not generally worry about the *international* security of themselves, their families, neighbors or friends except insofar as this may be comprehended in some idea of the security of the state or of states. International security, unlike, say, "law and order," is not a concept readily invoked in everyday thinking and language or applied to real persons. It has a distinctly technical or jargonesque ring. It encompasses the abstract "people" entailed in "states" and "systems" of states. There are good reasons why this should be so: international security is something which individuals cannot make available for themselves on a voluntaristic basis; states exist to prevent such self-help which might indeed amount to a state of nature. The role of the state is unique and nonsubstitutable. It is the magnitude of the resources that states bring into play that place international security essentially beyond the scope of private action and, so often, make catastrophic the dissociation between the interests of states and those of persons in this domain. Above and below the level of the state, voluntary action can ameliorate or aggravate problems of international security. A multiplicity of voluntary humanitarian organizations are more or less routinely engaged in trying to enhance the security of various groups across the world. At the other extreme, criminal organizations, operating on a global scale as e.g., in the drug trade, contribute significantly to the insecurity of persons and states.

Neither the special role of the state nor any pretended monopoly of the "legitimate use of force" should be taken so literally as to obscure important links in many instances between private violence and the state. Private violence is sometimes condoned or even incited by states, or coercion contracted out to private agencies which may range from mercenaries to vigilantes to criminal gangs and warlords" (as in South Africa's black townships in the last days of apartheid). In addition to the proliferation of firearms in private hands sometimes permitted by states, armed criminality escapes control in many countries, and what is more, it is increasingly integrated into politics: gangsterism and protection rackets being inseparable from the normal operation of government. This can evidently happen, as Russia suggests, without the state suffering a significant loss of legitimacy domestically or internationally. It is almost as if the surrender of the monopoly of the use of force is the indispensable condition for its legitimate use: the state cannot function without the sanction of armed criminal organizations. This has been the situation for years to some extent in drug-dealer dominated states like Colombia. Besides, legitimation is seldom entirely free of the threat of violence and intimidation by some citizens against others, as marginal populations well know.

Sam C. Nolutshungu

In recognizing a special role for states in the area of security, the point, is not to reassert received ideas about the moral character of states or their "true" purpose with respect to the suppression of private violence. Rather, it is to stress that such interventions involve an intricate entanglement of private and state interests and actors. Non-state activities generally presuppose a preponderant role for states which they try to influence and use, or else they divide and fill a space contingently vacated by the state but which is properly its own (as, e.g., in the case of warlordism and political banditry in Africa). A realistic view of international security requires an equally realistic account of the contemporary character and practice of states.

Several chapters have demonstrated that marginality has sometimes been created or exacerbated in the process of creating and consolidating states. Attempts to form modern states that rely on unitarist and centralizing nation-building ideologies have contributed significantly to the marginalization of some populations—reinforcing old prejudices or creating new ones, inciting hostility to forms of cultural expression and social organization deemed incompatible with the preferred national ideal. The implicit demand that such groups assimilate, by its stringent, often unfulfillable requirements, often betrays a logic of domination and exploitation that provokes conflict rather than unity, resistance of various kinds and degrees rather than willing assimilation. The dissolution of imperial systems resulting in the emergence of new would-be modern states has been the occasion in many instances for changes or challenges to what were previously settled status and power relations among populations within a territory, and in the case of partitions creating communities dissected by international boundaries and new borderlands that are often special sites of marginality.

Nationalism, nation-building, and state formation are all potentially—in many poly-ethnic and poly-cultural settings, *inherently*—marginalizing for some groups. The modern nation state is more unitarist and centralist than its predecessors but it is impossible to conceive of any form of state that does not, to some degree, draw lines of belonging—cultural, political, territorial and to some degree genealogical—that also define peripheries of exclusion and inferiorization. Marginality as linked to inequality and differential participation within a given political and economic space, and the accompanying vulnerability and insecurity, were well-known in pre-modern states and in political formations that preceded nation-states. State formation is very much a process of drawing conceptual frontiers of inclusion and exclusion. Moreover, non-state entities like ethnic groups—in their complex articulation to prevailing systems of power and states—also define themselves largely by the boundaries they maintain.[2] The insistence on a uniform high culture" that would include everybody may signal a particular source of intolerance as a characteristic feature of modern states.[3] It makes a very particular contribution to marginalization in the new states emerging out of the old empires, not least the Ottoman Empire as Bozarslan has shown .

Yet, the modern, nation-state in its very insistence on a common belonging asserts both a potential universality of membership and an individuation of persons that are fundamental to the extension of personal rights and to virtually all practical, contemporary notions of democracy. Nation-building in the context of the modern state asserts a collective identity that, ultimately, justifies the claim of individuals to equal treatment—or, perhaps, to equality, period. Hence the conflict with other identities, real or imagined and whether or not of comparable scope and salience. Identity, defined in terms of membership of a community, whether that is coextensive with the state or more parochial, invokes equality.[4] The critique of the (ideal-typical) modern state, in this regard, must be counter-balanced by a recognition of its inherently democracy seeking nature. I.e., it prefigures and, in many cases, enables democracy or, at least, the struggles for universal (rather than particularistic) enfranchisement or democratic citizenship.[5]

Can it be, then, that democratization, both in the current, immediate sense of "transitions to democracy" or in the richer perspective of the longer historical process of its emergence via the creation of modern nation-states necessarily produces marginality? A scandalous outcome, surely, to conclude that the advent of democracy suppresses the multitude of previously existing identities (politically relevant ones, at any rate) in favor of one centralizing (if also equalizing) identity? Evidently, marginality (like assimilation) is, in this light, a problem *for*, and quite often, *of* democracy, as well as other forms of rule. Leveau and Hopper provide pertinent evidence with respect to two established democracies.

Contemporary states stress the importance of shared outlooks and values, a common culture, a common political sociability. Democracies also pride themselves on tolerating, indeed, valuing difference (more so among individuals rather than groups however defined).There is not much consensus among democrats about the measure of diversity that, as a matter of fact, is either necessary for, or compatible with mutual comprehension, toleration, solidarity, and compassion.Consider, for example, the oft-stated diffidence about the chances of democracy in multi-ethnic countries (the Indian experience notwithstanding), or in countries where the contrasts of wealth and poverty are very great. All political systems, democracies no less than the others, have sought to attenuate the effects of such extremes, and have placed a high value on political integration both in the specifically functionalist sense of all the parts of the system being brought into harmony with each other, and in the sense of all members of the political community—whether subjects or citizens—coming fully within the sphere of effectiveness of the state, under its authority and into loyalty towards it and participating (whether equally or according to some principle of differentiation) in its system of obligations and entitlements. What measure of difference is necessary or possible in the process of integration is very much a political matter: incapable of being resolved *a priori*. It is settled contingently by the political action or inaction of those concerned. Divergence and conformity are always subject to the relations of domination that prevail and that impose the areas and forms of permissible difference. It is in the politics of this ordering that marginality is generated, reproduced—and resisted.

The imposition of a sense of common belonging and shared values facilitates social control but it has also been the basis of claims to solidarity justifying ameliorative collective action, typically through the agency of the state, in favor of various categories of citizens. The quest for unity and solidarity and the presumption of their attainability have been at the base of the systems of mutual economic support through the state which have been an important feature of political and economic life for a good part of this century. Now that these systems of support are being dismantled or severely curtailed in various countries, new marginal groups are being created. Social welfare systems whether of radical nationalist, democratic or socialist inspiration were part of a widely shared view which is now under attack but which is directly relevant to the situation of marginal populations. One aspect of that outlook was the belief in the creative use of the state to *deepen and broaden democracy* and to secure economic amelioration. Notions of progress were indissociable from the integration, indeed, unification of the national state. The other aspect was "progress" itself, which for those who embraced it, presented the same horizons of fulfillment for individuals within the same state, in rights and material advancement and in cultural attainment, however diverse might be their cultural or biological origins. Certainly, the practical implications of these commitments were never clear or universally agreed. But they were prominent on the political agenda of many countries.

The contemporary situation in the West, at least, is characterized by the discredit, in various quarters, for quite diverse reasons, of all these key elements. The provider-state has come under attack as a mere gobbler of resources that does not and cannot much relieve either misery or inequality. In the face of the persistence of inequality—against the background of substantial general improvement of material opportunities and living conditions for all in the industrial countries for most of the post World War II (but in recent years a sharp increase of inequality in many countries not matched by a comparable general improvement)—many question whether it was ever wise to place so high a value on equality or possible for the state to secure it. The

Conclusion

collapse of communism has reinforced skepticism both about the ameliorative power of states and about the idea of progress. A profound skepticism, if not cynicism, attaches to many ideals that had become central to the very idea of politics.

The removal of the Soviet Union as a potential threat to Western states has undermined the prestige of the state among those whose primary image of the state is that of a defender against enemies. In addition, a profound change in the capacity of states to influence national economic outcomes has been signalled by globalization which has reduced their power, or their ideological confidence, to intervene effectively to influence the movements of capital, jobs and incomes. Easy, then, to see the state as superfluous. There is, accordingly, no end of reminders of the obsolescence of the nation-state and of the transcendence of sovereignty. For some the nation state is too small as a theater of accumulation while for others it is much too large as a basis of meaningful identities (and solidarities?). A long peace, even one punctuated by moments of anxiety and excitement about crises in some areas of the world, has contributed to the prevalent *ennui* to which the state-as-protector as well as the state-as-provider has fallen victim.

Yet, the discredit of the state also provokes demands for the reassertion of its power against enemies within (including some marginal groups) and without, or to retrieve some of the economic security of the past. Those who have not yet had the full benefit of statehood are not discouraged in their claims to rights of participation within existing states, or, alternatively to states of their own: self-determination, autonomy or secession. At the same time, struggles for the control of state power lose none of their bloody ferocity.

When states are enfeebled or when their protector and provider roles are de-legitimated insecurity increases. The situation of marginal people is likely to deteriorate while their ranks are swollen by new categories of people threatened with exclusion from collective political and economic life. Ideological retreat from an ethos of solidarity and mutual help may do more harm than any quantifiable diminution of distributed assistance when it is accompanied by discourses of inculpation and stigmatization and a search for scapegoats.

What follows is, very often, a dramatic intensification of the politics of conformity and exclusion: both the demand from within the dominant population that marginals should be made to conform and those of marginal people that they should either be included on terms acceptable to themselves or left to affirm their own identities, and, sometimes, violently competitive claims of different categories facing marginalization or already marginal, for state recognition and support.

Sam C. Nolutshungu

The problem for marginal people is not, therefore, how to get rid of the state, not at any rate until an alternative to actually existing forms of political association is credibly devised or anarchism becomes a more persuasive option. Nor is it to supplant the macro-unity or identity at the level of culture and consciousness which the state proclaims across the particularities of race, class, culture, gender, or situation, but to define different, more inclusive and less arbitrary criteria and modalities for its realization; alternatively, where conditions permit, to create new states for those who feel excluded.

Regarding self-determination in the Wilsonian sense, the contributors to this work would concur with Gurr that conflict cannot be eliminated by reconstructing the state system so that territorial boundaries correspond more closely to the social and cultural boundaries among peoples."[6] They would also share the criticism made by Daniel Moynihan (and many others before him) of the doctrine of self-determination that has now acquired the status of a principle of international law.[7] Yet, as Hale shows, the plea for self-determination is an important feature of the struggle of indigenous groups. In these cases, it does not assert a right of secession but makes a radical demand for autonomy in defining the leadership and aims of liberation struggles. It also asserts collective rights over territory and to a measure of autonomy within the larger state, a kind of "internal sovereignty"—an approach that has advanced the furthest, in doctrine and practice, in Canada.[8] The case of Quebec suggests, however, that when issues are formulated in these terms, it may not be possible to satisfy simultaneously the aspirations to "self-determination" of "first nations" and nationalist French Canadians, and, indeed, to enhance the security of ethnic minorities and immigrants and recent immigrants.[9] In the struggle of the Ogoni people against both the multinational oil company, Shell, and the Federal Government of Nigeria, the demand for self-determination is a dramatic statement against both ecological degradation of Ogoniland due to oil extraction and neglect by government with regard to services and remedial measures against pollution.[10]

The right to secede is precisely what is primarily asserted by the claim to self-determination in many other cases, however, and although this may be an effective way of ending marginality for some groups under certain conditions it is not relevant for marginal people who do not occupy a discreet piece of territory or those who lack a shared sense of nationhood. It may be, however, that a greater willingness on the part of states to concede claims to regional autonomy might obviate the need for secession and pave the way for a redesign of states that would allow for divided sovereignty and permit a variable geometry of association between territories and collectivities within existing states, or, indeed, in new entities made up of several states, like the European Union.[11] Divided or shared sovereignty is, in fact, prefigured in

Conclusion

various, admittedly modest ways, in many contemporary international and transnational institutions, practices and conventions. As in federalism, it may produce jurisdictional disputes but these are not impossible to regulate and manage deliberatively. The real problem is that demands for self-determination and especially those that envisage secession tend to be formulated in absolute terms—the "self" is categoric and non-negotiable both in affirmation and in negation—in a mobilizational context that reflects and generates intense hostility on both sides, making the cooperation necessary for shared sovereignty difficult. This is in large part the work of ideology, in the sense, at least, of how people think and feel about identities and about states.

In the abstract, the claim to self-determination can be advanced on behalf of a heterogeneous, territorially-defined, population. In practice, however, whether advanced in the context of indigenous claims or in the national cases envisaged in the classical doctrine, self-determination asserts ethnic identity—the ethnic nation—as the supreme principle of statehood. The ethnicization of politics that it, therefore, represents sits uneasily with some very basic ways of thinking about democracy and political progress. Ironically, it is often the ethnicization of the state, explicit or under the pretense of universalism, that creates marginality and provokes some groups to a countervailing ethnic mobilization. Whether the assertion of ethnic identities and claims in opposition to domination "levels the playing field" or merely queers the pitch for good so far as democracy is concerned, is uncertain. Whichever is achieved, the road to it passes through a great deal of insecurity, violence and hate.

None of this is to deny that initiative and competence to act at the community level of the self-identified group are proper democratic concerns, or that government is more effective in alleviating problems when it cooperates with "local" efforts as Asiwaju argues with respect to once promising Nigerian initiatives regarding its borderlands. Yet a certain reserve is in order: as to the boundaries that "local" enshrines and to the associational life which it institutionalizes with its "most favored lords" who, as Leveau and Laitin suggest, can be both fire fighters and pyromaniacs and unrepresentative, all at the same time. Once again, there is a tension between two imperatives—of recognizing local particularities in order to integrate localities more effectively into the larger state, and of not encouraging that inveterate spirit of locality" against which John Stuart Mill rightly warned.

While problems may be relieved by policies of recognition of groups and locales, by devolution and the promotion of self-determination, the mere localization of the problem provides no decisive solution and may, sometimes, simply displace it to more hopeless sites of marginality and insecurity. That, after all, is one reason why, at the other remove, transnational political spaces

Sam C. Nolutshungu

indigenous peoples.

Democracies might be expected to create more scope for diversity and for managing the problems that arise from it, as they might also be expected to respond more effectively to the marginalization produced by economic change. The values that democracies proclaim, the capacity of diverse groups to mobilize and the possibility (in theory, at any rate), of making coalitions across all lines of cleavage, and a certain constructive opportunism of candidates and parties seeking election, might all be expected to work to ensure, in Dr Azikiwe's much-quoted saying, that "no condition is permanent."[12] The status of individual political rights—whatever may be the position of democracy on *collective* rights—gives significant protection in principle to members of marginal groups and provides scope for them to mobilize and agitate for their collective interests. Conversely, undemocratic systems may be expected to be less heedful of the rights of minorities.[13]

However, democracies in the real world are far from perfect and often fall well short of the principles they profess. They are subject to the domination of majorities (or, indeed, minorities who act on their behalf) that are much more stable than such a characterization would allow. The strong association of marginality with economic inequalities that change extremely slowly affects the capacity of marginal populations to make an impact on democratic politics. Designer models of democracy—any of the many variants of consociational democracy proposed in various situations—might improve the situation of marginal elites, in ways that consolidate the power of "most favored lords" . While in some cases such accommodation may result in tangible benefits for the marginal population as a whole, it would also favor the entrenchment (and perhaps the violent enforcement) of boundaries between marginal and other groups. In any event, if the full benefits of reciprocal elite accommodation on a footing of equality were conceded to a group, we would be inclined to wonder whether it was truly marginal in politics.

To say that democracy provides a better context for resolving problems of marginality may be no more profound than observing that national prosperity provides more opportunity for dealing with the problem of poverty. In most cases the problem is, of course, getting there: *achieving* democracy or prosperity. If democracies are, indeed, better placed to deal with marginality, then the prevalence of marginality in its different forms within mature democracies is discouraging.

On the other hand, some undemocratic states have had some success in protecting and incorporating previously excluded populations—enough to shift the question from the *a priori* to empirical investigation of the sources and dynamics of various forms of marginality in their detailed particularity.

Conclusion

Under what conditions have state initiatives been successful in reducing
marginality and increasing security for previously or potentially marginal
groups. How, in practice, do different forms of government and *different
democracies* work in this regard.One may, of course, still prefer, for all sorts of
cogent reasons, to be marginal in a democracy (as one might prefer to be poor
in a rich country) rather than anywhere else.Yet, it is important amid the
hybris in the West, encouraged by seemingly irresistible, universal waves of
emulative democratization, to avoid an uncritical attitude to democracy or, to
be exact, actually existing democra*cies*. One cannot be content, where democracy has not yet come, simply to wait for it to arrive and bestow its blessings
of universal inclusion and protection. On the contrary, struggles against
marginality and insecurity where there is no democracy may not only hasten
its advent but may contribute to democratic initiatives elsewhere and democracies might even find that there is something to be learned from such
struggles. At the same time we must guard against making excessive claims for
the liberating and equalizing effects of actually existing democracies in ways
that denegate real marginality and insecurity and de-legitimize the struggles
against them within democratic states.

Democracy does not operate without presuppositions, which define its
community and lay down the criteria of effective participation in it, over and
above the explicit legal rules of citizenship. Those relating to ethnic and
cultural nationhood and nationality are among the most troubling sources of
marginality. Democracy can, conceivably, exist without nationalism in its
worst forms, but it is difficult, in practice to exclude appeals to nationalism
and xenophobia completely from the rhetoric of political competition. Presuppositions may include notions about the nature of its own society and
culture in contrast to other peoples' that sometimes degenerate into familiar
forms of prejudice. Characterizations of "the people" of reference of the
democracy, or of the cultural values it is supposed to reflect and serve, only too
often become the vehicle through which discredited quintessentially exclusionary ways of thinking gain a place in the dominant political culture and
discourse.[14] Racism may thus remain an ineradicable feature of democracies.
Equally, cultural and civilizational representations of other peoples and states
rebound on the internal politics of multi-ethnic states in ways that increase
marginality and insecurity. The particular hostility to North Africans in
France is not unrelated to stereotypes of Arabs and Moslems, generally.

Economic doctrines also impact on the way democracy deals with marginality and can contribute to exclusion and stigmatization by the way they
distribute responsibilities for marginalities of various kinds. Victorian style
distinctions between the "deserving poor" and those thought to be improvi-
dent wretches who have brought their dismal fate upon themselves affect

democratic responses to marginality.[15] Economic ideologies—distinctions between doctrine, theory and ideology in practical politics are quite illusive, residing as they do, in the uses rather than the substance of ideas—have a bearing not only on what the democratic state considers it can, or cannot, usefully do to alleviate marginality and insecurity, but they also shape reciprocal perceptions and expectations, solidarities and antagonisms among groups and define the horizons of attainable improvement for different categories of people.

It is tempting to dream of a solution based on agreement on political values, or agreement to conform in political and economic terms while leaving every group to pursue its own cultural interests and identity—to draw a line between the private and public domains and enjoin all states and dominant populations to pay attention only to what is properly in the public domain while urging minorities to keep their cultural *differentiae* to themselves in the private domain. Unfortunately, such boundaries would have to be policed and would probably never be agreeable to all. Boundaries between "private" and "public" easily become contentious, as when a Moslem girl wears a traditional head scarf to school; they have become controversial and sometimes violent in the US in the conflict over abortion; and, above all, they feature in tragic ways in the current turmoil of some Moslem states today. Moreover, for the reasons already stated, the cultural would be impossible to disentangle from the economic and political in many cases both as an object acted upon by politics and economy and as the source of moral economic and political imperatives for public life. Even though constitutional and institutional reforms do help, they have to be re-negotiated over and over, and continually revalidated by political action.

There is not much ground for confidence that the problem could be solved by divesting political community of its cultural encumbrances and defining it purely in terms of participation in a system of rights and obligations of citizenship that would be neutral as between different cultures and sub-cultures in society. Real democracies have distinct cultural biases. Some agreement—some convergence—on substantive matters of policy, value and culture (in the sense of beliefs and their expression, ways of living and comportment, and so on), are necessary in addition to the formal procedures of democracy. Some consensus must be achieved on the content of democracy in substantive terms also. An exclusive focus on procedural aspects of democracy (even defined to include an appropriate *political* culture) may obfuscate a reality of general cultural oppression—in both the senses of suppression of some cultures by others and, perhaps more important, of domination and exploitation through culture.[16]

Conclusion

Changing peoples minds about marginal populations in their midst is all the more important because, for all the importance that we may attach to the role of the state, societal attitudes, sometimes in flagrant contrast to official intentions and policies, can encourage create and sustain marginality as Barany shows with respect to the East European Roma. Civil society is often as much in need of reform as the state. The adoption of a particular state form like democracy—if that could somehow be done in all cases—would not provide a permanent solution beyond the danger of reversal and reaction.

If it is impractical to count on democracy to provide the once-and-for-all institutional fix everywhere at once, attention might constructively focus on action as well as institutions, on, shall we say, process as well as structure. Marginality is clearly a world-wide phenomenon often exacerbated by global developments of all kinds. It affects people for whom the national political systems, be they democratic or otherwise, do not provide effective avenues of redress or effective action. In some cases, international organizations, transnational pressure groups and movements have been more effective than protest and agitation at the national level. Yet, the international and transnational space in which such actions unfold is one of very limited institutionalization and one to which democracy does not apply even figuratively. For many marginal groups, notably, migrants and refugees but also those who straddle boundaries or, like nomads, have to crisscross them to make their living, it is the very fact of national boundaries and sovereignty that is constraining and marginalizing. The appropriate political action approach would focus not only on the diversity of processes by which marginality is produced but on the resistances to it, and what is potentially more exciting, the mapping of the topology of the field of action across (or above?) the marginalizing frontiers—the alliances and solidarities that might be developed, the modes of struggle, and the incipient forms of institutionalization relevant to the alleviation of these forms and aspects of international insecurity. There already exists an impressive array of multinational humanitarian and, specifically, human rights organizations. The politics of their relationship to the international security activities of states on one hand, and those of persons and non-state entities on the other, might, as one example, provide insights into the nature and possibilities of that terrain. Needless to say, a political action approach does not have to focus exclusively on state structures or formal political institutions (or intergovernmental spaces) but can be applied to all the sites where marginality and insecurity are produced.

International security as it is ordinarily understood is a problem for states and marginality a problem for persons. The dichotomy is, of course, abusive but it makes a point. We have treated marginality as a problem of, or for, international security not because the fate of insecure populations of infinitely varied types around the world constitutes any immediate threat to any of the 299 important states whose concerns dominated, almost exclusively, even the academic study of international security for nearly half a century. All the analytical ingenuity at our command cannot make the danger of major war arising out of the situation of most of the marginal populations and their struggles, whether in the Balkans or Central Africa, the Middle and Near East or the Amazonian rain forests, appear other than remote. To be sure, some minor state, itself probably marginal by some criterion, may be in mortal danger. It may entangle its neighbors or spread the contagion of strife to them and to others by example. It is just conceivable that legitimation problems may produce, here and there a financial crisis of global significance as in the case of Mexico in the wake of the Chiapas revolt. Now and again, a marginal population may generate terrorists, or it may imperil some favored, or strategically situated, state, or it may incite to war two or more such states. It is always possible that ill-judged external interventions in such wars might raise the essentially internal conflicts arising out of marginality to much more dangerous levels, and so much more. Then, there is the oft-invoked danger of international terrorist movements (some with access to weapons of mass destruction) arising out of the revolts of marginalized populations—movements that could hurt strong and weak states alike both directly, by their acts of terror and, indirectly, by the effects of these attacks (or the fear of them) on civil liberties and the quality of political life generally. Yet, for international security as grand strategy there are other more pressing concerns. That, after all, is one of the senses in which these groups are marginal nationally and internationally, and one of the reasons why they remain so in all the other senses that we have explored in this book.

However, there are other reasons why these problems may be characterized as those of international security. The problems are global in incidence and show remarkable similarity in the types of people they affect both as marginalizers and marginalized; they provoke responses that are increasingly similar across the globe; they call for transnational as well as international ameliorative responses as much as many are provoked and exacerbated by forces operating on a world scale. Global communications provide a ready and effective means of dissemination of models of marginalization and violence as well as the ideas of cultural rectification, resistance and struggle that might be deployed against them. What remains true and may be unalterable, is that the valuations of these forms of insecurity by those in high politics and by ordinary people, especially those who have to endure them, are different. From the perspective of the everyday fears and hardships of people the world over, there are, one might say, more pressing concerns than grand strategy.

Conclusion

We have, nevertheless, been motivated by a desire to make conventional security thinking more sensitive to these preoccupations. It would be inconsistent, however, having begun by insisting that more attention be paid to the security interests of *persons* (specifically, marginal people), to end up by assimilating their needs to raison d'etat pure and simple. It is precisely at the point where the diversity of people and their interests are underrepresented by states that it becomes both necessary and gainful to explore and develop the scope that already exists and is likely to grow for new identities and solidarities to be forged across the traditional boundaries of national states, indeed, of nations and states. Theaters of effective political action emerge in the inter- and trans-state spaces which are created by both the normal development of international politics and economics and by the consequence of struggles that constantly overflow those boundaries, announcing a world politics. All things considered, the relation state-and-people is best left in its dialectical form. That, at any rate, is consistent with struggle and reform.

We argued in the Introduction that among states international security is not achieved through any system of dependable institutions or cogent rules but by contingent accommodations. That is even more emphatically true of the security of minorities and marginal populations. Enabling constitutional arrangements and institutional designs have a major role to play in making such accommodations possible and will, in their turn, be shaped by the movement of politics. But it is important to stress and to study directly the modes of political existence and the forms of struggle open to marginal populations beyond (and in spite of the limitations imposed by) such formal structures. *Both* would be appropriate directions of further inquiry in the light of the research and reflection reported in this work.

Notes

1. The European Union's increasingly restrictive definition of refugees has been severely criticized by the European Council for Refugees and the United Nations High Commissioner for Refugees. See Reuters, clari.net, November 23, 1995

2. See also Fredrik Barth ed., *Ethnic Groups and Boundaries: The Social Organization of Culture Difference*, London, George Allen and Unwin, 1970

3. See e.g., Ernest Gellner, *Nations and Nationalism*, Ithaca, Cornell University Press, 1983

4. There is a very valuable discussion of some of these issues from the point of view of normative theory in Charles Taylor, "The Politics of Recognition" in Amy Gutman ed., *Multiculturalism:Examining the Politics of Recognition* (Princeton, NJ, 1994), 25-73. The article by K. Anthony Appiah, "Identity, Authenticity, Survival: Multicultural Societies and Social Reproduction" in the same volume

Sam C. Nolutshungu

is also very germane, 149-163. Gutman poses the question in her introduction: "Can citizens with diverse identities be represented as equals if public institutions do not recognize our particular identities. . . . ". Another question needs to be asked also: "Can people be said to share an identity whatever the degree of inequality among them with regard to the realization of our more universally shared interests . . . ?" 3-4 Inequality suggests the inadequacy of the postulated identity as a description of those to whom it is applied. It is, then, partial, complemented for each member by other, perhaps, competing "identities". In this regard, identities, are, strictly speaking unshareable except at the level of the imagination or of political action and discourse that selectively *suppresses* differences and, above all, inequality. That is one reason, indeed, why they are, in current parlance, "socially constructed." Furthermore, "collective identity" is very difficult to distinguish from stereotyping (whether by oneself or by others, including one's chosen group or community) or conformity to *imposed* codes of (identifying) behavior. The essential point, here, is not so much the particularity of each individual's identity which many have stressed, but the multiplicity of collectivities, some embedded in others, some overlapping, with which an individual might identify or be identified. Some of these may relate to shared cultural attributes but others may concern life circumstances. Some of these are not positive though they gain "recognition" without difficulty, e.g., caste identities, "Untouchable"; or behavioral ones, like, sex offender, drug dealer, or hustler as well as those directly associated with class: poor, welfare-dependant, homeless, beggar, or, in many countries, illegal alien worker. All of these feature in a person's "dialogues" with others but are troubling precisely because the dialogues are of the deaf or between unequals, and because the identities" are not a matter of how people speak about, and to, each other alone but of the objective circumstances which provoke and inform their dialogues". Most of the chapters in this book place a heavy emphasis on life circumstances rather than "identities" while they implicitly acknowledge "recognition" as an issue for members of marginal populations in its own right and, as it were, for its own sake, but also as a *means*, i.e., as relevant to strategies of oppression and exploitation (over and above non- or misrecognition) and their overthrow. Here, the challenge to the dominant culture is not only to recognize people for who they think and say they are but also for what that culture has made them be. Right-wing, economically insecure whites may not be all that they think or say they are, but if they march with Le Pen or the Michigan militia, then more fortunate members of their societies might wish to know what it is that makes them what, in fact, they are.

5. "Universality" is, of course, always a potentiality which may require the assertion of particular identities to be fulfilled (to the extent that these do not negate its principle absolutely as, e.g., in secession from or overthrow of the would-be universal order). Of related interest, see Ann S. Orloff, Gender and Social Rights of Citizenship: The Comparative Analysis of State Policies and Gender Relations" *American Sociological Review*, 58,3 1993, 303-328

6. Gurr, *Minorities at Risk*, 323-4 .

Conclusion

After years of unspeakable violence it has proved impossible to base a peace in Bosnia on the application of such a principle: Bosnian Serbs and Moslems agreed in November 1995, in Dayton, Ohio, to live together in a state whose ramshackle structure is a tragic monument to the attempt to achieve this aim in the first place and, literally, "a portent of broached mischief to the unborn times."

7. D.P. Moynihan, *Pandaemonium*

8. See e.g., Michael D. Levin, *Ethnicity and Aboriginality*, Chapters 1,2 and 9

9. See, also, "Hésitations et contradictions du mouvement nationaliste québécois" and "Que faire de «premières nations»?" in *Le Monde Diplomatique*, July 1995, 7-8; In a referendum at the end of October 1995, Quebec voted to stay in the Union by the narrowest of margins, thanks largely to the non-French speaking voters although some 40 percent of French speakers are believed to have voted against secession. Reuters clari.net, October 30 and 31, 1995.

10. On Friday, November 10, 1995, the Government of General Sani Abatcha executed the leader of the Movement for the Survival of Ogoni Peoples, Ken Saro-Wiwa and eight others after their controversial conviction of inciting the murder of four pro-government chiefs. Reuters, clari.net, November 10, 1995.

11. Gidon Gottlieb, *Nation Against State: A new approach to ethnic conflicts and the decline of sovereignty* (New York, Council on Foreign Relations,1993) has some engaging proposals but all from a "nationalities" perspective which, needless to say, does not deal with other than "ethnic" situations.

12. Dr Nnamdi Azikiwe was the first President of Nigeria, 1960-67, a country in which the ethnicization of politics contributed massively to the breakdown of democracy in civil war.

13. Cf Gidon Gottlieb, *Nation Against State*, 2-3

14. See the very suggestive discussion in Alain Policar, "Racisme et antiracisme: un réexamen" in Gilles Ferreol (ed.), Intégration et Exclusion dans la Société Française Contemporaine, (Paris, Presses Universitaires de Lille, 1994), 23-58

15. See, e.g., Dan Ferrand-Bechmann La face cachée des solidarités" in Ferreol (ed.), *Intégration et Exclusion,*282-305

16. It may be asserted that in the long run—in the very long run, perhaps—the right procedures faithfully pursued will produce the right, or desirable result of, let us say, "a better life for all". However, that is matter of faith rather than demonstrable knowledge and the run may be too long to provide comfort for those who are marginal and insecure in the here and now.

INDEX

Index